Elements of
Managerial
Action

THE IRWIN SERIES IN MANAGEMENT

CONSULTING EDITOR   JOHN F. MEE   *Indiana University*

AMMER *Materials Management* rev. ed.
BRENNAN *Wage Administration: Plans, Practices, and Principles* rev. ed.
BROOM *Production Management* rev. ed.
CHAMPION & BRIDGES *Critical Incidents in Management* rev. ed.
EELLS & WALTON *Conceptual Foundations of Business* rev. ed.
FARMER & RICHMAN *Comparative Management and Economic Progress*
GREENE *Production Control: Systems and Decisions*
HANEY *Communication and Organizational Behavior: Text and Cases* rev. ed.
HOUSTON *Manager Development: Principles and Perspectives*
JONES *Executive Decision Making* rev. ed.
JUCIUS *Personnel Management* 7th ed.
JUCIUS, DEITZER, & SCHLENDER *Elements of Managerial Action* 3d ed.
LING *The Management of Personnel Relations: History and Origins*
MCDONOUGH & GARRETT *Management Systems: Working Concepts and Practices*
MEGGINSON *Personnel: A Behavioral Approach to Administration* rev. ed.
MOORE *Production Management* 6th ed.
MOORE & KIBBEY *Manufacturing: Materials and Processes*
MORRIS *The Analysis of Management Decisions* rev. ed.
NADLER *Work Design: A Systems Concept* rev. ed.
NIEBEL *Motion and Time Study* 5th ed.
ODIORNE *Personnel Administration by Objectives*
PATTON, LITTLEFIELD, & SELF *Job Evaluation: Text and Cases* 3d ed.
PRINCE *Information Systems for Management Planning and Control* rev. ed.
REED *Plant Layout: Factors, Principles, and Techniques*
RICHARDS & GREENLAW *Management: Decisions and Behavior* rev. ed.
ROSCOE *Project Economy*
ROSCOE & FREARK *Organization for Production: An Introduction to Industrial Management* 5th ed.
SEIMER *Cases in Industrial Management*
SIEGEL *Industrial Psychology* rev. ed.
SIMONDS & GRIMALDI *Safety Management: Accident Cost and Control* rev. ed.
SPRIEGEL & MYERS (eds.) *The Writings of the Gilbreths*
TERRY *Principles of Management* 6th ed.
THAYER *Communication and Communication Systems: In Organization, Management, and Interpersonal Relations*
TIMMS & POHLEN *The Production Function in Business: Decision Systems for Production and Operations Management* 3d ed.
VORIS *Production Control: Text and Cases* 3d ed.
WEBBER *Culture and Management: Text and Readings in Comparative Management*

Elements of Managerial Action

MICHAEL J. JUCIUS, Ph.D.
Professor of Management
The University of Arizona

BERNARD A. DEITZER, Ph.D.
Professor of Management
The University of Akron

WILLIAM E. SCHLENDER, Ph.D.
Dean, College of Business Administration
Cleveland State University

THIRD EDITION • 1973

RICHARD D. IRWIN, INC. Homewood, Illinois 60430
IRWIN-DORSEY LIMITED Georgetown, Ontario

Third Edition

First Printing, April 1973

ISBN 0-256-00261-4
Library of Congress Catalog Card No. 72–95391
Printed in the United States of America

46,422

To
Our
Families

Preface

THE COMPLEXITY of business operations and managerial activities continually increases. New problems, new solutions, and new insights attend such changes; and these have prompted an updated revision of the earlier editions.

No reason was found, however, to move from the guiding principle of the earlier editions: to provide an integrated and basic pattern of the functions, factors, and behavior of managing. Such a perspective and coverage—without encyclopedic minutiae—has been found useful by the authors both in the college classroom and in various executive development programs. The details of specific managerial tasks and relationships can best be grasped after one understands the total outline of the manager's job and role in an organization.

A manager is involved in a number of areas. These include the functions he performs as a manager, the factors he manages, the people he manages, his own behavioral complex, and the technical subject that he manages. The latter, though important, lies outside the scope of this book. An executive can be a success if he possesses superior skill in any one of the other areas, but his chances of success are much better if he develops his potential in all of them. It is with all these areas, therefore, that this text is concerned.

Numerous changes and additions have been made to the format of the earlier editions. New chapters on leadership, executive ethics, executive behavior, and trends in management have been included. In previously existing chapters, new information has been added on such matters as decision theories, management information systems, organization structures, the office of the president, management by objectives, appraisal methods, motivational practices, and behavioral relationships. In addition, many new illustrations, diagrams, and charts have been included.

This work is structured to be used alone or in conjunction with supplementary readings, a number of references of which are included in the bibliography. Questions and short cases—practically all of which are new—are appended to each chapter and may serve as pedagogical aids. Three extensive integrative cases at the end of the text may serve for broader discussion. These materials, or incidents presented by the students or practitioners, can also be used in connection with the materials in the text both in the academic class or in management development programs.

In writing this book, the authors are indebted to many. From the wealth of earlier writers and various associates they have developed and distilled many of their own views. They are particularly indebted to Dr. Ralph C. Davis, professor emeritus of The Ohio State University, for the patterns of his general theory of management. To their colleagues at The University of Arizona, Cleveland State University, and The Ohio State University they are obligated for much stimulating analysis of managerial topics. To Dean James W. Dunlap, Drs. Frank L. Simonetti, Karl A. Shilliff, David D. Van Fleet, and N. F. Davis—all of The University of Akron—they are grateful for both support and many helpful suggestions. Finally a special note of thanks is extended to Nancy Witsaman, and Susan Kostko, for their selfless assistance in preparing and editing the manuscript of this latest edition.

Of course, the authors assume full responsibility for their interpretations of the subject.

March 1973   MICHAEL J. JUCIUS
                                      BERNARD A. DEITZER
                                      WILLIAM E. SCHLENDER

Contents

1

The Field of
Management

Organized Group Effort

ONE OF THE most distinctive features of modern society is the pre-dominance of organized effort. Attainment of various objectives is seldom sought by individual effort. Rather, groups of people combine their efforts and resources so as to maximize the attainment of group and individual purposes.

Such arrangements are found in every phase of human life. Goods and services that satisfy our economic needs, for example, are principally produced and distributed by business units composed of more than one person. Again, the protection of our nation is a mission of a military organization consisting of millions of men and women. Similarly, our political parties, our religious affiliations, our unions, our charitable and welfare institutions, and our recreational and social activities are characterized by group efforts and relationships.

But groups in and of themselves are not enough to explain organizations. Rather it is in the human skills found in such groups. Very simply, organizations serve to assemble various talents, skills, ambitions, and special abilities. Thus, each organized group, whatever its purposes, brings together human skills and technical resources in a way that accomplishes more than could be done by the individuals acting independently.

But this bringing together of skills and resources is not accomplished automatically. For example, typists in an office do not automatically coordinate their efforts with those for whom they perform such services. Neither do production workers automatically synchronize their output with the efforts of salesmen. Nor do such specialists as engineers, accountants, or personnel managers auto-matically serve the needs of production units. And similarly in non-business areas such specialized experts as soldiers, athletes, minis-ters, and civil servants do not automatically work together in their respective spheres.

Managerial Specialists. Cooperation among and coordination of the foregoing specialists must be sought through the efforts of an-other type of specialist. The latter is responsible for getting the other experts to work together effectively. He must unite the tech-nicians of production, distribution, politics, recreation, or whatever the particular field may be. And he is as indispensable to effective organized human effort as are the technical experts themselves.

The "coordinator" expert is known by many names. In the politi-cal field he may be called president, governor, or mayor, to mention but a few. In the religious field, he may carry such titles as cardinal, bishop, abbot, or pope. In recreational areas, he may be called coach, manager, or director. And in the business field are found such titles as executive, superintendent, vice president, supervisor, and foreman.

Common to all these titles is the implication of group leadership. The task of each is to increase group effectiveness. Each should cause to elicit from a group more than the group could accomplish without such leadership, or more than the individuals therein could accomplish independently.

Acting in this leadership sense shall be termed here *managing*. While each leader—manager—must be technically equipped in a special area, such as politics, religion, recreation, and business, he must also add managerial capabilities to his technical and human skills.[1]

This book, then, is concerned with managerial phases of leader-ship, particularly in the field of business. It may be noted, however, that management practices would be generally similar in other areas of human activity.

Moreover, the term management is applied to all levels of leader-ship in a business enterprise. If the president manages the vice presidents, so do the latter manage those below them, and so on down to the foreman who manages his group of workers. Each is a manager of his particular group of subordinates. While there may

---

[1] In this text, the word manager is used to be a class term for all leaders, but on occasions use will be made of such commonly used synonyms as executives, supervisors, and administrators.

be differences in details of emphasis or coverage, as will be noted in later chapters, the essential features of the management phase of the leader's task at all levels are much the same.

To repeat, the manager is a specialist leading a group of technical experts or specialists. The chief engineer, for example, manages a team of engineers just as the drill press foreman manages a team of drill press operators. Each must possess managerial attributes that will permit him to optimize various goals of his particular team. These attributes include a fund of knowledge, a set of skills, and an acquaintanceship with functions which serve him in his managerial duties.

Scope of Discussion. How is this complement of managerial attributes and capacities acquired? For a long time it was felt—and still is in many companies—that managers either were born or could become so only after long years of practical experience. Such a stand is bound to result in managerial growth that is slow and expensive. There is growing recognition, however, that managers, like engineers or accountants, can be helped by formal training. This view has gained support because there is a growing body of information in regard to the knowledge, skills, and functions of management which can be passed on from manager to manager and from managerial generation to managerial generation.

The composition of the field of management may be briefly outlined in this chapter by seeking some general answers to the following questions:

1. With what broad areas must the manager be proficient?
2. What functions does a manager perform?
3. What factors must be considered in performing managerial functions?
4. How may managerial functions be performed?
5. What tools may be used in performing managerial functions?
6. Through what channels may managerial functions be performed?
7. What constraints limit managerial action?
8. How may managers be tested for degree of success?

Areas of Managerial Proficiency

A manager must develop proficiency in three major areas. To begin with, a given manager must know something about the technicalities of the field in which he is the leader. A sales supervisor, for example, must be skilled in the principles and practices of selling. An office manager is expected to know the technicalities of office procedures and machines. And the warehouse superintendent is expected to know the fields of storing and handling materials.

Next, every manager must work with and through people. Hence, each must have knowledge and skill pertinent to personnel and human relations. He must know how to procure, develop, maintain, and utilize the human factor. And he must be acquainted with the psychological, sociological, political, and ethical dimensions of human behavior.

Granted technical and human proficiency, what then? The manager must coordinate the work of various technicians into an effective team. Such coordination is attained by planning, organizing, directing, and controlling the work of others.[2] The manager does not do the work of others. To repeat, he plans, organizes, directs, and controls their work. These are the broad functions (activities) of a leader when he acts as a manager.

Although the first of these areas—the technical—is of vital interest to every manager, attention to it is beyond the scope of this book. The second of these areas—the human—will be explored in more detail in later chapters. The third area—the managerial functions—is of immediate interest now.

Functions of Management[3]

The managerial functions—planning, organizing, directing, and controlling—are now briefly described, but each will be examined more fully in later chapters.

Planning is the managerial function of determining in advance what a group or an individual should accomplish and how the goals are to be attained. It establishes goals, methods of accomplishing

---

[2] There are differences among various writers regarding the major classes into which the functions of management should be divided. As yet there is no conclusive evidence in full support of any classification. It is felt that the functions listed here provide a useful and widely accepted basis for discussion of the manager's job.

[3] This discussion of the functions of management does not mean that employees do not or cannot or should not participate in such functions. But if this book is to be kept in respectable bounds, emphasis will be on the role of the specialized manager.

them, and needed resources. Each level of an organization takes the plan of the level above it and either converts the plans for the level below or applies the plans as given. Planning is the original decision-making step of managerial action.

Organizing is the managerial function providing the various factors and resources necessary to carry out the plans after they have been programmed. Thus, an organization structure must be established to properly relate executives and subordinates. Procedures and systems must be established to carry out the projects specified in plans. Personnel, materials, tools, equipment, and other resources required to carry out plans must be procured. Organizing is in a sense the function of setting up the machine needed to operate the plans.

Directing is the managerial function of running the machine as it carries out desired plans. The manager as a director is comparable to the pilot flying a plane to its objective or to the captain on the bridge in the command of a ship as it proceeds on the planned course toward port. In this phase, management is engaged in actively supervising and motivating the organization as it operates in converting plans into results.

Controlling is the managerial function of evaluating organizational operations and results so that deviations from plan may be minimized or corrected. For example, management must assure itself that the right quantity of the right kind of output is coming out of various organization units at the right time. Or controls must be exercised to see that expenditures for various resources do not exceed planned budgets. By controls, management may take steps to realign current activities or may provide information to plan future activities more effectively.

These four, broad managerial functions are neither mutually exclusive nor always performed in an undeviating sequence. As will be seen more fully later, for example, planning must be performed with due respect for ultimate controlling, thus how one plans depends in part on how one can control. Or directing is often carried on in part concurrently with controlling. And, to cite one more instance, available resources, such as people, often determine limits to planning and organizing. While it is convenient, therefore, to discuss the functions of management under separate headings, in actual practice there is much overlapping and crisscrossing of these functions.

Factors of Management[4]

But what specifically is planned, organized, directed, and controlled? In all instances, it will be found that careful consideration must be given to the following factors:

1. Philosophy.   5. Human faculties.
2. Objectives.   6. Environmental factors.
3. Functions.   7. Procedures.
4. Policies.   8. Organization structure.

1. *Philosophy.* This refers to the basic guide that underlies all the actions of a manager. What does he believe, for example, is the justification for the existence of his particular business? What does he fundamentally think about his subordinates as people? What ethics and ideals guide him in making decisions regarding customers, stockholders, employees, and the community? Are his actions influenced by the golden rule or that of the devil take the hindmost? Whether he knows it or not, every executive has a basic philosophy of managerial action. Hence, it would seem the better part of wisdom to derive his philosophy through conscious analysis.

2. *Objectives.* Objectives refer to the goals that are to be sought. As a business institution, an enterprise must produce and distribute some worthwhile good or service. To its owners, a profit of a satisfactory amount over the life of the concern should be forthcoming. To its employees, satisfactory monetary and nonfinancial rewards should be forthcoming. And for the community in which it operates, various social values and responsibilities must be protected. Each subdivision of an enterprise has an impact upon these services, personal goals, and social purposes. How well these various goals are established and balanced relative to one another is dependent in part upon the philosophy and ethics that govern the thinking of the managers.

3. *Functions.* Functions refer to the activities by the performance of which it is proposed to attain desired objectives. Such functions may be grouped into three main categories: first, the technical, that is, those that are concerned with producing, distributing, financing, etc., goods and services; second, the managerial, that is, those concerned with planning, organizing, directing, and controlling the first category; and, third, the human, that is, those con-

---

[4] It might be well at this juncture to scan Figure 1–1 which serves to show graphically how factors of management are related to other dimensions of management.

cerned with procuring, developing, maintaining, and utilizing the human factor.

4. Policies. Policies are guidelines within whose boundaries functions must be performed if objectives are to be attained effectively. They are, in a sense, directives established in advance for the guidance of subordinates. Thus, a subordinate need not seek a decision from his superior about what to do if a policy governing the specific case has been established previously. The policy states the decision the executive would make were he to be asked personally.

5. Human Faculties. This factor recognizes the fact that the performance of functions must be entrusted directly or indirectly to human beings. Hence, it is imperative to specify, acquire, and develop the human skills needed to perform technical and managerial functions. And since human output is dependent as much perhaps upon willingness to work and attitude of mind as upon physical and mental ability, it is imperative to give attention to morale, motivation, and human relations matters.

6. Environmental Factors. This factor recognizes the fact that people are in turn aided and affected by physical, social, and political forces. Management must, therefore, give thought to, first, providing technical tools and physical environment that will favorably benefit workers and, second, making appropriate adjustments to social customs and political requirements.

7. Procedures. This term refers to the fact that functions and the people who perform them must be arranged in orderly sequences. Thus, many functions must be performed to make, let us say, a bicycle wheel. Unless these activities are arranged so that first things are done first, and so on, each advancing the completion of the wheel in efficient order, a wheel will not be completed with dispatch or economy. Similarly with functions of engineering, sales, or accounting, management must see that procedures for the detailed activities of each are properly related in orderly sequences.

8. Organization Structure. This factor provides for the invisible framework that ties together various technical and managerial experts and specialists. Thus, a line on an organization chart drawn downward from the name of sales manager to district sales manager informs all concerned of who has authority over whom and for what in this area.[5] Such downward lines have an upward flow which indi-

---

[5] As will be seen in a later chapter, detailed statements of what one has authority over or one is responsible for can only be spelled out in a job description.

cate who is responsible to whom and for what. In sum, the organization structure provides lines of authority and responsibility which help to tie the members of the group into a more effective team.

Methods of Management

All managers perform the managerial functions in respect to their technical areas and with consideration to the foregoing factors. But not all do these things in the same way, just as not all successful baseball players hit the regulation baseball in the same way. Some common differences in management "swinging" are worthy of note.

To begin with, managers use different methods in seeking solutions to their problems of planning, organizing, directing, and controlling. Some decide what to do in given cases on the basis of their own experiences. Some imitate the decisions and plans of others. And some attempt to apply scientific thinking to the solution of problems.

Another method of management has to do with the appeals used in dealing with subordinates. In some cases fear is employed in motivating subordinates, and in other cases an appeal is made to the positive drives of people. Along somewhat similar lines, some executives think constantly in terms of work to be accomplished while performing their managerial functions, while others are person-centered in their managerial outlook.

To cite another phase of methodology, there is the matter of the degree to which managers anticipate problems. It is not unusual, for example, to find some managers who are swamped with urgent problems that cry for solution. Indeed, problem "fires" are breaking out with such frequency that the manager never has time to think about a fireproof structure. The managerial approach here is that of curing existing problems. On the other hand, some managers seem adept at minimizing difficulties by anticipating problems. They prevent them from becoming very serious.

And, finally, managers use a variety of personal qualities and behavior in performing their functions. Some rely on personal magnetism, some on teaching and coaching ability, some on their rare judgment and forecasting ability, and some on their physical capacity to work long hours, years on end. In their behavior, too, managers differ. Thus some insist without exception upon protocol pertaining to their status in the organization, whereas at the other extreme some act the part of "one of the boys" without apparent loss of prestige or effectiveness.

Tools of Management

A variety of tools, of varying degrees of precision and complexity, are available to aid in the performance of managerial functions. A few are now mentioned merely to indicate something of their nature and variety.

A number of tools have had wide usage by managers. The organization chart is an example of a common tool. Often found, too, is the organization manual which fills out in detail the otherwise bare framework of an organization chart. What the foregoing does for the organization chart, such tools as system models, layout charts, policy manuals, standard practice instructions, and man-machine models do for the factor of procedures.

Increasingly, in his decision making, the executive is calling upon the tools of mathematics and statistics, electronic computers, data processing, and communication systems. In dealing with people, he is relying more and more upon the findings of such branches of the behavioral sciences as psychology, sociology, and anthropology. Most helpful to him in planning and controlling have been the tools of quantitative analysis as well as those of budgeting and accounting.

Channels of Management

It is only in the smallest groups that there would be but one manager supported by his single line of subordinates. Invariably there are several levels through which the top manager must act before the bottom operative level is reached.

A number of designs[6] are used to effectuate bottom-level coordination by a distantly removed top manager. A simple design is to have each of a successive series of managerial levels perform all the necessary planning, organizing, directing, and controlling for the level immediately below it—this is the so-called pure line organization. A more complex plan provides for taking from each executive the need for actual performance of part of one of his managerial tasks, such as planning or controlling. An assistant, for example, does the planning or controlling but gets approval of the appropriate line manager before submitting the plans or controls to the subordinates—here is the staff that goes to make up the line and staff organization structure. These relationships are usually formalized, but often many contacts between managers and between

---

[6] Examples of these are illustrated in Chapter 12.

line and staff are informal. And in very large organizations spread over wide geographical areas, authority over, and performance of managerial functions in the dispersed areas are in some companies centralized in a home office and in others decentralized among the various units.

Managerial Constraints

In performing his work, the manager operates under two major constraints: situational and resource. The first of these refers to the fact that various laws, customs, and institutions place limits on his freedom of action. Legally, there are rules, decisions, and directives of various political bodies that govern managerial action. Then there are social customs, traditions, and mores that can be transgressed only at greater or lesser peril. And finally, such institutional groups as governmental agencies, business associations, and unions set limits within which the manager must act.

Resource constraints refer to the fact that all managers are limited by available time, money, and skills. Time within which to make decisions is invariably less than would be desired. Or what manager has ever had enough money to support the various projects that could increase his effectiveness? And perhaps above all, who has ever possessed enough skill in such areas as economics, organizational know-how, motivation, systems design, and behavioral patterns to be unshakably certain of his decisions?

These constraints are certainly not cause for pessimism. To be sure, it would be fine if they could be removed. But by being fully aware of and alert to changes in situational factors, the manager can live wisely within them. He can certainly reduce foolish clashes with various groups, laws, and customs. And by increasing his skills in pertinent areas of required knowledge, he certainly can be reasonably effective and competitive in making decisions for his organization. He doesn't have to be perfect—only as good or better than his competitors.

Tests of Management

How is it possible to know in a given case if a manager is performing his managerial functions correctly? In one sense, the answer is the same as that for a baseball batter—how many hits is he making? In short, what kind of results is the manager getting?

Thus, one answer goes back directly to a comparison between predetermined goals and actual results. Are goods and services being purchased by customers in adequate quantities and at prices that permit costs to be so covered that reasonable profits are being earned? Are wages, salaries, and other *perquisites* for which people in the organization strive being adequately met? Is the community in which the company operates (and this refers to the nation as well as the municipal locality) not harmed but indeed enhanced by its operations?

Moreover, it may well be asked whether or not the foregoing results are being attained with consistency and a fair degree of stability. Then, too, is there a reasonable balance between the various competing objectives of owners, customers, employees, and the community? Obviously these are difficult tests to apply, yet they are the basic measures which are applied sooner or later to every manager.

An Integrated Picture

The foregoing has served to depict the many interacting facets of the phase of group action known as management. Each affects and is affected by the others. Each facet is part of a greater entity—no one of them can stand alone in explaining the success of a manager. Each must be carefully handled in relation to the others if a manager is to increase the chances of his success as a leader of a group.

With this overall view in mind, it is now possible to present a definition of management that integrates the various facets of this field. Management has reference to the field of human endeavor concerned with planning, organizing, directing, and controlling group effort so that the several objectives of the group and the individuals are attained to the optimum degree and with optimum efficiency.

The relationships between the parts of this definition have a static as well as a dynamic character. Viewed statically, one obtains a picture of an organization as of a given moment. A dynamic approach recognizes the fact that an organization is an ongoing institution. This contrast of views is not unlike the relationships between the parts of an automobile which is standing still and of the same automobile when it is in motion.

A static model of management is illustrated in Figure 1–1. Here it is seen that a manager's success is measured by the degree to which various objectives of the group and of the individuals are attained. His success in helping to attain these objectives is determined by his ability to coordinate the efforts of the members of the group. And his ability to coordinate is dependent largely upon his skill in performing the managerial functions of planning, organizing, directing, and controlling. But success in performance of managerial functions, in turn, is conditioned by how the manager deals with, first, various basic factors, and, second, human beings. The former will require appropriate technical knowledge and skills. The latter will call for appropriate behavior to motivate and inspire human beings to the highest degree possible.

FIGURE 1–1
A Static Management Model

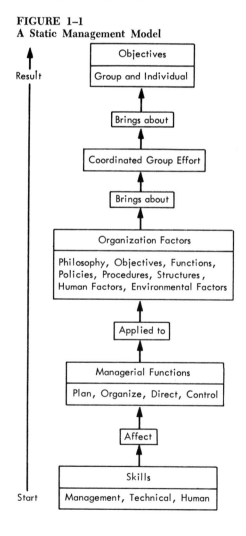

FIGURE 1–2
A Dynamic Management Model

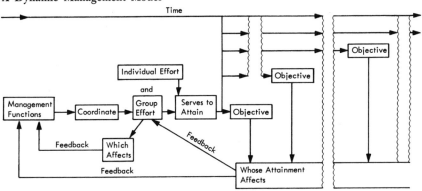

A dynamic model is illustrated very simply in Figure 1–2. Here, as in the case of the static model, it is seen that management functions coordinate group effort which serves to attain objectives. But there are two additional features contained in Figure 1–2. First, as one objective is attained, the managerial process and group effort are repeated continuously for additional objectives with the passage of time. Second, as an objective is attained or, is in the process of being attained, it reacts back on (there is a feedback to) group effort and management functions for succeeding objectives. Hence, there is a continuous, interacting, circular process of relationships between the various parts of an ongoing organization.

Summary

To summarize, managerial work encompasses three major areas: the functions the manager performs; the basic factors in regard to which he must develop appropriate skills in performing his functions; and the behavioral pattern he must adopt if he hopes to deal effectively with people as people. These three areas are taken up in subsequent parts of this book as follows:

1. The next three chapters are devoted to managerial leadership, philosophy, and decision making.
2. The second major section of this text consists of four chapters covering the basic functions of management.
3. The next six chapters are devoted to the basic factors which must be managed.

4. The next six chapters are concerned with a variety of human areas with which management is expected to deal.
5. The next five chapters focus on activities directly concerned with the effective utilization of the resource of management itself.
6. A final chapter summarizes some recent developments and possible trends in management.

What is said in any one of the subsequent chapters, it must be remembered, is but part of an integrated whole. No one chapter about, or facet of, management can stand alone. Only when the composite of functions, factors, and behavior is properly related can the full potential of management be successfully exploited for the common good. Management must be viewed as a multifaceted subject whose harmony is derived in a complete, integrated system.

QUESTIONS

1. Why do people work together in groups, and what must be true of such group operations if their results are to be optimized?
2. In what three large areas must every manager develop appropriate skills if he is to be most successful as a manager of a group?
3. What are the managerial functions, and what is the relationship of each of the functions to each other?
4. To what factors must managerial functions be applied no matter what the technical field is in any particular case?
5. Differentiate and show the relations among objectives, functions, and policies.
6. What are the various methods which might be used by a manager in performing his managerial functions?
7. What tests might be applied to determine how well a given manager is performing his managerial functions?
8. Illustrate by diagram the essential difference between a static model and a dynamic model of organizational relationships.

CASE 1-1

The president of a company, while attending a conference, had heard the following idea expressed: "If the business executive does not manage his company, then it will either fail or the management of the company will in part be taken over by the government, a union, and the employees informally. It will then be idle for management to complain that the prerogatives of management have been usurped."

Mulling over this idea in terms of the experiences of his own company, he agreed that the following had happened:

a) Various governmental agencies had enacted legislation affecting his wages, hours, and working conditions.
b) The union in his company also had a large voice in matters of wages, hours, and working conditions.
c) Employees subtly and informally established norms of output and standards of how work was to be done.

Yet he felt that when framed against the large financial risks he had undertaken in operating the business, the undermining of his managerial authority to run his business was decidedly unfair.

1. Why had these "noninvestors" interspersed themselves into the management of the business?
2. What views of management must the business executive take if he is to retain a broader hold on his "prerogatives"?

CASE 1–2

Bill Jones had been an ensign in the Navy. Now, Bill was a department head in a large branch store of a leading merchandising chain. He, along with six other department chiefs, reported to the store manager, who also held the title of vice president in the parent organization.

While in the military service, Bill had been taught that a junior officer had to be prepared to take over the position of his superior officer should this person become incapacitated under fire. Bill thought this was a good principle to follow in business. So he undertook a plan of action. First, he wrote down all of the managerial duties he had and then tried to look for an unofficial understudy for himself. Second, he took every opportunity to see how the store manager did his job. Third, he began—at what he thought were opportune times—to ask questions about the management practices of the store manager and of the department chiefs as they related to the store manager. And fourth, he wrote, rewrote, and revised, as he learned more, what he thought the job specification of the store manager ought to be.

His plan did not go unobserved. His fellow department chiefs thought he was pushy, and the store manager wondered sometimes if Bill was some kind of a spy planted in his store.

1. To what extent do you subscribe to this principle of managerial leadership?
2. What of Bill's plan for effectuating the principle?

2

Leadership

Introduction

PROBABLY no other area of management receives as much attention, investigation, and study as does leadership. Certainly, there are decisive reasons for this. For it is leadership that gives dynamism, vitality, and substance to an organization. It is the drive and force of leadership that galvanizes a firm and its people into materializing required and expected results. It is leadership that provides, and reflects, the character, soul, in fact, the very life itself of the institution.

Our purpose in this chapter will be to analyze and discuss both some theoretical and pragmatic aspects of leadership according to the following outline:

1. Definition of leadership.
2. The leader versus the manager concept.
3. Trait approach to leadership.
4. Skill approach to leadership.
5. Group approach to leadership.
6. Roles of leadership.
7. Styles of leadership.

Definition of Leadership

Theoretically leadership is a subset of the managerial function of directing. As such it serves alongside motivating and communicating as necessary skills of direction. In other words, in the act of or while directing the work group in the achievement of desired

17

objectives, the leader either simultaneously or alternatingly motivates, communicates, and leads.

Leadership, then, is a process in which a central figure guides and influences the activities of others in the pursuit of group and individual goals. Essential to this definition of leadership is the behavior of a pivotal individual around which a group gravitates and also performs certain tasks within an environment deemed conducive to the group's interest. Moreover, this concept of leadership focuses less on what the key figure is intrinsically composed of and more on what he extrinsically does.

The Leader versus the Manager Concept

This brings us to the point of the distinction between the terms manager and leader. Is there, in fact, a difference? To be sure, there are significant differences worthy of discussion. The definition of a manager insists that he enjoys a formal position on the organizational structure from which he plans, organizes, directs, and controls the resources and activities of a work group. Furthermore, he has the formal power of his office to support his position. Ideally, managership should be equated with leadership. Desirably the manager should be an effective leader. Leadership, furthermore, implies followership. It stresses personal influence and interaction between the leader and his followers. Leadership implies a genuine acceptance of the manager by his group. It is the inspirational force that makes realizable the objectives of management since the objectives are identified and agreed upon by the group within the context of the situation. Leadership implies an awareness of group norms and values, of individual goals and aspirations, as well as a deliberate structuring of a climate conducive to individual and exceptional performance and contribution.

Trait Approach to Leadership

Is there a constellation of personality traits that characterizes effective leadership? Much research and study has been devoted to learning what characteristics or traits differentiate the leader from the follower. But thus far evidence is inconclusive about traits exclusive to leadership.

Leadership, it seems, appears on the organizational scene in all sizes, colors, and shapes. One needs only to be acquainted with the leaders of a firm for a brief period of time before he realizes the varied differences in the personalities and related traits of its many managers. Organizations would be hard pressed for adequate leadership if all candidates for managerial posts had to satisfy the trait requirements of an ideal leadership profile. What needs to be recognized, however, is the different leadership requirements of the various levels of the firm. What may be an essential requirement at one level and in one situation may not be demanded of another. Obviously, a vice president of marketing would require a different mix of leadership skills than, say, a manager of the print shop.

The trait approach to leadership once found support particularly during the 1950s when some theorists and practitioners felt that leadership could be developed through training, personal experience, and also exposure to recognized leaders themselves. Composite lists of traits were developed and synthesized into profiles. These leadership profiles contained a range of qualitative attributes many of which were inconsistently definable. Examples of such traits were initiative, intelligence, judgment, aggressiveness, decisiveness, courage, cooperation, persistence, and so on. While recognized leaders exhibited many of these described traits, it was extremely difficult, if not impossible, to isolate those traits directly related to leader effectiveness. Hence, credulity in the trait approach could not be established.

On the other hand, it is unwise to totally discredit the trait theory in the light of more recent findings. Recently research[1] has revealed several traits that are significantly correlated with management performance ratings and organizational levels in several different organizations. These traits are intelligence, supervisory ability, initiative, self-assurance, and individuality.

Intelligence.   The level of an individual's intelligence is correlated to managerial success up to a certain cutoff point. Beyond this, individuals with higher intelligence scores are less likely to be successful as managers.

Supervisory Ability.   By this is meant "the effective utilization of whatever practices are indicated by the particular requirements of the situation."[2]

---

[1] Research is by Ghiselli as described in Alan C. Filley and Robert J. House, *Managerial Process and Organizational Behavior* (Glenview, Ill.: Scott, Foresman and Company, 1969), p. 398.

[2] Ibid., p. 398.

Initiative. This is the ability to think and act independently; to initiate action without being goaded by others.

Self-Assurance. This is defined as the extent to which the individual views himself and his own effectiveness in dealing with problems.

Individuality. This is the extent to which an individual pattern of traits is unique and dissimilar with patterns characteristic of many other individuals.

Skill Approach to Leadership

In contrast to the approach that emphasizes an identification of leadership traits (what a leader is) is the approach or focus on what a leader accomplishes (what he does in his leadership role). This analysis of leadership consequently shifts the discussion to the kinds of variant skills that leaders exhibit in the performance of their jobs. Skill in this sense is an acquired, a learned, rather than an intrinsic, quality.

In this context then, there are those basic skills on which leadership rests. These are technical, human, and conceptual skills. Technical skill refers to the leader's knowledge and ability of a specific technical field. It includes a functional mastery of the tools and techniques of a specialized field. A director of marketing or finance, for example, must have certain technical requirements for the job. It is recognized, however, that as leadership gravitates upward in the organization, there is a decided diminution of skill intensity.

Consequently, at the upper echelons of the organization, less technical and more managerial skill is required, while at the lower levels the reverse holds true.

The second skill requirement is the leader's ability to work with, inspire, and motivate the work group. The successful leader ranks high in the human relations field. He manifests a sensitivity to others. He evidences a feel for people at all levels of the organization. He is skillful in communicating with others and in making his behavior clear while simultaneously and accurately assessing the needs, the motivations, and the possible reactions of his subordinates.

The final of the three skill approaches is the need for conceptual skill. This skill involves the ability to visualize relationships, to manipulate abstract ideas, and to assess the probability of planned decisions and activities.

Summarily then, the need for technical skills diminishes as the leader ascends the structure; the need for human skill, while evident at all levels by the leader, is probably more important at lower levels where the frequency of human contact between leaders and subordinates is greater; while conceptual skills are more in demand at the higher levels where the effects of creative decision making, such as the identification of objectives, wise policy formulations, and the appraisal of management effort, are crucial to the operations of the firm.

Group Approach to Leadership

Within recent years another perspective of leadership has evolved. This is the examination of leadership as evinced from the study of the structure and functions of the group itself. Basically, there are two fundamental types of group functions: the task function and the human relations function.

The task function is concerned with the accomplishment of specific and definitive group goals such as the quantitative and qualitative aspects of the work itself. The human relations function, coincidentally, focuses on group behavior conducive to interpersonal cooperation, solidarity, the avoidance of conflict, and otherwise general group well-being. In this context then, leadership is seen as the performance of certain activities that assist the group in achieving its goals.

An interesting variation of the group approach may be seen in some leadership studies carried on at The Ohio State University. Here it was found that leadership behavior may be observed in terms of (1) initiation of structure and (2) consideration.[3]

Initiation of Structure. A leader who ranks high in this factor clearly defines his own role and makes certain it is understood by the followers. He clearly delineates relationships. Highly directive in character he, conversely, lets his subordinates know what is expected of them in their roles. The leader focuses on structural relationships and he functions within well-defined patterns of organization and established policies and procedures. Leadership, obviously, is task-oriented and highly structured around goal achievement.

Consideration. Highlighted in this dimension of leader behavior is a concern for the human relations aspects, not the toothy grin type, of the leadership function. The leader regards the comfort,

---

[3] See R. M. Stogdill and A. E. Coons, eds., *Leader Behavior, Its Description and Measurement.* Research Monograph No. 88, Columbus, Ohio: Bureau of Business Research, Ohio State University, 1957).

well-being, the status, and contributions of others. He is supportive of others. He recognizes the individual's personal worth and importance. He may allow for participation and decision-making involvement by the group members. Behavior here is indicative of friendship, mutual respect, and confidence between the leader and the led. This is the group maintenance aspect being exercised. These dimensions of leader behavior while relatively independent are neither inconsistent nor incompatible with each other and may appear in various degrees of combination. Again, initiation of structure and consideration are not individual traits of leadership but behavior that is manifested in a given situation with a given task and a given group.

Roles of Leadership

The role of a leader is a highly complex one. In the process of directing the work group, a number of roles, in varying degrees and intensity, may be played.

1. The leader is the representative. He assumes, speaks, and acts as the representative of the group. He acts as the official spokesman through which the flows of communication are channeled. Furthermore, he reinforces his representative role by maintaining cordial contact with his superior and other superiors in the organization.

2. The leader is the climate creator. He creates and nurtures the kind of working environment that encourages the best efforts of people and that unleashes talents, enthusiasm, and cooperation. It is the kind of climate that fosters individual development and personal growth, where people are aware of objectives and problems and where they are encouraged not only to commit themselves but also to be a willing participant in the determination of the outcome of events and activities.

3. The leader is a change agent. The leader as a planner, and as a director, necessarily becomes involved with change. He is sensitive to the changing needs of the organization and its people. He works toward planned change. He innovates it, applies it, and purposefully reduces resistance to its effects of application. He also reflects a high sense of adaptability to the force of change, internal and external, upon his own function, role, and on the existing order in the firm.

4. The leader is a goal emphasizer. He exhibits a concern for

goal realization. There is an emphasis on production output in order to achieve goals, an emphasis that is not inconsistent with the other desirable functions of leadership such as consideration for people. He applies, wherever required, necessary pressure to induce the desired contributions of his followers.

5. The leader is an activist. The leader is an activist, and activity requires the expenditure of energy. His energy is the catalyst that generates the drive to perform his required functions. Opportunities and dreams conjured up from behind a desk are nothing until they are physically activated. A manager may have intellect and knowledge, but these are meaningless until put to use with applications of energy.

6. The leader is an empathizer. Leaders recognize that their success is effectuated through others. Consequently, they develop a strong sense of social awareness and understanding of others. They are characterized by a sense of tolerance for individual differences that transcend race, color, or belief. They are positive rather than negative in their interpersonal relationships—displaying verve, enthusiasm, and voicing encouragement in the daily pursuit of objectives.

Styles of Leadership

It is now appropriate to discuss the matter of styles of leadership. This is done in this section by, first, noting various kinds of styles of leadership and, second, what forces influence style choices.

Kinds of Styles. Many managers find it difficult not only to *assess* their disposition to a particular leadership style but also, and fundamentally more critical, to adequately structure a positive framework for the *development* of an effective operational model of leadership.

In discussing leadership styles, the question inevitably arises as to whether a manager should be autocratic, participative, or free rein in his exercise of power.

An autocratic style refers to the leader's centralizing of authority and responsibility to himself. (See Figure 2–1.) This type of leader is highly directional and authoritarian in his relationships. Communications, including orders and commands, are mostly unilateral and stem downward from the leader to the group. Decision making is reserved for the leader.

A participative style, obversely, decentralizes authority and permits delegation of authority to subordinates. It allows for participa-

FIGURE 2–1
A Model of Leadership Styles

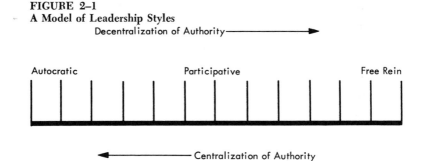

tion in decision making and accepts the contributions of the group. Communications are genuinely bilateral between the leader and the group. This style contributes to a group-based sense of responsibility. Basically supportive, it is generally endorsed over the authoritarian style because of its consistency with the spirit of personal freedom.

Free rein or laissez-faire management is exactly that. The manager avoids the use of power and relinquishes responsibility to the group for decision making. The group functions autonomously in determining goals and courses of action with only casual contact and support from the leader. Communications are group-generated and work upwards to the leader. This style is mostly leaderless in nature with little form and less structure. Obviously its use is narrowly restricted to specific work situations.

In reflecting on the above three styles there is no attempt here to critically evaluate each style. What is suggested, though, is an adoption of a flexible or situational, personal style that permits the leader to manage at various gradient points along a spectrum of power styles from autocratic through participative to free rein. Understandably, managers will, because of their individuality and personality, have a predilection for a particular style. What is being said here is that irrespective of a leader's operational style, consideration should be given an adoptive style that is reflective of certain values and forces in the leader himself, the group, the task to be accomplished, and the situation in which these factors take place.

Forces Affecting Styles. What are these certain identifiable, internal factors that will influence a manager's behavior? First of all, what is the leader's own value system and his perception of people in general? Does he believe in delegating authority, or does he feel that he's getting paid to make all the decisions. Secondly, what is his level of confidence in the subordinate's capability to make decisions? If he is unsure of, or is mistrustful of people, then he will be inclined toward closer rather than general supervision. Another factor is his own leadership inclination. Some managers function comfortably in a directive role, while others may be more comfortable when sharing responsibilities with the group. A final force in the leader's personality makeup is his tolerance for ambiguity. Some managers more than others require more predictability and surety of outcome in situations. Decentralizing one's authority requires relaxation of control over events and their outcomes.

There are also forces in the group which will affect leadership style. The leader may allow subordinates greater freedom of action if they evidence strong needs for independence in their work and if they are willing to assume responsibility for decision making. Another determinant is their identification with and response to the goals of the firm. Still another factor is their present level of knowledge and experience. Surely a willingness to accept responsibility must be accompanied by a reciprocal capacity to perform.

A third set of influential determinants focuses on certain variables in the organizational environment itself. How does top management feel about subordinate participation? What is its expected behavior of the manager? What is the degree of cohesiveness within the group? Does the unit function effectively as a team willing to work together in the delegated exercises of management? Another important factor is the nature and kind of decision-making opportunities. Is the group equipped to handle certain complex problems or should these complex problems be left in the province of the manager? And finally, there is the important variable of time. Many managers function in an environment of crisis. Their's is a "management by crisis," style which permits neither time nor latitude for delegating assignments to subordinates.

The above-mentioned determinants in the leader, the led, and the situation are some, but certainly not all, of the influential forces that can help decide whether a leader will be authoritarian or participative in his type of leadership. The successful leader, however, will carefully assess these forces relevant to his behavior and will manage accordingly.

In concluding this chapter it is hoped by now that the student has gained some appreciation of the importance of leadership in our society and in the organization. To be sure, the leader is a key figure in our economic and social life. It is leadership that inspires, that encourages, that motivates people into making a cooperative contribution to the ultimate success of the firm. In the final analysis, it can be said that our economic growth and progress are largely the result of the accumulated efforts of all our organizational leadership.

QUESTIONS

1. Why do you suppose it is difficult to accurately determine the factors that constitute effective leadership?
2. Distinguish the major differences between a "manager" and a "leader."
3. Describe the limitations of the trait approach to leadership.
4. Of what value is the skill approach to an understanding of leadership?
5. Discuss the two key variables of leadership—initiation of structure and consideration.
6. Identify and discuss some dimensions of leadership behavior.
7. Explain the situational theory of leadership. Identify the various elements in the operational model.

CASE 2–1

At a recent seminar there was a panel discussion on the ingredients of leadership. One of the panelists, a president of a small metal fabricating plant, observed that over the past 15 years he has heard all kinds of speeches and read all kinds of articles on what constitutes an effective manager. "I can name 20 or 30 personal traits that have been identified as required for the successful manager. I have sat in on sessions at which both the psychological and sociological factors of leadership were discussed. My staff, furthermore, has attended many leadership development programs. But I am not at all sure that these so-called learning experiences have made any difference in their personal behavior. I'm not even sure that personal characteristics or behavior can be changed through such approaches. Once a man reaches the age of 35 his behavior pattern and consequently his style of leadership is usually pretty well set."

1. Do you agree with the observations of the president of this company?
2. How would you respond to the president if his remarks had been addressed to you?

CASE 2–2

Ray Smith was one of the most productive sales "reps" ever to work out of the Pittsburgh district sales office of the Rohns Company. The Rohns Company produces and distributes a line of industrial products such as rubber packings, gaskets, and hoses for equipment maintenance purposes in the steel industry. Mechanical engineering was Ray's major in college and his technical expertise as a service representative was unquestioned. Highly analytical (his trademark was a miniaturized vest pocket slide rule), Ray successfully serviced several large industrial concerns and enjoyed an above-average income as a result.

The word "personality," however, seemed to be unknown to him. His reputation for being a "hard-nosed" salesman was well known throughout the sales office. Employees in the office generally avoided him whenever possible for fear of incurring his wrathful lectures on the quality of their work in sales order processing. His secretary confided that however effective, Mr. Smith was demanding and often inconsiderate in that frequently she remained after hours to complete sales correspondence.

The office personnel, including some of the other salesmen, generally felt that Ray was actually an obnoxious character who congratulated himself on his engineering background and mostly looked down his nose upon those from other disciplines such as industrial and chemical engineering. Business management was at the bottom of the list as adequate preparation for a career.

A further insight into Ray's behavior revealed that he was mostly unsmiling and unemotional and saw little humor in things. However, he was once known to be ecstatic when Michigan State—his alma mater—handily whipped Notre Dame in football. He never attended any of the office social functions—"much too busy"—and it was a known fact that while walking in the funeral cortege of the son of one of his fellow salesmen, Ray was heard telling the district manager about how he successfully closed a large order for rubber gaskets.

Later on, when the district manager retired, the New York headquarters office began searching for his replacement. Since Ray had the best record of the nine sales representatives, he seemed the likely candidate and readily accepted the position.

While discussing his new responsibilities, the corporate vice president of personnel talked to Ray about his personality and the need to be "more sensitive to and socially aware of" his people in the office. Ray agreed. Six months went by and there appeared to be no visible changes in his behavior patterns. However, at Christmas time, Ray attended the annual office party for the first time in years. He wore a paper hat; smiled broadly; danced the two-step with the office girls and made a genuine effort to mix socially. In fact, he was one of the last to leave the affair. The following workday he once again appeared to be his old unsmiling, demanding self.

1. On what basis was Ray Smith selected for the district manager's job? Evaluate this approach of selection.
2. Analyze and discuss Ray's leadership style.
3. Do you really think Ray can change his leadership style? If so, what program for change would you recommend?

3

Philosophy of Management

Scope of Discussion

ONE OF THE most fundamental aspects of management is the philosophy that underlies all of its activities. This has reference to the basic guidelines that direct the actions of a manager. It determines which course he will take when faced with a decision involving competing interests. For example, should he then consider himself to be primarily a representative of the owners of the business? Primarily concerned with protecting the continuity of the business? Primarily interested in the welfare of the employees? Primarily responsible for producing a service for the customers of the enterprise? Or primarily a compromiser to cover *all* of these interests?

How these broad questions are answered determines the way all activities in the enterprise are directed and emphasized. From the top of an organization to the very bottom, pressure is exerted to move in the direction indicated by its philosophy. That is why it has been said, for example, that an organization is but the shadow of its leaders and sometimes of one man. Either he integrates a group through basic guidelines or else the organization works against itself to its own defeat.

The purpose of this chapter is, therefore, to explore the ramifications of a philosophy of management. This is not done with a view of advocating a particular philosophy that the reader should adopt. Rather, it is done in the hope that the reader will be enabled to develop a better philosophy to serve as the foundation of his own managerial activities. To accomplish this task, the reader's attention is directed here to the philosophical aspects of this subject:

29

1. Meaning of philosophy.
2. Some historical trends.
3. Factors of philosophy.

4. Organizational aspects.
5. Communicating the philosophy.

Meaning of Philosophy

Various definitions have been proposed for the word philosophy. It has been defined by some as the reasoned science underlying a particular field of human interest or endeavor. Similar is the idea of philosophy as a scientific system. It has also been defined as the general laws of rational explanation for a given field. Broader and seemingly different in approach are definitions of philosophy that refer to it as an attitude of mind, an approach to problems, or a love of wisdom.

Careful consideration of these definitions reveals a common thread running through each of them. Philosophy has a use—that of providing a broad-gauged, basic guide to, or explanation of, action. Thus, a philosophy of life, for example, provides an individual with a basis for making decisions in matters that relate to how he shall live. When, for instance, a person has to decide between duty and friendship, his philosophy will dictate the choice. Or in determining how he shall live with his fellowman, his acceptance of the Golden Rule, let us say, determines the direction his actions will take.

Philosophy is in a sense the court of last resort. It is the *basic* guide. All else is built or predicated upon philosophy. Without a philosophy, man is like a tumbleweed, blown hither and yon by the slightest passing breeze. Man is troubled and insecure as well as ineffective under such conditions. Hence, a philosophy must be established to minimize bewilderment and avoid decisions based on expediency.

Applying these generalizations to the field of management, a philosophy here has reference to the basic guide to, explanation of, or justification for, the actions of business management.[1] If the philosophical foundation is weak or nonexistent, the life of the business will be subject to harmful insecurity. But if the philosophical foundation is strong and correct, the business will be guided with

---

[1] Inasmuch as this book is concerned with management in business, the subject of philosophy of management is discussed in terms of this institution. A general philosophy of management would hold true, however, no matter what the environment, type of institution, or economic system in which the management was being applied.

certainty through the daily welter of detail and through apparent chaos. To the leaders of such an enterprise will be drawn the loyalty and confidence of its employees. For teamwork is dependent in no small measure upon the feeling subordinates have that their superiors know what they are doing.

Some Historical Trends

A better appreciation of the meaning of management philosophy may be gained by reviewing some historical changes in the business world. This review makes no pretense of being exhaustive or precise in time divisions. Nevertheless some useful comments can be made by examining this subject under the following headings:

1. Prescientific management period.
2. Scientific management period.
3. Post–World War I period.
4. Post–World War II period.

1. Prescientific Management Period. In the United States, prior to about 1880, the philosophy of management was characterized by preoccupation with financial considerations. The test of management skill and success was invariably the degree to which profits were made or investment interests were advanced. A correct course of action could be ascertained by determining whether or not it favorably affected profits and property.

This belief was based on the idea that profits and ownership interests were the source of all other good. Perhaps working hours were long and working conditions were bad, but they would be much worse if profits were not protected. Social welfare and community affairs depended upon protecting the system that returned good profits to those who invested capital. Indeed, the ethics of the times justified and condoned the actions of men who are now often regarded as "robber barons" and cynical monopolists. But at the time, such men were regarded as true benefactors of society. Anyone who questioned their ethics, motives, and actions was a radical and troublemaker who lacked understanding of the real civic-minded segments of society.

Another philosophical attitude that prevailed during this time referred to the manner in which managerial decisions were made. How to make financial choices, how to deal with people, and how to plan or to implement plans were skills that a person either had or could be developed only through long years of experience. A manager was born or was made in the hot crucible of experience. He thus relied upon intuitive guidance when faced with a decision or knew what to do because he had been "through the mill." So, in a sense, he learned nothing from previous generations and could pass nothing on to succeeding generations as far as managerial skills were concerned.

2. *Scientific Management Period.* Roughly from 1880 to 1920, a number of individuals opposed much of the foregoing philosophy. These men believed, in the first place, that management was not solely an art, but a field with its own principles and logical relationships. They believed, too, that by study and experimentation these basic principles and relationships could be ascertained and codified. Moreover, they believed that the knowledge so acquired could be transmitted from generation to generation just as were the findings of chemistry and physics. And some believed, in the second place, that management was intended to serve the interests of employees, customers, and the community, as well as those of the owner.

Chief responsibility for advancing this view of management is accorded Frederick W. Taylor, who is commonly known as the "father of scientific management." He labored many years with his experiments and practical shopwork to develop and apply management principles. Because his work was based on controlled experiments, carefully collected data, and logical analysis, his efforts and their results were accorded the accolade of scientific management. Working with Taylor, or independently about the same time, were such sympathetic students of the movement in the United States as Henry Gantt, Frank and Lillian Gilbreth, Carl Barth, and Harrington Emerson.

One might think that this movement would have gained nearly universal support. But the contrary was true. To begin with, most industrial leaders were not convinced that management was a science equivalent, for example, to engineering. Moreover, those leaders that did borrow from the scientific management movement took only principles and practices that lent themselves to increasing labor output. As a consequence, labor generally turned against the entire movement as a device to enhance the owner's position at the expense of employees. Even the government was thereby persuaded to look with suspicion upon practices recommended by the proponents of scientific management. Due to these combined forces, the scientific movement was obstructed to such an extent that only a small group continued efforts in this direction. And those that did had to live down such epithets as "efficiency experts" which was bestowed upon practitioners who applied incorrectly or only partially the philosophy in the minds of the founders of the movement.

3. *Post–World War I Period.* As the efforts of this earlier period were examined by later students, it was seen that the good intentions and substantial contributions of the founders of scientific management had been beclouded by the way in which they had been interpreted or utilized by industry, labor, and the public. Part of the blame could undoubtedly be assessed against the founders of the scientific movement themselves for failure to emphasize the role of management as a benefactor of society. It had been assumed by the founders that this aspect of management's role would be self-apparent merely because it had been mentioned by the various founders.

Later students of management have given, therefore, much more attention to management's social responsibilities. While recognizing that the business manager is directing an economic institution, these students have given more open consideration to the place of this institution in the general scheme of society. Social as well as economic factors are to be considered when making managerial decisions. More and more, the thoughtful manager must ask himself how his economic enterprise fits into, contributes to, and is affected by the general welfare of society.

This is not intended to imply that business leaders were and are discarding capitalism and private property. Rather, this trend in management philosophizing recognizes the fact that managers must take the broad view of their responsibilities and opportunities if the private property aspect of business is to be protected. Thus to the economic phase of philosophy is being added a social and ethical dimension.

Somewhat as a corollary of the foregoing has been the growing trend classifying management as a profession. In part this is explained by the trend toward separating management from ownership, particularly in other than small businesses. Of greater import is the growing recognition that management does have characteristics of a profession. It has a body of principles, theories, and practices that require a high level and long period of training. It must follow, as indicated in the foregoing paragraph, a considered course of broad ethical conduct. It has opportunities for service beyond the mere call of financial rewards. And it has the potential, realized by some executives already, of attaining a prestige beyond that of a skilled trade or job.

4. *Post–World War II Period.* Since World War II there has been an acceleration of managerial interest in the human side of organization and of its expertise in decision-making processes. As to the former, there has been substantial concern for, first, the individual needs and identity of people in an organization, and, second, the behavioral impact of the manager on people. The first of these concerns seeks to serve various psychological, social, aspirational, and fulfillment goals of people. It recognizes that people are not only economic factors of production but have various personal needs that require managerial attention while they are working as well as after they leave the workplace. The second of these concerns recognizes that a manager affects his people not only by his organizational position of authority but also by his personal patterns of personality, attitudes toward people, consideration for others, perceptions of the value of human dignity, and democratic involvement in business relations.

On the other hand, there has been a sharpening improvement in the processes by which management makes decisions. Much progress is being made in removing decision making from the province of uncipherable intuition to analyzable and transferable methods. Gratifying results are being derived from such a variety of tools as mathematical models, statistical applications, organizational simulations, problem-solving techniques, group interaction experiments, and clinical techniques. And the tools are being applied not only to the handling of problems and factors within a business organization but also to relationships of a company to external systems and demands—ecology is a case in point. Such broad advances are serving to give the term scientific management a better claim to credibility.

Factors of Philosophy

This brief historical review serves to show the substantial progress made in fundamental thinking about management. And it also shows that a single explanation of management is inadequate. Rather, management philosophy must be eclectic. A number of facets and forces must be integrated into a basic explanation.

Among these are managerial, economic, psychological, sociological, political, ethical, and methodological components.

A basic premise of managerial philosophy is that there is a special area of human endeavor known as management. In the past, except for a few pioneers scattered through the pages of history, this view has had few adherents. In recent decades, however, this viewpoint has attracted increasing support and has inspired more confident followers. The manager, from this viewpoint, not only is a technical expert but also a managerial expert. He does not do the work of others but manages their work. He must, consequently, consciously seek to learn the secrets of this phase of his work and, once found, to apply them.

Management must establish bench marks as to the methodology it will apply in developing its skills. That management is solely an art, to be learned by practice and to be practiced by ear, is no longer generally believed. Instead, there is a national—indeed international—movement in the opposite direction. In this movement, management is recognized as a science even though, first, most of its laws as yet remain indistinct, and, second, the precise techniques of the physical sciences cannot be applied in the social sciences. This movement has also been advanced by almost universal acceptance of management training and executive development programs within the universities and business concerns themselves. And this movement has been given impetus by students in such fields as psychology, sociology, engineering, law, political science, military science, and religion.

This field of managing, in the business world, is done in the economic milieu. The manager, whether of high or low status, is a leader in an economic institution. His philosophy must take into consideration economic principles. He must understand the economic facts of life. Not until then can he transmit to others an appreciation of the basic reason of how and why the members of the group can hope to attain their own individual objectives. Whereas each member of a group may derive different satisfactions from a loaf of bread, for example, it is a primary imperative that the loaves be produced within the constraints of economic principles.

But men do not live by bread, or economic laws, alone. They are, to begin with, psychological creatures. They have feelings, emotions, sentiments, and attitudes. They are human beings as well as factors of production. As a consequence, their human traits, desires, impulses, joys, and sorrows must be considered in two important ways. How management acts toward subordinates depends, first, upon how it believes their psychological characteristics affect the application of their physiological, mental, and technical capacities and, second, upon how much it believes their psychological needs (as well as economic needs) must be satisfied in order to get optimum motivation.

But the individual is also a member of various groups both within and without the business enterprise—he has social interactions. These encompass his feelings toward others, his roles in various groups, and his status in these groups. His actions are seriously influenced by such group factors and forces. Hence management must adjust its behavioral style so that adverse group reactions are not aroused. And management's decision making must be based on the assumption that individuals have pride in and want to protect the interests of their group members.

The political phase of social relationships deserves special mention here. What role shall management play in the political arena? Shall it attempt to buy, as sometimes was true in the past, the favorable influence of governmental officials? Shall it encourage members of the management team to run for political office? Shall it seek to place its members in temporary governmental appointive and advisory positions? Shall it pursue plans that aim to educate the general public on the business and economic implications of proposed legislation, of the views of various candidates for public office, and of current laws and administrative rulings? Unless such questions are squarely faced and correctly answered, neither the ultimate good nor the particular enterprise will be well served.

But what is right and what is wrong in the economic, psychological, sociological, and political spheres of managerial philosophy? The answer must be sought in the higher area of ethics and, indeed, of religion. A search in these areas is by no means unrealistic or out of bounds. Through the centuries—directly and indirectly—the activities of business have been influenced by the then prevailing religious beliefs and forces. To mention the concept of the "just price" is a striking example of direct influence. And more recently such examples come to mind as the papal encyclicals on labor and as the opening of chapels within the factory and office grounds of some companies. Hence, ethical and religious standards are an inescapable phase of a managerial philosophy. Incidentally, Chapter 19 fully devotes itself to a discussion of the executive and ethics.

To summarize, a management philosophy must take into account a number of apparently diverse and unrelated forces and factors.

The task is difficult because by its very nature a philosophy does not have the precision of, let us say, a law of physics. Hence, people may differ in their philosophical views. But these differences are of minor importance compared to the error of leaving out of a philosophy consideration of any of the phases discussed in this section. Such omissions are a sure way for management to lose its rights of leadership. Conversely, when its philosophy is well rounded, management's role in society will be more secure and its contributions to human progress of a higher order.

Organizational Aspects

Some philosophical similarities and differences among managers may now be noted. Some of these are due to the vertical and horizontal segmentation of an organization. The formal and informal phases of an organization also reveal points of difference. And external and internal dimensions of an organization possess features worth noting in this connection.

1. *Organizational Segments.* At the top of an enterprise, there is more of a tendency to accept the broad, eclectic philosophy outlined in the preceding section. Moreover, it is at the top that the philosophy of an enterprise tends to be established and consciously kept in mind. As one moves toward the lower levels, the importance of the enterprise's philosophy becomes less apparent in the preoccupation with the daily details of actual work. There is greater concern with getting things done than with why the work has significance. Yet it is at the lower levels that the philosophical needs of management are greatest. Otherwise, employees and low-level supervisors perform without the saving grace of knowing "what it is all about."

Horizontally in an organization, there are usually found some philosophical differences. Line managers, on the one hand, tend to view their task in terms of the work for which they are responsible. They tend to be work-centered. Staff managers and other specialists, on the other hand, tend to be concerned with methodologies and with the means that serve the line managers. They tend to be idea-centered and people-centered. Of course, line managers should respect the views of the staff specialists, and vice versa. But they will not unless the top managers take precautions to cross-indoctrinate the horizontal segments of an organization.

2. *Formal and Informal Aspects.* Were one to consider only the formal structure of an enterprise, the philosophical basis of management might well emphasize such phases as the economic and

the methodological; and that has undoubtedly been done in most businesses. But, whether it is recognized or not, there are innumerable informal relations in every organization; and these relations tend to emphasize psychological, sociological, and ethical elements. The informal structures lay stress upon human patterns of leadership rather than technical authority. Interpersonal contacts and behavior are determined by feelings and social sentiments rather than by the demands of formal procedures and structures. Thus, a given executive may pay lip service to his immediate superiors, but his loyalty and confidence may lie with some executive in another part of the organization.

Ideally, of course, the formal and informal structures should coincide. This would tend to occur if the formal organization provided for psychological, sociological, and ethical needs as well as for the technical ones; but how to do this effectively in formal structures is as yet an unsolved problem. For the present, therefore, it seems wise to accept the informal organization as a useful means of helping to satisfy human needs within a business enterprise.

3. *Internal and External Aspects.* A word or two is needed on the fact that a manager has aspects of life beyond those related to the business enterprise. Of course, a sales manager, a supervisor of clerks, or a foreman of drill press operators should be indoctrinated with a philosophy consistent with that of their respective business concerns and with that of the profession of management. And, as described earlier, this philosophy should encompass such external relations as the nature and degree of participation in political and community affairs as they pertain to the business enterprise.

But there is another external area that demands a philosophical answer; that is the relationship that should exist between a manager's business life and his private life. When one views the lives of some executives, it seems obvious that they are not expected to have a private life—either that, or all elements of their private lives are expected to aid and abet the interests of the business. In such cases, the executive either divorces himself from a normal family life or dedicates his family to the interests of the business.

At the other extreme, and so far there is only a scattering of exponents at this end, is the philosophy that men work to live and should take the time to live. The idea finds expression in the rule that an executive should lock up his work when he leaves the office at night. Moreover, he should lock up when the rest of the workers do. If an executive has to take work home or work overtime, he has been overloaded, he has not been properly trained, or he is incompetent.

Perhaps the 40-hour week for managers is at present impractical. Nonetheless, development of conditions that would tend toward this should certainly be encouraged. If this is not done, the economic advantages of moving up the executive ladder may be offset by the medical, social, and family hazards of leadership.

Communicating the Philosophy

This discussion may now be directed to the manner of communicating the managerial philosophy. What does it avail to have a philosophy if it is not transmitted to others? Obviously, little if anything. So it is imperative to give thought to how a certain philosophy may be made to permeate the entire organization.

In simple terms, managers communicate their philosophy by, first, how they act and, second, talking about it. Of course, the former is the true test of one's philosophy. Do we really abide by the fundamental guides that we express? If we do, then the ultimate purpose of a philosophy is fulfilled. This need to live up to a philosophy is clearly expressed in the following statement of one company:

We believe in our free enterprise system because we believe in people. The basis of the free enterprise system is freedom for the individual to make his own choice on how he shall live his life. The importance of the individual and his personal liberty is the foundation stone of our concept of government as *servant* of the people—not their *master.*

With this basic concept we have become a great nation because each person could enjoy the fruits of his own labor in the form of spiritual and material rewards. Conversely, we believe that each individual must be responsible for the consequences of his own acts and decisions, and that he has a moral obligation to contribute, *voluntarily*, to the well-being of all, particularly the less fortunate who need the help of others.

Briefly, this sets forth our basic philosophy; it is in turn, I believe, based on and consistent with the moral law of Christianity. Our American system of free competitive enterprise has increased our production per man-hour so that we are able to produce in fewer working hours the goods and services which we need to support an ever-rising standard of living, and still have adequate time for recreation and annual vacations.

The results which we have obtained prove that only that system which permits fair profits and thereby encourages ingenuity, initiative, and the taking of financial risk for the hope of gain, produces a vigorous and growing economy. This is the kind of economy under which our company has grown steadily for nearly one hundred years; it is the kind of economy under which we hope to continue our growth and our service as we enter the second century of our company's history.

We believe that America has kept hope burning in the hearts of many peoples of the world. We feel that we have inspired this hope not so much by our material welfare as by the fact that spiritual values have flourished here more richly than elsewhere. Our freedom, our respect for individuals, our fairness, our teamwork, our good neighborliness have been traditional throughout the world.

Here we glorify the individual and his liberty. We believe that every society which has belittled the importance of the individual and has attempted to treat humanity in the mass has also eventually belittled religious teachings and faith amongst its people. To me this is an inevitable sequence. The Spirit of God does not reside in a group of people as such. The teachings of Christ invariably deal with the status of the individual. It is only the individual who can feel and live by religious faith. And it is only when individuals live by God's moral code that they can obtain and enjoy life's rich rewards!

If a company does not live up to its expressed philosophy, then all the beautiful words will be *only* beautiful words. The danger of not living up to an expressed philosophy can come from a source other than willful intent to say one thing but do another. Top management must recognize that after planning a philosophy it is necessary to organize, direct, and control functions. The president must live the philosophy and take pains to see that persons at subordinate levels live that philosophy, too. Only through an integrated effort can this method of transmitting the philosophy be successful.

In most cases, communication of philosophy must make use of the oral and printed word. Management must tell its story—clearly and continuously. It must repeat and repeat its philosophy through a variety of media and through all available channels. Such statements as the following, for example, which outline the basic beliefs and guides of a company, are simply stated but nonetheless powerful messages to all concerned:

Our company exists to serve three groups to whom we are primarily responsible:

Our Shareowners
Our Employees
Our Customers

We believe that management, the trustee of this responsibility, must serve each group fairly, never favoring one at the undue expense of the others.

We believe that to fulfill its responsibilities our company must operate a successful and profitable business.

We believe that to succeed we must design, manufacture, and sell products of the highest quality . . . products that the public wants, at prices it can afford to pay.

THIS, THEN, IS OUR CREED:

—To our shareowners we pledge a continuous effort to maintain earnings at a favorable level. We shall provide the highest possible return on their investment, while continuing our long-standing policy of reinvesting in the company a portion of each year's earnings to assure future growth and stability.

—To our employees we pledge the opportunity to earn wages equal to, or better than, the average for the community; a sound program of employee benefits; a policy of treating each individual with the respect and dignity due every human being, opportunity to grow and advance as our company grows. We shall work unceasingly to provide the greatest possible job security by a policy of product diversification, designed to avoid the hills and valleys of economic cycles.

—To our customers we pledge the finest products, at fair prices . . . products engineered and built to give lifetime satisfaction.

—Finally, we shall strive to serve our shareowners, employees, and customers justly and honestly . . . in keeping with our American tradition of democratic economic freedom.

Other devices for communication include executive training programs, conferences, and meetings of all kinds. Wherever groups are called together, it is well to open or conclude the meetings with a tie-in to basic company purposes and guides. This results in more than communication. It adds assurance that the leaders of the meetings will themselves precheck to see that what is done coincides with the company philosophy.

With this note on the importance of an integrated process, the discussion of a philosophy of management is closed. It is hoped that the necessity for such a philosophy has been shown. Moreover, it is hoped that the idea has been conveyed that such a philosophy is not an esoteric subject known only to gray-bearded patriarchs. Rather, part of the intent here has been to indicate that the subject has an aura of simplicity, which should be one of its strongest advantages. To be sure, no philosophy provides precise, quantitative guides to action. But a thoughtfully considered philosophy makes a constructive contribution to solving problems of organized effectiveness and personal needs and security.

QUESTIONS

1. Why is a philosophy of management an essential in business?
2. What views did the founders of the scientific management movement incorporate into their philosophy of management?
3. What is the strength and what is the weakness of a philosophy of business management constructed on an economic base?
4. Why is it argued that the ethical phase of a philosophy of business is closely related to religion?
5. In what respects, if any, are there differences of philosophical outlook or concern among the several levels of an organization?
6. Under what philosophical conditions might the formal and informal organization structures of a company be similar?
7. What relationships should exist between a manager's business life and his private life?
8. What suggestions can you make regarding ways and means of communicating a managerial philosophy?

CASE 3-1

In one of the departments of a small steel fabricator, metal parts are cut with the use of a gas torch. The cutting torches get their gas supplies from some common tanks located just outside of the building.

Recently an efficiency expert was brought into the company to suggest, if he could, ways to reduce costs and increase output. In the cutting department, he concluded that the torches could operate as efficiently and with less cost if the gas pressure of the torches was set at 15 pounds of pressure instead of the currently used 25 pounds of pressure.

When he made this suggestion, the superintendent pointed out that he was certain the employees would complain that their torches would not operate properly and would certainly go out of their way to prove that they were right.

Feeling certain of his suggestion, the expert asked that a deception be tried, one which he had found worked elsewhere. With the knowledge of the operating foreman, the pressure gauges were to be adjusted so that they read 25 pounds as the pressure was gradually lowered. This was to be a temporary expedient in that the correct gauge readings would be set as soon as the experiment had proved to be successful. In the meantime, if any employee complained or became suspicious, he was to be told that some of the new batches of gas were not quite up to par.

1. What is your opinion of such a deception?
2. What if it worked? Doesn't it meet the test that you can't argue with success?

CASE 3–2

The president of the All Sales Company had returned from a one-day conference of top executives concerned with the topic, "Business and Religion." He had been impressed with the talks, the discussions and arguments, and the seriousness of the executives who had expressed themselves on various aspects of the topic. On returning home, he came to the conclusion that the conference would have been a waste of time unless something were done along these lines in his own company. So he called together his top echelon of executives for an exchange of views.

He opened the meeting by telling the group some of the ideas that came up in the conference. Then he said he wanted his executives to express themselves on three opinions running through his mind (as well as others which they might suggest) as follows:

a) A minister should be hired in the personnel department to whom employees could come and talk over problems that they didn't feel comfortable in unburdening to the business staff. The minister would have no authority and would be there solely for personal counseling purposes on a voluntary basis.

b) A small chapellike room would be opened to which an employee could go during working hours for brief meditation. Such breaks, he thought, were just as relevant as coffee breaks.

c) And finally, he thought the company needed a stated expression on ethics which would be the basis for all interactions and suggested the following: Do right voluntarily.

1. What is your opinion of this man's excursion into religion and ethics?
2. How would you evaluate the specific proposals which he submitted for implementing his basic idea on religion and ethics?

4

Decision Making

Introduction

DECISION MAKING is, like philosophy, a pervasive aspect which deserves attention at the outset of study of management. Decisions are an inescapable part of everything a manager does or with which he is concerned. In planning, organizing, directing, and controlling a manager is constantly making decisions about the various factors, forces, and people with which he must deal. Indeed, the words decision maker could well be a synonym for manager. It might even be easy to conclude that something which all managers do all the time cannot be too complicated and therefore should merit no more than passing mention.

Such a conclusion might seem to find additional support in the simple definition of a decision as a choice between alternatives. But how are choices made? Don't alternatives themselves have to be decided upon? What means should be chosen to attain what ends? How do particular ends affect various alternative means? What assumptions and theories, what personal aspirations and drives, and what conditions and constraints govern choices? These questions are full of perplexities that characterize decision making as a complex subject worthy of searching study.

Attention in this chapter is, therefore, directed to the following phases of decision making:

1. General nature of decision making.
2. Major factors of decision making.
3. Subject matter of decision making.
4. Methods of decision making.
5. Resources of decision making.
6. Management information systems.

General Nature of Decision Making

To understand the nature of managerial decision making, it is desirable to survey its scope, implications, and components.

1. *Scope of Decision Making.* Defining decision making as a choosing among alternatives is useful chiefly as a springboard for more detailed analysis. To begin with, it is important to note that choices must be made among *ends* (goals or objectives) and the *means* of attaining them. Looking first at ends, choices invariably must be made among several, and often competing or somewhat divergent, objectives. Moreover, the choices must usually grade or rank (which involves decisions) a number of objectives which must be attained at the same time. It may be easy to say, for example, that the business executive must place profits as his basic goal. But if he attempts to maximize profits, he will soon find that others, such as customers and workers (with their own set of goals), will be dissatisfied. Hence the manager must seek a reasonable (less than maximum) profit so that reasonable (competitive) service can be rendered to the customer and reasonable (more than just minimum) wages are paid. He must, therefore, not *maximize*, but rather *optimize*, profits and, indeed, all objectives.

In actuality, decision making does not always begin with ends and then proceed to mean choices. The goals a manager can seek are limited in part by the means at his disposal. For example, the kind and quality of products which are to be marketed depend upon the methods a company can utilize in its selling program. As time goes on, selling methods can, and invariably, must be changed in line with the success in attaining objectives (for example, profits that can be plowed back into the business operations). So the relation between means and ends is reciprocal; ends depend upon means, means upon ends, consequently calling for new decisions regarding each other with the passage of time.

This continuous feature of decision making deserves emphasis. An executive does not make one decision and thereby gain relief from further decision making. Rather, every decision is a part of a stream of decisions, affected by past decisions, related to other current decisions, and of influence on future decisions. For example, the manager who is deciding how to discipline a subordinate should give consideration to past decisions in similar cases, to the immediate consequences of his present action, and to future implications (decisions he will subsequently be making) of his current decision.

2. Implications of Decision Making. The simple definition of decision making given earlier does not supply an answer to the question of methods and resources to be brought to bear in making a choice. If, for example, a coin is tossed into the air, either sheer guessing or probability theory may be used to decide whether to say "heads" or "tails" in a series of tosses. So it is for the executive: he may call the turn in the matter of his choices by using such methods as guesswork, past experience, logical reasoning, mathematical models and computations, and statistical calculations. And he may rely upon his own resources or seek the assistance of various experts, individually or in groups.

This brings us then to the matter of who is involved, and how, in decision making. To be sure, every manager, high or low, is a decision maker. But does he have full and exclusive domain in his own jurisdiction? Far from it. Each executive must be cognizant of three directions from which participants enter into his decision making. First, there are the superior executives whose decision must be given due weight. Second, there are subordinate layers of personnel whose views cannot be slighted. And third, there are one's peers whose reactions must be respected. For example, how budgeted funds are to be expended must be decided in the light of one's superior's wishes, subordinates' expectations, and peers' possible reactions.

It is imperative to note that the foregoing discussion has assumed that an executive recognizes every instance for which he must make a decision. This is not a valid assumption. The mere fact that one often has to cure problems implies that an earlier decision-making situation was not recognized; for, had it been, and had appropriate action been taken at the time, the later problem would not have transpired. One of the most important qualities of an executive is his ability to recognize that a situation has arisen or is about to arise that requires a decision. In other words, the good executive— like a good railroad engineer—sees the yellow signs which, reacted to in time, will make drastic action unnecessary should red signs appear.

Moreover, it is well to note that not deciding is itself a way of deciding. The executive who does nothing about changing sales methods, for example, has made a decision. As customer desires or fundamental channels of distribution change, doing nothing to change existing sales methods amounts to a change in sales methods relative to the new marketing conditions. Hence, the simple definition of decision making is useful only if, among other things, an executive is aware of the decision-making aspects of "no decisions."

3. Components of Decision Making. The nature of decision making can be better appreciated by examining a model such as that depicted in Figure 4–1. Here it is seen that managers (of vari-

FIGURE 4–1
A Model of Managerial Decision Making

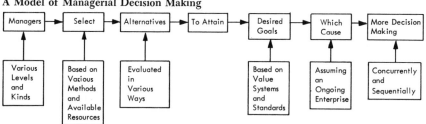

ous levels and kinds) make choices (based on various methods and available resources) among alternative means (evaluated in various ways) to attain goals (selected by appropriate value systems and standards). The process, in an ongoing enterprise, is then repeated in various concurrent and sequential stages.

A closer view of part of the choosing dimension, as illustrated in Figure 4–2, reveals some important aspects of decision making.

FIGURE 4–2
Information and Value Systems in Decision Making

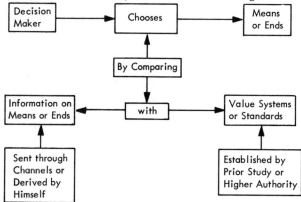

To make a choice, whether of means or ends, the characteristics of the alternatives available must be evaluated or tested against some standards (or value systems) established by prior study or by recourse to a higher authority. Information (inputs) on these matters must be derived from the manager's own experience or supplied to him through channels by his superiors, peers, or assistants. In choosing, for example, between a piecework plan or a bonus, time-saving plan of wage incentives for compensation purposes, an executive would have to compare the characteristics of each of these plans with the environmental and personnel conditions in his business. In this way, he can make that choice which is better for his company and people.

The ongoing feature of business calls for a flow of information to evaluate the effectiveness of decisions so that adjustments (new decisions), if needed, may be made. This process is termed the "feedback" or "follow-up" aspect of decision making. It requires a *sensor* to gather information about results of a decision, a *discriminator* to compare results with plans, and a *channel* to transmit messages from point to point. The sensor, discriminator, and channel may be a person or some instrument (such as a recording device, telephone, computer, statistical report, etc., or a combination thereof).

Feedback systems are of two major types: open end and closed end. The open end, the most common type, is illustrated in Figure 4–3. In this type, reports on performance are obtained only occasion-

FIGURE 4–3
An Open-End Feedback System

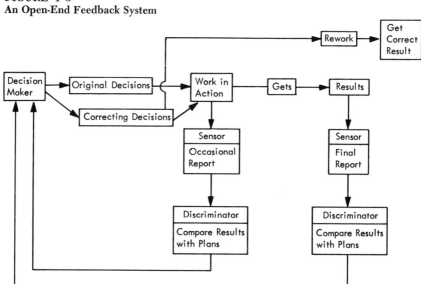

ally during work in process or only after a project is completed. Obviously, corrective action under this type is slow at times to the point that nothing much can be done to straighten out an operation that is going wrong or has gone wrong. In the closed-end type, illustrated in Figure 4–4, reports on performance are obtained con-

FIGURE 4–4
A Closed-End Feedback System

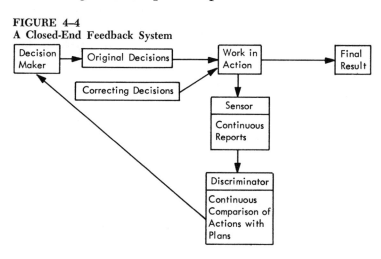

tinuously and concurrently as work proceeds. Consequently, corrective adjustments can be made before deviations from desired plans have become serious. Both types essentially place reliance upon flow of information, upon which successful decision making must necessarily depend.

Major Factors of Decision Making

The term managerial, when used in connection with decision making, implies that the decisions to be made will involve that part of a business which is concerned—as noted in an earlier chapter—with planning, organizing, directing, and controlling the work of others. This selection requires clarification and amplification in terms of who is excluded and why, what is included directly, and who indirectly affects or enters into managerial decision making.

1. *Exclusions.* Business decisions are by no means the exclusive domain of business managers (whether called administrators, executives, supervisors, or leaders). For example, union leaders, governmental agencies, and leaders of various social and community groups have much to say in various ways—sometimes generally and

sometimes specifically—about various business decisions. Full consideration of their processes of decision making would require a discussion too lengthy to include here; however, in a later subdivision of this section their influence upon managerial decision-making will be noted.

2. *Levels and Kinds of Decision Makers.* Obviously, all managers in a business organization make decisions. But their powers differ. In terms of their decision-making powers, managers may be classified according to *level* and *kind*.

Level refers, of course, to the hierarchy of organization structure. In most companies, for example, the president makes decisions for the entire company. Proceeding downward with successively narrower jurisdictional authority are various layers of managers, ending with the supervisor—the first level of management. From the point of view of level, therefore, decision making is largely a matter of the numbers over whom and for whom one makes decisions; it is a matter of how many people will be influenced by the choices an executive makes.

Kind refers, on the other hand, to the manner in which one's decisions affect others. This has reference to the concepts of "line" and "staff" which will be examined more fully in a later chapter. But for present purposes a simple example will be sufficient: A manager, such as the sales manager, has the authority to require his salesmen to follow the decisions he makes, let us say, in the matter of pricing policies. The market research manager, however, whose studies lead him to conclude that quantity rebates, let us say, will not significantly affect sales in his company, can only suggest that a rebate policy not be followed; he cannot enforce this conclusion because he has only "staff" authority.

This discussion must not be interpreted as one that separates executives into exclusive compartments. For one thing, an executive may well fall into all these compartments because of his informal relations with others, as will be noted in a later chapter. Thus, the vice president in charge of research and development is at the same time (formally) a high-level staff executive and (informally) one with much line influence. His authority in terms of organization level and of influence over others flows from his particular specialty. His decision-making powers and problems obviously are different from those of the supervisor of janitors, for example.

3. *Indirect Decision Makers.* In making decisions, an executive must weigh both the effect of his decisions upon others and the

reactions he may expect from others. This means that his decisions must be adjusted in accordance with, first, the decisions others will make because of his decisions or, second, the degree and kind of cooperation he can expect because of his decisions. The first factor, the decisions of others, is illustrated by the example of the industrial relations manager who is trying to determine what type of seniority clause he wants to bargain for with the union. He may want a clause in which seniority has minor weight for promotion, let us say, as compared with ability. But if he thinks that a strike might be called by the union over this issue, he may decide the price is too high. He, therefore, may propose a clause in which seniority and merit are given more nearly equal emphasis.

Even when direct decisions of others need not be considered, there is always the question of the acceptance which others will accord particular decisions. This is well exemplified by what may happen when a manufacturing or office process is changed. Technically, new equipment and a rearranged layout seem to be far superior to the old. But output does not come up to expectations. Soon it is realized that employees are the retarding factor; for fear of job loss or because of disturbed social relations, they are not furnishing the required cooperation. Until this cooperation is obtained, the resistance to change will be critical. Hindsight now tells the executive that in planning the change he should have had two plans, one for the technical side of the problem and one for the human side.

In brief, the decision maker himself is sooner or later affected by those who are affected by his decisions. He must weigh the direct decisions or indirect influence of others. This reciprocal relationship is difficult to evaluate in advance. But to the extent that allowances are made for the influence of others, the chances of jeopardizing the success of one's decisions are minimized.

Subject Matter of Decision Making

Subject matter raises a number of pertinent questions about decision making. The first question, not too difficult to answer, is, what subjects are the province of decision makers? Second, how does breadth or narrowness of subject matter affect decision making? And third, there is the very interesting question of what, if anything, is common to all subjects insofar as decision making is concerned?

In answer to the first of these questions, there are three large categories of subject matter with which the decision maker is concerned. To begin with, technical decisions must be made in such functional fields as production, sales, finance, engineering, accounting, and personnel. As every executive soon learns, these functional fields also require managerial decisions of planning, organizing, directing, and controlling. And both the functional and the managerial subjects involve decisions about such basic factors as objectives, policies, functions, procedures, people, and environmental matters. All of these areas (except the functional) are amplified in other chapters in this text; hence, at this juncture it is sufficient to note that every manager must have some competence in and appreciation of these basic subject areas.

The next question is, how does breadth of subject matter affect decision making? That there is some relationship is implied in such statements as the following:

We can't promote "X" until he learns to see problems on a company-wide basis.
We've got to see the "big picture."
There are too many specialists around here.
Potential for filling the big jobs is too scarce.

Presumably then, decision making at the supervisory levels or in staff units is somewhat different than at the upper levels of management. Taking a closer view, it may be deduced that lower and specialized levels have fewer different kinds of decisions to make, many of the decisions are repetitious, and all are invariably subject to some guidelines or restrictions from above. The upper levels are faced with more novel situations, have fewer guidelines to work with, and have more freedom of choice. Viewed in this way, it is not so much the subject matter itself which causes differences in decision making, but rather the conditions that surround the area of subject matter which falls within one's jurisdiction. The unknowns and variables with which one must contend when deciding whether or not to automate a process are different from and more numerous than those that, let us say, a man detailed to design electrical switches, must consider after an affirmative answer has been given by the higher executives in regard to the automation of a manufacturing process.

This brings us to the third question: what, if anything, is common to all decision making? Besides differences in decision making at various levels, there must also be similarities—or the executive ladder would indeed be a series of unrelated steps, and advancement would follow no logical pattern. Something must be learned at lower levels that is useful at higher levels. Does knowledge of subject matter at lower levels and in more restricted staff areas help one to make decisions as he progresses to higher levels? Yes, but this is by no means the critical factor. The innumerable instances of people moving successfully from one functional field to another (often unrelated) are proof of this. Do knowledge and skill in managing and in the factors common to all areas have a significant carry-over from lower to upper levels of management? Sophisticated research is not available to support an affirmative answer. But again personal experiences of many people seem to give credence to the thesis that those whose managerial skills make them successful managers at lower levels will be successful at higher levels also.

Is such success due to knowledge of subject matter or to skill in handling subject matter? At this juncture it is impossible to say, but certainly the methods one uses have much to do with successful decision making. The interest that has been shown in this aspect of decision making in recent years, and the pertinent findings that have been disclosed, would lead to a favorable opinion about the importance of methods in decision making. Hence, it is to this aspect that attention is turned in the next section.

Methods of Decision Making

Decision making as an act implies the use of methods. The second part of this section describes various methods which are being used widely or which have promise of wider use. But to place these methods in their proper perspective, it is desirable to make some general comments about methods and about viewpoints regarding methods.

1. *General Survey of Methods.* For a long time almost everybody believed—and undoubtedly many still do—that the method used in making decisions could be simply described but was beyond analysis. In short, a person either did or did not have judgment (ability to make decisions), and only practical experience could bring out this trait or demonstrate its absence. If one had judgment, he could make good decisions, and he deserved consideration for managerial advancement. If one didn't have it, this would soon be apparent, and further concern with such a person for managerial positions would be unwarranted.

As long as this belief prevailed, historical progress in decision making was precluded. Such a view is based on the thesis that there is no formal way to teach judgment. So reliance has to be placed upon the "school of hard knocks"; and only those who have "it" in them succeed. How "it" got in them and how "it" developed were beyond analysis. So there simply wasn't anything to be taught, and investments in teaching "judgment" would be futile. One generation of successful executives could neither teach nor transmit anything of its methods to the next. Each generation of executives had to build its methods from scratch.

Many now question this thesis. But our accumulated store of knowledge is still insufficient to discard this view entirely. Even now, many executives cannot tell how they arrived at a particularly successful decision. Even now, many problems arise to the solution of which one can only bring deep soul-searching. Even now, some executives still turn to soothsayers, fortune-tellers, and "star readers" because nothing else seems to be available. Even now, one hears of executives to whom a solution to a difficult problem came "out of the blue" after a good night's sleep. So respect for informalized judgment must be retained to some extent.

On what grounds do some question this thesis? A number of points can be cited. There seem to be logical, quantitative, and interdisciplinary arguments for believing that something useful and transmissible can be said about decision making.

Certainly there seems to be a logic to decision making. There is a method of reasoning from premises, for example, which can be taught. In this sense, the logic which is applicable in other forms of human activity—philosophy, law, and science—is pertinent to business organizations. If this be not granted then economics, which is universally accepted as a basis of business, can contribute nothing to business decisions. So the conclusion seems inevitable that one generation of business executives can learn from another and thereby build a progressively better system of decision making from the processes and principles of logical reasoning.

Increasingly, too, quantitative areas of human knowledge are making gratifying contributions to decision making, because managers must not only decide what to do but also how much of what to do. It is not enough to conclude—for example—that a wage increase is in order; the decision must establish a quantitative level to the increase. Nor is it enough, to cite another example, that an increase in the prices of a company's products is in order; the increase must be stated quantitatively giving due consideration to customer and competitor quantitative reactions. To these and similar decisions, various statistical, mathematical, graphical, and computational techniques and methods are making contributions of inestimable value. Some of these techniques and methods will be described in the next section. Certainly all are of a type that can be explained to and passed on to succeeding generations in improved form.

Findings of various experts working together also seem to justify the assertion that decision making is not an inexplicable activity. Merely to mention the emergence of operations research (discussed in the next section) is sufficient to indicate a new attitude toward decision making. Here, as well as in other examples of interdisciplinary cooperation and research, a fundamental thesis is that knowledge and skills developed and utilized in particular scientific areas can be combined effectively in the solution of business problems. Thus, what is learned in one area can be applied and extended in other areas. Indeed, chances for improvements in decision making seem to be increased when experts from other areas come together for the purposes of applying their skills jointly in the field of business.

To summarize, it is admitted that many things that happen in business are novel, unique, and highly abstract. In this area, the decision maker must rely upon intuition, hunch, judgment, and luck. But there are many things that are within the realm of systematic analysis. In this area, the decision makers would be wise to avail themselves of the growing body of logical, quantitative, and joint-effort knowledge and techniques.

2. Specific Methods. It is now appropriate to note the more common methods which are available to managerial decision makers. Obviously, this cannot be an exhaustive survey. All that can be done is to undertake some brief descriptions and make some brief comments. The order in which the methods are discussed implies no evaluation of importance. Included for discussion here are the following:

a)	Past experience.	*d*)	Simulation.
b)	The scientific method.	*e*)	Heuristic.
c)	Quantitative methods.		

a) *Past Experience.* One of the oldest and undoubtedly one of the most widely used methods of decision making is that of utilizing past experience—one's own or that of others. Keeping records—

in one's mind or on paper—of past decisions and their outcomes provides a useful means of deciding what to do—or not to do—in the future. So long as the new situation is not significantly different from a past situation, this method has much to commend it. Then a decision can be quickly made with good reason to expect success.

The major shortcomings of this method are twofold: dissimilarity between new and old situations, and accessibility blocks to past decisions. The first of these can be described by the statement often heard that things seldom happen exactly as they did in the past. To the extent that they differ, managers must make changes from, or discard entirely, old decisions. So using old decisions really involves another one—whether or not to use the old decision; and this may be just as difficult as starting anew. Despite the perplexing question of similarity between old and new situations, however, there seems to be little doubt that most executives will still rely on their experiences in the past.

Removal of the second of the shortcomings—accessibility blocks—requires systematic and cooperative effort. Unfortunately most experiences and decisions are locked in the recesses of one's mind or in the minds of others. To be sure, most managers can readily recall some of their past decisions, but usually only a small proportion of them. And the experiences of others (again only a very small sample) can be found in magazines, books, and other published materials. But most human experiences are unavailable for use.

b) The Scientific Method. As an imposing contrast to experience as a means of decision making is the growing use of the scientific method. This method is based upon facts, classified and organized through a series of logical steps. It gains its name, therefore, from the attempt to adopt the attitudes and processes of the physical scientist who seeks solutions to problems from data supplied by careful experiments. Similarly, the scientific organizational manager, faced with problems, seeks data that will serve to provide answers to his questions.

Although enthusiasm for scientific decision making is easy to generate, it has two serious weaknesses that should be noted. First, facts are difficult to obtain in the managerial field—particularly facts about people and about the future. Second, facts are difficult to obtain in time. Often, decisions must be reached within a time interval that permits little or no fact gathering.

Despite these shortcomings, the scientific method has the best hope for successful planning. Hence, it deserves fuller descriptions. This is done by viewing the following steps of the scientific method:

(1) Statement of purpose.
(2) Preliminary analysis.
(3) Suggested solutions.
(4) Testing and selection of alternatives.

(5) Testing selected solution.
(6) Application and follow-up.

(1) STATEMENT OF PURPOSE. The first step of the scientific method is to establish as precisely as possible one's purposes. The purpose may be either to accomplish particular objectives or to solve problems. The former is exemplified by such statements as "Sales are to be increased in the next period by 10 percent," or, "Accounting for customer accounts is to be converted to electronic equipment within two years." The latter is exemplified by such statements as, "How can collective bargaining be placed upon a factual basis?" or, "How should our decentralized warehouses be integrated into a more efficient distribution system?"

The statement of a problem is particularly difficult. To say, for example, that sales are low does not state a problem. Low sales are an undesirable result. The desired result—high sales—was not attained because some problem was not solved. What if one has—to cite a highly improbable situation—fallen into a bear trap? The "being in the bear trap" is a highly undesirable result. The problem now is how to get out. Thus, every problem has two major phases, first, where is one in relation to where he wants to be (his objective), and, second, how does one get from an undesirable point to a desired point.

Another facet of the "caught in the bear trap" situation is worth noting. One must develop a plan of getting out before he can keep from falling into future bear traps. This is well exemplified by human relations problems. One has to solve the current problem before he can prevent the difficulty from recurring. To be sure, two plans may have to be operated simultaneously; one, let us say, to remove unfavorable employee attitudes; and the other, to develop favorable attitudes. The point is that one plan alone could scarcely cure and prevent at the same time. Or to refer to the bear-trap situation, one cannot prevent oneself from falling into a bear trap into which one has already fallen. After one gets out (cure), he can try to keep from falling in again (prevention).

(2) PRELIMINARY ANALYSIS. An accurate statement of pur-

poses, objectives, problems, or questions is so important that whatever is determined in the foregoing step should be considered tentative until the case is examined more carefully. This is in line with the adage that a correct statement of a problem is half its solution.

Two suggestions are in order in making a preliminary analysis of a problem to be solved. First, it is well to know something of the people involved and the general circumstances in the problem area. One should be sure to have his "feet on the ground" or "to know the ropes" before plunging ahead. These are popular ways of stating that deciding, let us say, to convert an office operation from a manual to a machine setup should not be approached strictly from an engineering point of view. There are personal attitudes, organizational relationships, and actual or implied job rights to be considered.

Second, the views of interested and capable parties should be sought. This suggestion assures the adoption of the "principle of participation," as well as the inclusion of helpful, technical assistance. A decision is more likely to be successful if it is eventually executed by those who had some hand in its development, and if it was helped along by competent contributors. Moreover, this approach is reminiscent of the poem about the six blind men who "looked at" an elephant. Because each took a partial view, none had a correct picture of the animal; but, in combination, their individual impressions might form a picture of a complete elephant.

(3) SUGGESTED SOLUTIONS. With a clear fix on the problem, the next step in the scientific method is to establish possible solutions. This step, it must be admitted at the outset, has to fall back upon guess, educated hunch, experience, and judgment in the field of management. Until a larger store of managerial principles, knowledge, and tested relationships is accumulated, reliance has to be placed in this step upon managerial judgment and imagination.

Of interest in this connection are such notable developments as brain storming and creativity sessions. These seek by individual and group meetings to generate suggested solutions. The more that are generated, the better the chance that the list will contain the best possible decision.

(4) TESTING SELECTED ALTERNATIVES. Which of the suggested options should be adopted? The answer is simple—the one that will work best. But getting the answer is supremely difficult because it means getting the facts on each plan. How does one go about determining, for example, whether a 3-, 12-, or 20-factor plan of evaluating employees is best? Or whether, in collective bargaining,

employees will be offered a 10-, 15-, or 20-cent an hour increase? Suggestions on approaches to getting answers have been made in the preceding paragraphs of this chapter, so further discussion is unnecessary here.

Whatever method is used, however, they all tend to follow somewhat the same formula. The advantages and disadvantages of the several alternatives (suggested solutions) are weighed on the scales of available information. The option with the best net score is adjudged the one to be employed. In a sense, data decide the course to be followed. This might sound as though executive judgment were being discarded. On the contrary, much judgment is still necessary throughout all stages to insure that logical rules are being followed. Machines may "think," but only because a human mind tells them how to think and sees to it that the machine does not run off the track.

(5) Testing selected solutions. Having determined what is the best alternative, application of it would logically seem to be the next step. Often this is so; and indeed time limitations may require this. But where possible an intermediate stage of testing is desirable. This may be done on a trial basis in a limited area or on a "pilot plant" basis. The former provides a check to see whether or not the plan works out in practice as expected. An advertising plan may be checked in a local area before it is put into effect on a national scale. Or a training program may be tried out in a branch plant before it is installed companywide.

A "pilot operation" has similar advantages. An accounting systems may be operated under the jurisdiction of a consulting concern until all the "bugs" are worked out. Thus, the trial runs permit corrections to be made, unforeseen situations to be handled, and refinements to be included before final application under normal, full-operating conditions.

(6) Application and follow-up. The adopted decision should then be applied and continuously checked. To begin with, adequate instruction and guidance should be provided to see to it that a plan is operated as intended. It is unfortunate when a manager concludes that his work is largely done when he has made a good decision and that his subordinates can take over without further ado. This seems to be a strange point of view. If an executive has struggled for some period of time to arrive at a decision, how can he expect his subordinates to grasp the technicalities of its ramifications without careful supervision?

Next, it is desirable to check the degree of success attending the operation of an adopted plan. In the first place, checking will permit adjustments to be made so that the plan will better serve the purposes for which it was intended. Certainly, the so-called flexible budget, for example, is a plan whose usefulness depends upon changing the basis of the plan as fundamental conditions change during the period for which it was intended to be used. In the second place, checking will permit lessons to be learned that can be applied to the improvement of future decision making. So, year by year, better decisions will be developed because of close scrutiny of past successes and failures. For the real test of success is not perfection but gradual improvement. And this can be assured by good follow-up.

c) *Quantitative Methods.* A whole array of quantitative methods is increasingly being refined and made available to the managerial decision maker. Through quantitative tools, from simple records such as account books through advanced mathematical abstractions, the hands of the decision maker are being strengthened. The usefulness of some of these, such as accounting and various statistical methods, is so well accepted and known that further discussion here is unnecessary. So attention will be directed to more recent developments.

One of the most interesting contributions to decision making is in the area of probability theory. Here mathematical devices for computing probabilities, and the logical idea of probability, are gaining increasing acceptance from managers. One may consider, for example, the case of a prospective strike. What should management do about it—take the strike or make concessions? The best possible answer cannot be determined without a consideration of probabilities: What are the chances that the strike will last one week, two weeks, three weeks, etc.? And what percentage of one's customers will be willing to wait for deliveries as the strike goes through one, two, or "X" weeks? Estimating probabilities and feeding the estimates into revenue and loss data helps management to determine the best course of action in such a situation.

A useful device for incorporating probability calculations into available choices is the so-called decision tree, illustrated in Figure 4–5. Here it is seen that a company has a choice of making and selling sleds or skis. In either case, its sales may be large or limited. What is the probability of each class of sales and how does it influence the ultimate decision? As seen in the figure, volume of sales has been estimated for each level of sales for each of the two prod-

FIGURE 4–5
A Decision Tree

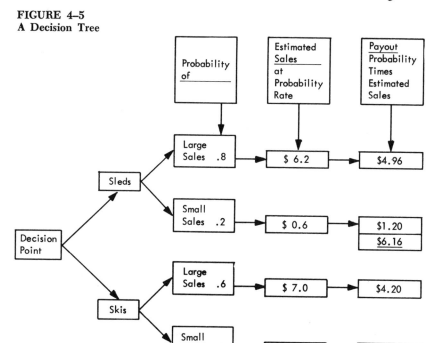

ucts. But the full value of these sales should not be used to compare the two products because the probability of making each of them is less than 100 percent. Hence, each sales estimate is multiplied by the probability of making the sale to arrive at its probable value or as this figure is called, its payout. Carrying out these calculations, the payout for sleds is $6.16 while that for skis is $5.40. The decision is, therefore, in favor of sleds, even though skis have an estimated, large sale of $7, which, however, is offset by its lower probability of being attained.

This illustration of the probability method leads to the point that business decisions are often like the decisions one makes in playing games. And naturally enough, many people—both practitioners and, particularly, students—have recognized the applicability of game theory to decision making in business. In games there are probabilities of winning and losing, the strategies to be used depend upon the moves the "opponent" may make, and there is a continual need for new decisions as the game proceeds. Business operates under similar conditions. Take the case of a company that is thinking of entering a new market area. What are the probabilities of success? How are they affected by varying amounts of investment that might be applied? What will competitors do in regard to prices, services, and advertising to counter this move into their territory? How must we adjust and readjust to their reactions? Game and probability theory can provide some aid in this very serious "game" of business.

The foregoing has hinted at the fact that decision making is not a matter of absolutes. No manager should expect, for example, simply to maximize sales or profits or minimize expenses or losses. He must maximize or minimize over a period of time and with due consideration for other objectives. In the matter of time, for example, maximizing profits may mean making decisions which result in very low profits, or no profits, currently but with a view to better profits later. To do otherwise might mean good profits now but none later, so that over the years the total profit would be less than satisfactory. In the matter of balancing objectives, a manager who attempts to maximize profits might well find that he has minimized wages or service to customers to such an extent that the quality and salability of the product are harmed and expected maximum profits are not realized. So instead he must make decisions that "optimize" profits, that is, decisions that result in less than maximum attainment but nevertheless are realistic in view of the fact that other objectives (those involving sales and personnel, as cases in point) have to be realized to a reasonable extent. So the wise manager makes decisions that optimize, not maximize, objective attainment.

In this matter of having to decide within limits, management can also have recourse to the method of linear programming. This method applies in situations in which given resources might be used in a variety of ways. What is the best way of allocating the resources, recognizing that the resources have limitations of capacity and that the ways in which they might be used depend upon the objectives to be sought? For example, a company has facilities that can be used to make tents or sleeping bags. It can make tents only, or sleeping bags only, or both in restricted quantities, and the returns on each product are not the same. Would restriction to one or the other, or some combination of both, yield the best results? Linear programming, executed either graphically or mathematically, serves to produce an answer which would otherwise be forthcoming only by luck or by cumbersome and time-consuming approximations.

In these quantitative aspects of decision making, information is so basic that much thought is being given to the theory of information sources, flow, usage, and requirements. Terms in current use, such as information input and output, feedback, and systems, are indicative of the significance accorded to information in decision making. What is happening here is a recognition of the fact that to make decisions, appropriate information must be obtained before things happen, during an activity, and after the action has been completed.

The importance of well-structured flows of information has been impressed upon executives by the characteristics of electronic computers. These contributors to decision making are fully effective only if they are proficiently programmed. They cannot "think" for themselves. If executives are to derive useful information and guidance (outputs) from computers, information and instructions (inputs) must be appropriately fed into them. Considerable thought must be given, therefore, to the kinds and forms of information that computers can digest, as well as to the timing by which various quantities of information will be fed into the system. Thus the computer can make tremendous numbers of calculations quickly, accurately, and usefully only if the flow of information into it is carefully systematized.

d) *Simulation.* Another method of decision making which is of interest is that of simulation or model building. A simple example is the use of charts of how systems operate or might operate (for example, a hiring procedure, a manufacturing line, a channel of distribution, or a budget-building procedure). A more refined example is the use of three-dimensional scale models of projected manufacturing processes and layouts. Of more recent origin and on a more sophisticated plane is the use of computers programmed to simulate such situations as a revised distribution system, a new warehousing plan, or a control plan for jet airline operations.

An interesting example of model building is the use of business games to develop and improve executive decision-making skills. These games require preparation of a series of case materials simulating business situations about which participants must make "decisions" which affect all parts of the business. "Judges" evaluate the effect of the decisions on sales, profits, costs, customers, competitors, etc. Then the participants make new decisions which again are evaluated. At the end of the "game," the final scores of the various participants are reported. A session of analysis and constructive criticism is then conducted. Thus practice is gained under conditions that simulate real problems. And there is added value in the analysis which is derived from the critique session.

e) *Heuristic.* As already noted, some of management's decisions are made in situations that are unique and very abstract. In these cases, expert and experienced guesswork is often the only way to get an answer. But there is growing interest in "heuristic" approaches. These are used when objectives are tangled or inconsistent, forces at work are neutralizing, logic is illogical, and indeed the situation seemingly cannot even be comprehensively defined. (See Figure 4–6 for the heuristic approach to problems.) Under

FIGURE 4–6
Heuristic Program for Solving Ill-Structured Problems

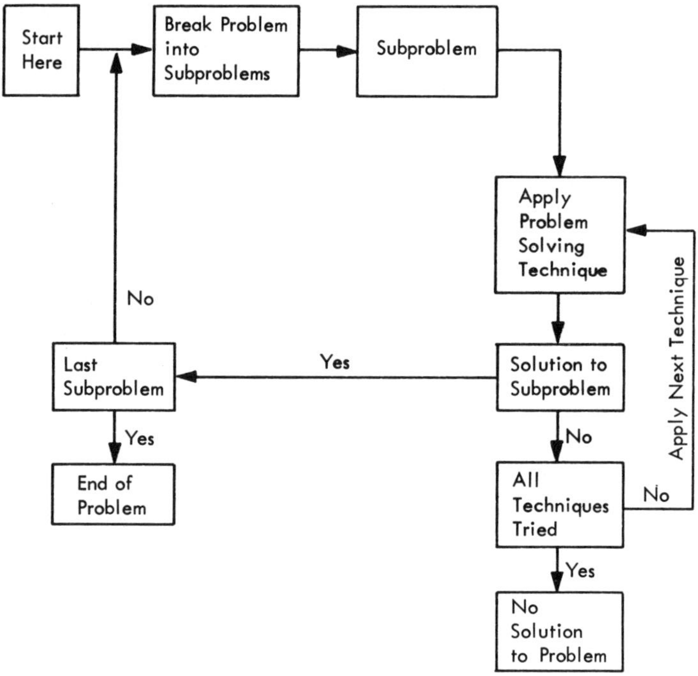

such conditions, the real question is, what can be done (what decisions will serve) to continue the life of the business or maintain the status quo? The most imperative objective is "staying alive." In such instances, we don't know what should be done—or not done—so that perpetuation of the business or some part thereof is insured. As an example, a company may not be sure which, if any, investments in research will pay off, yet it had better decide to invest in research anyway, because not to is a sure way of heading for business disaster.

Resources of Decision Making

A variety of resources can be brought to bear upon decision-making problems. These resources may be classified as knowledge areas, developmental factors, organizational factors, and technical tools.

There are few fields of human knowledge which cannot make some contribution to managerial decision making. To review them all, therefore, would involve compiling an encyclopedia. But practically, there are some which stand out as important contributors. Obviously an executive must have some background in the technical area in which he operates, for example, production, sales, finance, accounting, engineering. He must also have knowledge in planning, organizing, directing, and controlling the work of others. Then there are numerous supporting fields with which he must have varying degrees of acquaintance, for example, economics, law, logic, philosophy, ethics, mathematics, language areas, and psychology. Obviously the extent and depth of acquaintance must be different for different executives. So each must seek proficiency according to his own personal and job needs.

As a developmental factor, the potential of executive training can be a significant resource in decision making. Reference has already been made to the developmental value of business games. Few would argue against the need for training in the areas mentioned in the previous paragraph. Other programs will be discussed in a later chapter, but it is well to note that some of the most obvious skills of executives can stand strengthening. For example, training executives to be better listeners, better readers, and more sensitive to the feelings of others has a considerable influence upon their success in dealing with problems and with people.

Furthermore, good organization structures, policies, standard practice instructions and procedures are most helpful in allocating responsibility for decisions as well as insuring better decisions. Later parts of this text will devote much attention to these factors.

Finally, a major and more recent technical tool, in the form of computerized management information systems, has facilitated appreciably the decision-making capability of management. This tool is considered important enough to merit specialized attention in the following section.

Management Information Systems

Management information systems (MIS) are basically networks of data processing procedures developed and integrated, within the organization, to provide management, at various levels, with necessary information for subsequent decision making. A system is simply a set of interrelated and integrated parts or subsystems. The business enterprise itself may be usefully viewed as a system of interrelated and functional subsystems such as production, personnel, marketing, and so on, depending, of course, on the nature of the

FIGURE 4–7
A General Business System Model

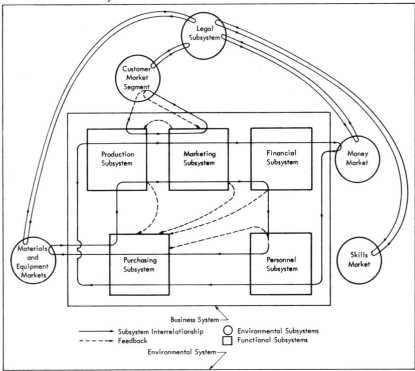

Reproduced with permission from Howard L. Timms and Michael F. Pohlen, *The Production Function in Business* (3d ed.; Homewood, Ill.: Richard D. Irwin, Inc., 1970.), p. 104.

business. Figure 4–7 represents a general business system model with feedback loops between the various functions.

Management information, in the formal sense, is relevant knowledge that is garnered for specific useful purposes. It is the end product, or result, of a process in which data input is processed to produce information output.

Furthermore, there is a distinct data processing operation which produces this information output. The operation consists of four basic steps of data processing:

1. *Data Origination.* Data is collected from original source documents such as sales orders, invoices, payroll timecards, and so on.
2. *Data Input.* Originated data requires processing. Source data are recorded either manually or mechanically on punched cards or punched paper tapes. Proper recording requires deciding on the kind of data to be processed as well as validating the accuracy of the data.
3. *Data Processing.* After data has been recorded, they are manipulated by storing, calculating, summarizing, and storing on paper documents, microfilm, or magnetized media.
4. *Data Retrieval and Reproduction.* Data is recovered from the original stored data as, and when, needed and then duplicated on such media as punched cards, punched paper tapes, and magnetic tapes.

Operationally, then it (MIS) is a system that integrates routine computer applications such as purchasing materials, controlling inventories, processing payroll, accounts payable and receivable, researching aspects of the market, to name a few, and then arranges and stores this data (within a framework of relationships) that is immediately retrievable by management for use in decision making.

1. *The Use of the Computer.* Important for the student to remember is that a management information system does not necessarily have to be computerized to be effective. Using a computer does not automatically guarantee the improvement of information. The fundamental test of any information system is the quality and adequacy of the information. Does it serve its purpose? Automation will not improve inadequate and inaccurate data. As a general rule, it appears, though, that the computer is most applicable in processing information that (1) has a number of interacting variables; (2) has reasonably accurate values placed on the coefficients of the equations (results of calculations are no more accurate than the assumptions upon which these calculations are made); (3) necessitates speed in processing the data to provide management

with data prior to decision making; and (4) is repetitive in character since the cost of an information system can be substantial.[1]

Traditional information processing systems in the early days before computerization were independent of other systems in the firm. Data collection processes were mostly slow and arduous. Computerization, however, has magnified the timeliness of business information. In fact, the present sophistication of automatic processing equipment has made management information systems realizable to the point where the firm not only has capability to process a massive volume of, say, accounting transactions but also can process information requests and provide reports on a demand basis. Figure 4–8 suggests that a management information system goes beyond the traditional record-keeping function. The upward pointing arrows in Figure 4–8 are meant to suggest that the same data ob-

FIGURE 4–8
Management Information System

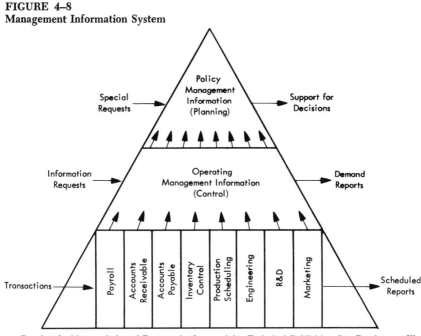

tained for routine accounting purposes can be selected and transformed for management control purposes. Consequently there is

---

[1] Adapted from John Dearden, *Computers in Business Management* (Homewood, Ill.: Dow Jones-Irwin, Inc., 1966), pp. 121–22.

an evolvement from conventional or traditional applications to the use of the same information at the middle management level for control purposes and at the general management or executive level for planning purposes.[2]

2. Kinds of Information Systems.[3] It is generally recognized that there are three major information systems and many minor systems in a productive enterprise. A major system is one that affects the entire structure of an organization while a minor system is limited to a single functional part of the firm.

3. Major Information Systems. There are three major information systems: logistics information, financial information, and personnel information. These three systems have several characteristics in common, "they exist in nearly all companies; they affect almost all parts of the business; they usually involve handling large amounts of data; and they are principally concerned with recurring documentary, internal, and historical data."[4]

a) Logistics information system. This system is concerned with information about the physical flow of goods through an organization. It includes such subsystems as a procurement information system, a raw materials inventory control system, a production scheduling and control system, a finished goods inventory control system, and a distribution system. It is most adaptable to computerization since the timing of information and the need to handle a large volume of data quickly and accurately are critical to the effective functioning of a logistic system.

b) Financial information system. The basis for this system is the flow of dollars through the organization. The financial information system is composed of such subsystems as a general accounting system, a standard cost accounting system, a manufacturing expense budget and reporting system, and a budgetary control system. Most financial systems are readily adaptable to computer usage because of the large volume of historical recurring data.

c) Personnel information system. The personnel information system is concerned with the flow of information about the people of the firm. Personnel data is largely recurring, documentary, internal, and historical. Some data, however, is obtained from ex-

---

[2] Robert V. Head, "Management Information Systems: A Critical Appraisal," *Datamation*, Vol. 13 (May 1967), pp. 23–27.

[3] This section adapted freely from Dearden, *Computers in Business Management*, pp. 118–20.

[4] Ibid., p. 119.

ternal sources. A personnel information system (see Figure 4–9) is in turn composed of procedurized subsystems such as recruiting, testing, and selecting, evaluation of management and employee per-

FIGURE 4–9
Personnel Information System

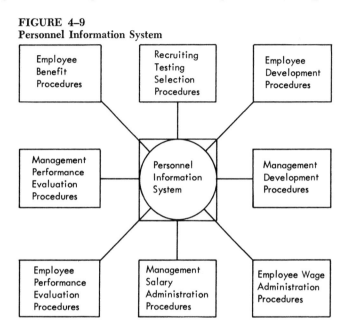

formance, management and employee development, management and employee salary and wage administration, and employee benefit administration procedures.

4. *Minor Information Systems.* In addition to the three major systems within the firm, there are also other minor systems, an example of which is the marketing system. This system is minor in the sense that it applies to a limited area of the firm and will contain data regarding a customer's marketing history, demographic data and projections of population and income, competitive data regarding actual and estimated sales volume of competitors, and so on. Additionally, the data bank could be utilized for the development of sales forecasting models.

5. *Evaluation of Management Information Systems.* The development of management information systems has resulted in a growing technological field with a range of specialized jobs such as programmers and analysts who are regularly fitting new applications to computer-based systems. This is only the beginning. The future will see a continual and ever-expanding application of information technology which, while requiring the manager to develop the necessary functional knowledge and skills of MIS, will nevertheless extrapolate extensively his decision-making capabilities.

Summary

The purpose of the foregoing discussion has not been to provide specific rules or practices of decision making. This would require at least several volumes. Instead, the aim has been to establish a perspective. Decision making must be seen and appreciated as a total complex of a number of interrelated parts and dimensions. Only then do specific techniques make sense, and only then can their potential be fully realized.

As noted at the outset of this chapter, such a perspective was once considered illogical, if it was thought about at all. But in recent years, there has been growing recognition that decision making needs scrutiny and study. This view rejects the idea that decision makers learn only by making decisions. It assumes instead that by examining processes, methods, resources, and situational factors, improvements can be made in decision making. Hence, the purpose of this chapter has been to draw an outline of the full dimensions of decision making. It is hoped that as various facets of management are taken up in subsequent chapters, they will be viewed not only in terms of their technical content, but also as areas which affect and are affected by managerial decisions.

QUESTIONS

1. Define the term decision making and then note some of the reasons why decision making is difficult for any manager.
2. Differentiate between maximize and optimize, and then discuss the relation of these terms to the goal aspect of decision making.
3. Of what significance are standards and value systems to the process of decision making?
4. How does follow-up or feedback contribute to managerial decision making?
5. How does the breadth or narrowness of subject matter with which a manager must deal affect his decision making?
6. List and describe the steps of the scientific method of decision making.
7. Why is the application of probability theory and methods indispensable to decision making?

8. If a company locates a store at location "X," based on past experience the store can make $4,000 per month if it is successful or lose $1,000 per month if it is not successful. If the company locates a store at "Y," it could make $6,000 per month if the store is successful or lose $1,200 if the store is not successful.

   a) Where should the company locate if the manager is an optimist? A pessimist?

   b) Where should the company locate if the probability of success at "X" is one half and the probability of success at "Y" is one third?

9. Given the following data, if business is good a company could make $700,000; if business is bad, the company could make $400,000. If the probability that business is good is .3, calculate expected value. What is the expected value if the probability that business is good was increased to .8?

10. What resources may be brought to bear upon decision-making problems?

11. Define what is meant by management information systems.

12. Identify the basic steps of data processing.

13. Of what value is the computer in MIS?

14. Discuss the various kinds of information systems within the firm.

CASE 4–1

While calling on a purchasing agent, a salesman of industrial lift trucks had carefully and expertly described the qualities of his line, the services made available by his company, and the competitive aspects of its prices. During the presentation, the sales manager and the chief engineer of the company came into the purchasing agent's office. Upon being introduced to the salesman, and being told about his line and company, the sales manager asked the salesman how far his company was prepared to go in reciprocal purchasing, and the chief engineer asked the salesman how many years his company guaranteed to have parts available after a model was discontinued.

To neither question had his company given the salesman a specific answer.

Later, during a salesmen's training session, the salesman related this incident to illustrate a problem that other salesmen might encounter.

But he had to face the issues then and there in the purchasing agent's office. And when he returned to his home office, his own

sales manager gave the questions careful consideration since they
were likely to be encountered in the future.

1. In making a decision in these instances, what methods of decision
   making could have been used by the salesman on the spot? By
   the sales manager later? During the sales training session?
2. If the salesman had answered "I don't know, but I'll find out," to
   what extent would he have made a wise or unwise decision?

CASE 4–2

Sharp Penn had over the years built a reputation and a nice living
out of custom-made golf clubs. Some promoters came to him with
the proposition that his designs could be turned into a real money
maker. This would involve mass production and mass distribution
of his designs under some popular golfer other than his own
name. Penn would have an interest in the business but not a controlling one.

The proposition caused Penn to do some serious soul-searching.
Why was he in business? To whom did he have responsibilities?
Would he be used by the promoters?

After considering a variety of angles, he told the proposed syndi-
cate managers, "Thank you, no."

They immediately countered with the following arguments:

a) Look at all the people who will be denied the pleasure of using
   your clubs.
b) Look at all the new jobs your new company would create
   for many people.
c) Look at the earnings and estate that will accrue to you and
   yours.

They implied as subtly as they could that he was self-centered and
selfish if he didn't come into the project.

1. What are the various angles that enter into this matter of why and
   to what extent a person devotes his life to a business enterprise?
2. What decision do you think Penn ought to reach?

5

Planning

Introduction

In the preceding chapters, attention was directed to the general scope, philosophy, and decision-making aspects of management. This survey provided a basic foundation for an understanding of management. It is now time to examine in more details the functions and factors of management. In the next four chapters, therefore, concern is with the managerial functions, that is, planning, organizing, directing, and controlling. Afterwards several chapters are devoted to various important factors to which the functions are applied. In actual practice, a manager performs the functions in direct relation to the factors; the two are inseparable. But for purposes here of economy in presentation, it is preferable to separate the two.

In the current chapter, the survey of the managerial function of planning is taken up under the following headings:

1. Nature of planning.
2. Subject matter of planning.
3. Factors affecting planning.
4. Guides to effective planning.
5. Managing the planning.

Nature of Planning

As defined earlier, planning is the managerial function of determining in advance what a group should accomplish and how the goals are to be attained. This does not imply that nonmanagers do not plan—they certainly do; but they plan for themselves not others. A manager plans the work of others. He is doing what Frederick W. Taylor argued was essential to effective organizational success; that is, planning should be separated from performance. The manager should specialize in planning the work of the group, and the members of the group should specialize in performing the work as planned.[1]

Planning, thus, has three key ideas. It is done in advance of work. It is to be done for others by a specialist. And it has a contribution to make to group effort. Each of these deserves more than mere mention.

1. *The Predetermination Phase.* Planning, in the first place, is something which must be done before something else. Its justification lies in the simple fact that work will be more efficiently performed if the work is first planned. This aspect of planning can be seen by examining, first, the contributions of planning, and second, the time aspects of planning.

a) Planning Contributions. The justification of planning must be found in its possible contributions. To begin with, it has the advantages of specialization in its favor. Generally speaking, anyone who specializes in a subject, function, or methodology will be better than a nonspecialist. So the manager who specializes in planning work is more apt to be better at planning than a worker who does both the planning and the work. For example, anyone who has performed time and motion studies knows how poorly employees execute operations designed by themselves. To be sure, this does not mean that only managers should plan. Employees can often provide useful planning ideas.

In the next place, planning contributes to effectiveness because all details of work and their relationships are worked out in advance. Not only are the best of details selected and designed but they are arranged in proper sequence. This is of utmost importance. Planning enhances ultimate coordination. Doing the right thing by each member of an organization implies that specific actions are properly

---

[1] The contention is often heard, and often supported by case studies, that productivity is higher when subordinates help plan as well as do their work. It is reasoned that this is so because employees, first, have much job knowledge that is useful in planning and, second, cooperate better when their advice is sought.

But it is also well to be aware of the fact that employees often neither trust the fairness of management's plans nor have confidence in management's planning skills. Under such conditions it is not surprising that employee productivity would be low; and not until the conditions are changed by giving employees a voice in managerial decisions which affect their jobs and interests would improvements in productivity be made.

related to each other. For an advertising and sales promotion campaign to be "right," for example, not only must the message be right but it must be coordinated in time with the production of goods and their distribution to wholesale and retail outlets. This kind of rightness is best achieved through planning.

And finally, planning contributes to work effectiveness by handling possible obstructions to contemplated work projects. Planning seeks to anticipate and thereby remove obstacles, difficulties, and problems which stand in the way of attaining goals. Advance steps can be taken to eliminate, circumvent, or minimize undesirable conditions that would otherwise adversely affect work efficiency. By being alert, for example, to a possibility of a strike by a supplier's employees, of changes in styles or consumer preferences, or of governmental regulations affecting one's products, adjustments can be made much more effectively before rather than after one is actually in production.

b) Time Aspects. The effectiveness of planning is also related to the factor of time. Since planning implies a time predetermination, it would seem that the more time that is allowed for planning, the better the planning should be. In part this is so. If a company proposes, let us assume, to revamp its marketing channels and policies, the appropriate plans cannot be devised overnight. At least months would be required for such changes to be planned successfully. But in part, the longer the interval of time between planning and performance, the less confidence can one place in a plan. The trouble lies in the fact that a plan by its very nature is a forecast or is based on a forecast of the future. The degree of success with which one can forecast obviously grows less the farther one looks into the future. And by the time a plan is converted into action, the conditions for which one planned are likely to have changed considerably. This might be cause for pessimism about planning were it not for two facts. First, if one does not forecast he will invariably be worse off than if he does. No forecasts are really forecasts that conditions won't change. And, second, techniques of forecasting are continuously being improved so that however uncertain long-range forecasting may be, it is gradually becoming more accurate.

So forward planning is the modern theme, even though every planner knows he cannot forecast accurately. But he is getting better and he is also learning more about how to handle the probability aspects of his forecasts. So he plans. Some of his plans are based on periods of just a few days, some shop and sales quotas are cases in point. Some plans are based weeks and months ahead; budgets, production programs, sales estimates, and financial requirements are examples. And some plans are worked into time spans of 5, 10, and 20 years; growth plans, personnel needs, research projections, and financial flows are of this nature.

2. *The Specialist Phase.* Planning, in the second place, is done for others by a specialist. Except in financial matters, most planning was for a long time left to chance, to subordinates, or to spur-of-the-moment decisions. It was already discussed, that not until Taylor's time was there disagreement with this approach. But even then the assumption of the planning function by management was restricted, in the thinking of the day, to industrial tasks at the shop level. In this area there was strong support for the notion that workers who had almost universally planned their own work were poor planners. The workers neither set good standards of output nor determined the best way to do their jobs. Numerous experiments by Taylor, his associates, and his followers proved the shortcomings of planning by the performers (the workers.)

Gradually the conclusion was accepted that someone else should do the planning. That "someone else" being the manager. He is supposed to specialize in thinking through, in advance, the action that is to take place in the future. In a small organization this does not cause much of a problem because there will be only one manager to do the planning or, at the most, just a few.

But what if there are many managers at different levels and covering various specialties and functional areas? In such instances, planning must be carefully organized or there will be costly duplications of effort or unfilled gaps. In general, the design of planning has called for horizontal and vertical allocations of duties. Horizontally, planning responsibilities are companywide and cover longer periods of time at the top of an organization and gradually are reduced in subject matter and time spans as one moves to the lower organizational levels.

A few illustrations are worth noting in this connection. The range of planning responsibilities is illustrated in Figure 5-1. Here it is seen that the president is responsible for companywide planning but the lower executives have narrower ranges of responsibility. The time span of planning responsibilities is illustrated in Figure 5-2. Here it is seen that the president of a company is responsible for plans that extend from several months to several years; whereas

FIGURE 5–1
Extent of Planning Responsibilities

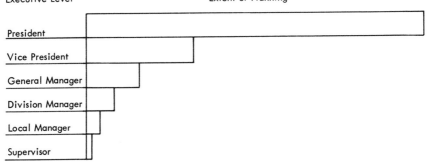

FIGURE 5–2
Time Planning Responsibilities

the time span of lower executives tends to be of much shorter duration. And the nature of planning responsibilities is illustrated in Figure 5–3. Here it is seen that the president is responsible for broad, qualitative predeterminations of objectives, policies, functions, procedures, organization structures, people, and environmental matters;

FIGURE 5–3
Specifics of Planning Responsibility

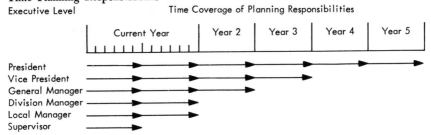

whereas the lower executives tend to establish more detailed, quantitative plans for these factors.

And finally, it should be noted that the work of the various planning specialists must be integrated into a unified, systematic, coordinated plan. An example is shown in Figure 5–4. Here it is visible

FIGURE 5–4
Model of Planning, Production, and Distribution Cycle

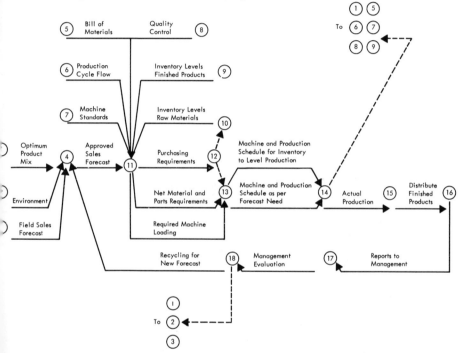

that various plans covering forecasts, products, quality, costs, rates, machines, etc., ultimately result in the actual production and distribution of goods. The effectiveness of the latter being largely dependent upon the effectiveness of a multitude of prior, detailed plans.

3.   *The Group-Action Phase.*   Planning, in the third place, has a contribution to make to group effort. It should provide the basis for group action. This is done, to begin with, by a clear statement of the common and personal objectives of the group. All will thereby know in what directions efforts are expected to be made. And this

pulling together is on a firm foundation when the planning also specifies what is to be done, how, and by whom.

Thus, planning is a positive factor in increasing the efficiency of the group. But planning also contributes to group effort by increasing the effectiveness of the managerial functions of organizing, directing, and controlling. For example, organizing simply becomes a hit-or-miss proposition unless plans are carefully established. Or controlling must take the major part of a manager's time if he does not do a good job of preplanning. Indeed, the amount of time that is spent on planning can well reduce the time that is spent on the other functions of management.

The favorable aspects of planning may be illustrated in the field of exploration. When explorers return home, they invariably have many tales of adventures with which to regale their listeners. And the tales reveal incidents that could easily have resulted in disaster if they had not been handled fortuitously and successfully on the spot. After the "exciting" parts of the tales have been told, the explorers invariably point out that they would just as soon have avoided the adventures. They conclude that more planning might have served to anticipate the troubles, the adventures, and the risks of disaster. Similarly, where business life is concerned, planning can serve to reduce hazards which otherwise would have to be dealt with on an uncertain, curative basis.

Subject Matter of Planning

It is now important to determine the subjects to which planning may be applied. There are three major areas, as follows, each of which will be discussed in this section:

1. Managerial functions.   3. Specific projects.
2. Basic business factors.

1. *Managerial Functions.* Planning has already been enumerated as one of the major managerial functions. Planning has been stated to precede organizing, directing, and controlling. In this sense, organizing provides the resources to carry out the plans of planning, directing then carries them out, and controlling aids in comparing the degree to which plans have been successful and determining what corrective action needs to be taken in regard to future plans.

But if organizing, directing, and controlling are to be well performed by an executive, he must plan these functions. Before an organization structure can be installed, for example, it must be designed, that is, planned. Before an executive can direct the activities of his subordinates, he must determine how he shall behave toward them, that is, plan his behavior. And before he can evaluate and measure performance, he will have to design a system of control, that is, plan his controls. And as will be discussed more fully later in this chapter, an executive must also plan his planning.

Planning for planning and planning for organizing, directing, and controlling should be given the time and resources they deserve particularly as companies grow and business becomes more complex. Such organization units as staff planning departments and such methods as operations research are definite proof that this trend is taking place in larger companies. But smaller companies must also find time for such planning—however on a more informal basis or through intercompany cooperation—if their operations are to be conducted with greater success.

2. *Basic Business Factors.* The basic factors found in every business situation constitute another significant area of planning. Certainly, only by means of planning can the following be properly established:

a) The objectives to be sought.
b) The policies to be followed.
c) The organizational and procedural structures to be used.
d) The human faculties to be employed.
e) The environmental factors to be handled.

As an example, Figure 5–5 provides a simple outline of factor planning. This shows selected items for each factor, the responsible executive, and the dates by which preliminary and final plans must be completed. Of course, detailed statements of each factor would have to be derived. For example, output would be expressed in quantitative terms for each product manufactured and sold by style and type.

All of these will be considered in some detail in subsequent chapters, so little more than mention of them is needed here. It should be noted that such difficult questions as how the customer's dollar should be divided among the various contributors in a company must be attacked by careful planning, or else answers must be sought by strife and privilege. And equally needful is planning to attack problems of policies, functions, organization structure, proce-

FIGURE 5-5
Responsibility for Factor Planning

Plan of Objectives:	Responsibility of—	Preliminary Plans by—	Final Plans by—
Sales	VP—sales	June 1	July 1
Production programs..	VP—production	June 15	July 15
Cost limits:			
Production	Production mgr.	June 20	July 10
Sales	Sales mgr.	June 15	July 10
Overhead	Controller	June 25	July 10
Plans of Policies:			
Profit expectations	Executive VP.		
Pricing	Sales mgr.	June 10	June 25
Marketing channels ...	Marketing mgr.	June 10	June 25
Advertising themes ...	Advertising mgr.	June 10	June 20
Financial	Financial mgr.	June 20	June 25
Plans of Organizing:			
Executive lines	Executive VP.	May 1	May 15
Staff units	Organiz. plan. mgr.	May 1	May 15
Systems design	Systems plan. mgr.	May 1	May 15
Purchasing goals	Purchasing mgr.	June 25	July 20
Environmental:			
Social relations	Public relations	May 1	May 15
Political relations	Executive com.	May 10	May 15
Competitive			
strategies	Executive com.	May 10	May 20

dures, etc. By planning in this area of basic business factors, the foundation and structure of an effective business machine is established.

3. Specific Projects. Planning is also intended to serve in the area of specific projects. Certainly, it may be the broad plan of a company to earn in the coming year a certain profit, by the manufacture of a given product, and by its distribution through a certain marketing channel. But many "little" plans will be needed to carry out the broad plans. A foreman in the factory will need a plan to carry out his end of production, a sales supervisor will need a plan to persuade customers to buy in quantities equal to quotas, and the service manager will need a plan to repair products returned by customers.

To illustrate the practicality of scientific planning, an example may be cited of time and cost estimates beginning with research and development activities through to a completed product. Figures 5-6, 5-7, and 5-8 depict various stages of planning and of comparisons of actual results with plans. They illustrate the Program Evaluation and Review Technique—popularly known as PERT—developed to aid in the planning and control of time schedules of the Polaris submarine program. When cost estimates are added to PERT, as illustrated in Figures 5–7 and 5–8, the technique is designated as PERT/Cost System.

The first major step of PERT is taken by relating in some time sequence the various events which are essential in the ultimate completion of a project. Thus, in Figure 5–6 are shown (by circles)

FIGURE 5–6
The Network of Expected Times
PERT NETWORK
Showing Precedence
of Activities (Tasks)

3 TIME ESTIMATES
FOR EACH ACTIVITY
• Optimistic
• Most Likely
• Pessimistic
"Expected Time" t_e

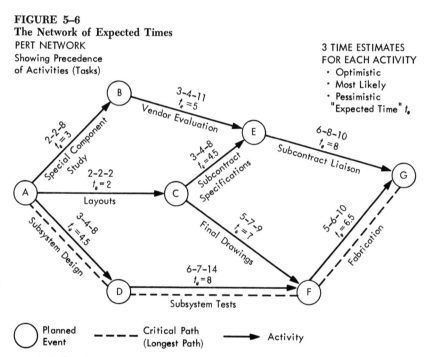

○ Planned Event   - - - - Critical Path (Longest Path)   ⟶ Activity

$t_c = \dfrac{t_o + 4t_m + t_p}{6}$; To find the longest path through the network, the series sums of t_r values are compared.

Source: *The PERT/Cost System*, a pamphlet of the U.S. Department of the Navy, October 1961.

the various events and (by arrows) relations between events to complete project "G." Along each arrow are also indicated three numbers which represent the optimistic, most likely, and pessimistic time estimates, respectively, for completing a particular activity. Then a t_e or "expected time" is calculated for each activity. Then from among the various activity arrows, there is shown—by a light line—the path of events which represent the longest time period from the beginning of the total project to its ultimate completion.

Since cost estimates are essential to good planning, these too are incorporated in PERT, as shown in Figure 5–7. Here the dollar estimates are recorded in small rectangles above each activity line.

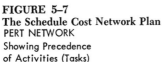

FIGURE 5–7
The Schedule Cost Network Plan
PERT NETWORK
Showing Precedence
of Activities (Tasks)

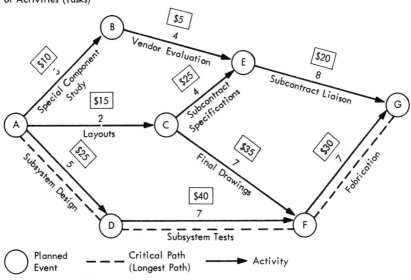

Source: *The PERT/Cost System,* a pamphlet of the U.S. Department of the Navy, October 1961.

As the project which has been planned gets under way, actual results can be fed into the chart, as illustrated in Figure 5–8. Thus, it is seen here that planned event *B* has been completed and has cost $8 (000's omitted) whereas the budgeted estimate was $10. The *AB* activity has taken more time than was estimated. Activity *BE* has taken up the estimated time and cost but as yet has not resulted in a completed *E*. Of all the parts of the plan, only activity *AD*—which is on the critical path network—requires special attention, because it has run a week over estimate. Thus, activities *DF* and *FG* will need to be completed ahead of their "estimated time" if the total project is to be completed on time.

So this area recognizes that planning is not all high-level, broad, and complicated. Much, if not most of it, is of a minor, routine, and simple character. Much is concerned with day-to-day specific tasks. Much planning can therefore be established in the form of standing orders, standard practice instructions, rules and regula-

FIGURE 5–8
The Schedule Cost Network, Plan and Status

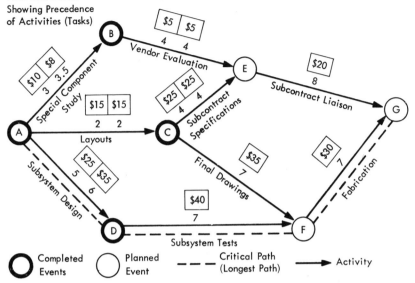

PERT NETWORK
Showing Precedence
of Activities (Tasks)

| ◯ Completed Events | ◯ Planned Event | - - - Critical Path (Longest Path) | ⟶ Activity |

Source: *The PERT/Cost System,* a pamphlet of the U. S. Department of the Navy, October 1961.

tions, and the like. But, nonetheless, such planning is important to the success of any concern, and provision should be made for its proper development and usage.

Factors Affecting Planning

The nature of planning in any company will be affected by a number of factors. Among these are the following:

1. Skill and attitude of management.
2. Time and resources available.
3. Types of problems encountered.
4. Environmental, social, and human conditions.
5. Uses and usage of plans.

Perhaps the most significant factor affecting planning in a company is the skill and attitude of management. What can one expect in a company in which the chief executive goes to fortune-tellers in order to make decisions regarding the future? Fantastic as this may sound, such cases are not figments of the imagination. Or how much scientific planning can be expected in a company in which the top executives are set against mathematics and statistics in marshaling data and information? Perhaps as silly, at the other extreme, are those who want every decision buttressed by vast arrays and schedules and charts and formulas of "data." Obviously, then, the key to good planning lies in the skill and attitude of top management toward planning.

Somewhat akin to the foregoing factor are the time and resources available to perform the planning function. The time aspect has a number of phases, such as the following:

1. Time available to establish a plan before putting it into effect.
2. Time the plan should go into effect.
3. Time interval to be covered by the plan.
4. Time the plan should be revised or made void.

The resources aspect also has a number of conditioning phases, such as the following:

1. Funds available to invest in planning.
2. Availability of trained or trainable planning personnel.
3. Availability of technical facilities for planning.
4. Degree of sympathy and understanding of personnel who are expected to use the plans.

Space is too limited to explore all of these phases. It is perhaps enough to note that the precision of planning cannot be any greater than the time or resources available for planning, nor should it be any greater than the capacities of those who are to use the plans. Obviously, if only a week is available to plan a system of warehousing distribution, it would be futile to employ the involved techniques of operations research in developing the plan.

The types of problems to be encountered present another factor affecting managerial planning. Some problems have only a few variables to be solved, whereas others have numerous interdependent and interaffecting variables. As an example of the former, establishing an employee-suggestion system while posing some important questions is not an overly difficult task to accomplish. But establishing a plan of distribution from a warehouse setup of several units to a number of retail outlets is another matter. It would have to be determined whether or not each warehouse would carry a full complement of products, make shipments to each retail outlet, bill each retail outlet separately, and take orders from each outlet but ship from another warehouse. To optimize the relationships among warehouses, products carried, distances covered, and retail outlets involves a set of factors that will task unaided human skills but provides an excellent problem for electronic computers.

Planning is also affected by environmental, social, and human conditions. As one illustration of this, planning in the field of labor-management relations was not particularly difficult in the days when labor legislation was practically nonexistent and labor unions were usually impotent. But under present-day conditions of involved labor laws, strong unions, and alert labor, management must expend much time and effort and apply itself skillfully and diligently to problems in this area. And to cite another example in this area, a company with branch plants and offices scattered throughout the world must plan its operations in the light of social, political, and all environmental conditions in the various areas. Thus, policies that might be very effective in the United States, let us say, would be disastrous in the Near East, Japan, or Italy.

Another factor affecting planning is the uses to which it is to be put and how it is to be carried out. Is planning primarily intended to be foresighted or hindsighted? Too often, plans are used largely as control devices to determine how well or poorly executives have accomplished their work. As a consequence, a negative atmosphere of fear revolves around such plans as budgets. On the other hand, emphasis upon providing correct solutions for future or current operations may be the purpose of plans, so that budgets, for example, are viewed in a constructive and positive light.

Guides to Effective Planning

If the managerial function of planning is to be performed effectively, certain tests or guides should be kept in mind. Perhaps the most significant test relates to the matter of objectives. At all stages of planning it is imperative to keep in mind the purposes which, it is hoped, will be achieved thereby. This is so because the ultimate success of a plan depends upon the degree to which it achieves desired objectives. If results are below objectives, the plan has to that amount failed. Thus a plan is a way to an end and should be so viewed. Indeed, this emphasis upon objectives is supported by those who assign to management by objectives—to be discussed in a later chapter—a major role in all phases of management, particularly planning.

A plan must provide a definite route to desired goals, yet it must have some degree of flexibility. A financial budget expresses in monetary terms how much is to be expended in some future period for various items in order to accomplish particular purposes. But during that period variations may occur from conditions that had been expected. The budget will then be unrealistic. The answer to this is to make the budget "flexible" to begin with. That is, the plan should be established to provide for deviations from expected conditions. Thus, the budget is stable in that it establishes a financial route to desired objectives. But it is flexible in that the route can be varied by fixed amounts if conditions vary during the budgeted period.

A plan should also be sound in terms of basic strategy. It should among other things give due consideration to the following:

1. Conditions expected to prevail during the time it is effective.
2. Attitudes of personnel by whom it is to be used.
3. Priority and importance of problems to be solved.
4. Nature of obstacles—personal, legal, political, etc.—to be faced.
5. Avenues of escape or change, if unforeseen emergencies develop.

A plan can become a straitjacket of failure unless it is designed with the foregoing strategical safeguards in mind.

Finally a good plan should be clear and understandable. A plan may be clear to the planner. But is it equally clear to the intended user? The planner should make certain that his plan either is expressed in clear terms or is communicated to the user so that the latter knows what is expected of him. And if it is clear to the user, does he understand and have confidence in the plan? Again, the planner has the responsibility to transmit a plan so that users believe in its efficacy and fairness.

Managing the Planning

Plans are not self-executing. Hence they must be managed. And this, like any other project, requires planning, organizing, directing, and controlling.

To be a good planner, a manager should plan his planning. This admonition is a justification for much that has been said in this chapter. To repeat briefly, a good planner checks out his method of planning. He is aware of available tools of planning. He knows what areas and factors will require planning. He allows enough time and resources for planning. And he gives thought to the conditions, obstacles, and guides affecting planning. In short, he plans

FIGURE 5–9
The Planning Process

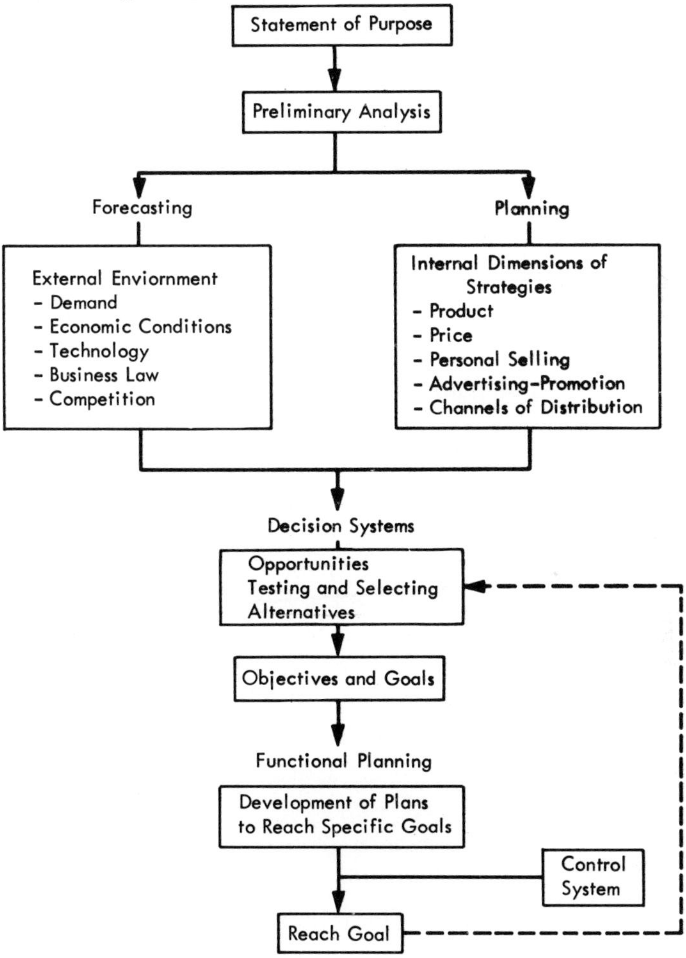

his planning in the light of the elements of the planning process as shown in Figure 5–9.

Next, planning involves an organizing phase. To begin with, planning should incorporate a precise determination of who is to be responsible for the completion of each part of the plan. Each of the responsible parties should be informed of the person to whom he is accountable for results, the times at which he is expected to report on progress, and the manner in which reports are to be submitted. And determinations should be made of how and in what manner the responsibilities of each person are to be finally discharged.

Plans also require directional management. Each executive, manager, and supervisor must interpret and communicate planning information to his respective subordinates. This may call for instruction and indoctrination in the meaning and purposes of the planning. Various motivational efforts may be required to get subordinates to effectively support the plans. Provision should be made for constant and timely information on progress in executing planning. In this manner, interruptions to planning can be caught before they become serious and thereby appropriate corrective action taken. The planning in this context is an indispensable part of effective direction.

Finally, by adequate controls the full value of planning may be attained. Results of plans should be carefully measured against desired objectives. For example, did actual sales equal planned sales, actual cost of sales equal budgeted costs, and actual profits equal hoped-for profits? After deviations of actual from planned results are computed, an analysis should be made of causes for deviation. The why's and wherefore's are the real value of postoperational control. They provide, first of all, a basis for rewarding the successful planners and penalizing the failures. And they provide, in the second place, a basis for improving planning in the future. The latter of these purposes is more important. Unless control of planning can lead to improvement, it really has little to contribute to successful management and, in turn, to successful operations of an enterprise.

QUESTIONS

1. What are the three key ideas involved in managerial planning?
2. How does the element of time enter into the planning function?
3. How does top management planning differ from planning at lower organizational levels in terms of extent, time coverage, and time spans?
4. What contributions does planning make to group action?
5. What values do you see in the PERT/Cost System of planning and control?
6. The nature of planning in any company tends to be affected by what factors or conditions?
7. By what tests may the effectiveness of the managerial function of planning be evaluated?
8. What is meant by managing the planning? Why is this significant?

CASE 5–1

The Readem Meter Company made a variety of meters for measuring and recording electrical information. After the various parts of a meter were stamped out or machined, they had to be assembled, various wiring operations performed, and then adjustment and inspection work performed. In performing these operations there seemed to be no consistent system or sequence in doing the work. Indeed, various job lots going through at the same time were often done differently by various work crews.

To illustrate, as well as to cite the undesirability of the situation which brought on the need for a decision, in one group of workers the three aspects of assemble, wire and solder, and adjust and test, respectively, were being done by people who specialized in one of these tasks. In another group, working on another lot, there was a shifting of workers from one task to another as they tired of doing the same thing over and over again. The problem came to a head because it was decided by the methods department that specialization would be the most efficient way and should be adopted by all groups.

This decision angered group two because they liked the flexibility of their changing-around plan. But at the same time, it also angered group one because they were not told they could not shift should they decide to do so, a fact which earlier had not entered their minds.

1. What has been overlooked in this planning of a procedure?
2. How can changes or orders not to change be made more effectively?

CASE 5–2

John Smith had developed an "atom counter" device to measure the thickness of various materials while they were moving through various stages of production. He organized a company to produce and distribute this device. In several years, he had seen the company grow from a one-man organization to one in which more than five hundred were employed. And he had, as a consequence, seen his own job change from that of an inventor to that of a full-time executive.

Although he has a capable staff of executives directing the several divisions of the company, he still feels himself overburdened. So he has decided to hire someone to give him, personally, a variety of assistance. But in thinking about the kind of person to hire, he has concluded that he had better have a good picture of, first, the job he wants the assistant to do for him and, second, the relation of the assistant to his top executives. In this stage of planning, he began by reviewing in his mind his own job and his relation to his subordinate top executives.

1. What is your opinion of Mr. Smith's method of planning to shift some of the work load from his own shoulders?

2. What managerial functions and which business factors might be shifted (and in what relationship to himself and his executives) to the new staff assistant?

6

Organizing

Introduction

ORGANIZING, as noted earlier, is the managerial function of marshaling various factors and resources necessary to carry out plans. It is based upon the managerial function of planning. It precedes the managerial functions of directing and controlling. In a sense, it sets up the machine which will be directed and controlled in carrying out established plans.

The "machine" of organizing has a number of important parts. An organization structure must be established by which various executives and subordinates are tied together into an effective framework. Procedures of various kinds must be designed and established. Personnel must be hired and trained to staff the structures and procedures. And various materials, tools, equipment, and resources must be procured. Each of these will be discussed in this chapter.

Organization Structure

Organization structure is the invisible framework that, formally and informally, establishes the authority, responsibility, status, and roles of each person in relation to all other persons in the group as shown in Figure 6–1. It specifies which individuals and what general areas are subordinate to which superiors. Or, viewed from the superior's point of view, it specifies who has jurisdiction over whom and, in general terms, for what. It also defines the interpersonal relationships that will exist between individuals in various jurisdictional levels and divisions.

FIGURE 6–1
Lines of Authority and Responsibility in Organization Structure

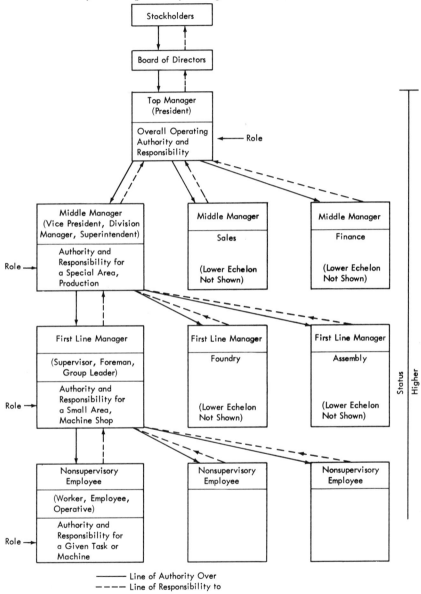

Organization structure is intended to promote coordination of
the members of the group. By appropriate assignments of authority
and responsibility, each person will carry out his part of preestablished plans in proper relation to the parts of others in the group.
In an effective organization structure such coordination will take

place even though various members of the group are separated geographically, do their work at different times, and perform a variety of specialized tasks. Thereby, an executive may direct and communicate with a team of specialists even though they are widely separated spatially, in time, and in their respective tasks.

If the factor of organization structure is to be utilized effectively, its features and characteristics should be fully understood. In subsequent chapters, various aspects of this subject will be treated more fully, but for the present a brief discussion of the following points will suffice:

1. Types of structures.
2. Authority and responsibility relationships.
3. Factors of structural design.

1. *Types of Structures.* Organization structures are both formal and informal. In this section attention is first directed to the formal types and then to the informal.

a) *Formal Organization Structure.* The formal organization structure is that which has been expressly established to spell out who has authority over whom, and for what, as illustrated in Chapter 12, Figure 12–1. Such specifications are of three kinds, to which have been given the names line, functional, and line and staff. The characteristics of each, their relative advantages, and areas of best usage will be reviewed.

(1) LINE STRUCTURE. In the pure line structure each executive has complete authority over all his subordinates. He is subject only to the commands of his immediate supervisor. There are no advisers, experts, or staffs to help him in his work or to "interfere" with his authority. He must do for himself—or get help from his superior—all that is necessary to command his unit effectively.

This form of structure has important advantages. Since each person reports to one and only one superior, the line of command is clear, misunderstandings need not plague anyone, and "buck passing" is impossible. Moreover, decisions within any unit can be made faster since there is no need for consultations with various experts.

But the line structure has a major disadvantage. A line executive must be able to take care of all the varied details and complexities that arise in his jurisdiction. But few executives can be expert in all fields of needed knowledge. So a pure line structure suffers from a lack of specialized leadership.

Its sphere of effectiveness is limited to the following conditions:

first, a company is fairly small and its problems are relatively simple and unchanging; second, well-rounded executives are available; and, third, undivided authority is absolutely essential.

(2) FUNCTIONAL STRUCTURES. The functional structure is intended to supply the specialists lacking in the line structure. In this form, each specialist has authority only over his specialty. In turn, each subordinate reports to several specialists, but to each only for his respective area of specialization, as illustrated in Chapter 12, Figure 12–2.

The advantage of this form lies in its specialization. Each executive would be a specialist, would be concerned only with his specialization when dealing with subordinates, and would in turn report to a specialist. As a consequence, there should be specialized managerial direction of various technical subjects.

But what happens when a subordinate reports to several specialists, even though to each for something different? The answer in practice, except in a few isolated cases, has been unsatisfactory. Lines of authority, though clear on paper, are seldom as clear in practice. Subordinates are never quite sure to which superior to report. Uncertainty and delay of action are the consequences. Moreover, the various specialized executives tend to "politic" for advantageous positions, yet tend to "pass the buck" when unsatisfactory results have occurred.

So this form of structure has not gained any general use. It is occasionally adopted in emergencies or in complex situations (such as automated processes) when direct authority must be given to a specialized executive. But as a general practice such specialized leadership must not be bought at the price of divided leadership. Yet functional structures can be built into an organization structure so that both single accountability and specialized leadership are attained. This is the case in the line and staff form.

(3) LINE AND STAFF STRUCTURES. The line and staff structure provides for single accountability in the line with specialized service through the staff, as illustrated in Chapter 12, Figure 12–3. The staff provides services which the line may accept or reject, unless the superior of the line orders acceptance of the service. The staff does not have authority on its own to force the line to accept its services.

This form has the advantages of the pure line and the pure functional, but a minimum of their disadvantages. It has the advantages, first, of a clear and undivided chain of command and, second, of a group of specialized staffs. Its disadvantages are, first, that line executives sometimes refuse to listen to staff people even when their advice is good; and, second, that staff people sometimes try to force their services on the line. These disadvantages are not difficult to minimize.

Because of the relative superiority of this form of structure, it is the most widely used. Its design will be more fully explored in later chapters.

b) *Informal Organization Structure.* The formal structures are not the only ones which set out lines of authority, responsibility, communications, status, and roles. There also exist in all companies informal structures. No matter how much one might try, moreover, these informal relations cannot be eliminated. It is desirable, therefore, to describe their nature and to note some common types.

An informal relationship exists when a given person ascribes to another a higher or lower place in the structure than that accorded in the formal structure. Let us take, as an example, the sales supervisor of hypothetical region "A." He, according to the organization chart, is in charge of this region, with specified authority to plan, organize, direct, and control the work of those assigned to his territory. But quite a few of his men discuss their sales problems with the supervisor of region "B" because they hold supervisor "B" in high respect and feel that he is "going up" in the organization. Thus, "B" is the informal leader of a number of salesmen in region "A."

Such deviations from the formal lines of authority may be of a number of kinds. Upward, a subordinate may go to a superior of his superior or to some staff executive for guidance, help or leadership. This subordinate may be at the worker level or anywhere in the executive ranks. Or, looking downward, a superior may short-circuit his immediate subordinate to reach lower levels in an organization. Similarly, people in one chain of command may contact informally other chains of command instead of going through designated channels of contact.

Such deviations may take place for a number of reasons. It may be time-consuming to go through channels when a friendly visit can accomplish desired results much more quickly, though without formal approval. Or, as noted in the foregoing, a designated point of contact is avoided because of a lack of confidence in it or respect for it. In other cases, a particular individual may be sought out because he has appealing personal qualities of understanding, sympathy, and wisdom. In still other cases, the positions of a person in terms of title, location, office, appointments, or proximity to "the chief" may make contacts with him selfishly satisfying. And finally, conditions often change so rapidly that it is better to handle them through flexible informality.

Too little is yet known about informal structures. Their existence is well known; the "grapevine" is more than common proof of this. But how to use them is another matter. Perhaps at present the best advice is to find out, if possible, the cause of important deviation from the formal. Then, it can be decided whether to minimize the cause or to let the informal relationship continue, as the better way out. Sometimes the informal is best both for executives and the attitudes of subordinates.

2. *Authority and Responsibility Relationships.* An organization structure, as mentioned, serves to denote who has authority over whom for what. This involves matters of authority, responsibility, and work divisions, subjects to which attention is directed more fully later but to which some brief comments are in order now.

a) Authority. Authority may be defined briefly as the right to command obedience from others. It has two sources. Authority may be delegated from above or earned from below. The ultimate source from above is that which society delegates. Thus, in our society the right to command others is derived through the devices of private property and legislative permissions. Some businesses may be started simply if one has the necessary capital, but most, in addition, have to obtain permission from local, state, or federal agencies.

Once society's authority to proceed is obtained, authority is delegated by owners through successive echelons of the organization structure to the ultimate working level. Thus, the owners of an enterprise delegate authority to a board of directors, then to a president who, in turn, delegates authority through the various subordinate executive levels.

Right to command seems to imply harshness. If obedience depended solely upon such rights to give orders, the system would be unpalatable to most individuals. But obedience may be given willingly. Superiors may earn from below a "right to command." Subordinates voluntarily submit to and respect executive commands when they become convinced that they personally gain from such relationships.

b) Responsibility. Responsibility is the reverse of the coin of authority. It has reference to the obligations of individuals. For example, the office manager has authority over the office, the office help, and the work of the office. He, in turn, is responsible for all of this to someone. To be sure, his subordinates may do the actual work of the office, so they are obligated to him. He may discipline them for poor performance or reward them for excellent performance. But his superior will hold him responsible for office performance.

Responsibility thus has a number of interesting facets. First, it implies an obligation for something to someone. Second, the obligation should be matched with commensurate authority. And third, each level of an organization is responsible to its superior not only for its own work but also for the work of the levels below it. Taking the case of the office manager, this may be summed up by saying that he has authority over the office yet is responsible to his superior for what all his subordinates do or don't do.

c) *Divisions of Work.* But over what kinds and amounts of work should a person be made responsible or given authority? First, and so obviously common that it is easy to overlook, is the division between the work of *managing* others and the work *of* the others. As a simple example, the manager of the foundry has work which differs from that of the molders. And the manager of the foundry has work that is different from the work of other executives such as the factory manager, the chief engineer, and the personnel manager.

But among workers or executives at the same level, the work of any organization may be divided up in different ways. Let us assume, for example, that a company is in the meat-packing business. It might set up divisions of the organization on the basis of the following:

a) Products: pork, beef, and lamb.
b) Functions: production, sales, finance, etc.
c) Geographical areas: Eastern, Southern, and Western Divisions.
d) Customers: wholesale, retail, and institutional.
e) Processes or equipment: cutting, by-product, or packaging.

Generally, as a company grows, various combinations of all of these bases of divisions would be employed in setting up the organization structure.

3. **Factors of Structural Design.** The design of structure adopted in any given case should give consideration to several perti-

nent factors. These include the purposes and philosophy of top management, available personnel, size and location, and desirable characteristics in a structure.

a) Philosophy and Purposes. Organizational design is basically determined by what one hopes to accomplish and how he hopes to accomplish his goals. Indeed, every businessman seeks to make a profit. But does he propose to do this by performing a superior service, encouraging employee participation, promoting full product lines, innovating technological advances, establishing nationwide distribution, or what? To be Number 1 or Number 2 in a business area tends to call for organizational effort and relationships that are more complex than when one's aims are more modest.

Furthermore, structural design is determined in part by a management's philosophy. How closely, for example, does management propose to adhere to the golden rule, or shall it let the devil take the hindmost? How much does it trust the honesty and fairness of employees, suppliers, customers, and competitors? Will it cut corners in serving customers, take advantage of marginal suppliers, and always be on the lookout for contractural loopholes? Obviously how such questions are answered will determine in part how authority is delegated to and divided among various subordinate executives on the organizational chart.

b) Available Personnel. An ideal structure may be designed on paper, but adjustments may have to be made because of who is available to fill the various positions. On paper, it may have been desirable, let us say, to make a place for a director of sales research. But no one may be available or can be procured to fill this position. As a consequence, the work of research may be temporarily combined with that of the sales manager.

On the other hand, a position may be retained in a structure because it is unwise to move or remove the incumbent. Assume that it were found desirable in the ideal design to assign hitherto separate sales traffic and production traffic departments to a major traffic division. Assume further that the manager of neither of these units is qualified to move up, yet each has long seniority and will be pensioned in a few years. In this case, it would be wise to retain the current setup until time makes possible the installation of the more effective design.

c) Size and Location. The design of structure is seriously affected by the size and location of an enterprise. It is not generally considered wise for a small and young company to decentralize rapidly. Some of the advantages of such a firm are its flexibility and economy of operation. Department heads may have the decision-making ability to lead their own departments but have not had the opportunity to develop the perspective and objectivity to make decisions for several functions.

As a company grows, however, and as its work is spread over many locations, the organization structure must be expanded in size and complexity. Structural units will have to be added, not only to take care of the added work but also to control the managers of the added work. As a simple illustration, the president of a growing organization becomes more and more a manager of managers and has less and less direct contact with the lower levels of the structure. Moreover, he must establish various staff organization units, not only to help his subordinates manage but also to help him manage the subordinate managers.

The structure of such an enterprise grows horizontally and vertically. If it is not to turn into an unwieldy monster, the president must adopt devices to extend his powers of control. He himself and his subordinate executives will have to rely on such tools as policies, budgets, standard practice instructions, speedy communications, and carefully planned projects. When executives add such tools to their managerial arsenals, they can extend their limited spans of control and thereby reduce the number of echelons through which their controls and communications need travel.

d) Desirable Characteristics. Structural design should be checked against a number of tests. First and foremost is whether or not a selected design will serve to attain most effectively and in the simplest possible fashion the purposes for which the enterprise has been established. The design should also be relatively stable, so that provision is made so far as possible for replacing executives who drop out of the organization. The design should make provision on the one hand for short-run changes in volume of business and, on the other hand, for long-run growth or contraction. And, finally, the design selected should be made known to all concerned so that each understands his place in the structure.

Procedural Structures

The organization structure diagrams the relationships between various individuals and divisions that have authority and responsibility for particular areas of work. But this structure does no work. The work of an organization is accomplished through its procedures or, as some prefer to call them, its processes, systems, or operational flows. Hence, in the organizing phase of management, careful attention must be directed to the designing of procedures or systems through which managerial plans are to be executed. More detailed analysis of procedures will be made in a later chapter, so for present purposes, a brief review of the following aspects of the subject will be sufficient:

1. Nature of procedures.
2. Building procedures.
3. Factors of procedural design.

1. *Nature of Procedures.* Defined very simply, a procedure is an arrangement of functions (activities) intended to achieve some objective. A production procedure, for example, is an arrangement of functions intended to manufacture a product. This procedure (system) may consist of a number of subsidiary procedures (subsystem) intended to manufacture a part or to contribute to processing materials, parts, or subassemblies.

For a procedure to be effective, more is needed than just a series of functions. First, the arrangement must be orderly and logical. And, second, each step of the procedure must be adequately staffed with personnel and operated with appropriate tools or machines in an appropriate environment. In diagram form, an effective procedure may be charted as follows:[1]

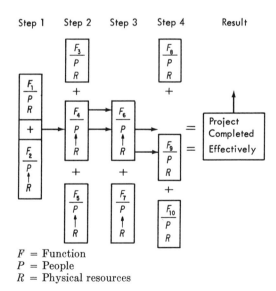

F = Function
P = People
R = Physical resources

---

[1] This procedure is diagrammed in another way in Chapter 11, Figure 11–2.

In this diagram, it is seen that a procedure is built of, and around, functions. To be effective, some functions of a procedure must be performed before others, that is, in sequence. Other functions must be performed at the same time, that is, concurrently. For example, step 1 takes place before step 2; that is, there is a sequence to the procedure. But functions 3, 4, and 5 are to take place at the same time; that is, there is a concurrence of events in a procedure. Hence, in designing a procedure it is necessary to ascertain not only what functions must be performed but also their order of performance, concurrently and sequentially.

Another task of procedural design is to determine the human and technical resources required to perform each specified function. What skills, knowledge, and experience are needed to perform F_1, F_2, etc.? And what tools, machines, and environment should be provided so that each function can be performed most effectively and economically? Several answers to such questions will be touched on later in this chapter and more fully explored in subsequent chapters; hence, further discussion here is not needed.

The foregoing diagram can serve to bring out another significant feature of procedures. Let us assume that the procedure illustrates the making of a wheel: step 1 is that of making hubs; step 2, making spokes; step 3, making rims; and step 4, assembling the hubs, spokes, and rims. Each step consists of two or more functions. This is the manufacturing procedure. But what goes on in each function? How do units of work pass from manufacturing stage to manufacturing stage? And how do various specialists such as engineers, cost accountants, and inspectors relate themselves to this procedure? Broadly speaking, answers to these questions would show that in every procedure there are, first, internally, subfunctional or motion divisions and, second, externally, various co-related procedures.

The internal nature of procedures is well exemplified by motion analysis of factory and office functions. Micromotion study and the therbligs of the Gilbreths are noteworthy examples. Thus, in the process of making a wheel, step 1 is that of making a hub, and F_2 is that of drilling holes. At this point of procedural design it is necessary to ascertain and specify the sequence of motions an operator should follow in picking up the material to be drilled, handling the materials, and releasing them after drilling. If management, or a designated staff specialist, does not design this phase of a procedure, then the worker will have to work it out for himself.

Better practice suggests that the former assume responsibility for such designs.

The external nature of procedures may be illustrated by reference to the work of inspection, transportation, and production control units. Using inspection as an example, in the manufacturing procedure outlined above it will be necessary to add appropriate quality controls. The decision may be to inspect only after F_2, F_6, and F_9. On the blueprint for the manufacturing procedure would be added, in some identifying manner, marks for inspection points. For example, the letter I could be shown adjacent to R under F_2, F_6, and F_9. Similar identifying letters or symbols could be shown for transportation, production control, or other associated functions.

To summarize, organizing a procedure requires that functions, personnel, and technical resources be arranged in an orderly, logical, and complementary fashion. Each procedure (system), as has been seen, consists of three procedural parts (subsystem): first, the primary procedure itself; second, the internal phases of each function of the primary procedure; and, third, the external procedures or functions that are related to the primary procedure.

2. Building Procedures. Attention needs to be turned now to the basic processes by which procedures are built. These consist of two major stages, functional analysis and functional differentiation. In the former stage, the functions needed to complete a project are determined. In the latter stage, the functions specified by analysis are grouped into orderly arrangements.

Functional analysis, as the term implies, means "breaking up" a whole into its parts. To illustrate, making a wheel or selling a wheel may be looked upon as a "whole." Such "wholes" are not accomplished or achieved all at once. Each is attained only through the performance of a series of steps. And each step—as in walking a mile—can be taken one at a time. It is the task of functional analysis to ascertain what these steps are.

Functional differentiation is intended to establish the functions determined by functional analysis into an orderly arrangement. Orderliness connotes three significant aspects: similarity, time, and place. So differentiation groups functions according to their similarity, to the time at which they should be performed, and to the place at which they should be performed, as illustrated in Chapter 11, Figures 11–3 and 11–5. Much thought must be expended in examining various possible combinations to ascertain which arrangement will be the most effective and economical in completing specific projects.

3. **Factors of Procedural Design.** This section on organizing the procedural structures of an enterprise may be brought to a close by commenting briefly upon some pertinent factors of procedural design. These factors may be summarized under the headings of the importance of logical thinking, the need of adequate coverage, and the tests of a good procedure.

a) *Logical Thinking.* From what has already been said, it is obvious that designing procedures is not an easy task. Great skill and much experience are needed to establish procedures that will serve to carry out plans economically and effectively. Yet when one views the actual world, it is surprising how often procedural design is left to operative workers themselves, or how often procedures have just grown "like Topsy."

Much constructive thought has been given to procedural design in a few areas such as routine factory and office work. Here motion study has made significant contributions to how work should be done, and here engineering has successfully coped with process-layout problems. But elsewhere, in sales work, in management processes, and in administrative relations, only isolated work has been done in systems development. Yet here are areas in which confusion is built on confusion because procedural development has been left to chance.

Yet the logical methods of procedural design employed successfully in shopwork are just as applicable in other areas. To be sure, it may take more time to analyze and differentiate the procedures through which the president of a company can communicate with the lowest levels of an organization. Or it may be more difficult to design a procedure by which the work of a personnel department (staff) is integrated with that of a foundry (line). But difficulty or time consumption should not stand in the way when one contemplates the losses which could be minimized by expenditures of logical thought. Particularly as an organization grows is such logical thought necessary if the economies and advantages of growth are not to be more than offset by the losses and costs of poorly designed managerial and organizational procedures.

b) *Adequate Coverage.* Another factor of procedural design is that of adequate coverage. This has two phases: types of procedures and tools of procedures.

As noted in the immediately preceding section and also in earlier sections of this chapter, designing procedures involves more than just primary projects in such areas as production or sales. As noted in connection with the diagram of the procedure for making wheels, internal and external procedural relationships are involved. It is necessary to see that adequate provision is made for these types of procedures. Then too, it has been suggested that procedures need to be established for other areas of the enterprise, if full coverage of procedures is to be provided.

A quick check on adequate coverage of types of procedures can be made if a list of possible procedures is kept at hand. Such a list could be based upon the following classification:

1. Operative, to cover the work done by operative employees in production, sales, office, etc.
2. Functional, to cover the work done in the various functional and technical divisions of a company.
3. Managerial, to cover the work done by:
    a) Various echelons of a company such as administrative, middle management, and supervisory.
4. Regional (if any), to cover the work done by:
    a) Home office as opposed or related to branch office or plant operations.
    b) Particular regional requirements within the domestic area or in given international sections.

The second phase of adequate coverage is related to the tools used in procedures. Mention already has been made of blueprints and layout sheets in procedural design. These are very useful in visualizing actual or contemplated systems. Of similar nature are the more complicated three-dimensional models of factory or office layouts. Other tools of procedural design include orders, instructions, communications, records, and reports. Through appropriate attention to designs and implementation of these instruments, procedures can be established that will tend to serve an enterprise with much greater effectiveness.

c)   Desirable Features. The design of a procedure, to be termed good, should incorporate a number of features. The primary test of goodness is attainment of objectives economically and effectively. A good hiring procedure is one that serves to select good employees at a low cost and when needed. So the designer should have this question uppermost in his mind as he thinks about every function in a procedure, about whether or not it should be included, and how, when and where—and the question is, will it serve to contribute to the desired objective, economically and effectively?

Then, too, a procedure should be stable, flexible, growth directed, balanced, and related. A stable procedure is one that is not being constantly changed for whim or fancy, or with every passing force. Yet a procedure must be flexible enough to take care of current and short-run changes in volume of business. Moreover, a procedure should be subject to expansion or contraction as long-run forces dictate the need for such changes. Balance refers to provision of appropriate manpower and resources—but no more and no less—to implement performance of specified functions. And relatedness has reference to the design of a procedure so that it fits in, and is complementary with, related procedures.

But no matter how well a procedure is designed, it is futile unless it is known and understood. This may seem so obvious that to mention it seems inane. But one does not have to have much experience in the practical world to soon note how often this prerequisite is not met. Workers, supervisors, and, indeed, top executives often do not satisfactorily understand where and how they fit into the procedures that surround them. And until they do, either the procedures or the persons involved will suffer needlessly. Hence, the designer of a procedure should also concern himself with seeing to it that instructions are available to all involved as to how and why the given procedure operates as it does. For example, Figure 6–2 neatly illustrates how various forms and reports move through a given operational process.

Assembling a Staff

A large task of organizing is concerned with assembling a staff to work in the organization structures and procedural structures whose purpose it is to carry out the plans of an enterprise. Assembling a staff—both operative and managerial—involves three major phases as follows:

1. Specification of personnel requirements.

2. Procurement of personnel.
3. Training of personnel.

FIGURE 6-2
A Chart of Steps in a Selected Procedure

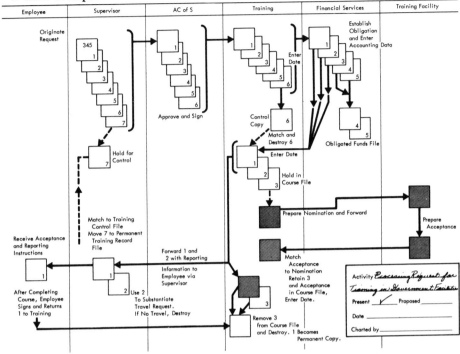

Employee	Supervisor	AC of S	Training	Financial Services	Training Facility

Adapted from a training manual of the U.S. Civil Service Commission.

1. *Specification of Personnel Requirements*. Two broad areas of problems call for solution in assembling personnel: first, quantity of personnel needed and, second, kinds of personnel.

The problem of quantity of personnel must be solved for both operative and managerial groups. In each case, quantity may be computed by waiting until vacancies occur or by forecasting needs in advance. The latter method is to be preferred because staff can usually be hired, without emergency haste, in time to keep operations going with a minimum of loss. And much has been done in the area of operative employees to use the forecasting method effectively. This is possible when statistical techniques serve to disclose within a practical range of probability, first, how much labor will be needed to carry out estimated sales and production programs; and, second, how much of the present working force will have to be replaced because of normal labor turnover. The task of estimating managerial requirements is not as easy, yet steps can be taken—

as will be noted in a later chapter—to make reasonably accurate forecasts of managerial turnover.

The problem of kind of personnel is best solved through a good program of job specifications for both operative and managerial personnel. Such specifications should indicate, first, what is done on particular jobs; and, second, what qualities a person should possess to fulfill the requirements of the jobs. Detailed analysis will be made of personnel qualities later, particularly in relation to executive position, but for the present it is sufficient that such specifications, to be useful, should cover the following qualities:

1.	Physical.	4.	Sociological.
2.	Mental.	5.	Ethical.
3.	Psychological.	6.	Behavioral.

The first two of these qualities are generally accepted and known. Obviously, in varying degrees for different jobs, physical ability and mental skills are required. And, increasingly, the impact of psychological and social qualities upon job success is being recognized. Certainly a person's inward poise and psychological balance, as well as his social ability to get along with others, affect his productivity and that of his fellow workers.

The last two of these qualities are being given deserved recognition, too, but as yet in only a minority of cases. The matter of the attitude of fairness and empathy one has toward his subordinates will certainly influence their effectiveness. An executive may give the impression that labor is a commodity, a cost factor, or, at the other extreme, a valuable partner in a business effort. And in return he will get a reaction reflecting his attitude. Similarly in behavior, an executive may be autocratic or democratic, to cite but two possible types of behavior. And in return he will get a different reaction from each. It is desirable, therefore, that a job specification indicate the type of attitude and behavior toward which executives in particular should strive in the performance of their jobs. And, of course, in selecting executives, candidates with potentials in the required directions should be sought.

2.   *Procurement of Personnel.* Procurement of personnel, once requirements are established, can proceed along fairly standardized lines. Suggested here are knowledge of sources of labor supply and screening procedures for candidates.

a)   Sources. Sources of labor supply are many and of varying usefulness. Broadly speaking, the sources are internal or external.

Internal sources include present employees, active or on leave. This source should be well combed if good material is not to be over-looked and if morale of employees is not to be lost because of the hiring factor. Procedures and records should be established that will serve to bring to light all who are deserving of consideration when vacancies occur or are expected to occur. Of course, when companies expand at a rapid rate, or when the present force has little potential for growth, the internal source will prove inadequate.

The external source includes such diverse types as advertising, scouting, employment agencies, consulting concerns, and college recruiting. Each has usefulness, although not of equal value at all times and for all companies and for all classes of vacancies. Hence, it is desirable to keep records of how useful such sources have been in the past and to keep abreast of how good each source is at present and may be in the future.

b) Screening. Screening has reference to the procedures and policies used to select desirable candidates out of a group of applicants. Such screening usually involves such hurdles as application blanks, reference letter, interviewing, psychological tests, and physical examinations. The detail and thoroughness of each step will depend upon the importance of the job to be filled and the attitude management has toward the practical usefulness of each.

How screening (or selecting, procuring, or hiring—to use common synonyms) may be done can be seen by perusing standard texts on the subject. And some fuller comments will be made in a later chapter. It is worth underscoring here, however, that perhaps there is no more significant function of organizing than that of procuring good people. With a good staff, many inadequacies and poor designs can be made to work with some degree of effectiveness. Without a good staff, the best of structures and technical resources will be misused to the point of excessive cost if not outright failure.

3. Training of Personnel. Organizing a good team is incomplete without a good program of training and education. This is necessary, in the first place, to transmute the potential of an individual into actual ability to do what is needed. Thus a person has, let us say, a potential to manage. But this potentiality must be developed so that he actually can manage. Training is necessary, in the second place, because conditions change. New machines are designed and installed, new processes are laid out, new products are taken on, and new territories may be invaded. As a consequence, present (as well as new) employees and executives must be trained so that their knowledge and skills will be adapted to, and increased in line with, the new responsibilities.

Training can be accomplished by "doing" or under some formal plan. For a long time practically all training was by practical experience. Then came a trend toward formal schooling in such areas as engineering, chemistry, and accounting. More recently there are signs that the management area is being included among those that call for formal school training. In addition to school training, more and more companies are turning to formal in-plant programs. Executive development programs of various types, trade courses, and apprentice programs are just a few examples of company training programs. Such programs are recognition of the fact that enough skilled employees—operative or management—cannot be obtained just by hiring, nor skill of employees maintained at an effective level without training. All of these are recognition also of the fact that since employees are bound to learn on the job anyhow, they may as well learn the correct way.

Technical Resources

Finally, organizing an enterprise calls for the assembly of appropriate kinds and quantities of technical resources. Such factors as tools, machines, buildings, materials, supplies, and working conditions must be available to carry out intended plans. To this task will be brought the services of such experts as engineers, chemists, purchasing agents, production control technicians, and stores keepers. Behind them stand the custodians and providers of funds—finance experts, accountants and controllers, the board of directors, and ultimately the stockholders and various creditors.

This phase of organizing obviously goes into subjects whose adequate treatment calls for more space and knowledge than is available here. Hence, beyond mere mention of this significant part of organizing and beyond a very low bow to its importance, further examination of it is left to those who have so capably and fully explored the various aspects of the technical area.

QUESTIONS

1. What is meant by the term organizing and what are kinds of factors that are organized?
2. What disadvantages are attached to the functional form of organization structure?

3. Under what conditions would the use of the line and staff form of organization structure (in part, if not in whole) be desirable?

4. For what reasons may the informal organization structure deviate from the channels and lines depicted by the formal organization structure?

5. What are the sources of authority in an organization? Which, if any, is to be preferred? Why?

6. What is a procedure, and what are the basic processes by which procedures are built?

7. What features should a procedure possess if it is to be said to be a good one?

8. List and describe the major phases of assembling a staff needed to carry out the plans of an enterprise.

CASE 6–1

A company which has all its facilities and staff in one location desires to establish branches elsewhere not only for purposes of expansion but also to disperse some of its home operations. Of the numerous organizational problems that it faces, a major one is that of how to handle the research and development activities.

Briefly, the company wants to retain research and development in the home location yet place in the branches research and development specifically pertinent to those branches. In making such a split, it wants to assure itself that local facilities for research and development, while contributing to the needs of the respective branches, do not become a set of dissimilar satellites. In other words, while recognizing the need for individuality and regional creativity, the company wants some restraints, to avoid duplication, and agreement on how research and development are to be operated.

1. What suggestions do you have for the organization of research and development in this case?

2. Would you answer differently if the function in question had been of a more routine nature, say plant maintenance and repair services?

CASE 6–2

The Soft Leather Company was not unionized, and its owner desired to keep it that way. To reduce the chances of being organized, he felt, among other things, that employee dissatisfaction should be kept at a minimum.

To forestall grievances from building up, he decided to set up a special committee whose task it would be, first, to know what employees were thinking and, second, to have at hand the best available plans for dealing with employee attitudes and goals. This committee was to be composed of himself, the factory superintendent, his general office manager (who also acted as personnel manager), and two operative employees.

He gave particular thought to the qualifications which the employees should possess who were to serve on the committee. He decided to have the two elected by the entire working force from a slate of 8 candidates, screened from a list of 15 employees nominated by the employees themselves. The eight were to be screened by a consulting psychologist on the basis of their basic mental and personality qualifications. Presumably their technical background in the shop was checked out by the nominating procedure.

The reasons for the screening were that the owner wanted to be sure that the two employees who were finally selected would be, first, capable of taking some university courses in pertinent fields which he thought would be desirable and, second, capable of gaining better perspectives from visitations to other factories to which he wanted to send them.

By this plan of selection, the two employees on the committee would have good practical experience, acceptance by their fellow workers, and a broadened outlook. They would thus be able to offer advice from the veiwpoint of the employees yet understand company problems from both a theoretical and industry angle.

1. What is your opinion of the plan of selecting the employee members of the committee?
2. With whose objectives is the owner concerned here?

7

Directing

Introduction

DIRECTING is the managerial function of running the organization
(or any subdivision) as it actively carries out plans. Defined earlier,
this activity is comparable to that performed by the pilot flying
a plane to an airport or by the captain on the bridge in command
of a ship as it proceeds toward port. The airline pilot presumably
is flying in accordance with a plan that had been prepared before
takeoff. And the captain is guiding his ship according to a preestablished course. In business, too, there is a directing phase in which
an executive commands his organizational ship.

This active phase of management, as the term implies, "directs"
the group toward goals established in an earlier phase of planning.
The executive issues orders and instructions to his subordinates so
that proper course is maintained or undesirable deviations are corrected. He senses the temper of his crew and takes needed action
to curb faulty performance or to reward superior effort. He motivates his subordinates so that optimum action is stimulated. And
he keeps appropriate records current so that future evaluations
of his current actions and those of his organization can be made
in terms of pertinent data and information.

The kind and amount of direction depends largely upon the kind
and amount of prior executive planning and organizing. The less
of the latter, the more of the former. And, vice versa, the more
thorough the planning and organizing, the fewer are the unexpected
problems and the fewer the on-the-spot decisions that the executive
will be forced to meet as he actively guides his team to desired

objectives. Assuming then that planning and organizing have been handled in an effective manner, the directional phase of an executive's job would consist of the following subphases:

1. Translating plans of superiors into immediate plans and orders.
2. Issuing specific orders, instructions, and communications.
3. Supervision and evaluation of current efforts.
4. Motivation of current efforts.

Translation of Superior Plans

An executive does not, of course, operate his unit independently of others. As shown in Figure 7–1, he has been well designated as

FIGURE 7–1
The Organizational Relationships of the Supervisor

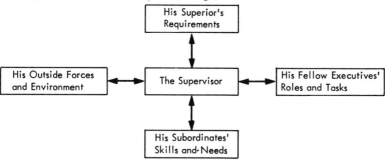

the "man in the middle." His work and that of his unit must fit into the plans of his superior. He must, in other words, be a good member of the team. Consequently, he must take the plans, projects, orders, and instructions of his superior and translate them into plans, projects, orders, and instructions for his subordinates that complement those of his superior. And he must adjust to such outside elements as the community or unions. To do this correctly, he must keep in mind, first, the expectations of his superior; second, the potential abilities of his subordinates; third, the roles of his fellow executives; and fourth, outside forces.

1. *Expectations of Superiors.* Good teamwork begins with a proper understanding of what an executive's superior expects to accomplish technically and humanly. Technical expectations of accomplishments may be expressed in terms of results, methods, or both. Thus, a sales executive may be told that he is expected to

sell "X" dollars of merchandise during the next month within a budget of "Y" dollars. Beyond that quota and budget he may be given no further orders as to what methods or policies he is to pursue. Such a bare order is seldom given, although some companies claim that they manage by objective alone. If they do, then executives are held responsible solely for results, not for how they are obtained.

Generally, however, superiors either informally or formally expect subordinates to follow prescribed methods in pursuing established goals. Informally, the sales manager may assume that subordinate sales supervisors will use the right methods because he trusts them. His trust is based on the fact that he has selected supervisors who have learned his methods; he has not promoted those who failed to learn from him. Or formally, the sales manager may spell out through policies, selling manuals, and training sessions how he expects his supervisors to conduct their operations. In this way, he seeks to assure himself of uniform and effective performance.

But very important are the human expectations that must be learned. Does one's superior view himself as a superior personally as well as organizationally, as one whose status must be fully respected, or as one for whom protocol is important? Does or does he not like flattery? Are his feelings easily hurt? These questions illustrate the point that there are behavioral patterns and expectations that must be deduced by every subordinate executive.

Each executive level is informed from above in technical and human terms what is expected of it. Such expectations, particularly the behavioral, are seldom crystal clear. This is so because it is impossible for a superior to spell out all of his expectations or because he himself is unaware of his personal sentiments. But clearer pictures of various aspects of supervisory human relations could be obtained if such questionnaires as that illustrated in Figure 7–2 were adopted.

Most executives must, therefore, spend a good deal of time trying to ascertain the exact wishes of their superiors. Indeed, so much time is spent "looking up" that not enough time or consideration is given to "looking down." The question may be raised as to why a subordinate doesn't ask, if he is not sure of his exact obligations. The answer is simple; subordinates do not like to admit that they couldn't get a clear picture from their superior, nor do they like to make the boss feel that he isn't giving clear orders and thus incur his possible animosity.

FIGURE 7–2

Supervisory Practices Questionnaire

I. The 12 statements listed below describe some of the ways in which supervision is being exercised in the part of the organization in which you work. Complete each statement, thinking not only of your own supervisor but also of others who make up the management team directly closest to you. (Circle) the response which best completes each statement. Please do not omit any statements.

	1	2	3	4	5
A. The extent to which employees are *kept informed* on what they need to know about what is going on is _____	Rather Unsatisfactory	Just Adequate	Mostly Satisfactory	Quite Satisfactory	Highly Satisfactory
B. The extent to which employees do *influence* supervisors on decisions and policies where their experience and knowledge should carry weight is _____	Rather Unsatisfactory	Just Adequate	Mostly Satisfactory	Quite Satisfactory	Highly Satisfactory
C. The extent to which employees are given opportunity and encouragement to *exercise judgment* and make decisions is _____	Rather Unsatisfactory	Just Adequate	Mostly Satisfactory	Quite Satisfactory	Highly Satisfactory
D. The extent to which employees are encouraged to work hard and to do a *high quality* job is _____	Rather Unsatisfactory	Just Adequate	Mostly Satisfactory	Quite Satisfactory	Highly Satisfactory
E. The extent to which employees receive *guidance* and assistance from supervisors is _____	Rather Unsatisfactory	Just Adequate	Mostly Satisfactory	Quite Satisfactory	Highly Satisfactory
F. The extent to which employees know and accept the current *objectives* of this part of the organization is _____	Rather Unsatisfactory	Just Adequate	Mostly Satisfactory	Quite Satisfactory	Highly Satisfactory
G. The extent to which *waste* and unnecessary work are avoided and manpower and money are used wisely is _____	Rather Unsatisfactory	Just Adequate	Mostly Satisfactory	Quite Satisfactory	Highly Satisfactory
H. The extent to which supervisors are judging and *appraising* employee performance fairly is _____	Rather Unsatisfactory	Just Adequate	Mostly Satisfactory	Quite Satisfactory	Highly Satisfactory
I. The extent to which the most *capable* employees are the ones selected for new opportunities is _____	Rather Unsatisfactory	Just Adequate	Mostly Satisfactory	Quite Satisfactory	Highly Satisfactory
J. The extent to which employees are treated as being *responsible* people capable of getting their work done properly is _____	Rather Unsatisfactory	Just Adequate	Mostly Satisfactory	Quite Satisfactory	Highly Satisfactory
K. The extent to which employees in the organization support each other in order to achieve *teamwork* is _____	Rather Unsatisfactory	Just Adequate	Mostly Satisfactory	Quite Satisfactory	Highly Satisfactory
L. The extent to which employees can exercise the *authority* necessary to carry out their jobs is _____	Rather Unsatisfactory	Just Adequate	Mostly Satisfactory	Quite Satisfactory	Highly Satisfactory

II. Which 3 of the above 12 items have improved the most in the past 6 months? (Circle) 3 letters.

A   B   C   D   E   F   G   H   I   J   K   L

III. Which 3 of the 12 items would you like to see the biggest improvement in the next 6 months? (Circle) 3 letters.

A   B   C   D   E   F   G   H   I   J   K   L

"Building More Effective Organizational Units," U.S. Postal Service, p. 43.

2. *The Abilities of Subordinates.* Translating expectations of superiors involves a good grasp of the abilities of one's subordinates. How many subordinates do I have, what are their skills, how reliable are they, what are their attitudes and expectations, and what is the current state of their morale, are questions for which each executive must have good answers in this stage of management.

This is a phase of his job that never ends. He cannot rely upon yesterday's status in these matters to hold true today or tomorrow. He must constantly have his finger on the pulse of each employee. He should know which ones are giving and which are standing still or regressing. He should know what types and amounts of motivation will work currently for each subordinate. He should know the load of work each is carrying and how much more, if any, each can be made to carry.

As he stands on the bridge of his organization unit, this interpretation of his men must be based on what they can do now, not what they can be made to do on future trips. To be sure, a particular subordinate may show signs of potential for advancement in accepting increased responsibilities, and another subordinate seems somewhat "under the weather." But for the present, a particularly difficult assignment should not be given to the former but assigned to the latter. How the potential of the former or the temporary illness of the latter should be handled are questions apart from that of immediate direction of the ship.

This does not imply that in directing his group, an executive cannot seek current objectives along with future objectives. This is a problem that forever faces every executive. How far should he go in sacrificing (or balancing) present goals against future goals (or vice versa)? Should he, for example, give the growing executive some or all of the work he might well assign to the ailing employee? If he does, current results are bound to suffer. But future voyages can be made in greater safety.

3. *Roles of Fellow Executives.* Translation involves knowledge of the roles and expectations of related team members. How a given supervisor interprets the instructions of his superior depends upon what the supervisor thinks other supervisors and staff people are being told to do. Else, like a pilot flying in a fog who knows that others are in the same fog but without adequate restrictions, he will soon be overdoing parts of his job, underdoing others, while constantly in a state of frustrating tension and fear.

Of course, a superior may specify exactly what each subordinate is to do, and then he alone is presumably responsible for team co-ordination. Each executive does what he is told to do and as long as he follows instructions there is little danger of collisions. Such centralized controls are rather cumbersome, time-consuming, and costly. Seldom is such a degree of managerial control exercised.

Instead, executives at the same level, or given executives and service or staff units, often are expected in more or less large measure to cooperate among themselves. Such cooperation is perhaps best built upon a foundation of frequent contacts. Thus, a traffic manager, for example, should make it a point to meet frequently with those he serves, such as the production manager, purchasing agent, sales manager, and shipping department supervisor. And cross contacts should include occasions when time is available to discuss each other's views and plans without the pressures of immediate decisions or difficulties. Cultivating acquaintanceship and understanding under these conditions will serve to preserve and enhance teamwork in times of stress.

4. Outside Forces. And increasingly, consideration must be given to various outside groups such as governmental agencies, community groups, unions, and ecological groups. Business can no longer be viewed as an organization protected by high walls and a moat. But these environmental and outside forces involve such complicated relationships that their consideration can be taken up here only to the extent of recognizing their existence.

Issuing Commands

Having translated the desires of his superior, however expressed, an executive then engages in the actual direction of his group. He issues commands to his team as it works away. Issuance of commands in the process of direction may be discussed in terms of the following phases of the subject:

1. Establishing specific work units.
2. Selecting specific individuals for assignments.
3. Communicating assignments to individuals.

1. Establishing Work Units. Issuing good commands presupposes that the kind and amount of work blocked out fits the individual in question in a particular time span. If a clerk, for example, is asked to check the accuracy of extensions on a batch of purchase orders, the assignment should have given due consideration to quantity of work, quality, and time allowed.

Work units differ in terms of, first, degree of accuracy of measurement and, second, possibility of predetermination. In the matter of accuracy of measurement, some assignments can be stated with a high degree of accuracy. Into this category fall such tasks as most production jobs and many office jobs. At the other end of the scale are such tasks as creative planning, most managerial assignments, and various research projects. When a research engineer, for example, is assigned the task of trying to develop an antiknock gasoline, how long this will take can scarcely be determined in advance. Consequently, the work unit must remain scientifically indeterminate as far as time is concerned, though some time limit may be arbitrarily established.

Determination of work units may also be considered from the viewpoint of their possibility of preestablishment. Some assignments can be decided in advance of actual performance; these would fall in the scope of the managerial function of planning. Included here would be such diverse devices of order giving as standard practice instructions, process and layout charts, procedural manuals, working policies, and operating directions. Where these are available, direct order giving can be greatly simplified. The subordinate need only be told to proceed with a given task, since the why's and wherefore's are contained in the aforementioned devices.

No matter how much predetermination goes into establishing work units, the executive still will have many decisions to make in the active phase of direction. He still, like the captain of a ship, must stand on the bridge and issue commands. To be sure, he—like the captain—may have planned his whole course, may have many assistants to help him coordinate, and have available many devices to inform him quickly of current conditions. But the system of organization and management is as yet not automatic, nor can all contingencies be foreseen. So he, like the captain, must be ready, from his store of experience and judgment, to weigh current developments and issue work assignments on the spur of the moment.

2. *Selecting Specific Individuals.*[1] With the work units established, the next logical step in issuing commands is to select the in-

---

[1] It is well to note here that sequences of steps to be followed as suggested throughout this text are not intended to imply that a rigid one, two, three, four series is mandatory. Often steps have to be repeated, some must be redone, some must be done out of order, some done simultaneously, and sometimes the whole sequence must be gone through more than once. For purposes of discussion, the various possible combinations cannot be covered here, but even though space and time permitted, any attempt to do so would be unduly repetitious and boring.

dividual upon whom the assignment is to be placed. This is stated as the next logical step, because the work load should determine personnel requirements. Often, however, these steps are reversed. What is available determines how work shall be divided.

Individual selections should be based upon three major considerations: capacity to do the job, present versus future considerations, and effect upon interpersonal relationships and morale. The first of these is usually the easiest of the three to weigh. An executive should have a good picture of the technical skills and abilities of his subordinates. This picture should have been obtained through his associations with his subordinates, through observation, and through reviews of ratings, progress, and records of performance. Moreover, each picture should be painted with appropriate colors of an individual's likes and dislikes, his emotional and social makeup, his drives, his training and experience, and his potential for growth. With this picture in mind, or written out on paper, an executive should be able to ascertain which work units are best assigned to which individuals in terms of technical competence.

But technical competence is not the sole test for allocating work to particular individuals. Perhaps John Doe is the best draftsman, let us say, and a particularly difficult drawing should logically be assigned to him. But organizational stability will not be achieved unless younger and less versatile draftsmen are given an opportunity to work on tough assignments. So at the expense of not getting as finished a drawing as quickly, and with more supervision time from the chief draftsman, Richard Roe, a less skilled draftsman, is assigned the job in question. This is an example of balancing future advantages against current advantages in making work assignments.

And finally, individual selections should give consideration to interpersonal reactions. What will happen if the John Does are always given difficult or choice assignments? Or the Richard Roes? Either the Does or the Roes will feel varying degrees of resentment. Hence, the reactions of subordinates must be weighed when making particular assignments. Obviously, it cannot be expected that everyone will be pleased no matter what is done. But assignments should not be made solely on grounds of technical competence or training needs.

3. *Communicating Assignments.* The critical stage of direction is now at hand: the captain actually issues commands from the bridge and the executive actually tells his subordinates what to do.

On the surface this seems to amount simply to issuing an order, that is, telling someone to do some particular thing. If subordinates then did what they were told to do, this phase of direction could very quickly be passed over. But things don't happen so nicely. Unless assignments are made with finesse, they are not carried out as desired. There are a number of matters to which an executive should give thought in order to communicate his wishes effectively. In what ways may orders be issued? How detailed should they be? Through whom should they be issued?

To consider the first of these questions, orders may be issued in a number of ways. To begin with, they may be oral or written. An executive may prefer for simplicity's sake to issue oral commands. But these are ephemeral, easily misunderstood, and just as easily forgotten. More and more, particularly as a company grows, the practice is followed of putting orders in writing. This gives a permanent record, which overcomes the disadvantages of the oral though it is a bit more costly to prepare and issue. And orders may be issued in advance of immediate performance or only when performance is immediately expected. The former method gives the subordinate some time for preparation, the latter does not. Often, like the captain on the bridge, there is no time for allowance between command and performance.

How detailed should orders be? A simple, but incomplete, answer is detailed enough to serve to get the job done. A fuller answer must look into the components of an order, which include the following:

1. Authority to proceed.
2. Description of what is to be done.
3. Instructions on how the what is to be done.

All of these must actually be in each order, or implied in the previous training and experience of subordinates and the previous relationship of the superior with his subordinates.

A few illustrations will serve to bring out the possible combinations. Assume first that an entirely new job is being undertaken. Then the executive must cover all three components of an order: authority, work description, and instruction. Assume now that the job in question is similar to one that has previously been done effectively by the person to whom the assignment is to be made. In this case, the first component alone needs to be handled by the executive because the second two have previously been covered. Between these extremes would be various cases in which past experience and relationships would call for varying degrees of description and instruction. So the simple answer to the question of how much detail in an order is not as naïve as it may sound. An executive must figure out how much of each component of order giving is enough to serve to get the job done in each case.

The third question raised in connection with communicating assignments is that of through whom orders should be issued. The executive of each group should be the source of all orders for his immediate subordinates. But he need not personally communicate every order. He may have staff assistants or subordinates through whom he may channel his orders. All in his organizational unit must understand, however, that the order is his, and not that of someone who is acting on his own. As a warning, the executive should be alert for any of his staff who are assuming order-giving prerogatives because of their position as communicators of orders.

Another source of problems in communicating orders lies in the contacts of service departments or of those in other departments who precede a given department in a procedure that cuts across departmental lines. What should a subordinate do when he receives a communication from a service unit such as engineering or personnel? The communication may place the subordinate in a position of having to decide whether to follow the communication of a staff unit or of having to go to his superior for a decision. In either event, it places the subordinate in a position of embarrassment. Except in emergencies, the questionable communication should have been cleared up at higher levels.

Another example of conflicting orders arises when a person performing an earlier step in a procedure begins to think that he has authority over those that follow him. Does the balance-of-stores clerk, for example, who has the duty of issuing purchase requisitions on standard-run materials when they reach preestablished minimum ordering points, have authority over the buyers? Of course, he doesn't in a pure organizational sense. But since the balance-of-stores clerk has to do something before the buyers can proceed, the latter are placed in a position where procedural authority seems to take precedence over organizational authority. Here is a common and delicate situation, which indicates the need of educating the balance-of-stores clerks and the buyers on their respective rights, duties, and relationship to their superiors and to each other.

Supervision and Evaluation of Current Efforts

A major part of the managerial job is that of supervising and evaluating current efforts and conditions. This is a "watching over" function of an executive. As work is actively progressing he observes the work, the workers, and the working conditions. He observes with a view to determining whether or not deviations from plans are occurring and, if they are, what needs to be done to put operations back on desired course. So supervision may be examined in terms of the following:

1. Meaning and scope of supervision.
2. Measurements of supervision.
3. Corrective actions of supervision.

1. *Meaning and Scope of Supervision.* Supervision has been defined in part as a watching over process. But what is watched and how is it watched? As noted in the foregoing, an executive must know what is going on, who is doing what, and what the working conditions are. Where these are all relatively in the open, the supervisor can observe without too much difficulty and obtain a fairly clear and accurate picture. A tennis coach, for example, can see during a game who is winning, how his team members are playing, and the condition of the court and of the weather. Similarly, in some business operations, a supervisor can get an equally good picture of what is going on.

Some business situations, like situations in other fields or professions, are not as easy to observe. Salesmen in the field, an engineer working out an experiment, or an executive thinking are a few illustrations of situations in which the superiors would be hard put to know with any degree of precision what is going on merely by looking.

So the expressions "watching over" or "looking at," when used to describe supervision, include more than just personal observation. The executive may surround himself with a variety of assistants and devices to observe. He may, on the one hand, employ specialists to help him see what is going on. The cost accountant gives him information on costs, the inspector on quality, the personnel manager on employee attitudes, the economist on the economic conditions, etc. And, on the other hand, he may utilize mechanical devices to help him observe. Automatic counters may report quantities; control panels may report output, quality, and conditions; telephones and telegraph may communicate a variety of information; and television may permit him to observe a wide range of scattered operations.

Thus, supervision must be based upon a picture of what is going on. Such picture taking presupposes an appreciation of what shots to take and what to do with them after they are taken. The next two divisions of this section take up these matters.

2. *Measurements of Supervision.* Attention is now directed to the question of the measurements that are made by supervision. These measurements involve, first, factors of measurement; second, units of measurement; and, third, measurement standards.

A variety of factors are measured in supervision. The following list is illustrative:

1. Quantity of work.	5. Attitude of workers.
2. Quality of work.	6. Working conditions.
3. Costs.	7. Economic factors.
4. Time of performance.	8. Political and social conditions.

Of course, the significance of these factors will vary according to the level and functional division of a company. Certainly political and social conditions would be much more significant at the top of an organization than they would at the bottom. And quantity and quality of work would be subject to more specific scrutiny than would be desirable or feasible in a research laboratory. So, the emphasis would have to be adjusted to the particular situation of each executive.

Measuring units are also diverse and not all equally applicable. Examples include the following:

1. Physical units of output.
2. Weight or container lots of output.
3. Productivity per hour, per man, or per dollar.
4. Costs per unit of input or output.
5. Quality measures of hardness, conductivity, ductility, color, appearance, etc.
6. Units of working conditions such as temperature, humidity, dust content, etc.
7. Units of personal behavior and attitude such as morale surveys, absenteeism, tardiness, grievances, disciplinary action, and merit rating.

These units are intended to give quantitative expression to the factors being measured. It is obvious that it means nothing to speak, for example, of production unless some quantitative definition of production is also expressed. An executive can see that employee efforts are being exerted to produce, but he must also "see" how much is being produced. So, units for various aspects of current activity must be established if an executive is to measure what is going on.

In addition to units of measurement, it is also necessary to establish standards of performance. An executive must know how much of each factor is an acceptable quantity of performance. How many pieces per hour, how much cost per unit, how many absences per month, and how much humidity in the air are examples of standards of performance. Some standards can be set to a high level of accuracy; whereas others, such as how subordinates feel, are little more than arbitrary guesses. Nevertheless, without some standard an executive cannot supervise very effectively. Without standards, he can only wait until projects are completed to determine whether an activity was good or bad—and there will be no active direction.

3. *Corrective Actions of Supervision.* The purpose of the preceding observation and measurement is to determine what action, if any, the executive should take as his ship is proceeding to its destination. All of the preceding has been intended to give him on-the-spot information of how current progress conforms with pre-established plans. With this information at hand, he is in a better position to decide what should be done currently to get the ship back on a course that will take it to the desired port.

This is the sphere of corrective action. What can be done as activities are currently being carried on depends upon the amount of deviation, how long the deviation has been allowed to take place, and the time and resources to make corrections. If, for example, a bad case of spoilage is not discovered until a production run is almost completed, current corrective action will be ineffective. Here the trip is practically completed, the ship has missed its port. Had a better system of observation been employed—let us say, such a system as statistical quality control—the executive could have detected the start of an undesirable deviation in quality very early. He could have ascertained the cause of the undesirable trend and issued orders to remove the cause. And the ship would have been back on desired course with a minimum loss.

Obviously, in the case of current operations, time is usually of the essence. A pilot who notices a vibration in a wing cannot run an experiment to ascertain what type or design of metal could best absorb the cause of such a vibration. He must decide on the spot whether to land as soon as possible or to go on to his destination, and what adjustments in power he should make as he proceeds. And so, too, must an executive decide who notices that the work of one of his subordinates is below expectations on an important task that must be completed before the day is over. The executive cannot go back in time and decide to put another man on the job; he must make some decision that will serve to get the job done in the available time.

Motivation of Current Efforts

No matter how much technology is brought into the business picture, the human factor will always remain a dominant factor in business operations. And this factor constitutes perhaps the most significant area of concern to an executive as he directs the work of his organization unit. To build an effective team, the executive has presumably selected and trained his subordinates so that the required skills and experiences are at hand. But that is not enough; his subordinates must contribute their efforts willingly and with loyal enthusiasm. They must be motivated.

Such motivation may come in part from within an employee himself and in part from his superiors, his associates, and his group environment. The self-motivation part should be obtained through the process of selection and enhanced through the processes of training and education. But for purposes of current supervision, these opportunities for motivation are gone except insofar as employees may be shifted on the spot from job to job or given quick instructions.

Motivation while work is being carried on must concern itself with factors that affect willingness, enthusiasm, and loyalty at the moment. Of particular significance here are the following:

1. Grievances—detection and treatment.
2. Appropriate disciplinary action.
3. Positive motivation.

This order of listing is not intended as an indication of order of importance.

1. *Grievances.* If current operations are to proceed smoothly, the disturbing influence of employee dissatisfaction must be minimized, if not removed. The executive must be alert to signs of discontent and then take appropriate action to reduce its effects.

a) Grievance Detection. Handling grievances during operations involves their detection and then their treatment. Except when a person openly expresses his dissatisfaction, we cannot as yet determine dissatisfaction directly. Instead, we must guess at it either through the behavior of people or from the results they produce.

Observation of behavior is a most fruitful source of information when used skillfully. It is surprising how much people tell us by their behavior—particularly by their changing trends in behavior. A particular employee usually is smiling, but now he isn't; another has been very tidy in dress, but now isn't; another was invariably prompt in getting to work, but now is tardy; and another has worked with enthusiasm, but now is a laggard. These are signs that something is happening and so obvious that any good executive should notice them.

Records of performance and results are also useful indirect measures of grievances, if kept currently. Information on quantity of output, quality, costs, and on-time performance can indicate possible areas of dissatisfaction. When the records disclose undesirable trends, the cause may be in the area of grievances. If prompt reports are received or personal observation is made of these matters, an executive can be put on his guard before too much damage has been done.

b) Grievance Treatment. What to do about grievances depends upon their nature. It is to be remembered, too, that we are dealing here with the area of direction while actively engaged in current operations. Under these conditions, the possibilities of action are not too great. The executive must take some action currently and more drastic steps later. It is not unlike a case of first aid now and hospitalization later.

Having detected a grievance (or a possible source of one) perhaps the most useful thing an executive can do is lend a sympathetic ear to the aggrieved and assure him of a full hearing at the first available moment.

An executive must be able to convince the group of his trustworthiness. To do this on the spot is a large order for anyone. The answer to this is that current trust must be based upon past fairness. If an executive is to obtain current cooperation in the face of a grievance to be handled later, he must have proved himself fair in the past. Getting desirable results in a current treatment of a grievance depends less upon what is done currently than upon what has been done in the past.

Since time is short, current grievance treatment must be of a palliative nature. If the causes underlying complaints are not too deep, immediate corrections can be made. A raise may be granted or some poor working condition corrected. More serious complaints will have to wait until the ship gets into port. The aggrieved may or may not put up with promises of future consideration of their complaints. If they strike then, operations stop, and the managerial function of direction must be replaced immediately by applicable managerial functions of planning and organizing.

2. *Appropriate Disciplinary Action.* Motivation may have to be of a negative nature. Employees may have to be prodded by the devices of fear and penalties. An executive may use this device when he concludes that fear is needed either to correct or to prevent an undesirable deviation. He must feel that failures in the particular circumstances will best yield to a probable or actual penalty.

But what penalties should be applied during active direction? Very simply, those that will produce the desired results. To apply this principle is not nearly as simple. It is not as easily measured as the problem of how much heat is required to raise the temperature of pure water from, let us say, 69° F. to 70° F. People differ in their reactions to penalties, so the amount of penalties for the same situation would have to vary from person to person. And, indeed, the same person would need a different amount of disciplinary action from time to time. Moreover, there is no scientific way of determining dosages for different individuals and cases. Nevertheless, it is best to follow the practice of uniform penalties for similar infractions because grievances tend to flow when variable penalties are applied in allowing for individual differences.

When work is in progress, an executive may assign a penalty but delay its application until a project is completed. This may be necessary in order to serve, let us say, a customer on time. Much might be lost if a valued employee, who deserved a penalty, were laid off in the middle of an important job. So the use of disciplinary action in the phase of managerial direction does not imply that such action must be taken immediately upon discovery of an employee failure. Judgment should dictate the timing of the application of the penalty.

3. Positive Motivation. Attention is now turned to ways and means of spurring employees to more effective results by appeals to positive and constructive forces. Taking up positive motivation last does not mean that it is the least important. This subject will receive fuller treatment in Chapter 18, hence only a few points will be noted here.

Use of positive motivation effectively assumes that conditions in general have been worked out satisfactorily. Good employees are working under good conditions and under good supervision. To this complex may now be added positive motivation. Appeals are to be made to employees so that they work harder than they might otherwise.

What are these positive motivators? They are satisfactions that flow from pride in work well done; craftsmanship; the commendations of superiors, fellow workers, and friends; and the full exercise of one's faculties and skills. So the motivators may be grouped into the following classes:

1. Those concerned with actually participating in the work.
2. Those related to the results of having worked.
3. Those related to what others think of what is being done or is being accomplished.

The effectiveness of these stimulators will vary from individual to individual. Positive motivation should give great weight to individual differences. An executive should stress with each of his subordinates the appeal that is most effective. To some, it may be that of the rewards to be obtained, to another the attitude of associates, and to still another that of the work itself.

The application of positive motivation is significantly conditioned by the effectiveness of communications. How well does an executive convey to his subordinates the ideas of cause and effect of positive motivation? How does he convince employees that if they work harder, they will achieve a variety of satisfactions? Answers to these questions depend in large measure upon an executive's skill in communication to be discussed more fully in Chapter 20.

Summary

The variety of subject matter taken up in this chapter is proof enough that managerial direction is not a simple activity. Much lies behind the simple act of an executive's walking through his department, just as much lies behind the waving of a baton by an orchestra leader. The score may have been planned, the orchestra organized. Yet, as the leader stands before his group, and as the executive walks through his department, plans must be translated to immediate decisions, orders must be issued, results currently supervised and evaluated, and the efforts of the group variously motivated. Direction is thus a complex managerial activity, but nonetheless one which upon analysis falls into relatively neat divisions and compartments. Thus examined and structured, it becomes an activity that can be performed with a high degree of effectiveness and personal satisfaction.

QUESTIONS

1. What is the function of directing and what is its relation to the other managerial functions?
2. For an executive to translate correctly the plans of his superiors, what must he ascertain and also keep in mind?
3. Selecting an individual to whom work is to be assigned should be based upon what major considerations?
4. Why is it essential in the directional phase of management to be mindful of the roles and responsibilities of one's colleagues?
5. What is the difference between factors of measurement and units of measurement in supervision? In your answer give a few examples of each.
6. What role can supervision play in the detection of grievances, and upon what does success in detection depend?
7. Since disciplinary action is based essentially upon prodding by fear, what good, if anything, can be said for it as a tool of management?
8. What is the relation between positive motivation and communication?

CASE 7-1

Billy Capri, one of the best machine operators in the department, nonetheless was also one of the boys when it came to being on the side of the employees. He knew and practiced all the tricks to keep ahead of Joe "Gumshoe" Silver, the departmental supervisor. When Joe retired, Billy was promoted to the supervisory position. He got this job because management rated him very high on managerial potential and he had done a superior job as an operative.

Billy soon found out that his relations with the boys (or better, theirs with him) had changed. They took pleasure in pulling tricks on him. They warned each other by secret signals when he walked around the machines unobtrusively (as he thought). Or they figured out ways to look like they were working when they weren't. And they would come up with time-wasting gripes that did no one any good.

To counter all of this, Billy finally called the men together and said "I'm your supervisor. I know what you're doing to me. I didn't realize what we we're doing to Old Joe with our tricks when I was one of you, and now I know. He had a job to do too. Do you want to cooperate with me? Do you want me to get tough? Or do you want to get a new supervisor who may have no liking for any of us or our problems?"

1. Is Billy a good supervisor?
2. What suggestions for improvement do you have to offer Billy?

CASE 7–2

A supervisor in a given case has to assign the same kind of work to four workers. The first worker is a long-service man who has had experience on practically all of the various jobs in his department. The second worker has had some experience but still has much to learn. The third is a better-than-average worker and a very important informal leader among the workers on technical matters. And the fourth worker is new, having been in the department and with the company less than a month.

The job in question is one which has not been done in this department before, it is very technical, and getting it done right and on time is very important to the company.

1. If you were the supervisor, how would you transmit this order to each of the employees?
2. If the job were one that had been worked on before would your answer be the same? Why or why not?

8
Controlling

Nature and Scope

IN THE FIRST chapter, the manager is described as the specialist who seeks to coordinate the efforts of other specialists. He does this by planning, organizing, directing, and controlling the work of others. Thus far, attention here has been concerned with the first three of these functions. Now, concern is with controlling.

Simply defined, control is the managerial function of seeing to it that projects are completed as planned, organized, and directed. This amounts to seeing that each person does the right thing, at the right time, at the right place, and with the right resources.

Thus, control is particularly concerned with coordination. As a consequence, some use the term as a synonym for coordination. Indeed, some are so impressed with the significance of control that they use it as an equivalent for management. Consequently, one often encounters such terms as financial control, material control, sales control, quality control, and personnel control. In these instances, control is really given the meaning of management; thus, financial control is essentially financial management, material control is material management, etc. Control is thus intended to imply authority over, and responsibility for, the work in the field of finance, materials, sales, quality, and personnel. It is felt here, however, that control defines a portion—albeit a major portion—of the work of management. To facilitate understanding of the function of control, it is discussed in this chapter under the following major headings: (1) how controls are exercised, (2) factors controlled, and (3) who controls.

How Controls Are Exercised

Perhaps the best approach to the study of control is to see how controls are exercised. This may be done by seeking answers to three major questions, as follows: (1) What specifically does a manager do when he controls? (2) What devices are used in controlling? (3) What specifically is controlled?

1. *Functions of Control.*[1] Control, as already implied, is performed in relation to something else. The next major section of this chapter discusses the factors that are subject to control. But to illustrate the functions of control, the activities-of-subordinates factor is here taken as an example.

Controlling activities fall into three stages. Thus, some control activities take place before the activities to be controlled are performed, some take place during the actual performance of the activities to be controlled, and some take place after the actual performance of the activities to be controlled. Diagrammatically, this can be shown as follows, using a sales function as the function to be controlled:

Time
————————————————————————————————————►

| Preliminary Control | Concurrent Control (Sales Activity) | Post–Control |

a) Preliminary Control. Preliminary control refers to managerial control functions performed prior to the performance of a

[1] Although practically all writers on management include control as one of the major functions of management, there is very little agreement on the subfunctions of control. This is largely due to the fact that, as noted earlier, managers seldom, if ever, follow a strict order of "plan, organize, direct, and control." Rather there is much crisscrossing, reciprocating, and interaction among these basic functions. So, it is practically impossible to say where a given function begins and ends.

The student will soon notice that the present authors have assigned a number of subfunctions and tasks to control which, it can readily be argued, should be assigned to planning or direction. This is not the place to argue the merits of where some of these subfunctions might be best assigned. That they are debatable is admitted. But for the sake of providing a practical picture of what happens in control, rather than seeking to establish a picture of "pure" control, a number of subfunctions are considered to be a part of control, the allocation of which might well be objected to by some.

specific function. If, for example, specific sales activities are to be properly related to specific production and specific promotional activities, some preliminary controls are in order.

But is this not planning? In a sense perhaps, but basic planning differs significantly from, and must precede, the preliminaries of control.

Planning, once again, provides a basic plan of action. In its original or creative stage, planning determines broadly such things as the objectives of the sales activities, the major tasks to be performed in selling, the financial and human resources, and the time periods in which selling efforts are to be emphasized. Such planning thus establishes a model scheme of what management hopes will take place. It is a mental visualization beforehand of what the salesmen will do in actual contact with the customer. It does not list specific times and places of action for each salesman.

Next, the large, original, or creative sales plan must be broken down into specific assignments and determinations. The basic sales plan may specify, for example, that "X" units of sales effort are to be applied during the month of July. But specifically where, by whom, and when should the sales effort be applied? The answers are supplied by predetermining where specific salesmen should be at specific times.

Preliminary control answers these questions through the subfunctions of routing, scheduling, preparation, and dispatching. By means of *routing*, specific salesmen are told where they are expected to be. And by means of *scheduling*, they are told when they are to be at specific places.

It is not enough to work out advance routings and schedules. Good preliminary control also makes certain that resources will be available to go over the routes at the times scheduled. Let us assume that a salesman is scheduled to be in town "X" on July 3. Management should precheck to see whether:

1. A salesman, properly qualified, is available to meet this schedule.
2. Transportation is available to bring him into town "X" by July.
3. Living accommodations are available to the salesman.
4. Customers will not be unavailable because of a holiday, company policies, or special events.
5. Promotional materials, price lists, factory availability lists, etc., will be in the salesman's hand.

Such prechecking is considered here as *"preparation."* It might seem preferable to allow each salesman to make these preparations for himself. Many companies do follow this practice. The point is that if the salesman does these for himself, his actual time for selling is reduced to that extent. Of course, there are occasions when preparations and, indeed, specific routing and scheduling, by other than the salesman would be unrealistic and impractical.

After routing, scheduling, and preparation are attended to, preliminary control ends with appropriate release of authority—dispatching—to the operating parties. In the salesman case, orders should be dispatched to carry out the selling plans. While precise dispatching may not be important in selling, its significance in other areas, such as production, cannot be overestimated. Careful dispatching in an assembly-type, continuous plant such as that of automobiles is absolutely essential. Without it, the most careful engineering, routing, scheduling, and preparation would be voided in short order. The chaos that would result is too painful to contemplate.

b) Concurrent Control. Concurrent control refers to managerial control functions performed during the same time as the function to be controlled. First, it is necessary to instruct the employee concerned in how work is to be accomplished. With experienced workers, instruction can be waived on the assumption that the salesman taken as an illustration in the foregoing knows how to sell.

Concurrently, too, the supervisor—and every executive for that matter—should evaluate performance and take whatever action is necessary to keep his subordinates on the path dictated by plans. Essentially this is a comparison process; results are measured against objectives. If an employee is deviating negatively from the established course, the supervisor should initiate motivational or corrective action. But to measure results, the supervisor must be receiving current information on progress; concurrent action cannot take place after the ship has piled up on the rocks. This feedback of information can be readily accomplished with some types of operations, such as production. It is extremely difficult with such work as selling. In the latter case, concurrent comparison may have to be entrusted to the operators themselves.

Concurrent evaluation should seek to measure not only negative deviations. Where positive, wholesome, and favorable improvements are taking place, management should be alert, first, to apply currently the reasons therefor to other operations; and, second, to reward appropriately those responsible. When management is as quick to reward as it is to penalize, employees develop a more favorable attitude toward controls.

c) *Postcontrol.* In postcontrol, management is performing control functions after the activities to be controlled have been performed. For example, the sales efforts for the month of July have been completed. How did sales compare with planned quotas, were costs of sales above or below estimates, was more or less supervisory attention needed than estimated, and has morale of salesmen gone up or down? Comparison between results and objectives (or call it evaluation, appraisal, audit, measurement, or inspection if you will) is a significant part of postcontrol.

Such comparisons will show either no deviations from plan, or favorable or unfavorable deviations. In the case of no deviations, presumably management has no reason for changing plans in the future for similar operations. If deviations are noted, then management must seek the reasons for the deviations. Unfavorable results presumably are caused by the presence of undesirable causes or the absence of positive factors. In the future, the former must be removed and the latter supplied. Favorable deviations presumably are caused by factors that had not been anticipated. In the future, management should seek to plan for the inclusion of the favorable forces. Penalties for failure and rewards for success are part of managerial action after comparison has indicated deviations from plans. Not all deviations are caused by operating personnel. The original plans of management may have been at fault and may call in the future for extensive revision.

In both concurrent control and postcontrol, information on operating results is of utmost importance. In one way or another, the manager must get such information by a process of follow-up, or to use a more popular term currently, feedback. As defined in an earlier chapter, such feedback may be of an open-end or closed-end type. In the open-end type, as illustrated in Figure 3–3, information on performance and final operating results tends to come back occasionally, such as the daily or weekly field reports of a salesman. In the closed-end type, as illustrated in Figure 3–4, information comes back constantly, such as a temperature record on a furnace. Moreover, in the closed-end type arrangements are made so that appropriate instructions to the point of performance can be given when the feedback denotes that undesirable deviations from plans are taking place. Obviously, the closed-end type has advantages for purposes of managerial control but unfortunately getting continuous recordings on performance are still impossible in many fields of business activity.

2. *Devices of Control.* Functions of control are not self-executing. They are exercised through devices and by people.

Perhaps the simplest device of control is that of personal observation. By merely observing the work of his group, an executive can determine, for example, whether or not progress is up to standard and, if not, what corrective action should be taken. Personal observation is obviously limited, however, by the ability of an executive to be present in person to see what is going on. To expand his powers of observation, the executive in such instances takes the obvious step of asking his subordinates to keep records of their work. As a consequence, the executive can check records of what is going on or can have summarizing reports sent to his desk. In that way, the work of an organization spread over a wide area can be encompassed by the executive.

To expedite the transmission of reports and records, various aids can be employed. The telephone, telautograph, and pneumatic tube are devices that can be usefully employed to increase the speed with which control information is exchanged between executive and subordinates. Increasing in use are the fantastic electronic devices which gather, analyze, and summarize information at a speed that defies the imagination. In minutes the executive is supplied with data that previously took days and even weeks to accumulate. Figure 8–1 illustrates the use of a computer in this connection. Other mechanical control devices include such aids as order control boards, graphical summaries, blueprints, and standard practice instructions.

Another group of control devices relates to interpersonal communications. The executive can sharpen his control through appropriate use of orders, commands, and instructions. Either orally or through policies and directives, subordinates can be given directions as to how to conform with desired plans. The efficacy of these devices can be enhanced by appropriate techniques of motivation and disciplinary action. That is to say that there are human relations aspects to control as well as the purely mechanical phases. Indeed, to the extent that subordinates can be trained and motivated to act in accordance with desired plans, the amount of executive attention and need for mechanical transmission of information can be reduced.

And, finally, control can be performed more effectively through appropriate devices of procedures and organization structure. Not

FIGURE 8–1
Computerized Shop Control System

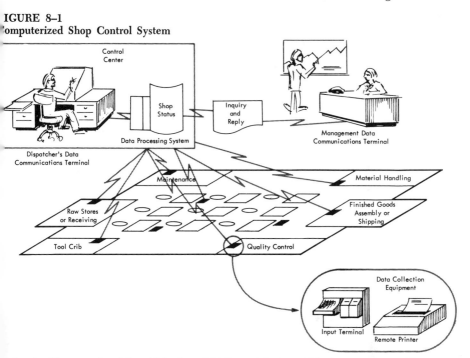

Reprinted by permission of the publisher from AMA Research Study 77, *EDP Applications for the Manufacturing Function,* © 1966 by the American Management Association, Inc.

only is it necessary to perform functions of control, but they should be arranged in effective sequences. Such sequences should not only tie together the control functions themselves but also relate them correctly to the activities to be controlled. In similar vein, control functions must be assigned to well-related units of the organization structure. In that way responsibility of performing control functions will be placed without gaps in, or overlapping of, authority for control.

This interrelation of factors, procedures, and organization is aptly illustrated in Figure 8–2. Here it is seen that in the case of budgetary processes, their control must be preceded by appropriate preplanning and budget preparation. And the movement of various stages in the processes through various organizational units must be specifically indicated. As a consequence, all those involved in this process are informed definitely of the order of their responsibility and something of the nature of their work in budgetary control.

Another good example of the systems aspect of control is illustrated in Figure 8–3. Here it is apparent that good control has to

FIGURE 8–2
An Integrated Plan of Factors, Procedures, and Organizational Elements

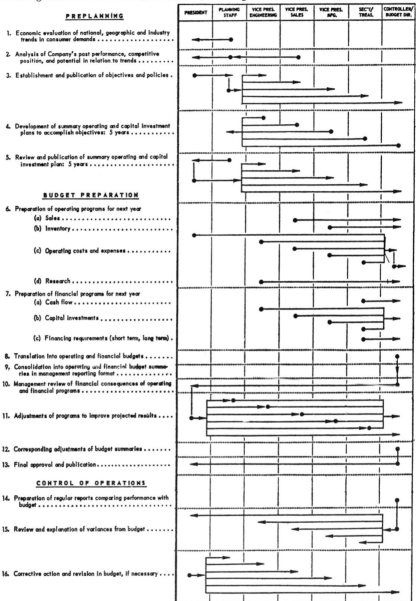

Reprinted by permission of the publisher from AMA Management Bulletin No. 74, *Budgeting General and Administrative Expenses*, © 1966 by the American Management Association, Inc.

FIGURE 8-3
A Systems Concept of Manufacturing Control

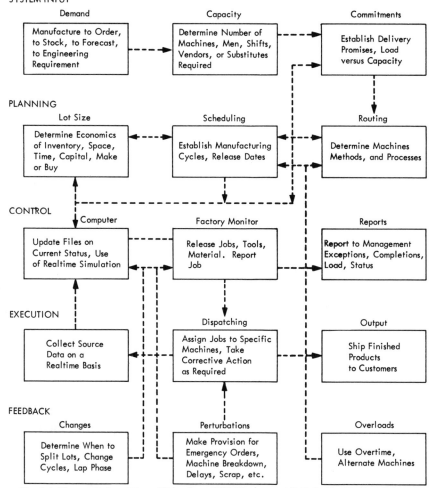

Reprinted by permission of the publisher from AMA Management Bulletin No. 24, *Control through Information*, © 1963 by the American Management Association, Inc.

be preceded by a good arrangement of system inputs and planning. Then comes appropriate execution and feedback. The whole system is best designed as an integrated relationship if control is to be properly executed.

3. *Elements of Control.* When control is exercised, what specifically is controlled? What, for example, is controlled in the case of production control? A little thought will soon show that certainly production itself is not controlled. Rather, something else is "con-

trolled," which in turn serves to control production. And that "something else" is some unit or element that can be measured.

A variety of elements are available to serve control purposes. Time is a commonly used control element. Thus, projects must be completed on particular dates. Comparisons will show whether or not progress is on schedule. Units of output are another universal control element. Measure how much is being produced or sold, and you are helping to "control" production or sales. Standards of length, width, area, hardness, strength, appearance, and color are examples of quality control elements. The financial unit has long been used to provide a measuring device for expenditures, costs, and returns of particular projects and plans. Lastly, though much less concrete, abstract measures of personality and behavior have been used in relation to personnel control.

It is imperative to grasp the meaning of this concept of control elements. The term control is used so invariably with the thing controlled that we assume that the thing itself is controlled directly. But this is not so. To control production or sales, for example, some measurable element of these areas is controlled—time, quantity, cost. If a good unit of measure is not employed or is difficult to establish, as is time in the field of human behavior, control itself breaks down or cannot contribute much to managerial efficiency.

Factors Controlled

Having drawn this somewhat detailed picture of the process of control, it is now appropriate to focus attention on the factors or subjects that are controlled. The factors may be visualized more clearly if the relations of the various parts of a going business enterprise are first charted. Verbally, this can be expressed by stating that objectives are achieved by working on projects through the performance of functions in properly designed procedures and organization structures aided by human resources and physical resources. In diagrammatic form, this is shown in Figure 8–4.

If desired objectives are to be accomplished, control can and should be exercised in relation to everything that contributes to, or affects, attainment of the objectives. In the last analysis, the objectives themselves serve as the ultimate test of control. If, for example, an objective of a businessman has been to earn a million dollars in a given year, this becomes the yardstick against which results are finally measured. Obviously, this yardstick is utterly use-

FIGURE 8–4
Relation of Factors in the Business Enterprise

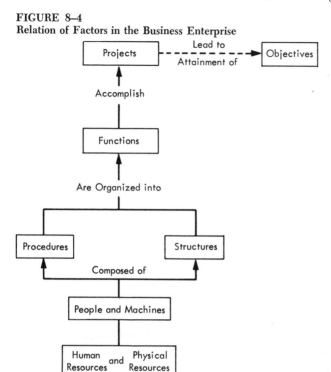

less, however, as a control over what happens on any given day to any given person. Other control elements are needed here.

Working back then from objectives, it is only reasonable to ask what it is that is intended to help earn the million dollars. The answer presumably is a variety of projects. These, then, must be controlled. Here will be found sales projects, production projects, financial projects, engineering projects, accounting projects, research projects, transportation projects, etc. Each will be assigned an individual number or name as illustrated in Figure 8–5. And each will be controlled as noted earlier in this chapter.

To stop here with control might be sufficient in simple situations. In most companies control would go beyond this stage. Referring to the enterprise diagram, control would be performed in relation to functions, procedures, structures, people, or resources. An example of each is given in the following list:

1. Functions: control of the work done by an operator performing the function of selling a particular commodity in a particular town.

FIGURE 8–5
A Progress Chart

	October				November				December			
	1	2	3	4	1	2	3	4	1	2	3	4
Project A			Indicates Starting Time			Over-All Progress			Scheduled Finishing Time		Current Date	
Project B												
Project C												
Project D												
Project E												

2. Procedures: a sequence of selling operations from planning the sales, to selecting and training salesmen, to the actual selling, and through evaluation of results could be controlled in total.

3. Structures: the work done in each organization unit such as the engineering department or sales department, and subdivisions thereof, could be subject to control.

4. Personnel: each person on his job makes an excellent unit of control, particularly at the supervisory level.

5. Resources: control may revolve about—

    a) Machines: each drill press, cash register, workbench, or truck, for example, may be controlled.

    b) Materials: each class of materials or supplies in each store-room or department could well be considered for purposes of control.

How far back and into what detail control will be exercised will largely be dependent upon how important it is to regulate and restrain details. If possible losses or gains are great, obviously it will pay to spend more on control. If losses or gains are small, then it would be foolish to spend more on control than controls can save.

It might be noted, too, that how much control is exercised depends upon how much planning is originally done. To reemphasize, the less planning management does, the more it will have to control, and vice versa. Whether emphasis should or can be placed upon planning or controlling depends upon the situation, the skills and attitudes of management, and the nature of the problems faced.

Who Controls

It is now appropriate to examine the question of who specifically controls. Of course, it has been argued earlier that controlling is a function of every executive. Indeed, it can even be argued that every person—whether a manager or not—performs a certain amount of control or self-control. But from an organizational point of view there are a number of ways by which and through which managerial controlling may be performed. Discussion of these may be conveniently taken up under the following headings: (1) internal control of each organization unit, (2) staff control relationships, (3) informal controls, and (4) external control forces.

1. *Internal Control of Each Organization Unit.* Each executive, no matter what ramifications of control may be developed in an organization, must to a greater or lesser extent be responsible for controlling his own unit. The simplest plan, of course, is for each executive to perform in relation to his subordinates all necessary control functions. Prior to, during, and after the performance of work, the executive concerns himself with control functions outlined earlier in this chapter. By performing control functions himself, the executive can keep in closer contact with his subordinates, evaluate more intimately his own planning, and minimize the amount of record keeping both by himself and by his subordinates.

The internal control of each unit may also be accomplished by the appointment of a staff assistant or through control procedures. The assistant may keep records of work progress, check quantity of output against program quantities, check quality of work against standards, compile reports, and analyze deviations of actual from planned action. Or, the executive may design procedures that serve to control his subordinates. Report forms, statistical and graphical displays, and routines regarding how and when to report are useful control devices.

2. *Staff Control Relationships.* As an enterprise grows, it is usually found desirable to establish separate organization units to

perform control functions. A rather common example of an interdepartmental control unit is the production control department. Very simply, it is responsible for taking care of details necessary to get customer orders through the many departments of a factory.

For example, if Customer Smith ordered 100 No. 18 wheels to be shipped on June 30, let us say, it would arrange to have the hub, spoke, rim, and assembly departments work on their respective parts of this order at the right time. A production control unit, by keeping appropriate records of other customer orders in the factory, and of available capacity of the various manufacturing departments, can fit Customer Smith's order into the maze with efficiency and with due consideration for all the variables involved. Other examples of staff units concerned with operative projects are sales control units, engineering control units, and transportation dispatching units.

The top levels of an organization may also have administrative control staffs. Such units are responsible for coordinating the efforts of the major divisions of an enterprise. To illustrate the work of such staffs, let us take the case of a company that has decided to introduce a new model of its product every year on October 1. Working back from that date, it is necessary to calculate how much time each department—engineering, sales promotion, sales, production, finance, personnel, etc.—will need to carry out its share of this annual project. Starting and finishing times for each department must be calculated. And checks will have to be made to see that each department keeps to the scheduled times. All of this would be the responsibility of an administrative control unit, reporting to the president or executive vice president. This staff unit relieves the top executive of all the details of coordination, thus freeing him to concentrate on creative planning and high-level policy making.

Staff control units may also be established to assist in the control of particular factors or resources in a company. For example, the cost department is responsible for, among other things, gathering cost data, comparing them with cost estimates, and making recommendations for cost reductions. The inspection department is another staff unit that assists in quality control, through its work of comparing quality of output with standards of quality. A standards department may be established to check on the maintenance of all types of mechanical, chemical, engineering, and specification standards. And, to cite but one more example, the auditing department is responsible for checking financial expenditures and accounting records to see that honesty and accuracy are maintained in all parts of the business. Such staff control units as these are desirably established on an independent basis, because their work cuts across the activities of many departments and because their integrity can best be safeguarded by separating them from the units they are intended to control.

3. *Informal Controls.* The managerial function of control may be performed in part in a number of informal ways. For example, the insignia or perquisites of an executive are useful in regulating and restraining the activities of subordinates along desired lines. Such things as executive titles, large and expensively furnished offices, and special privileges accorded executives serve to command the respect and obedience of subordinates. Or, the establishment of various precedents, traditions, and protocol serves the same purpose. Certain types of speech, of social activity, of precedence of speaking, and of expected courtesies are other examples of informal control devices.

Though not stated in any manual of organization or of office procedures, informal controls are nonetheless very significant in their own way. A person who transgresses the informal folkways of an organization can be effectively stopped from further progress in the company. Moreover, he will fail to get his daily work done with success because cooperation of various parties will not be forthcoming. The importance of these informal controls is seen in the warning that any newcomer to a business situation should learn the ropes before taking important action. Of course, informal controls have positive value in that they set limits within which people know they can move freely without inhibiting fears.

4. *External Control Forces.* And, finally, forces and controls of a variety of kinds outside an organization itself may affect managerial controlling. Common to all enterprises are, of course, governmental legislation, judicial decisions, and rulings and procedures of administrative bodies which surround practically every managerial action. Then, too, various community agencies—welfare groups, trade associations, educational institutions, unions, churches, etc.—have their impact upon the controls management can and does exercise. Along somewhat similar lines, the social mores and customs of the community (local and national) in which a business operates have a tremendous effect upon the kinds of, and the degree of, controls that can be exercised by management. And it is well to note

that favorable or unfavorable public relations have an important impact upon management controls.

These external factors and forces are often overlooked in studies of managerial controls. This oversight may be due to the fact that the work of an office supervisor seems to be concerned solely with what happens within the four walls of the office. He is controlling the flow of work through the office procedures of his company. But it is soon apparent that much of what he does is influenced by the external controls listed in the preceding paragraph. And the same influence is felt by every other executive in the company. Hence, in exercising managerial controls, the import and significance of these external forces should be carefully weighed and taken into account.

QUESTIONS

1. What are the relations between control, coordination, and management?
2. What subfunctions (subsystems) are performed in preliminary control? What is meant by each?
3. What devices may be used in the exercise of control?
4. Specifically, what is controlled when control is being exercised?
5. What is the relation of control to objectives, procedures, and resources?
6. Who may control, and over what would their jurisdiction extend?
7. What are staff control units and why do they evolve?
8. What are examples of external controls that may affect a business enterprise?

CASE 8–1

When the Missile Age Toy Company was small, it had no trouble controlling the flow of orders through the shop so that manufacturing was efficient and customer orders went out on time. Now that it has grown in size, it seems that orders going through the factory are not always processed efficiently and deliveries to customers are delayed often enough so that costly returns by customers are incurred. As a consequence, a thorough review of the control system in the factory has been undertaken to determine what is wrong and what improvements might be suggested.

In actually tracing how an order proceeds through the factory, the following was found:

a) The sales department informs the shop that a given customer wants a given quantity of a particular style of toy shipped on a certain date.

b) The control department in the shop figures out from past orders of a similar kind, what parts and processes are needed to complete the toy, and also schedules the completion date for each part for each department in the shop.

c) The supervisors in each department figure out how the order scheduled into their departments would best fit into the load of work already assigned and then they turn over the work orders to the workers at the appropriate times.

d) Each worker gets what tools and materials and supplies are needed to do the jobs assigned to him.

e) The supervisors report to the control unit as each job lot is finished.

f) The control unit checks the reports as they are finished against the customer promised date. It expedites (goes into the shop and pushes) those jobs whose parts are falling behind schedule.

1. What specific steps of control are not being performed well?
2. What suggestions for improvement do you have to offer?

CASE 8–2

John Barkem is the superintendent of a manufacturing plant and has under him 15 foremen. Several months ago he assigned Joe Correr to the position of foundry foreman. Joe has a degree in metallurgy and has been with the company four years. He tackled his job enthusiastically and soon was brimful of changes which were resulting in significant technical improvements.

But in going over the semiannual morale survey and reports on grievances, Barkem found that morale in the foundry has tended downward noticeably. On closer examination in the foundry, he also found such things as unanswered employee requests for position changes, failure to hold group meetings on safety and suggestions, and undue delays in handling grievances. Upon raising these matters with Joe Correr, Barkem was told by Joe that he thought he should be sure that technical matters and production were in hand first (which they were because of what he had done) before he worried about some of these "personal matters," as he put it. And on being asked if he had taken an evening course in human relations and psychology (as had been suggested when he was appointed to the foremanship position), Joe admitted that he had not because he had spent all of his time in the evenings working on the technical matters.

1. To what extent is Joe right in putting personnel matters, and the preparation for handling them, low on his priority list?
2. Since production seems to be so satisfactory, isn't this justification for what Joe did?

9

Objectives

Introduction

ANY ORGANIZATION exists to attain objectives. In the case of business organizations, for example, the earning of profits is a generally recognized objective. This simple statement does not do justice, however, to numerous other types, uses, and implications of objectives in business. Nor does it disclose managerial responsibilities imposed by this important factor in the operations of organizations. Hence, this chapter is concerned with the following aspects of objectives in the business organization:

1. Nature of objectives.
2. Kinds of objectives.
3. Uses of objectives.
4. Responsibility for objectives.
5. Criteria of sound objectives.
6. Maintaining objectives.

Nature of Objectives

Earlier it was mentioned that the attainment of objectives justifies the existence of a business organization. If a business does not satisfactorily attain objectives it will sooner or later cease to exist. Basically, then, what are these objectives?

Objectives are those results which are considered valuable, needful, or useful. Specific examples of objectives are profits, goods and services, salaries and wages, job security, control of markets, industry leadership, and so on.

Regularly, however, in the operations of a firm, objectives are alternately called ideals, purposes, goals, targets, and missions. Pragmatically, there is nothing wrong with this as long as everybody has a clear understanding of the meaning intended. Semantically speaking though, the major differences among these seemingly equivalent terms are that a purpose identifies the reason why a firm is in business, an objective indicates what it desires to achieve, while a policy tells how it conducts its activities in order to accomplish its purpose and attain its objectives.

Kinds of Objectives

Most organizations have more than one objective, although some objectives are usually more significant than others. Consequently, it is possible to classify objectives in several ways. Since the reason for determination of objectives is chiefly to do a better job of managing, it is helpful to establish those classifications which would be most meaningful in planning, organizing, directing, and controlling the activities. Discussion here will therefore center on (1) the kinds of organization values or service provided, and (2) the length of time required for their achievement.

1. *Value or Service Basis of Objectives.* The value or service basis of objectives may be further classified as to economic, profit, personal, social, and secondary operational.

a) *Economic Service Objectives.* The primary or basic mission of the business firm is to produce and distribute certain economic products or services which the customer will buy. Since this economic service is the reason why the company exists, these objectives may be considered primary. Accomplishment in an efficient and economical manner of the primary objectives tends to assure the survival of the firm, provided the objectives themselves are selected on the basis of customer needs and wants. (An additional provision is that the objectives are legitimate. A firm might continue to operate on the basis of illegitimate objectives simply because there were customers who would be willing to purchase its goods or services. An example would be a firm which produced and sold bootleg liquor.) Since it is the customer who ultimately makes possible the profitability (financial success) of the concern, the organization must create and distribute the desired values to its customers. Trade will inevitably flow to the firm that demonstrates that it is making available more for the price of its product or service than its competitors are.

The growing social consciousness of business leadership has created a climate in which certain objectives appear worthy of being raised to the level of primary importance for the organization—for example, the creation of employment opportunities. The temptation to state these as primary objectives of the firm must be resisted, however, since they will probably come about because of management's concentration on primary economic objectives. If the assumption is made that it is the company's first obligation to create jobs, the values to the customer could be relegated to secondary consideration, and the competitive position of the organization could be affected adversely.

The development of sound basic economic objectives is not always simple, even if pitfalls such as described in the preceding paragraph are avoided. It is easy to state that economic service to the customer is the primary objective, but actually pursue another goal instead, such as maximizing the return on sales. When performance is appraised in terms of an annual accounting period, for example, there may arise a real question as to whether the two objectives are always in consonance. An executive may find that his performance is rated as deficient even though he has genuinely provided service. On the other hand, he may fail to give adequate service to customers but be considered successful if he has made a handsome return on sales for that period. Naturally, in these circumstances the executive soon detects the objective that counts with his superiors and guides himself accordingly.

The economic service expected of a business firm is often stated in a broad way in its legal authorization by the state to engage in business. Thus a company might be granted authorization to carry on a business, at a profit, for the purpose of providing television broadcasting services to the public, but the management would still have to make decisions as to the kinds of programs it would plan to provide—entertainment, educational, news, and others. The objectives decided upon would then suggest the kinds of policies, organization (including staffing), and means of direction and control which need to be developed to attain those goals.

  b) Profit as an Objective. A common conception of *the objective* of a company is profit. Although this has been viewed earlier as an oversimplification, it can nevertheless be said that an objective of the organizational mechanism is a profit resulting from its operations. A profit is necessary for the continued survival of the business, and therefore it qualifies as an economic value which the organization renders to itself. It is true that profit is also an objective of other interests—the stockholders, partners, or proprietors of firms. But to the extent that the organization as such must provide, through its operations, the wherewithal necessary to its continued existence, profit must be considered to be an economic value which it provides for itself.

It is easy to engage in debate about whether profit is a return (reward) for good operation rather than an objective. It is contended that profit is a measure of how well other primary economic service objectives are attained. Nevertheless, it is imperative to recognize the fundamental importance of the objective of service. Business is an institution by means of which society seeks to satisfy the desires of its members for goods and services. To those who help attain the service objectives various personal rewards are forthcoming such as profits, wages, and other personal satisfactions. Consequently, benefits to the public, management, and the employee are derived from achieving the service objective. The position taken here, then, is that profit is a basic objective for which the organization quite properly strives. But to make it the *primary* objective, to the exclusion of others discussed above, makes it impractical to use the primary objective as a point of departure for managing. The objective of "production and distribution of a complete line of canned seafoods for the gourmet market" is a more meaningful objective for planning than is the simply stated goal of "profit." One more thought may be added. A firm may be able to operate for several years without making a profit (although it certainly will continue to expect to achieve a profit before many years have passed). But it is far less likely that a firm can operate for even a fraction of a year without producing and selling an economic good or service.

c)   Personal Objectives. Management well realizes that other interests must be served as a consequence of its operation. Individuals make up the organization, and every individual expects to acquire certain values from his association with the organization. Because the organization cannot function well without the cooperation of these individuals, it must take as its obligation the satisfaction, in reasonable degree, of the personal objectives of all individuals in the organization. Thus the stockholder or owner has as a personal objective the receipt of a healthy dividend which should result from the company's obtaining a profit. The manager and nonmanager alike have certain objectives which they seek to attain through their association with the firm. Some of these objectives are: desired salary levels, opportunity for promotion, achievement of status, recognition, and other values. The fact that the executives do have personal objectives presents a problem in their determination of the organizational objectives. The latter can easily be affected by the personal aims of the executives. It is not difficult to imagine the rationalization possible to define a personal objective as an organizational one. The ambitious chief executive can easily accept as an enterprise goal "becoming the leader in the industry."

Personal objectives are very real and must be taken into consideration in the management of the company. When pressure of influence is brought to bear on acquiring them to the point where basic organizational objectives are not properly met because of the influence of either personal goals or a group's goal, the health of the organization may be at stake. It has occasionally happened, for example, that a company's labor costs have constantly grown because of repeated wage increases (a group goal) with the consequences that the increased costs have had to be reflected in consumer prices, and the company has effectively priced itself out of the market. Similarly, emphasis on certain personal executive goals to the detriment of company welfare can cripple or bring about the demise of a company.

d) *Social Objectives.* What the firm expects, or feels obligated, to supply to society generally constitutes its social objectives. Some of these social objectives, and the manner in which they are achieved, are prescribed by the government through legislative action. For example, pension plans, unemployment compensation, accident losses, and health care are funded by various taxes. Such government influence may take place on the local, state, or national level.

A firm frequently assumes voluntarily obligations to the community in which it is located. Top management may follow a policy of participation in such civic undertakings as a community fund drive, antipollution programs, or the backing of a hospital construction program. It may establish a foundation devoted to raising educational and cultural standards of schools, a community, or the entire country. In this manner a business firm behaves as a conscientious citizen of the community, and with its resources contributes very important values to society in general.

e) *Secondary Operational Objectives.* Secondary operational objectives are the company's goals with respect to economy and effectiveness of operation. Economy refers to the cost at which the service or product is produced and distributed; effectiveness refers

FIGURE 9-1
Company Principles and Objectives

OUR PRINCIPLES

We believe that people have within their own hands the tools to fashion their own destinies.

We believe that by working together people can develop an economy of abundance which will provide a maximum of opportunity, freedom, and security for all.

OUR OBJECTIVES

Motivated by these principles, and with an abiding faith in the worth and dignity of every human being, the Boards of Directors of the Nationwide Insurance Companies have adopted the following objectives as the official guide for the administration and operation of the Companies:

1 To provide people—individually and in groups—with the best possible insurance protection for their economic and personal welfare; and to provide this protection at the lowest possible cost consistent with the maintenance of efficiently operated, financially sound, growing companies.

2 To invest policyholder and other funds so as to build financial security, and at the same time make a meaningful contribution to fulfillment of human and social needs.

3 To operate as consumer-oriented companies whose products and services reflect high sensitivity to the changing wants and needs of people.

4 To further insurance practices which are fair and equitable to policyholders, shareholders, agents, employees, and the public.

5 To encourage policyholders to participate in the activities of their insurance companies.

6 To invite the active sponsorship of groups of people joined together for their mutual achievement and benefit.

7 To provide Nationwide employees and agents with opportunities and incentives for self-expression and personal growth —in economic stature, in mind, and in spirit.

8 To act as a good corporate citizen by participating responsibly in economic, social, and industry matters affecting the public interest.

Reproduced by permission of Nationwide Insurance Companies, Columbus, Ohio.

to the production and distribution functions being rendered when required, and in the right quantity and quality.

2. Time Basis of Objectives. Not only may objectives be classified as to coverage but also they may be classified as to the span of time within which their achievement is expected. As such we may distinguish ultimate (or long-term) intermediate, short-term, and immediate objectives.

a) Ultimate Objectives. Ultimate objectives are broad goals which are continuously sought, permanently in view, and never satisfied. They are basic to all other goals, are broad-gauge in nature, and represent the aims of the firm over its business life. Figure 9–1 is an illustration of ultimate objectives. The ultimate, or long-term, objectives primarily are guides or goals for the highest echelons of management; while more immediate challenges are required at lower levels. Here is another typical example of ultimate objectives:

To provide for customers a high-quality product at a fair price.

To provide for employees working conditions, fair wages, and other forms of compensation which are equal to or better than those of other firms in the community.

To provide for our stockholders an equitable return on their ownership investment.

To accept our fair share of responsibilities as a good citizen of the community, and to strive to promote the economic well-being of the community.

b) Intermediate Objectives. These are objectives of a specific nature, indicating definite programs or projects having dimensions and an ending point. They are those objectives which are sought in the near future, usually in the 5- to 10-year range. The standard may be in the form of market penetration. In the case of an appliance company the intermediate objective may be to have 30 percent of the market for its products at the end of the next five years. The current penetration may be 22 percent of that market. The intermediate goals are apt to be expressed as sales, production, or financial criteria. Figure 9–2 illustrates how the intermediate operational, social, and financial goals of a particular firm are subintegrated with the ultimate objectives of this firm.

c) Short-Term Objectives. These objectives relate to those values which the company hopes to attain in the next accounting period or so. It may be in the next calendar year or the next quarter.

FIGURE 9–2
Intermediate Objectives

FIGURE 9–3
Short-Term Objectives

Babcock & Wilcox

OBJECTIVES

To produce by technological leadership the maximum profits consistent with good asset management.

To develop and maintain a social, economic, and political environment favorable for the Company.

* GOALS

'OPERATIONAL

1. Develop quantitative performance standards for all divisions and subsidiaries.
2. Review inventory management systems in all operating divisions and subsidiaries and establish more effective systems where necessary.
3. Review production control systems in all operating divisions and subsidiaries and establish more effective systems where necessary.
4. Implement a Corporate program for personnel development, including manpower inventories and management training.
5. Identify and begin to implement the management information system required by the Corporation.
6. Increase external support for the R&D Division to 20% of total funding.
7. Prepare a Corporate Development Plan.

*SOCIAL

1. Recruit and train minority-group employees at the rate of 1% of total employment per year.
2. Establish a program to insure continuing compliance with local standards for pollution control.
3. Define additional programs to improve the environment in which the Corporation and its divisions and subsidiaries operate.

*FINANCIAL

1. Realize income from operations before tax equal to 12% of sales.
2. Increase net income to 15% of stockholders' equity.

Babcock & Wilcox
Power Generation Division

OBJECTIVES

To obtain the maximum return on investment from participation in those markets best served by Division resources.

To develop new and improve existing products to permit maximum profitable growth.

* GOALS

OPERATIONAL

1. By year end, complete all steps defined in the Reorganization Action Plan.
2. By May 1, 1970, issue a Comprehensive Division Systems Plan and Schedule, and by year end be at least on this schedule.
3. Implement a Strategic Manpower Plan to define the actions required to develop, train and maintain a capable and efficient work force. Complete the skills inventory and manpower backup programs by July 1970.
4. Develop a Comprehensive Business Plan by August 15, 1970, for each department and for the Division as a unit.
5. Achieve a minimum overall 5 percent average productivity improvement for 1970 based on the current Estimated/Actual (E/A) shop manhour performance, and by year end achieve a Division E/A 10 percent greater than year end 1969.
6. Reduce year-end 1970 raw material inventory by 30 percent from year-end 1969 inventory.
7. Implement the Engineered Standards Program and achieve 55 percent Engineered Standards coverage by year end 1970, and be on schedule relative to the total plan.
8. Develop by June 1970 a total facilities capability and department allocation plan.
9. Obtain an average increase in erection and construction sales of 8 percent annually (constant dollars) for the 1970–1974 period.
10. Reduce the cumulative guarantee costs 20 percent by 1974.

* SOCIAL

The social goals of the Division are identical to the social goals of the Company.

* FINANCIAL

The Division will assist and take all prudent action to enable the Company to meet the financial goals.

Source: The Babcock and Wilcox Company, Corporate Headquarters, New York. Used by permission.

It may apply to the next month. They are objectives which must be quite precise and which are usually subject to careful measurement. Thus an automobile company announced that it had scheduled for production in a given month 40,000 units. This is a short-term objective. At the end of the month the company could check the actual production and determine that its goal was achieved. Figure 9–3 further illustrates how the short-term objectives of a division of this firm are subintegrated into the intermediate objectives of this firm.

d) Immediate Objectives. These refer to those goals or aims which are established for a work shift, a day, or some part of a day. Thus, we may set up a daily quota of production for a punch-press operator. This had been established as the production required that day to achieve that month's and that year's production goals, so as to move in a planned way toward the intermediate and long-term objectives. This finite objective, however, must be set at the operative level for each employee, as the long-term objectives furnish too little guidance for him in his work.

Uses of Objectives

Objectives are of utmost significance in the performance of managerial functions. Here, in this section, attention is paid to the uses of objectives in managerial planning, organizing, directing, and controlling, as well as the institutional identity given by objectives.

1. *Managerial Planning.* Objectives assist the group in determining what planning activities will be wasteful as well as contributive to a sound course of action. The objective of a certain publishing firm, for example, was the establishment of a market for a new magazine dealing with the field of fine arts. A listing of the purposes which it was to serve, to whom it would appeal, the content involved, and similar items, gave specific purpose to the planning effort of the groups involved and facilitated coordination with a minimum of wasted effort.

2. *Managerial Organizing.* Clearly stated objectives will assist in the organizing of activities assigned to a job, project, department, or division. Appropriate resources, authority-responsibility assignments, and channels of communication can be established. What kinds of and how many people should be assigned to a project, for example, can effectively be set only when the objectives of the project are clearly determined. Conversely, inefficient or duplicative organizational units and resources can be quickly spotted by determining to what objective they are or are not related.

3. *Managerial Directing.* One of the common complaints of employees at various levels is that they do not know what the boss expects of them. On the other hand, when they know what the goals of a company and its various units are, it becomes easier for them to be a part of the team which willingly strives for organizational success.

The sense of achievement, of contributing something significant, is a personal need of all of us. A goal, properly set, represents a challenge. There is an anticipated satisfaction in accomplishing that goal, whether it be an individual or a group goal, which causes people to respond in a positive way. If there is no clear goal which provides a sense of accomplishment as a reward for its attainment, then motivation is, to that extent, adversely affected. The salesman who is simply admonished to "go out and sell" does not have as clear a target as does the salesman who is aware that he ought to sell 50 machines over a given time period. Furthermore, if an added motivational device is to be used, such as a bonus for the sale of all machines over 50, then surely a specific and reasonable objective is a necessity.

Incidentally, many organizations are utilizing what is known as management by objectives as a basis for developing managerial talent. Briefly a management by objectives (MBO) program consists of the following sequential steps:[2]

1. Management initially identifies the corporate objectives or goals.
2. These objectives are formulated for the firm, then scaled downward into subobjectives and sub-subobjectives for departments, divisions, and work units. (See Figure 9–4 for an illustration of the integration of individual with organizational goals.)
3. The supervisors and their subordinates mutually set personal goals for accomplishment. These are first developed, then written out and communicated to the involved and responsible parties.
4. Periodic appraisals are used to analyze progress.
5. There is a discussion of variances in goal achievement, and a mutually agreed upon prescription of activities for successful goal accomplishment is developed for the future.

---

[2] See Chapter 23, "Appraisal of Executives," for a treatment of management by objectives as a managerial appraisal technique.

FIGURE 9–4
Integration of Individual Goals with Those of the Organization

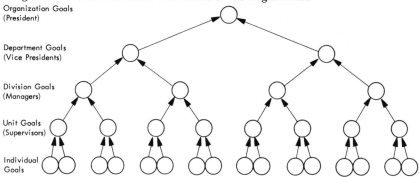

Management development seems to be facilitated through such interaction since there is evidence that MBO programming:

1. Fosters both communication and cooperation between managers who, first of all, set and then work regularly toward achieving company and unit goals.
2. Identifies and then integrates the goals of the individual with those of the organization.
3. Facilitates personal development by localizing specific areas for development that are congruous to the defined objectives.
4. Stimulates individual efforts of employees who are working toward common objectives which are consistent, realizable, and accepted.

   4. Managerial Controlling. Objectives aid measurably in exercising control. Some executives have stated that the only thing that counts is results. They mean that whether or not the company's or a man's efforts have been properly applied can be seen in the end results of those efforts. While this may be an oversimplification, it does show that the ultimate standard or criterion, by which effort is measured, is the objective which was to be achieved. When standards for accomplishments of projects or phases of an overall program are set, they become objectives which act as building blocks toward overall objectives. Comparison of performance to these objectives thus becomes a means of measurement of progress toward program completion as shown in Figure 9–5.

   5. Institutional Identity. Objectives give identity to the organization and assist in relating it to those groups upon which its survival depends. For example, General Electric's advertised objective of "Progress Is Our Most Important Product" serves as a unique

FIGURE 9-5
Model of Relationship Objectives to Planning and Control (the function of planning is to determine objectives for the corporation as well as the subsequent determination and integration of necessary subobjectives and finally the activities themselves that initiate the chainlike process.)

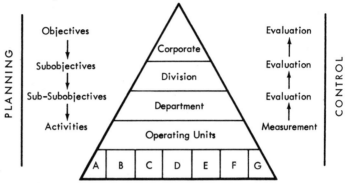

objective of the business, inviting challenge and comparison by both the consumer and the public.

Responsibility for Objectives

Objectives, obviously, are not self-generating. They arise out of the conscious deliberations of the owners of the firm, and over time are influenced by both management and employees as the objectives themselves are being implemented. Furthermore, the economic, social, and political climates concurrently exercise a profound influence on those objectives. This section, then, concerns itself with the responsibility for the formulation and interpretation of objectives within the milieu of both the firm and the climates within which it functions.

1. Actions of Owners. In any system of government embracing the concept of private property, the primary source of the objectives of a firm is the ownership group. These are the stockholders in a corporation, partners in a partnership, members in a cooperative, and the entrepreneur in a proprietorship. In the initial stages of formation of all of these forms of business the objectives are likely to be sharply and clearly defined, as in the case of a service station operator who sets up his own station so as to be free and independent of supervision.

All too often, however, the original objectives become lost or hazy as the firm continues in existence. The ownership body changes; new members entering to replace older ones. New ideas and new emphasis or interpretations of the objectives cause a change, perhaps subtly or overtly, in the direction and purpose of the venture. These changes may not be reflected in the stated objectives, but they may be reflected in the operations and activities directed toward attainment of objectives. Consequently, it may happen that while the owners adhere to the stated objectives, management at some critical level changes the direction of efforts. In a large cooperative enterprise, for example, the president continues to enunciate "service to members" while his staff continues to strive for more efficient operations based upon an increasing-of-profit concept.

In all firms it is imperative that the owners or board of directors remain active in seeing that their concept of the objectives is sharpened, crystallized, and completely communicated to all employees, managerial and operative. This means a continuing appraisal of the firm in terms of these objectives.

2. *Actions of Management.* Where the managers are the owners, the above applies. Where the managers are hired employees of the owners, these men act as individuals and are able to strongly influence not only the carrying out of the objectives but also the formulation of the objectives. In such a case, care must be taken to make certain that management focuses on the *organizational* rather than their *personal* objectives.

The philosophy of a particular manager can have a deciding effect upon objectives. Where a manager believes in decentralized, democratic leadership, he will delegate vast amounts of authority and responsibility to his subordinates, and they, in turn, will pass them down the chain of command. Such wide delegation brings great responsibility to the top management to see that all subordinates have a clear grasp of the firm's objectives and are motivated to strive to achieve those goals. This requires, then, of the firm a continual program of redefinition and communication of objectives to all the people of the organization.

3. *Actions of Employees.* Employees directly and indirectly affect the objectives of a firm, both in their formulation and, more obviously, in their satisfaction. Certainly it is clear that an organization could not set up objectives that had little or no motivational value to the employees of the firm. If, for example, a firm were to announce that its sole objective is to maximize the return on absentee stockholder's capital, how could it expect to thereby win

the support of the employees—especially since the actions of management which would have an important bearing on successful attainment of such an objective would probably adversely affect employee morale. An example of such action would be the decision to pay below-area wages in order to reduce costs so as to maximize profits.

Consequently, in this day of considerable labor relations activity, it is likely that progressive managements will seek to establish, for their firms, objectives having an appeal to the employees. A customer service objective will have much more appeal to the employees than will one that seeks to maximize the return on sales or capital. The inclusion, in a statement of objectives, of an objective of providing stable employment at competitive wages will have similar, even greater, appeal to employees. This may explain, in part, the present tendency to state multiple objectives, many with an employee relations value.

4. *Influence of Environmental Factors.* Many environmental factors affect the establishment or modification of organizational objectives. Some of the more significant ones are considered here, among them economic and political environmental forces, as well as others.

The general business climate will affect the objectives of a company. Objectives of a firm born in a depression period will often reflect those deteriorated economic conditions. The firm will probably accent survival and the creation of value, rather than maximization or return on capital or sales. The promoters may have been looking for a way to make a living—not a speculative profit, or even, particularly, an investment. They may well have set as their goal a break-even operation with attainment of a minimal market position.

On the other hand, if a firm is created in a period of general prosperity, there is some tendency to be more optimistic about its future and to set goals that reflect the more satisfactory business climate. It is thus likely that the objectives of the company will stress obtaining a good return on sales and/or capital. Indeed, the boom may be such as to make it possible for a firm to "skim the cream from the market" by producing values without much concern for high-quality standards, or delivery promises, or price. It is not likely that many firms entering business life with these standards of product acceptance will continue to succeed. Some do, however, survive and succeed mainly by recognizing the changes that must inevitably occur in market conditions, and they react by increasing product values before it is too late. One might infer that many firms created in boom conditions with a "get rich quick" objective, in effect change the emphasis of their goals in advance of impending changes in market conditions, with the result that they continue to prosper after the boom is over. The above relationships of economic conditions to goals can be said to apply to an existing concern also, insofar as the going concern may also redirect the emphasis on objectives as times change.

Conditions such as monopoly or acute competition can also affect the objectives set by a firm. Management operating under the latter condition will have good reason for taking as realistic objectives the provision of high-quality product, outstanding customer service, lower price, or some combination of all three. Its objectives will need to be concerned with survival and growth among strong competitors. A company under monopolistic or near-monopolistic conditions does not have the same pressure from the marketplace to stress values. It can afford to put greater emphasis on obtaining a better rate of return on invested capital. An effective limit to the maximization of return is the fear of action that may be taken against a monopolistic concern. In fact, many firms that have reached a position of substantial command of a particular market have demonstrated a very high regard for the interest of the general public and their customers, and their objectives indicate this consciousness.

The political environment in the nation, state, and locality must be considered, too, in shaping company objectives. In a free economy the individual firm has a wide latitude in determining the goals it will strive to achieve. In a regimented economy the goals will be more limited or will be set for the enterprise. In the Soviet Union, for example, the objectives of an enterprise are usually well defined by the specific trust that controls that segment of the economy.

All economies have some limiting factors stemming from political considerations, and management will be aware of the political climate in which it operates. In the United States, society as expressed through the administrative, legislative, and judicial branches of the government has created an environment affording a relatively wide latitude of operation to private enterprise. It has, however, earmarked certain types of activities as illegal and has set certain conditions—for example, minimum wages—which place restraints on management.

While age and size of a firm may be less influential than are

economic and political conditions, they are nevertheless general factors that affect the objectives of a company. A large firm tends to
be perpetually in the eye of the public. Its conduct has to be more
circumspect than does that of its smaller business sister. Then, too,
its objectives will tend to reflect a greater social awareness than
will those set by smaller competitors. Should it elect to emphasize
the maximizing or return on invested capital, it will spend much
time and money to actively inform the public why it feels this attention to financial return is required. Witness the resources devoted
by giant companies to programs of economic education. Notice, also,
the public pronouncements of the officials of the very large firms.
Observe the funds that firms such as General Motors, Standard Oil
of New Jersey, and Du Pont devote to educational research and
scholarships. These are all evidence of an acute awareness by the
large firm of its social responsibilities. Usually, its objectives reflect
the social impact of its gross operations.

The older firm is also more apt to demonstrate in its statements
of objectives an awareness of more than a monetary interest. It,
too, will set objectives that have social significance. It will become
more willing to consider continuity not only of its own operations
but also of employment opportunities within the firm. More attention will be devoted to development of product and of manpower.
More consideration will be given to growth and to leadership of
its industry. But in its earlier struggles it had to be acutely aware
of return on invested capital; it had to concentrate much attention
on increasing the return on capital so that further growth could
be financed. Only by obtaining a healthy return on its capital could
it induce new investors to commit their funds to the business. Only
in this way could it display the financial solvency which lenders
require in order to extend loans to the firm. As these needs were
met, however, more and more attention could be given to other
objectives—increasing values for customers, providing good working conditions, becoming a leader in the industry, and so on. With
age came greater awareness of the firm's place in society and a
greater willingness to accent those objectives that would contribute
to the customers, the employees, and society in general.

5. *Aids to Establishment of Objectives.* Certain scientific management techniques or tools are of some assistance in molding objectives. The technique of market research is of considerable aid in
spelling out a practical objective of product quality. It also assists
in devising an objective or objectives for the distribution of the
product. In determining intermediate and short-term goals, market

analysis and economic analysis can give realistic data from which to draw in shaping market goals for the near future.

Improved production control techniques provide knowledge that can be materially helpful in setting production goals or targets. Time and motion study and time and duty analysis give insight into practical output standards (immediate objectives) for individual employees. Job evaluation produces accurate job descriptions, which can be very fruitful in developing objectives that run the gamut of employee activities.

The attainment of all objectives is dependent upon the modern use of progressive, scientific management tools. What does it gain a firm to set up high-sounding objectives that are soon shown to be obviously unattainable? It is better practice to use the devices of scientific management to develop objectives that can be realistically depended upon as achievable.

Criteria of Sound Objectives

If fullest benefits are to be derived from objectives, they should possess certain desirable characteristics. Some of these are as follows:

1. *Acceptable.* To be effective, an objective must be acceptable to the people whose actions are involved in its achievement. This means that an organizational objective must be meaningful to the members of the organization. The more acceptable the objective is, the greater the probable successful accomplishment of it. In many cases, what is basically involved is depicting the objective in terms that make it as acceptable as possible to the membership or employees of the enterprise. This may mean that we state our objective of providing an adequate return on invested capital to include a comment on why this is important to all concerned with the enterprise, viz.:

It is the objective of this company to earn an adequate return on invested capital to the end that the enterprise may continue to prosper and grow, providing opportunities for an increasing number of employees to earn a livelihood.

To state a capital earnings objective in the above terms is to make it more acceptable to the bulk of employees who do not own stock in the firm and are thus less likely to want to work hard to earn a return for stockholders for whom they have no particular feeling.

2. *Attainable.* To be effective, an objective must be attainable within a reasonable time. If an objective is such that the people who work for its attainment cannot at some time tell whether they have or have not achieved it, it will soon lose its effectiveness. This means essentially that the overall, long-term objectives of the firm must be translated into intermediate and more specific objectives, which will provide yardsticks against which progress of the firm and its individual employees may be measured. Thus, an objective of becoming the leader in an industry must be translated into attainable objectives, such as "the company must have 30 percent of its product market within 5 years, 50 percent in 10 years, and 70 percent in 20 years." This is an objective which should represent something that is potentially attainable. It can be determined in five years what percent of the market the firm has, and everyone connected with the firm can then know whether or not the objective was attained. The goals do not have to be reached; the important point is that they must be *capable* of being attained.

3. *Motivational.* To be effective, an objective must have inspirational qualities which motivate all personnel to want to strive to achieve it. The objective of the Nationwide Insurance Companies has been expressed as "In Service with People." This is the sort of objective that has the quality of inspiring employees to want to create and distribute values for the patrons of the firm. It has been further developed to show in what specific ways the firm will be operated, so as to maximize the values that are available to its patrons. These patrons are men and women just like the employees (and in fact include very many employees). Mutuality of interest is created between the user of the firm's services and the providers of the services. Thus, the more the providers create, value-wise, the greater the satisfaction of the customers, who include the very producers of such values.

4. *Simple.* To be effective, an objective must be as simply and clearly stated as is possible. There should be a minimum of objectives as far as the individual employee is concerned. Each should be briefly and clearly stated and yet give complete meaning to the expression of purpose.

5. *Communicated.* To be effective, an objective must be communicated to all who are concerned with its achievement. Such communication must not only be initially well done but must also be continuously maintained with the employee. This does not mean a multiplicity of signs strung before workplaces. It means that in

its continuing communications, oral and written, with employees, management must take every opportunity to stress the goals for which the firm and its employees are striving.

Maintaining Objectives

As the firm continues in existence, it will be necessary to periodically reexamine the objectives to determine if changes are dictated because of evolution in the business environment. The basic, original objectives must be constantly reappraised to be certain that they are still pertinent.

While, again, the board of directors of a corporation or the owners of other forms of enterprise must be the ones to reappraise the objectives, management must take the lead in identifying the need for such reappraisal. It may well be that management will be the group that detects the changing environment that is requiring a reexamination of the original objectives. Again, a new management may come into the firm, and it will be very desirable for that new man or group to meet with the owners to either reaffirm the original objectives or evolve new ones. One need only peruse current business news items to see how changes in ownership or top management of a concern are accompanied by alterations in both general and specific objectives.

Through continuing appraisal of the firm's progress, through annual audits and other means of examination, management will give emphasis to objectives. The progress of the whole, and of each individual who is a part of the enterprise, must be judged against the criterion of the company objective. "What has Mr. Blank done to help achieve the organizational objectives?" is at the heart of each merit rating or performance appraisal. Thus, in its daily determination of progress, management must consciously look at the objectives. This alone will be a great stimulant to the achievement of these goals.

QUESTIONS

1. How does a firm determine its objectives? To what extent are influences external to the firm involved?
2. What kinds of objectives can be identified for a business organization? Can the general classification used in this chapter be applied to nonbusiness organizations?

3. What is meant by the statement that objectives are values?
4. Identify the advantages which accrue from a clear formulation and statement of objectives.
5. What are the dangers in confusing personal objectives with basic economic service objectives?
6. How could you ascertain whether objectives on one level are consistent with objectives on all other levels?
7. Identify and discuss the various criteria of sound objectives.
8. Must all objectives be in complete harmony with each other? Can, for example, personal objectives always be in complete accord with other organizational objectives?
9. Suggest ways in which objectives can be effectively communicated to all members of the organization.

CASE 9–1

The Rural Insurance Company is a multiple line firm that presently markets life insurance as well as several property and liability coverages such as auto and homeowners. The history of Rural is one of farm orientation. Located in a rather small community and founded in the early 1900s by a group of wealthy farmers, its original purpose was to provide low-cost crop and property insurance to farmers who were considered select risks. The company's name and its advertisings and promotions (its advertising logo, a scythe-bearing farmer) were all geared toward strengthening its image as a financially sound, yet progressive, farm-oriented group. Its board of directors, over the years, inevitably was a mix of rural farmers, country bankers, and dairymen.

As the automobile became popular, the firm added this coverage; and later on, in the late thirties, it added life insurance to its portfolio of products.

As time and rural America gave way to the city, President Hiram Jones uncomfortably saw Rural's growth (in terms of premium income) stabilize and then gradually begin to decline. In an attempt to solve what Jones felt was an apparent marketing problem, he hired the services of a marketing consultant.

After several interviews with Mr. Jones and his vice presidents of underwriting, claims, and sales, the consultant, in a formal report, stressed the need for Rural to improve the identification of objectives at all operating levels. He further recommended that every employee and every manager agree with his immediate superior at the beginning of each quarter on what the employees or, in the case of a manager, the departmental work objectives will be. The report also recommended an appraisal be held at the end of each quarter to determine just how well the stated objectives were being met. Each new quarter was to begin with new attempts and resolutions to improve these objectives.

1. Do you feel the consultant's diagnosis and recommendations were appropriate for Rural?
2. Are there any other, and possibly more basic, problems in this case?
3. If you were Mr. Jones, what would be your plan of action?

CASE 9–2

The Pluto Chrome Tool Company over the years has enjoyed an excellent reputation for its line of high-quality, chrome alloy ratchet and flat wrenches. The published objectives of this Southwestern firm are:

a) To manufacture and distribute wrenches of the highest quality material and workmanship;

b) To pay above-average wages in the industry and to provide stability of employment to all employees;

c) To be a good corporate citizen of the community; and

d) To yield the maximum rate of return to its shareholders.

For about 10 years, Pluto has been the major supplier of wrenches to a national retail chain that marketed them under its private brand label. Sales to this chain accounted for about 70 percent of total business, and it was a recognized fact that this one major account was responsible for Pluto's success and growth.

Recently, however, the national chain store informed Pluto that it has decided to eliminate merchandising the chrome-alloy wrenches in favor of much cheaper, chrome-plated wrenches. "Quality in wrenches no longer counts with the user, and we can sell just as many, perhaps more, wrenches of lesser quality and cost."

1. What effect do you think the decision of the national chain will have on Pluto's objectives? What about its name?
2. In analyzing Pluto's objectives, do you see any conflict among its stated objectives?

10

Policies

Scope of Discussion

IN MANAGING the work of others, the executive is essentially making decisions. When he plans, for example, he is deciding upon some objectives rather than others, and he decides upon certain courses of action and excludes others. Or when he organizes, he uses certain resources and structures while rejecting others. And when he directs and controls, he is constantly making choices among supervisory and evaluation procedures. As a consequence, management is thought of by some as being the process of decision making (discussed in Chapter 4).

If one analyzes the situations about which the manager makes decisions, it is found that they can be divided into two distinct classes. First, some situations encountered are unique. Each is different from others, so that each has to be handled on its own merits. As a consequence, a separate and individual decision-making effort must be made by the manager. Second, some situations encountered are very similar to cases met in the past and are very likely to be met in the future. Each of these cases could be decided separately and individually. But it would seem much wiser to establish a standard decision and apply it to the same type of situation.

Such standard decisions for recurring, similar situations are provided by policies. Policies are among the most useful tools of management. Through policies, the manager affects the work of many people, and is in turn affected by them every day of his executive life. Such a significant tool should be thoroughly understood if it is to be used properly. To provide the basis for such understanding is the purpose of this chapter. The discussion here is concerned with the following phases of policies:

1. Nature of policies.
2. Purposes of policies.
3. Coverage of policies.

4. Establishment of policies.
5. Characteristics of policies.
6. Control of policies.

Nature of Policies

Policies are guides to action in that they provide standard decisions for recurring problems of a similar nature. They serve to keep action in line with desired objectives. This concept can be better understood if, first, policies are compared with other guides to action; second, attention is directed to what they are and are not; and third, some thought is devoted to what they can and cannot do.

A number of "guides to action" are used by management. For example, a philosophy of management provides a basic guide to action. Principles are commonly followed as guides to action. Rules and regulations are often-encountered guides to action. How do these differ?

There is no universal agreement as to the exclusive domain of these guides. To illustrate, the "Golden Rule" is more akin to a philosophy than to the specific rule of a "No Smoking" sign. It is possible, however, to grade these terms as to a general, if overlapping, degree of universality and specificity of application. A philosophy is the broadest guide, covering in general terms every situation an executive may encounter—"Do unto others as you want others to do unto you" is an example. A rule is a guide pertaining to a specific situation—"Do not smoke here" is an example. A principle is not as broad as a philosophy but has general application in a given area—"Locate a retail store where the pattern of consumer purchases is of greatest density" is an example. A policy is usually based on a principle and reflects a managerial decision based thereon. For example, it may be decided that "Future retail store locations shall be selected only at sites at which consumer traffic is at the rate of 'X' amount of density." Diagrammatically, the relationship among these various guides may be shown as follows:

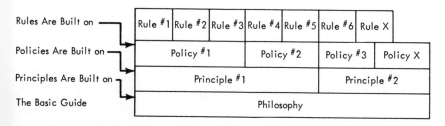

The relationship between these terms may also be seen in the hierarchy of definitions contained in Figure 10–1.

FIGURE 10–1
A Hierarchy of Managerial Nomenclature

Level of Abstraction

Philosophy	. . . A system of thought that explains basic business problems and supplies the basis for an intelligent approach to their solution.
Principle	. . . A fundamental truth, an accepted guide or rule of conduct, action, or thought.
Objective	. . . An end to be achieved; a result to be accomplished.
Policy	. . . A guide to be followed in performing activities to achieve desired objectives.
Rule	. . . A mandatory, prescribed course of action or conduct to be followed in a specific situation or localized environment.

A better insight into the meaning of policies can also be gained by seeing what they are not. Thus, policies are guides to action, but they are not the action itself. A policy governs work but does not do the work. It is equivalent in this sense to a highway. Those who stay on the right highway are guided in their travels to their destinations. The highway does no traveling but does serve to guide the travelers. This is true of policies. For example, a certain office manager follows the policy of selecting employees only from those who have a high school certificate. In his selection activities (the work) his policy governs by immediately rejecting those who are not high school graduates. The selection procedure is applied only to those who are graduates.

Nor are policies objectives. They are intended to guide action to objectives but are not objectives themselves. Thus, the policy is like a radio beam which guides a plane to an airport—it guides to an objective but it is neither the objective nor does it fly.

One more point will serve to clarify the meaning of policies. They cannot think for themselves nor replace good management. To begin with, managers must develop policies for eventual application by their subordinates. Policy development, like all decision making, requires careful thinking and planning. It is essential, therefore, that policies be designed to suit the particular situations to which they are to be applied. This leads to the point that policies cannot apply themselves. Subordinates must be informed about existing policies, the situations to which they are to be applied, and how they are to be followed. Only then will their full potential be realized.

In summary, then, policies are guides (based upon principles) for making decisions and taking action in recurring situations, in ways that will lead more successfully to desired objectives. In diagram form, the role of policies can be shown as follows:

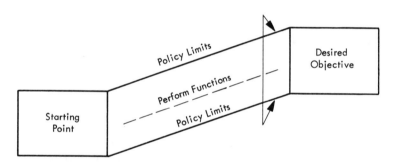

By performing functions within the prescribed policy limits, desired objectives will be attained economically and effectively. Policies are contributors to more effective management, and not a substitute for management.

Purposes of Policies

Once again, policies provide uniform and consistent guidance in the care of problems, questions, or situations that recur frequently. Thus they are useful to both manager and managed. Their usefulness to each may be seen in cases in which policies are not used and when they are used.

Without policies, the manager reduces his effectiveness in a number of ways. He has to take time to rethink a decision every time a problem recurs. Inconsistency may result since he may decide a given case one way one day and another way in the future. Moreover, he has to make himself available to subordinates while handing down decisions—a great demand on his limited time.

Without policies, the managed are subject to a number of disadvantages. To begin with, a subordinate must decide for himself what to do in a given case or refer the case to his superior. If he decides for himself, he may be handling something beyond his personal capacities; something outside his authority; or something that involves other organizational units. If he refers the case upwards, he may be repetitiously wasting the time of his superior and himself; shrinking from acting in a situation within his capabilities; and failing to develop his own skills.

But with policies, both may make impressive gains. The manager increases his managerial powers geographically and timewise. Through policies he can be in several geographical places at the same time. He can simultaneously provide answers to a number of his subordinates who may literally be hundreds of miles apart. Or he can through policies "speak out" from time to time without being present.

These powers are refined too because the manager can give better thought to arriving at good policies. Since he doesn't have to see subordinates on every decision, he has more time for planning policies. He also has more time for other executive functions such as organizing, directing, and controlling. Moreover, he assures himself that his decisions are uniform and consistent among his subordinates and over time.

With policies, the managed too have much to gain. Initiative of subordinates is encouraged because they are free to act within policy limits. A constructive atmosphere evolves with the knowledge of knowing what can be done under various conditions. The subordinate does not have the feeling that his superior is constantly breathing down his neck. And he has an inward assurance that his superior has given his decisions planned consideration rather than off-the-cuff opinions.

Fundamentally, policies enhance organizational effectiveness in reaching its objectives. Both managerial and managed participants of the organization can through policies perform their specialized responsibilities much more efficiently and with more personal satisfaction. All of this serves to increase the probabilities of organizational success.

Coverage of Policies

It is now appropriate to see where and for what subjects policies may be used. In general terms, policies should cover any situations that tend to repeat themselves. In this sense, it could be well said that there are few subjects, if any, that could not benefit from the establishment of policies. A study of all possible areas is, therefore, beyond the scope of this book. But some attention to this subject of coverage is desirable and can be conveniently undertaken under the headings of, first, organizational areas to which they pertain and, second, kinds of functions which they are intended to guide.

1. *Organizational Coverage.* This category classifies policies according to organizational relationships. It may be subdivided into three parts:

1. External policies, or those that guide the organization in relation to various outside groups and agencies.
2. Internal vertical policies, or those which, starting from the top, guide successively the various subordinate subdivisions of an organization.
3. Internal horizontal policies, or those that serve to coordinate various organizational units at the same level.

As the term implies, external policies guide an organization in relation to various outside groups and agencies. They are necessary because an enterprise does not operate in a vacuum. Various dealings and contacts are had with governmental, community, business, and union agencies. Merely by way of illustration, such policy questions as the following will have to be answered:

a) To what extent should company officials and technical experts be "loaned" to agencies of the federal government?
b) To what extent should financial contributions be made to charitable and educational institutions?
c) To what extent should the company participate in such business groups as trade associations and chambers of commerce?
d) What position should be taken in relation to unions and collective bargaining?

Internal policies of the "vertical" type pertain to those that are intended to guide lower levels of the organization. To begin with, broad company policies must be established that serve to guide the entire organization. Just as objectives should be identified for each echelon in the organization, so should accompanying policies

be formulated which will facilitate the achievement of those objectives. Then divisions and subdivisions to the lowest level will have
policies appropriate for themselves and consistent with higher level
policies. (See Figure 10–2 for the relationship of policies to organizational principles and objectives.)

FIGURE 10–2
Relationship of Policies to Organizational Principles and Objectives

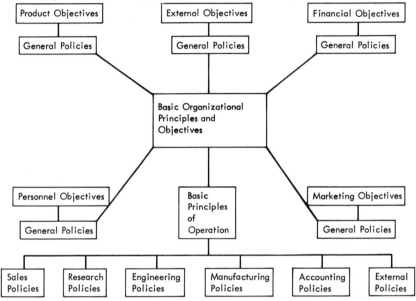

For example, it may be company policy to subsidize education
programs carried on by its employees, executive or operative. The
engineering division, in line with the broad policy but tailoring a
guide to its particular needs, may set a policy which states that
in addition to paying tuition fees of staff members taking formal
school courses, the company may send selected personnel at company expense to do postgraduate work. By the establishment of
companywide policies, guidance of a uniform nature is provided
which permits lower levels to write policies that fit their particular
needs.

Internal policies of the "horizontal" type serve to guide the horizontal relations among various departments. For example, it may
be the stated policy of the company that no department should
install a policy until it has determined that the policy is consistent
with policies in other departments. To cite an illustration, if the

policy of manufacturing is to stress simplification of product, it would be unwise for salesmen to follow a policy of stressing diversification of lines. Another area of horizontal policies is that which guides staff departments in their relations with those they serve. As an illustration of such a policy question, if the personnel department is assigned the task of hiring, should line departments be made to accept candidates submitted by the personnel department? Obviously, if there is to be coordination between departments at the same level, policies can serve to achieve this form of integrated effort.

2. *Functional Coverage.* This category classifies policies according to the functions to which they pertain. It may be divided into two large classes: policies of managerial functions and those of operative functions.

Policies of managerial functions are established to guide in the performance of planning, organizing, directing, and controlling. Recurring problems are invariably encountered in connection with each of these functions. It is just as sensible to establish uniform guidelines for these functions as it is for other types of functions. For example, in the matter of managerial planning, such questions as the following are constantly repeating themselves: What should the time period of planning be? Who should be responsible for forecasting the future? Should employees be asked to participate in planning? And how formally should plans be expressed? To establish policies for such recurring planning situations would be highly desirable. And the same would be true for the other managerial functions.

Policies of operative functions are established to guide in the performance of specialized activities. For example, in the field of sales there is need for policies on such constantly recurring problems as what price systems will be used, what kinds of advertising media will be employed, what allowance shall there be for returned merchandise, and whether private or national brands will be pushed. Or, in the case of accounting work, it will be necessary to establish guidelines in such matters as depreciation methods, inventory valuation methods, allowances for reserves and contingencies, and write-offs of bond discounts. Similarly, in other specialized function areas such as public relations, engineering, personnel, and production, policies should be established to guide their performance. (Figure 10–3 is descriptive of some of the areas in which policies are established.)

FIGURE 10-3
Some Possible Major Functional Policies of the Business Firm

Personnel Policies:
1. Compensate employees at higher than prevailing rates in the industry.
2. Provide training and developmental opportunities for all employees.
3. Promote, wherever possible, from within the firm.
4. Bear all the financial costs of employee health and welfare programs.

Marketing Policies:
1. Distribute products on a national and international level.
2. Advertise only in media directed to the medical profession.
3. Sell a product line of various types and sizes.
4. Keep total expenditures for sales and advertising expenses within 15 percent of gross dollar sales.

Finance Policies:
1. Secure capital whenever required by borrowing from long-term creditors.
2. Use profits rather than borrowed funds as a source of additional capital to finance the firm's expansion.
3. Pay regular and stable dividends on both common and preferred stock.
4. Issue preferred stock in preference to common stock as a source of capital.

Production Policies:
1. Manufacture products at safety tolerances exceeding industry and governmental standards.
2. Maintain rigid quality control tests at all stages of production.
3. Manufacture products only in the domestic United States.
4. Locate branch production facilities in cities of less than 200,000 population but in densely populated geographical regions.

Establishment of Policies

Undoubtedly, policies become established in many instances simply through informal evolution. Everyone "knows" without being told, and without knowing where it originated, that a certain type of decision is to be made in certain types of situations. Such policies are another example of the informal aspects found in every organization. To attempt to explain how such informal policies come to be established would be to explore the unconscious, the traditional, and the darkened corridors of past, unwritten history. This attempt is, therefore, not made here. But useful comments can be made about formal methods of establishing policies. In particular, attention is now turned, first, to responsibility for establishing policies and, second, to steps taken in establishing policies.

1. *Responsibility.* Enough has already been said to indicate that every executive is responsible for establishing policies. For the work in his jurisdictional limits, each executive should be held responsible for setting appropriate policies. It is imperative that each executive, however, be alert to three important warnings. He should be sure that his policies are, first, in line with those of his superiors; second, in line with those of other departments; and, third, within the scope of his authority limits. The first two points have been noted earlier in this chapter in another connection. The third needs further comment.

It may sound simple to lay down the rule that an executive should restrict himself to establishment of policies that pertain strictly to his own department. But this is not so easy in practice, because on any subject for which a supervisor might have need of a policy in his department, other supervisors would have an equal need. For example, disciplinary penalties are needed in all departments of a company but must be applied locally. Each supervisor needs disciplinary policies; but if each established his own, the total result would be inconsistent disciplinary action with its attendant undesirable features. Since it is generally true that all supervisors have about the same kinds of problems, it may be concluded that although all executives should establish policies, the lower one lies in an organization, the less likely that he will—because of the third limitation mentioned above—have reason to establish policies. Policies will be established by the higher levels; the lower levels will see to it that they are properly applied.

Another serious question of who shall establish policies arises when a company operates in several geographical locations. Then it is faced with deciding to what extent and over what subjects, if any, decentralized units will have authority to establish policies for themselves. The general question of local autonomy will be sufficiently explored in the chapter on organization structure; hence, it is necessary here merely to review the alternative patterns of policy establishment. At one extreme, some companies follow the practice of making the home office responsible for all policy determinations. This certainly should result in uniform policies, but in addition to placing a heavy burden on the home office, it reduces the advantages flowing from local flexibility and initiative. At the other extreme, some companies refer practically all policy making to each of the local units and merely check the local units through results achieved. This plan takes advantage of local talent and conditions, requires a higher level of executive talent in the local units, and lessens day-to-day control of the home office over the local units. Perhaps most companies with decentralized operations operate between these two extremes. They follow the plan of having the home office establish some policies (such as price, financing, and basic personnel); and the local officers establish other policies within the framework of home office guides. (See Figure 10–4 for the policy functions of the executive personnel of the organization.)

2. Steps. However responsibility for policy establishment may be divided, there are a number of steps that should be followed in their establishment. The first is that of determining what policies are needed. A simple way of doing this is for each executive to ask himself every time a decision has to be made whether or not the same situation is likely to be encountered again. If it is not, a policy would obviously be unnecessary. If it is, and recurrences are likely to be frequent, setting a policy is desirable. By this plan, over a period of time, a full complement of policies could be established. But waiting for time to turn up all situations requiring policies will result in wasted opportunities and unnecessary continuance of inconsistent practices.

Another plan of determining policy needs is to make surveys of problem areas. Questionnaires, interviews, conferences, schools, etc., may be used to determine what problems executives have encountered, are encountering, and expect to encounter. Attitude surveys among employees, consumer surveys, and consultant appraisals are also useful to determine problem areas. From such formal plans

FIGURE 10–4
Policy Functions of Chief Executive, Managers and Staff

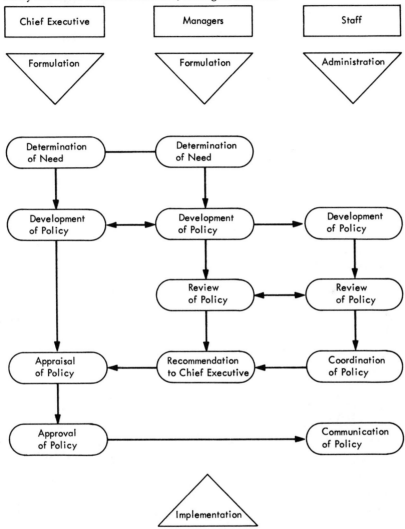

Reprinted by permission of the publisher from AMA Research Study No. 76, *Management Policies I*, © 1966 by the American Management Association, Inc.

of investigation, it is possible to determine situations for which policy guidance is needed.

The next step in policy establishment is that of verbalizing. Here it is necessary to phrase the policy so that it expresses what the executive wants done, and conveys that expression to the policy user. It must be remembered that the policy represents the executive; the executive will not be present when the user interprets the policy; hence, the policy must express what the executive would have stated had he personally been in the presence of the policy user.

A third step of policy establishment is that of issuance. Undoubtedly, many policies are issued by word of mouth. Although simple and quick, this practice has many weaknesses. Misunderstandings, misinterpretations, changes, nonuniform interpretations by different users, and neglect are some of its undesirable features.

Written policies are the obvious improvement. They require more time in preparation and proper filing care. But the advantages are weighty. The executive who writes out policies is usually more careful than the one who merely speaks them. Written policies are not lost as easily, are likely to be more comprehensive and consistent, and are more certain to be used by those who need them. Written policies can be quickly audited and evaluated, and they provide an excellent manual for instruction of new supervisors or review sessions with old, experienced hands.

A final step of policy establishment is that of policy appraisal. Some system should be formulated to provide for auditing of policies to determine which should be changed or dropped, where improvements are needed, and what other factors of management need investigation. A variety of appraisal methods are available. These are discussed later on in the section on control of policies.

Characteristics of Policies

It is now appropriate to inquire into the question of what constitutes a "good" policy. The best way to answer this question is by having a set of bench marks for testing policies. Thus, in order for policies to be considered good, they should have the following characteristics:

1. Objectivity.
2. Relationship to other objectives.
3. Complementariness.
4. Stability and flexibility.
5. Fairness and honesty.
6. Being known, understood, and accepted.

1. *Objectivity.* It was mentioned earlier that policies are supposed to guide action to desired objectives. Obviously then, there is no more significant test of a policy than that of its serving to attain its purported objective. Like a radio beam which is supposed to guide a pilot to a particular airport, a policy is supposed to guide business action to particular goals. In either event, if the guide is not beamed to the target, it can be most ineffective, if not dangerous.

Hence, every policy should be given the "objectivity" test. Does each policy aim directly at desired objectives, so that those who follow them will neither ramble aimlessly en route nor fail to arrive at the desired goal? To illustrate, if a company produces and distributes a low-quality product, it would be wasteful to establish employee selection policies—as some companies do—stating that only high school graduates will be accepted for employment. Conversely, if quality standards are high, it is unwise to fail to set restrictive hiring policies. In either event, the policies mentioned would not serve to guide action to desired goals.

To illustrate this test further, take the case of the company that expects its salesmen to provide technical advice to its customers as well as to sell. Such a company should be sure that its compensation policies, for example, are related to these twin responsibilities. The salesmen should be compensated for their nonselling and selling activities. On the other hand, in the case of a company in which selling is the sole function of the sales force, the compensation policy would not have to make an allowance for nonselling activities.

2. *Relationship to Other Objectives.* Practically all policies serve to attain—or affect—several objectives at the same time. Hence, another significant test of any policy is the degree to which it concurrently serves these objectives. As an example of this test, let us take the case of the company that has the policy of hiring only high school graduates. Let us assume that this policy serves to advance the goals of producing or distributing the commodities of the company. But what if there are not enough challenging jobs to which high school graduates can eventually be promoted? Then the policy fails to serve personal objectives, even though it serves the company objectives. Eventually personal dissatisfaction will obstruct effective attainment of company goals.

Furthermore, such a policy may fail to take account of community obligations. What about the non-high school graduates in the community? Shall they become a charge of the community for whose sustenance a tax shall be loaded upon us? Shall the company take an interest in welfare problems and educational matters so that all eligible members in the community have an opportunity to acquire a high school education? Whatever the final answer, policies can scarcely pass the complementary test if they do not weigh community obligations and implications.

Finally, the efficiency aspect of all policies should be tested. A policy should guide action to a desired goal. But it should do so effectively. An illustrative example is laying out a road between two towns. When a person takes the road from town "A" to go to town "B," he also expects it to lead him to "B" by the shortest feasible route (unless, of course, his desire is to ramble as a tourist, but then his primary objective is touring, not getting places). So, too, in business, a policy should not merely guide—it should guide effectively.

3. *Complementariness.* A policy cannot be said to be a good one unless it does not conflict with other related policies, vertically or horizontally. To begin with, this means that a given policy should coincide with those of the organizational division to which it is subordinate. Assume, for example, that it is the policy of a given division head to encourage initiative, experimentation, and search for improved methods. Then a subordinate executive who proposed a policy to the effect that members of his unit must not deviate from standard practice instructions will be guilty of establishing a noncomplementary policy.

In establishing policies, it is necessary to look downward, too, in order to determine the complementariness of a policy. Thus, the proposed policy noted in the preceding paragraph would be running contrary to policies which have informed the employees, for example, that in dealing with customers any action should be taken that would clear up customer dissatisfaction on the spot. Or employees may have been told previously that in the heat of emergencies, their individual judgment should be followed to take corrective action. Obviously, the newly stated policy would be in contradiction to this.

Lastly, a policy should be in line with other policies in other departments. There must be horizontal conformity. Assume a case in which a union contract contained a clause to the effect that operative promotions would be based on seniority, if the test of ability to do the job could be met. Then, it would be unwise for the employment department to claim in its hiring ads that opportunities for skilled and ambitious employees were unlimited. Nor would the following policies be complementary: quality of product shall be stressed in our advertising; check quality of output only in final inspection; and, primary considerations in purchasing shall be on price and delivery time.

4. Stability and Flexibility. Policies should meet the tests of stability and flexibility. Stability implies constancy. A policy should remain in effect without change, unless fundamental conditions change or objectives are changed. Otherwise, like a radio beam that varies from day to day, the varying policy will serve only to confuse those who attempt to be guided by it.

Stability can be assured by including all policies in a policy manual. In that event, a policy can be expected to be in effect as long as it is included in the manual. Revisions, of course, can still be made. But people are less likely to make nonessential and fanciful changes when they must go through the steps of first removing older policies and getting approval for the inclusion of the newer ones.

Flexibility has reference to some degree of exception to the prescribed limits of a policy. But deviations from prescribed limits should be permitted only under adequate protection. Thus, a policy might state that only high school graduates should be considered for employment. Such a policy would exclude good candidates who do not hold a high school certificate. Now if the policy were to permit exceptions, the otherwise excluded candidates could be employed. Such exceptions can be provided in three ways, as follows:

a) Exceptions can be stated in the policy itself. For example, in the cited case such a phrase as "high school graduates or equivalent" would make the policy flexible.

b) Exceptions can be made by noting what extra authorizations (such as signature of immediate supervisor) are needed to go beyond stated limits.

c) Exceptions can be made through normal channels, but those taking nonprescribed channels must be prepared to suffer the consequences if their action proves unwise.

Such safeguards are necessary, or else a policy would be so wide that it would be useless as a guide. A radio beam is useful, for example, because it provides a narrow guide between two points. To widen the beam would allow the pilot to ramble to such an extent that he would either hit an obstruction before reaching his objective or pass the objective when he should have reached it.

Diagrammatically, an overly flexible policy can be illustrated as follows:

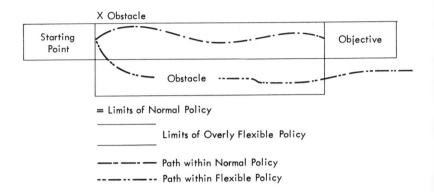

Without some flexibility in exceptional cases, however, executive initiative is stifled, opportunities for executives to exercise powers of judgment will be missed, and special cases cannot be handled without time-consuming conferences. Unfortunately, there is no scientific way of determining how much flexibility should be built into policies. This is a matter that can only be settled in each policy on its merits, with due consideration for all conditioning factors.

5. Fairness and Honesty. This test of policies is essentially a test of the fairness of the objective to which they are guides. Policies are means to help attain ends—particular objectives. So a fair and honest policy is one that leads to fair and honest objectives.

Essentially, this is a question of determining that the attainment of a given objective does not unfairly affect other objectives. It might seem fair to produce a high-quality product. Yet, the degree of quality put into the product should not be at the expense of the employees or the stockholders. Or, to overcharge customers or underpay employees or undercompensate investors are examples of unfairness.

This test is perhaps the most difficult of all to apply to a policy. To be sure, few people would admit that they are unfair, want to be unfair, or want more than their fair share in a common enterprise. Yet, few of us can agree on what a fair division is in a given instance. It is so easy to say, for example, that a company should give due regard in its policies to community obligations. But how much consideration is too little, how much is too much, and how much is just right? Perhaps the golden rule is at the present time the only practical guide that can be given in attempting to apply the test of fairness.

6. *Being Known, Understood, and Accepted.* Finally, a policy must pass the test of being known, understood, and accepted.

It would seem that applying the test of being known is belaboring the obvious. Certainly, policies cannot guide if people do not know about them. Yet, time after time, situations will be encountered in which subordinates did not know of the existence of policies. Hence, through printed communications, conferences, or direct person-to-person contacts, policies should be transmitted to those affected by them or expected to use them. And over the course of time, checks should be made to review policies with all interested parties.

But to knowledge of policies must be added understanding and acceptance. People must know why policies are established and the reasons behind their adoption. At one time, such understanding and acceptance were not as necessary as now. People were expected to follow policies, "or else." Times have, however, changed. Enthusiastic cooperation, loyalty, and positive willingness to follow policies can be expected only of those who understand and accept them. These tests of policies—particularly that of acceptance—may seem to put subordinates in the driver's seat. It is well to remember that the production of free, informed, and intelligent people invariably surpasses that of nonthinking drones. Moreover, it is personally more pleasurable to associate with equals than with slaves. So, executives find that their positive reactions are emphasized and negative tensions are reduced when operating under conditions in which subordinates know, understand, and accept their policies.

Control of Policies

Like any other organizational aspect, policies require control. Some suggestions for control are made in regard to (1) appraisal of policies, and (2) responsibility for control.

1. *Appraisal of Policies.* Some system should be formulated to provide for auditing of policies to determine which should be changed or dropped, where improvements are needed, and what other factors of management need investigation. A variety of appraisal methods are available.

a) Some policies should come up for review at specific time intervals. Wage policies are an example. Checks should be made periodically to see that these are in line with community rates.

b) All policies should be subject to some degree of review annually. Policies of each department or division may be subject to review when annual or special expenditure budget requests are made.

c) Spot or overall appraisals of policies may be made by outside consultants. This could be done either after trouble has developed somewhere, or preferably, as a preventative, constructive measure.

d) Policies should be reviewed whenever an executive submits new plans, new objectives, or major revisions for the operation of his division.

2. *Responsibility for Control.* Policy control is usually a shared responsibility. Of course, every executive should be responsible for checking the operational effectiveness of policies. He should be prepared to submit in his plans suggested changes, revisions, or additions to his policies. In addition, organizational responsibility may be given to special staff units concerned with accounting procedures, systems analysis, or organizational studies to make independent audits of policies in various departments. Outside agencies may also be invited to make spot or overall checks. And finally, policy reviews are often performed by a top-level committee. In a decentralized organization such a committee, with the aid of competent staff, will insure thorough audits and a consistency of branch policies with the policy position of the home office.

Perhaps it is well to emphasize the control over policies that should be exercised by direct executive supervision. An executive can thereby assure himself that policies are being adhered to by all concerned. Such supervision would include attention to the following points: (1) seeing that all concerned are aware of pertinent policies; (2) checking that all understand the policies and the need for them; (3) checking how policies are actually being applied; and (4) requiring reports on important policy results or exceptions to policy rules.

Such attention serves to control policies at their most vital point, that of execution. Obviously, an executive cannot check the application of every policy with each subordinate. Such an attempt, if successful, would obviate the need for policies. But spot checks of policies will serve to provide a needed and useful plan of control.

QUESTIONS

1. Distinguish among objective, policy, rule, and philosophy.
2. What are the major advantages of adequate policies for the chief executive of the organization? For the first-level supervisor?
3. How can policies aid management in decentralizing the organization?
4. Give examples of an external vertical policy and an internal vertical policy.
5. Give examples of managerial functional policies and operative functional policies.
6. How can policy appraisal be carried out effectively? Who, in your opinion, should be responsible for policy appraisal?
7. The executive vice president of a medium-sized firm commented that he did not believe in a written statement of policies because it would "hamper the dynamic effectiveness of the concern by restricting decisions to a narrow sphere; furthermore, all conditions for which policies are needed cannot be anticipated anyway." Evaluate his statement.
8. Discuss what you feel are the more important characteristics of policies.

CASE 10–1

The Republic Shoe Company, a retail shoe system, had been under organizational pressure by a national union. Particularly sensitive to organizational attempts was the warehousing operation which employed approximately 300 people in receiving, storage, and shipping activities. The firm never had a personnel officer. Basic employee activities were handled by the payroll office. Neither did it have written personnel policies. The president felt it was time they did. He hired a consultant who after six months of intensive investigation and preparation delivered a well-constructed, comprehensive personnel policy manual. The president was obviously pleased. As he handed the consultant his check for his efforts, he remarked, "Now, I'll just put this in my desk drawer and if the union ever wins a bargaining election and appears here with their contract, I'll have a better one to negotiate for."

1. What is wrong with the president's thinking in this situation?
2. What values accrue from communicating policies to those affected by them?

CASE 10–2

A branch of the Western Savings and Loan Association has been serving the western area for over 30 years, with assets totaling $125,000,000, putting Western Savings and Loan Association in the top 5 savings and loan banks in the state. Services include home and construction loans, passbook savings, and certificates of deposit. Western offers four certificates, plus variations on the $10,000, 6 percent certificate. One of these variations is called a monthly income account, where the money on deposit earns a compounded interest of 6.18 percent. This total amount is divided by 12, and a monthly income check is sent on the last working day of the month or the dividend is credited back to the account. The savings accounts and certificates are numbered in different series by the assistant vice president in charge of savings (savings officer). The savings officer also talks to each new savings (or certificate) customer and sets up his new account, including data such as his name, address, social security number, date of maturity, and special instructions as to whether to send a check or to credit the earnings back to the account. He then takes the information to a teller who puts everything on a computer card, checks the printout against the original setup, and cross-references the material.

In January 1971, the savings officer transposed a "5" instead of a "3" on the last figure of an account number for a certificate of deposit for Mrs. Jane Smith for a $15,000 mail dividend check (this is a 6 percent certificate). Since the computer had no "5" yet, it accepted all the information, the account was declared correct and the information was put into core storage. The following day and two certificates later, the Cara Nome Society bought a 6 percent certificate for $15,000. When this information was put on the computer, it was rejected because the computer already had a "5." An inquiry resulted in information leading to the mix-up. A change was then put through to correct the Jane Smith number, which should have ended in 3, not 5.

Seemingly the change was effected and the incident forgotten until May, and five checks later, when a teller was sorting the mail and asked if Jane Smith had two certificates. The savings officer was in charge of typing and mailing the dividend checks. He checked and found that Jane Smith had only one certificate but was receiving a check from *her* certificate and also that of the Cara Nome Society. Mrs. Smith had forged the Cara Nome Society, signed her signature, and cashed both checks. This continued until June, when both checks were stopped. In the meantime, the savings officer went on "a little trip to talk friend-to-friend about the money." The discussion revealed that "Since the checks were mailed to me, they belong to me, so I spent them," said Jane Smith. She had no intention of returning the money. At this point, the branch manager (and vice president) was informed of the situation for the first time. Since he did not want to "bother the company lawyer with such little things"—($1,170)—he had the savings officer write a letter to Jane Smith asking for the money back. The four tellers were told to "forget you know anything about this."

In the following week, a letter was received from Jane Smith saying she wanted to see the checks. She was invited to see the checks, and she declared loud enough for everyone in the office to hear that she had no intention of repaying the money.

A teller was told to put a "hold" on her account (a "hold" means no withdrawals from the account from that branch). When the accounting supervisor asked if a "hold" should be put on all branches, the branch manager replied, "If I want your opinion, I'll ask for it." The accounting supervisor walked away, and the teller voluntarily placed a "hold" on that account. The outcome is still awaited.

1. Identify the specific problems that seem to arise out of policy considerations in this case.

2. If you were branch manager, what action would you have taken in this situation?

11

Functions and Procedures

Scope of Discussion

THE ATTAINMENT of objectives is directly accomplished by the performance of functions arranged in procedures or systems.[1] This is true of every phase of business operations. In the factory, for example, the worker who operates a drill press performs a bit of work—defined as a function—which makes its contribution to the procedure of completing a product. In the office, a clerk who records the costs of drilling operations is performing a function (act) that plays its small, but important, role in a control procedure (system).

This brief description of functions and procedures raises a very important question. If functions get work done, what is the role of such other factors as objectives, policies, organization structure, and environmental factors? Functions get work done directly; the others indirectly affect the accomplishment of work. Thus, to cite but one relationship, objectives determine what functions must be performed, but objectives can only be attained through functions. As an example, the functions performed in a fine fur salon will differ in degree and to some extent in kind from those performed in the bargain basement of a department store. Similarly, such factors as policies, organization structure, and environmental factors will have an interdependent relation with functions and procedures. But it will be the functions, properly arranged in procedures, that will

---

[1] Very common is the use of the term system as a synonym for procedure. Also the term subsystems is used to connote the same idea as subprocedures, minor functional groupings, and procedural subdivisions. Hence, these terms will be used in the same sense in the present discussion.

immediately and directly get work done, that is, serve to attain desired objectives.

In order to gain a useful picture of functions and procedures, these subjects are discussed in this chapter under the following major headings:

1. Nature of functions and procedures.
2. Building procedures.
3. A systems approach to procedure building.
4. Factors of procedural design.

Nature of Functions and Procedures

In an earlier chapter it was observed a procedure may be simply defined as an arrangement of functions intended to achieve some objective. More detailed analysis of this simple statement is needed if the nature of functions and procedures is to be fully understood. Such an analysis is made here in terms of what functions and procedures are and are not, their essential features, and their basic components.

1. *Definitions.* The terms functions and procedures do not have universally accepted connotations. The term function, in particular, is subject to a variety of usages. To some it connotes purpose—thus, what is the function, meaning purpose, of an office building? The answer then is, to provide sheltered space. To some it connotes how something or someone acts. In the case of the office building, function would refer to the way in which the roof and walls, for example, provide shelter against undesirable weather conditions. And to some, functions connote what action is performed in reference to how a given action is performed. Thus, in the office building case, the building merely functions as protection against the weather.

Obviously, communications will be hopelessly entangled if function is defined in the mind of one person as purpose, in the mind of another as act, and in the mind of a third as how to act. In this book, functions are defined as acts. The purposes for which the functions or acts are performed are generally referred to as objectives.[2] How the acts are performed will be discussed in connection with such topics as standard practice instructions, procedural designs, motion study, and functional specifications.

------

[2] The term objectives has as common synonyms such words as goals, ends, missions, projects, values, and tasks.

But function, in itself, even when defined as an act, can be confusing. Selling, for example, is often referred to as a function. On close inspection, it is found to consist of subfunctions, such as locating leads, delivering a sales talk, and closing the deal. Are these pure functions and the overall performance of selling a conglomeration of functions? Or how about the function of producing a wheel? Is it a function, or is making wheels a *combination* of the functions of making spokes, rims, and hubs? There is no absolute answer to these questions. Each business must construct its own classification of levels of, or classes of, functions, as will be suggested later in this section.

The foregoing does lead to the point that subfunctions or detailed functions must be arranged into orderly relationships if selling or producing are to attain their respective objectives. And such orderly arrangements are referred to as procedures. Or to reverse the starting point, procedures may be defined as orderly and logical arrangements of functions. Thus, an accounting procedure is an orderly arrangement for gathering, analyzing, classifying, interpreting, and presenting financial data on the operations and condition of a business enterprise.

2. Essential Features.   The desirable features of a good procedure of functions are: orderliness, adequate staffing, and appropriate implementation and environment.

a) Orderliness in Procedures.   Orderly and logical arrangements are an essential feature of any effective procedure. This means that each function of a procedure must be performed at the right time and right place in relation to any other function. Time and place are the important ingredients of orderliness.

In the matter of time, two questions must be answered to design an effective procedure. First, what functions must be performed one after another, that is, in sequence? Second, what functions must be performed at the same time, that is, concurrently? These are illustrated in Figure 11–1.

This figure shows that F_1 and F_2; F_3, F_4, and F_5; F_6 and F_7; and F_8, F_9, and F_{10} are performed concurrently and are referred to as steps 1, 2, 3, and 4, respectively. Then step 1 is shown as being followed in sequence by steps 2, 3, and 4. The result is the effective completion of the specific project "X."

It is also desirable to indicate how long each function should take in the execution of the procedure. In that event, a drawing such as that in Figure 11–2 would be useful.

FIGURE 11-1

$Step\ 1 \longrightarrow Step\ 2 \longrightarrow Step\ 3 \longrightarrow Step\ 4 \longrightarrow Objective\ ``X"$

	$\dfrac{F_3}{P}$	$\dfrac{F_6}{P}$	$\dfrac{F_8}{P}$	Project
	R	R	R	Completed
	$+$	$+$	$+$	on time
$\dfrac{F_1}{P}$	$\dfrac{F_4}{P}$	$\dfrac{F_7}{P}$	$\dfrac{F_9}{P}$	and
R	R	R	R	effectively
$+$	$+$		$+$	
$\dfrac{F_2}{P}$	$\dfrac{F_5}{P}$		$\dfrac{F_{10}}{P}$	
R	R		R	

F = Functions
P = Personnel
R = Implementation

This chart provides a picture, first, of concurrent and sequential relationships; second, of the time taken in each part of the procedure; and, third, of the time relationship among parts. As a result, the respective duties involved should be performed not only in the right order but also in the right time allowances.

But place as well as time must be provided for if an orderly procedure is to be designed. Ideally, each function should be placed in space adjacent to the one it succeeds, the one it precedes, and the ones with which it is performed concurrently. Assume, for example, that function No. 5 in project X is performed concurrently with F_4 and F_3, but after F_1 and F_2 and before F_6 and F_7. Then it should be physically located, as illustrated in Figure 11–3. In addition, the

FIGURE 11-2

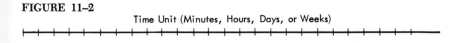
Time Unit (Minutes, Hours, Days, or Weeks)

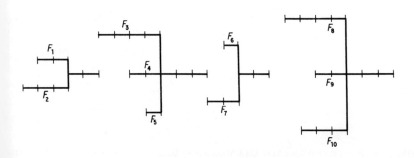

FIGURE 11–3

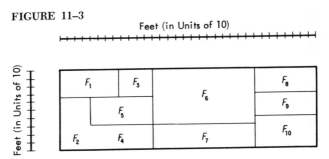

physical layout should provide a scaled measurement of the space required for each of the functions as illustrated in Figure 11–3.

This ideal arrangement will work out only if there is enough volume to utilize fully the space for each of these functions on project X. In actual practice, this works out in what is termed continuous manufacturing or process type industries.

An example of an automated process in manufacturing is illustrated in model form in Figure 11–4. In large-scale automobile manufacturing it is both desirable and feasible to arrange each function in its appropriate concurrent and sequential place physically. Thus,

FIGURE 11–4
A Model of an Automated Production Line

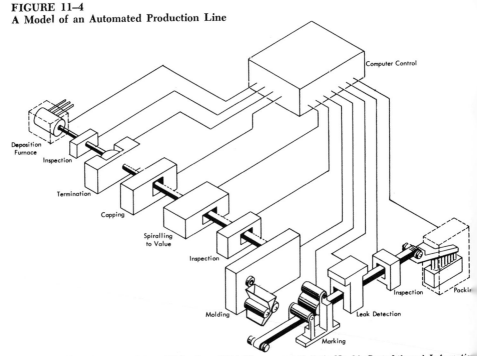

if an F_5 must be performed at the beginning of an assembly line and another F_5 must be performed at the end, space provisions for each will be provided at the beginning and end.

Very often, volume is not large enough to keep several locations of a function fully utilized. Or F_5, for example, may be performed not only on project X but also on projects Y and Z, but not always at the same time or in the same sequence in each of the projects. In such instances it would be uneconomical to provide separate and adjacent facilities for F_5. Instead, F_5 would be placed, not as shown in Figure 11-3, but in what would be the best location considering all the possible projects a company undertakes. Indeed, specific areas might be flexible enough to handle particular groups of functions, depending upon the projects that have to be worked on from time to time. Such an arrangement is common under conditions of intermittent manufacturing or job shop work and is illustrated in Figure 11-5.

FIGURE 11-5

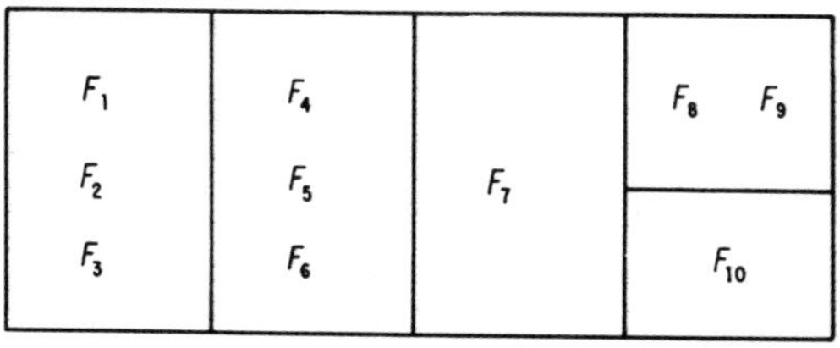

The determining factors in space arrangements are volume and standardization. If the volume of work on given projects is sufficient, then space can be allocated to each step of the procedure necessary to complete the given projects. It is standardized volume that makes possible straight-line operations, whether they be in the factory, office, or warehouse. When standardized volume is insufficient to keep a line fully occupied, then spatial arrangements of procedures must be based on similarity of equipment or machines rather than upon procedural flow. In the spatial arrangement based on equipment or machines, procedures are adjusted to the machines rather than the machines and space to the procedures.

b) Staffing of Procedures. Except in automation, functions and procedures are not self-effectuating. People are necessary to perform functions and to operate the procedures. The task of staffing procedures involves two major phases: first, determining how much staff is required; and, second, developing and maintaining an adequate staff.

Looking first at the matter of how much staff is required, the formula to solve the problem is simple to state, but its application is difficult. Staff needs can be calculated as follows:

$$\frac{\text{Minutes to Perform a Function} \times \text{Number of Repetitions}}{\text{Working Minutes/Day}}$$
$$= \text{Number of Workers for the Function}$$

If, for example, it takes three minutes to perform function No. 1 and function No. 1 is repeated 320 times, then in a given working day of eight hours, two workers will be needed, calculated as follows:

$$\frac{3 \times 320}{480} = \frac{960}{480} = 2$$

Calculating the time to perform a function or estimating the number of repetitions is far from simple. Anyone who has made time studies of factory or office operations knows how difficult it is to get agreement on time allowances. Or, anyone who has been responsible for determining how much distance along an assembly line given operators are to be responsible, knows how quickly the charge of "stretch out" is raised. And few executives are unaware of the difficulty of estimating the volume of work that can be expected in future weeks and months, let alone years. So the problem of calculating staff needs calls for a good deal of judgment, and often for juggling personnel from one procedure to another as demands in the various procedures change.

Staffing a procedure in terms of developing and maintaining an adequate labor force is largely a problem in personnel management. This deserves a much fuller treatment than can be undertaken here. It may be noted here, however, that a clear picture of functions and procedures stated in terms of job specifications is indispensable in hiring and training good people. A job specification can be useful in showing the skills, knowledge, and experience required to perform given functions. Candidates may then be selected who possess either the needed qualities or the potential to develop the needed qualities. Training can be made more effective because the difference between job needs and employee capacities can be more quickly ascertained.

c) *Appropriate Implementation and Environment.* If people are needed to perform functions, so are machines to make such performance more effective. Indeed, the trend is ever away from the human being to the machine as a performer. The human being increasingly becomes a machine tender, adjuster, and repairer. This is to be desired because a machine can do work faster, more accurately, and without tiring. When machines are devised—as is done in automation—which control working machines, man can be replaced and procedures made completely automatic.

How the problem of implementation is solved depends mainly upon the volume of repetitions of a given procedure and the comparative costs of various ways of doing the job. A simple calculation in the office, for example, can be done in the head of a clerk. An occasional, difficult calculation can be effectively done with pencil and paper. As the number of calculations increases, the same function may successively be implemented by a slide rule, machine calculator, tabulating equipment and, finally, electronic computers. After all, multiplying 5,280 by 35 can be done by an abacus or a computer, but each has a place that is most effective for it alone. They are not readily interchangeable. Hence, the executive must determine when an operation has reached a stage that warrants the investment in a more complex and costly machine which, however, reduces the unit cost of the job.

The emphasis on environment is recognition of the fact that the effectiveness of procedures depends in part upon the air, humidity, light, heat, noise, and vibrations that surround them. In some instances, these environmental factors are not too significant, or would be too costly to control, relative to the value that would be received. For example, a roof and four walls are enough for a steel mill. But in some food and pharmaceutical industries, environmental factors must be controlled to the closest of tolerances; and in office operations, it is being increasingly found that temperature control in summer as well as in winter is desirable if functions are to be performed as effectively as possible.

Building Procedures

This study of procedures can now be turned to the matter of how procedures are designed or built. Essentially two major steps are needed: first, finding out the functions that will be needed in a procedure; and, second, putting together the functions so discovered. The first step is known as functional analysis, and the second as functional differentiation.

1. *Functional Analysis.* Functional analysis is a process of

analyzing—a dividing up—of a whole into its parts. Its task is to determine the parts out of which a whole procedure is eventually to be constructed. It determines, for example, the specific functions that must be performed, let us say, to make a wheel or to sell a wheel. Its nature can be better seen by noting, first, the detail into which functions may be divided and, second, the methods by which it may be carried on.

a) Functional Details. Breaking up a functional whole can be carried to very elementary stages. To an outsider, making a wheel, for example, may consist simply of making hubs, spokes, and rims and then assembling the parts. But much, much more goes on than that. The part of making hubs will be broken down into such functions as rough-forming the hub, drilling the holes, finishing the forming, and painting. But drilling the holes, let us say, will be divided into such elements as pick up part, place in machine, operate machine, remove from machine, and inspect. These elements themselves, moreover, may be divided into still finer elements. The Gilbreths, for example, would have said that the elements just mentioned could be divided into basic motions called therbligs (Gilbreth spelled backwards), as follows:

1. Search.	10. Inspect.
2. Find.	11. Preposition.
3. Select.	12. Release load.
4. Group.	13. Transport empty.
5. Transport loaded.	14. Rest.
6. Position.	15. Unavoidable delay.
7. Assemble.	16. Avoidable delay.
8. Use.	17. Plan.
9. Disassemble.	18. Hold.

Perhaps these therbligs could be subdivided still further, but it is doubtful that this would serve any useful purpose. Indeed, for most business operations, therblig subdivisions would not be worth ascertaining. Some large subdivision will ordinarily suffice.

Functional analysis tends to bring out three types of functional details. First, in every procedure there are direct subfunctional or motion divisions. In the process of making a wheel, for example, there are steps of making hubs, spokes, and rims, which can be subdivided if desired into therbligs. Second, there impinge externally upon every procedure various assisting functions. Thus, wheels must be transported and inspected, and information about the operations communicated to various persons and properly recorded. And, third, every procedure is subject to managerial functions. Thus, the work of wheel makers and those who assist them must be planned, organized, directed, and controlled.

b) Methods of Functional Analysis. A variety of methods is available by which to analyze procedures into their functional elements. Perhaps the simplest is introspection. When a job has to be done—to make a wheel, let us say—one reviews in his mind the various functions that will have to be performed. While simplicity itself, this method of functional analysis has serious shortcomings. It is easy to overlook or completely forget some functions. In addition, from time to time as similar jobs come in, the same set of functions is not arrived at in setting up job orders. As a consequence, either the wheels do not look alike or more time and energy are required to make them look alike. When particular jobs are simple or infrequently repeated, this method of analysis is satisfactory.

Somewhat similar to introspection, is that of referring to records showing what was done on past jobs. Then, as similar requests are received, it is a simple matter to refer to the files and copy down the listing of functions from the appropriate historical record. This system of functional analysis has long been a favorite in many factories. When past orders have been effectively accomplished, this system is commendable. But when past orders have been set up on the basis of what workers or management just thought "out of their heads" was a good plan, it is more than likely that past mistakes are merely being repeated.

A more logical plan of functional analysis is to utilize a trained analyst to observe work situations and record his findings for further study. On a work sheet, the analyst notes the various activities that he sees the person performing, whether he be a factory hand, office worker, or a member of management.[3] For example, the study chart

---

[3] C. L. Shartle, *Executive Performance and Leadership* (Englewood Cliffs, N.J.: Prentice-Hall, Inc.), p. 86.

A listing of the work patterns found useful in analyzing the work of executives is shown as follows:

1. Inspection.	8. Supervision of technical operations.
2. Investigation and research.	9. Personal activities.
3. Planning.	10. Public relations.
4. Preparing procedures.	11. Professional consultation.
5. Coordination.	12. Negotiations.
6. Evaluation.	13. Scheduling, routing, and dispatching.
7. Interpretation of plans and procedures.	14. Technical and professional operations.

of a given factory operation showed the elements performed, time taken, tools used, and which hand did the work. This is illustrated in Figure 11–6.

FIGURE 11–6

Element	Time	Left Hand	Right Hand	Tool
Pick up piece	04	...	X	
Place in fixture	03	X	X	
Tighten fixture	08	X	X	Hammer
Operate machine	70	...	X	
Loosen fixture	04	X	X	Hammer
Remove piece	03	X	...	
Set piece in box	03	X	...	

This type of plan is much more accurate than the others mentioned thus far but, of course, it is more costly and time-consuming.

Even more accurate, but requiring more skill and cost, is the micromotion plan of functional analysis. This involves the use of the movie technique of recording the movements of an operator in performing a job. After recording, the picture is viewed over and over again until the analyst can summarize on paper what has actually transpired. Revisions of the present method are then devised by comparing the method used with principles of motion previously derived. Anyone who has used this method is thoroughly convinced that the development of effective procedures cannot be left to operators themselves. But it is also obvious that the cost of this method precludes its usage for anything but situations in which savings are likely to be correspondingly high.

2. Functional Differentiation. The various functions found by means of functional analysis are then arranged into orderly procedures by the process of functional differentiation. To see how this is done, attention is directed, first, to tests of orderliness and, second, to common types of orderly groupings.

a) Test of Orderliness. The ultimate test of orderliness is, of course, the effectiveness with which a given procedure attains objectives, economically and effectively. But how does one go about building a procedure that will meet this ultimate test? In general, it will be found that the answer lies in giving attention to time of performance, place of performance, and similarity of functions. These have been discussed earlier in this chapter so reference to that discussion is advised.

Arrangement of procedures is basically some compromise of time, space, and similarity. The compromise is determined by cost and results. Which arrangement will give the required results in the shortest time and at the lowest cost? The volume of work to be done and the degree to which particular repetitions can be standardized will be important factors in determining the arrangements to be adopted.

b) Common Types of Orderly Groupings. It is desirable at this point to describe briefly some of the common types of procedures. In general, procedures may be classed as managerial or operative.

Managerial procedures can be grouped in a variety of ways. For present purposes, they are reviewed in terms of basic managerial functions, line and staff relationship, and organizational levels.

In examining managerial procedures, it is wise to start with the systems used to perform the basic functions of planning, organizing, directing, and controlling. Each executive should outline the steps he takes in performing these basic functions. Through what stages does the sales manager go in planning a future sales campaign, in planning how his salesmen are to be trained, or in planning an evaluation program for efforts of salesmen? Through what stages does the accountant go in organizing his department, the chief engineer in directing his technicians, or the personnel manager in evaluating his personnel programs? Such surveys would go far in deriving better managerial procedures, eliminating duplications, and filling any gaps.

Another phase of managerial procedures is that pertaining to line and staff relationships. This is indeed a difficult as well as controversial area of procedural design. Assume for the moment a president who has been doing his own planning, organizing, directing, and controlling, but now appoints an assistant to help him in his duties. Two important questions must be carefully answered. First, which of his procedures should be assigned to his assistant; and, second, how should his subordinate vice presidents be routed through his administrative assistant? Unless these questions are carefully delineated in procedural instructions, the vice presidents as well as the administrative assistant may get wrong impressions of their status and roles.

Similar difficulties can be readily cited in the case of such a staff department as personnel. It is one thing to establish a personnel department and to state it is a staff unit intended to serve other departments. On the other hand, this statement is absolutely inadequate in indicating who does what, say, when hiring an accountant. Through what steps is an applicant selected, and who is responsible for each step? Obviously, this is a procedural matter, which can scarcely be settled by an organization chart.

Procedural relationships between line and staff must always be devised whenever decentralized operations are involved. At one time, this seemed to be resolved in most companies by making each branch plant or office a more-or-less independent operating unit except for essential financial reports. With the development of electronic computers and common language communication devices, however, the trend has been back to the centralized home plant or office as the record keeper and procedural operator for the branch plants. Hence, the problem of how procedures should be established between home and branch units is a dynamic one that usually goes through a number of stages as a company grows, expands, and becomes more complicated to the point that investments are warranted in sophisticated, high-speed, data processing equipment.

Managerial procedures must also be devised by which work flows between levels of an organization structure are effectuated. It is not enough to say that a given vice president has authority over a certain number of managers, or that a particular supervisor is responsible to a specific superintendent. Much more important in a practical, working-day sense are the procedures by which a superior reaches his subordinates and the subordinates reach their respective superiors. A case in point is communications. One reason that industry generally has done a poor job of communicating is that communications have been covered as an organization assignment. But few have worked out definite procedures for communications on different subjects, so that each executive knows what he must specifically do in working with subordinate levels, and each subordinate knows his procedural rights and responsibilities upward.

Operative procedures can be grouped in a number of ways. Perhaps the most common division is in accordance with the basic functions of a business. Thus, it is common to find production, sales, financial, accounting, engineering, and personnel procedures. As a company grows, or because products are particularly significant, production procedures may be classified—as in the case of meat packing—into pork, beef, mutton, and by-product procedures. Again, even these may be divided into regional procedures if several plants or distribution units are established in widely separated areas. Sometimes procedures are built around essential machine operations or processes. In the metal-trades industry, for example, it is not uncommon to find a foundry, rough machinery, finishing machinery, and assembly department.

In establishing operative procedures, there is also the question of the hierarchy of procedures. Should major procedures be on the functional basis with subprocedures in the declining order of products, geographical area, and then processes? Or should the major procedures be in product or geographical areas, with subprocedures put on a machinery and process basis? Usually the answer depends upon which of the bases is most significant in terms of complexity, skills required for their performance, investments required, service to consumers, or effect upon business success. No single answer serves all companies equally well.

A Systems Approach to Procedure Building

From what has been said thus far about procedures, it is apparent that building a procedure involves concern for a number of interacting factors. In small, stable, and low investment businesses, it is possible to deal with procedures in an informal, casual manner. But as companies have grown in size and as investments in procedural technology have sky-rocketed, procedural management has gained high recognition, new stature, and even a new name, that of management and business systems.

This development recognizes that all of the elements involved in the operation of a business must be carefully planned into a unified, integrated system. The various procedures, subprocedures, and sub-subprocedures must be interlocked with due recognition for the interaction of all these parts. Thus, to make wheels, for example, calls for a wheel-making procedure, to be sure, but how does this tie in with procedures for making sales forecasts for wheels, inventory controls for wheel components, billing of wheel customers, hiring and training employees to make wheels, calculating payrolls for these employees, compiling various executive and control reports on wheels, and so forth.

It is not possible here in a page or two to design such a system any more than it is possible in an engineering text to show all of the designs, let us say, for a Golden Gate Bridge. But it is possible and desirable here to illustrate such a design in model form and to make a few comments about a particular design. In Figure 11–7 there is shown a model of a system of management planning and

FIGURE 11–7
Model of a System of Management Planning and Control

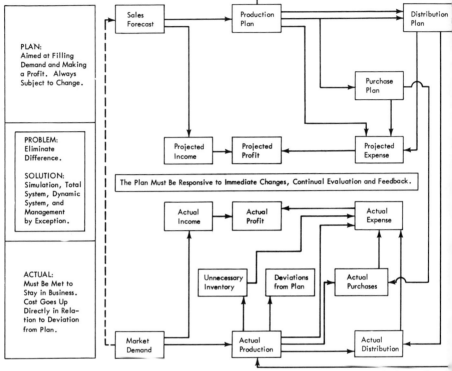

Reprinted by permission of the publisher from AMA Management Bulletin No. 36, *Case Studies in Compu* *Based Management*, © 1966 by the American Management Association, Inc.

control. Here it is seen that the first task of management in undertaking a project is to simulate how a job is to be done and what can be expected in the way of results. At this stage, planning should work out ways and means so that projected income and profits are attainable. Then management must follow through on actual surveillance of production, sales, inventories, purchases, expense control, and various deviations that arise from plans. The feedback from activities and results should provide a basis for taking whatever corrective action is deemed desirable.

Factors of Procedural Design

It is now desirable to describe and comment upon a number of factors which are particularly significant in the design of procedures. These factors may be grouped under the headings of, first, the importance of logical thinking; second, the need for full procedural coverage; and, third, identification of certain desirable features that procedures should have.

1. Logical Thinking. From what has been said thus far, it should be apparent that procedural design is neither easy nor something that can be left to amateurs. To be sure, it is easy to leave this task to amateurs, but the results of this practice are seldom very happy. Note what happens when one learns how to play golf or tennis by himself. The swing that one develops by himself is usually so poor, as evidenced by his scores, that the player eventually turns to an expert for help. The "pro" studies the player's form, shakes his head, and prescribes a new set of swings.

The amateur is unhappy with his old swing but no happier with the new. It takes time to learn the new habits, and during much of that time the scores may be worse than they were under the old method. He can scarcely believe that the new method is superior. But if he sticks with his lessons, his score improves, and so does his appreciation of the new procedures; and he rues the day that he undertook to teach himself. He champions the "old pro" system of learning to all who will listen.

Yet, in business we often continue to follow the "learn it yourself" principle. This is in spite of what is apparent to anyone who has participated in sports (and what executive hasn't?), and what Frederick Taylor preached over 60 years ago when he advocated eloquently the separation of planning from performance. Taylor, through his various experiments in procedural design, and the Gilbreths, through their micromotion developments, proved that an expert can devise procedures that far surpass those devised by workers themselves. But these logical and "scientific" methods involve time and painstaking efforts. Most executives seem to be unwilling to make these investments, or they are perhaps hopeful that by some miracle their procedural needs will be answered.

This advocacy of professional design of procedures does not mean that suggestions should not be sought from operatives. On the contrary, a good suggestion plan is an excellent way of getting ideas on how to improve existing procedures. Nevertheless, the main vehicle of developing procedures should be managers themselves and staff specialists appointed for that purpose.

Logic demands, too, that executives realize that organization structure is not a substitute for procedures. Work is done through procedures, not organization structures. Yet, some companies make a fetish out of the design of organization structure and do little or nothing about scientific procedural design. Then they wonder why results are poor, and can think of nothing else to do than to redesign the organization structure. If ever a choice has to be made, concentrate on procedural design. Of course, a choice does not have to be made. But it is nevertheless wise to emphasize procedures, and then one will be surprised how organizational difficulties seem to disappear.

2. *Procedural Coverage.* It is also important in the design of procedures to be sure that all needed procedures are provided. This can be accomplished through a plan of procedural control and by devising and suggested list of procedures.

There are companies that have established departments of procedural and system design. It is their purpose either to design procedures, or to assist various executives in the process of designing their own procedures. It is, thereby, possible to be assured of having better and more complete coverage when some one unit takes a primary interest in procedures. On the other hand, when procedures are everybody's business, and a secondary interest at that, it is a good idea to call in an outside consulting agency to audit procedures and to make suggestions on changes or additions.

A review of procedures can also be accomplished if a check list is prepared. Such a list could cover the work done in various areas and on various subjects. From what has been said before, such a list could be based on such a classification as follows:

1. Managerial areas.
   a) Functional work of planning, organizing, directing, and controlling.
   b) Line and staff responsibilities.
   c) Work of the several organization levels.
   d) Work of centralized and decentralized units.
2. Operative areas.
   a) Functional fields of production, sales, finance, engineering, etc.
   b) Product divisions.
   c) Process divisions.
   d) Machinery and equipment divisions.
   e) Geographical divisions.

Of course, these would be expanded to show considerable detail under each. For example, if a company produced a hundred different products, the product class would carry the hundred names. Someone should check to see that adequate procedures are outlined for each of the products so itemized. Indeed, a check should be made to see that for each part that goes into each and every product there is a suitable and effective procedure. All of this, to repeat, takes time, but there is no shortcut to the design of effective procedures.

3. Desirable Features. This chapter can perhaps be summed up in no better way than by taking up the question of how one can know whether his procedures are "good." In part, the answer is simple—a procedure is good when it serves to attain desired objectives, economically and effectively. A sales procedure is good when goods are sold in adequate volume and at relatively low cost or an engineering procedure is good when product and process designs are laid out, economically and effectively.

But certain tests can be applied without always waiting to see how a procedure actually works out. For one thing, a procedure should be relatively stable. It should not be changed so often that various participants are not sure of what the procedure is.

Change, however, is an inevitable characteristic of all life, including that of business. Hence, provision should be made in a procedure for changes due to increases or decreases in volume, improved materials and machines, and new ways of doing things. Provision for short-run volume changes may call for a complete revamping of procedures. Such complete changes may also be necessitated by new developments in machines or methods. The process of change can be made orderly in advance by requiring that all procedures be put down in the form of writing and that changes of such specifications are to be made only through approved procedures of change.

Procedures should also meet the tests of balance and relatedness. On the one hand, each step in a procedure should be provided with adequate manpower and technical resources. As suggested earlier, the amount of personnel, space, and equipment should be calculated, so that the correct amounts can be calculated for each step. In this way, no step will be over- or undersupplied. On the other hand, each step should be correctly related to all others in terms of time and space. As mentioned earlier, it is also important to check that the steps of a procedure are performed in proper geographical relation to one another.

Standards of performance and control should be established for each step in a procedure. How much is expected from each step, the quality thereof, and upon whom responsibility is to be placed should be carefully determined and spelled out. It is a frustrating experience to be a part of a procedure for which such standards have not been specified. One never knows for what he is really responsible, so he seeks in advance to insulate himself from possible blame. Effort that should be expended on operating a procedure is expended instead upon building up excuses and defenses.

A good procedure is also properly tied into the organization structure. No matter through what or how many organizational units a procedure may run, there is a minimum of misunderstanding among the various organization units regarding their respective results. This test can be met by superimposing a given procedure upon the organization chart. The dual chart can then be reviewed to see if there are any disagreements over respective responsibilities and jurisdictions. In other words, the procedures are thereby tested before they are put into effect, and not afterward, with the inevitable bickering, evasions, and alibis.

Finally, a procedure must be known, understood, and accepted if it is to be termed good. Obvious though this may seem, these standards are not always met. It seems to many executives that procedures will make themselves known and understood just because they developed them. Far from it. Steps must be taken at least to see that each person involved in a procedure knows what he is supposed to do. Better still, he should be given the opportunity to understand that his share in the procedure is significant and worthwhile. His acceptance of the procedure will thereby serve to increase his willingness to participate in it.

QUESTIONS

1. What is the relationship among objectives, functions, and procedures?
2. What features must be built into a procedure if it is to be termed orderly?
3. What factors or conditions determine the space arrangements of a procedure in the floor plan of a company?
4. How does one go about calculating how many people are needed to staff a procedure?
5. What is the relationship between functional analysis and functional differentiation in the building of procedures?
6. How does logical thinking contribute to the building of procedures?

7. Into what classes or groups may procedures at the managerial level be divided?

8. What features must be built into a procedure if the procedure is to be considered a good one?

CASE 11–1

In the machine shop of the Makall Company, there was a time when a separate grinder operator was needed for each grinder. Subsequently, though, by devising a certain type of control device for the machines, engineering made it possible for the machine to continue to grind automatically with little or no attention from the operator after a part was positioned in the machine. As a consequence, management decided to have one operator run two machines. While one machine was functioning, the operator would move over to the second and get it operating properly. Then he would alternate between the two; making adjustments, taking out parts, inserting new ones, and making necessary inspections as required. This practice neither overburdened the operator nor resulted in a decline in quality or quantity of output. Indeed, efficiency and incentive pay rose correspondingly.

After conducting time and motion studies as well as installing a new control device, it was further determined that one operator could efficiently run three machines. So this arrangement was established.

Again after some more automatic refinements, it was concluded that one operator could effectively run six machines. But in order to make the adjustment more smoothly, it was decided to change over to a four-machine arrangement first, and then step up one by one to the six-machine arrangement.

When the employees heard about this plan, they were vehement in their opposition. They claimed it would be too unsafe, too full of nervous tension for the operator, and an unfair infringement of their job security.

1. What factors determine the efficiency of a procedure?

2. What are the limiting factors on how much technical equipment can be loaded onto an employee?

CASE 11–2

A careful program of functional analysis has disclosed that research is performed in every division of a given company at present.

There is research of some kind in the manufacturing division, research in the personnel division, commercial research in the marketing division, research in the controller's division, research in the engineering division, and a top-level research and development division.

When this information was reported at a meeting of the executive committee, the controller expressed the opinion that it might well be desirable to bring all these research units together in one research unit. He felt this would bring about the same results that were achieved when the once-decentralized stenographers were brought together into a centralized stenographic pool.

He had no sooner concluded his statement when several dissenting voices were arguing that research was different and should be intimately attached to the major divisions served. The only one who came to the support of the controller was the director of research and development who thought that all research needed expert, sophisticated direction and encouragement—meaning his.

1. Upon what are the various arguments for functional differentiation in this case being based?
2. What base seems most applicable in this case?

12

Organization Structure

Scope of Discussion

Organizing was defined previously as a major function of management. It has to do with providing appropriate organization structures, procedures and systems, personnel, and material and technical resources. In this chapter, concern is with the topic of organization structure which is discussed under the following headings:

1. Nature and purpose of organization structure.
2. Types of organization structure.
3. Departmentation.
4. Organization levels and span of control.
5. Factors in structural design.
6. Control of organization structure.
7. Newer concepts in organization structure.

Nature and Purpose of Organization Structure

An organization—any organization—essentially is a group of people working together with a view to attaining desired objectives. Unfortunately, in the case of human beings, this "working together" does not automatically take place. Instead, it is necessary to provide some mechanisms of coordination and control.

One of these mechanisms is the organization structure. It shows who in an organization has authority over whom and, conversely, who is responsible to whom. It provides an invisible framework that serves to unify all of the people in working together toward

215

common goals. It provides also for executive control of the various units in the organization. And it is a vehicle for exercising leadership.

The framework of an organization structure is not an inert, static arrangement. Rather, it delineates the working relationship between the various team members and organizational units. Moreover, the lines of authority and responsibility from higher and lower levels and between units at the same level constitute lines of communication. These communication lines are, in a sense, channels of information flows which, both horizontally and vertically, insure a dynamic interaction among all the members.

Organization structure provides, therefore, an indispensable tool of coordination in human organizations. Some animal societies— bees and ants, for example—get along without such structures. But human beings need a structure to insure coordination. Thus, the structure of authority-responsibility relationships of work, decisions, and of flows of communication is a necessary coordinating device for organized human groups.

Types of Organization Structure

Organization structures may be either informal or formal. The informal refers to relationships which exist between people and organization units but are not slated, charted, or defined in any company document. Incidentally, this type will be discussed at length in Chapter 15.

The formal structure refers to the relationships which have been designated by some definite document of the company, usually an organization chart or organization manual. The various types of formal structure have been described in Chapter 6, so it is necessary here only to briefly review the characteristics of the three most common types: the line, the functional, and the line and staff.

1. *Line Organization.* Each executive in a line organization has a comprehensive responsibility and authority concerning all activities directly or indirectly related to his primary area. Authority extends in a direct line from supervisor to subordinate down to the operating level, with each executive having jurisdiction over, and responsibility for, performance of all activities necessary to his primary function (authority and responsibility are discussed in depth in Chapter 13). One result of this is that there is little or no specialization in such organization. Single accountability exists;

that is, a subordinate reports to only one boss with a direct line of command between them. Figure 12–1 illustrates a simple line structure.

FIGURE 12–1
Line Organization

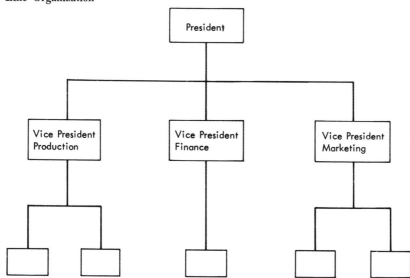

The line organization is therefore simple to understand and to operate. Since a line executive has no other person to consult except his own supervisor, decisions can be made with a minimum of delay. By the same token, evasion of responsibility, or "buck-passing," is minimized. Such direct and undiluted authority insures managerial flexibility and quick decision making.

But the line structure has a serious weakness. It lacks specialized leadership. And if a company is to grow and subsequently accomplish all its many and complex activities, then specialized leadership is a definite requirement.

2. Functional Organization. Specialization of leadership was designed at its highest level by Frederick W. Taylor in the early days of "scientific management." In his functional organization he proposed that specialized functional foremen, eight in number, be placed over each worker. In that way, each worker would get expert attention for the particular parts of his job. The diagram in Figure 12–2 shows, partially, a functional type of organization structure.

The functional form has both advantages and disadvantages. Ob-

FIGURE 12–2
Functional Organization

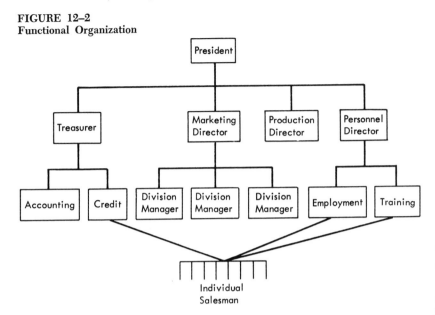

viously specialized leadership is its overriding advantage. On the other hand, it results in dual accountability in that a person reports to more than one superior. Theoretically, he reports to different superiors for different purposes, but in practice, too often he is not certain to whom he reports and for what purpose. The result is organizational confusion.

Hence, the major contribution of the functional form is to help understand better and operate more effectively the line and staff type.

3. *Line and Staff Organization.* The line and staff type of organization represents a favorable combination of the line and functional types of organization. Single accountability, so basic to sound vertical relationships, is preserved, since there is only one boss to whom any individual is directly responsible. Specialized staff advice and assistance are, nonetheless, available to any unit of the organization requiring them. Figure 12–3 is a typical example.

In this type of organization the service of the functional specialist can be developed to a fine degree. Yet, the advantage of single accountability is maintained. Maximum effectiveness of effort is made possible because every individual takes orders from and reports to only one boss. A corollary of this is that "passing the buck" is made difficult since the scope of one's responsibilities can be more

FIGURE 12-3
Organization with Line and Staff Relationships

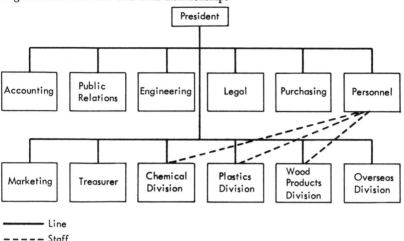

—————— Line

— — — — Staff

clearly defined. Another advantage is this—line executives are allowed to devote more of their time to their own specialty, that of
securing effective performance of their primary function.

The possible disadvantages of the line and staff form are twofold.
Staff units may attempt to usurp line authority, and line units may
fail to take advantage of staff services. But these are human failings
and not an inherent weakness of the line and staff form as such.

Departmentation

As soon as two or more individuals are engaged in an enterprise, some division of the work becomes necessary. Since the
organization is the mechanism set up to carry out the work, any
work to be done should be arranged in the most logical and effective manner. The division of the work in an organization into the
most logical units is called departmentation. Departmentation is a
basic element in the organizing process and as such is essential
to effective relationships between superior and subordinate. Departmentation is arrived at through functional analyses and functional differentiation.

Functional analysis is the examination of the objectives of the
organization as a whole and for each unit, and of the work to be
done in order to achieve such objectives. It consists of breaking
down the duties of each job and examining each duty to determine

its relationship to other duties, its relevance to the organizational unit, and the requirements for its performance.

Functional differentiation consists of grouping in an orderly pattern the activities that have been analyzed. They are grouped to facilitate their execution. In arranging these duties, management must give real consideration to the position in which these duties can best be performed, and to the proper sequence of their performance as well.[1]

Departmentation, then, classifies and groups the work to be done into manageable units. There are essentially five bases for grouping, with a sixth basis being some combination of the first five:

1. Functions.   4. Geography.
2. Product.   5. Customer.
3. Processes or equipment.   6. Combinations of above.

1. *Departmentation by Functions.* Similarity of functions is the most frequently used basis for departmentizing. Functions that are alike are grouped into individual organization units. Thus, it would be logical to group all sales activities together, even though selling might be concerned with different products, customers, and territories. Such classification and arrangement take advantage of specialization. It is true that sales activities may later be grouped further on additional bases as the entire sales function expands and the need for specialization of sales according to customer or product develops. Primarily, however, many activities are departmentized by function.

2. *Departmentation by Product.* Another common base of departmentation is to group functions pertaining to specific products in a company. An example is the division of operations of a meat-packing company into such major units as beef, pork, and lamb products. Some automobile firms departmentize major divisions on the basis of make of automobiles, such as Plymouth, Dodge, Chrysler, and Imperial. A rubber company may classify its major units into rubber products (such as footwear and rubberized

---

[1] Functional arrangement as described here is sometimes criticized by students of organization on the ground that the definition of jobs and departments creates a structure which discourages coordination among functions. Those within a functional unit, it is contended, become so preoccupied with effective performance in their unit that they fail to see their role in and relationship to other units and to the whole organization. Sound procedures, however, should effectively integrate the various functions into a total balanced and coordinated system, with each function making its specialized contribution to the objectives of the firm.

fabrics) and plastics. Concentration of all efforts peculiar to a particular product or service is thus made practical (Figure 12–4).

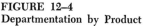

FIGURE 12–4
Departmentation by Product

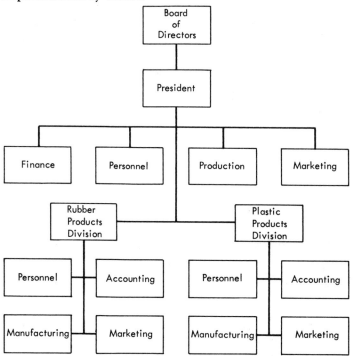

Departmentation by product not only permits the maximum use of managerial expertise and specialized knowledge but also permits the exaction of profit responsibility from the product department managers. This is a natural consequence since under departmentation by product, all activities necessary to both the production and distribution of goods and services are combined within the same organizational subdivision of the firm.

3. *Departmentation by Processes or Equipment.* This type of departmentation is often employed to permit certain economic advantages resulting from bringing manpower and materials together to carry out a particular operation that is part of a process. Activities may be arranged logically on the basis of processes or equipment employed. The two are grouped together because, for all practical purposes, similarity of equipment will involve similarity of processes—the two being quite interrelated. For example, an oil re-

finery operation requires the effective combination of equipment and technological processes. Process departmentation is also evident in the steel industry where companies are organized by discovery, extraction, processing, fabricating, and distribution groups.

4. *Geographical Departmentation.* Many firms use this type when its operations are physically dispersed in different locations (Figure 12-5). Thus a firm may divide its sales operations into the

FIGURE 12-5
Geographical Departmentation

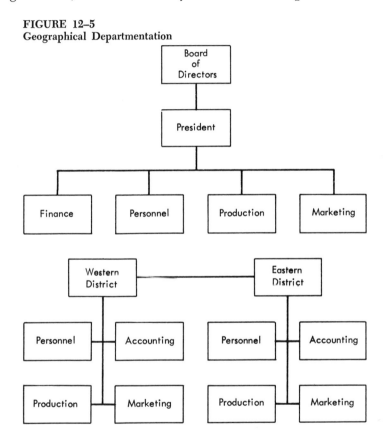

eastern, western, and southern divisions. A baking company may divide the work of its delivery men on the basis of geographical areas of the city or county. Officers of a police force may be assigned to patrol certain sections of the city. Note that in these instances the work may have been, and usually is, first differentiated on a functional similarity basis (sales, delivery, patrol).

5. *Departmentation by Type of Customer.* Here the type of customer is central to the manner in which activities are grouped.

For example, a firm may departmentize its sales activities into retail, wholesale, and institutional selling units. A bank may divide its loan function into such categories as commercial loan, mortgage loan, and personal loan departments. The personal loan department may be further subdivided into consumer loan, personal loan, and auto loan sections.

6. Combination Departmentation. As has perhaps already been evident from the above discussion, numerous firms have differentiated their work on a combination of bases. Thus, in the two examples of departmentation according to type of customer cited earlier, major units had first been formed on the basis of similarity of activities (sales and loans). On the other hand, a very large concern may even departmentize some of its activities on a geographical basis before going on to make further breakdowns among sales and production activities. This is true of foreign subsidiaries, particularly.

It should be remembered that as a phase of organizing, the end result of departmentation should be suitable conditions for effective performance. Adhering to one basis for departmentizing would, in the case of most large concerns (and many medium and small ones as well), create a stilted and ponderous mechanism, indeed. The test is whether the functional differentiation is the most effective and economical, relative to the goals to be achieved.

Organizational Levels and Span of Control

When the manager of a unit assigns some of his managerial duties and authority to a lower level unit, another level in the organization comes into existence. Obviously, where a manager has a large number of varied managerial activities to perform, such development of organizational levels tends to proceed at a more rapid pace. Figure 12–6 illustrates this development or devolution from the earliest stage of organization to a theoretical line organization of some size.

The number of organizational levels is closely related to the number of individuals, managerial or operative, which executives are capable of supervising, that is, their respective span of control. This is discussed now in terms of (1) the concept of span of control, (2) the Graicunas theory, (3) the problems of a narrow span of control, and (4) the narrow versus a wider span of control.

1. The Concept of Span of Control. Span of control refers to the number of individuals an executive can personally supervise with effectiveness. The number varies between operative employees

FIGURE 12–6
Devolution of Line Organization

Early Stage

Middle Stage

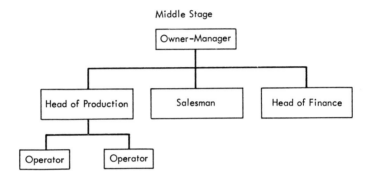

Advanced Stage

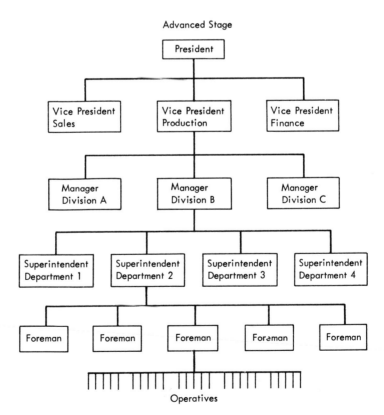

and managerial employees. As a rule of thumb, a span of 10 to 30 is generally indicated for operative and from 3 to 8 for managerial employees. This is true because of the nature of the work involved. In operative jobs the employees are usually trained to perform their activities in a set way. Once they attain proficiency, their work requires control of a somewhat routine nature. Contacts necessary in performance of their jobs are usually simple in nature and made briefly and directly with their supervisor. When interpersonal contacts are made at the operative level, they do not normally require frequent coordination by the supervisor but are usually routinized by procedure.

The administrative activities of managers above the first level of supervision are more complex; the effective span tends to be limited to fewer subordinates. Complexity of executive duties tends to increase as one moves higher in the organization.

At upper managerial levels span tends to be much less extensive. Managerial work is less standardized and involves much decision making. The managerial functions must be supervised and integrated with activities of other subordinate executives. Supervision and coordination of all executives on the same level in a division require frequent personal contacts, both between superior and subordinate and, often, among subordinates. Thus, a superior must devote proportionately more of his time to each of his subordinate executives than must a first-line supervisor to each of his operative subordinates.

2. Graicunas Theory. This fact of organization led to the Graicunas theory regarding the span of control.[2] This theory states that as the number of subordinate executives is increased arithmetically, the resulting relationships among executives tend to increase geometrically. The theoretical increase in relationships is illustrated in Table 12–1.

Thus, it is seen that if a supervisor who has seven subordinates adds one more subordinate, the number increase is one but the number of relationships that are added is 570. Obviously, this means a very large increase in responsibilities which, if not now, will shortly become impossible for the superior to handle.

3. Problems Involved in Narrow Span of Control. But keeping a narrow span of control means that more levels must be added

---

[2] V. A. Graicunas, "Relationship in Organization," in L. Gulick and L. Urwick (eds.), *Papers on the Science of Administration* (New York: Columbia University, 1937).

TABLE 12–1
Total Possible Number of Relationships
with Increasing Number of Subordinates

Number of Subordinates	Number of Possible Relationships
3	18
4	44
5	100
6	222
7	490
8	1,080

to an organization as it grows. This increases such managerial problems as: (1) layering, (2) difficulty of communicating accurately, (3) supervisory expense, and (4) unfavorable effect on morale.

Layering refers to inflexibility in performing managerial duties brought on by numerous organizational levels. Cross contacts between individuals in different units must be routed through the formal chain of command as shown in Figure 12–7. A bridge of

FIGURE 12–7
Effect of Layering in Communications

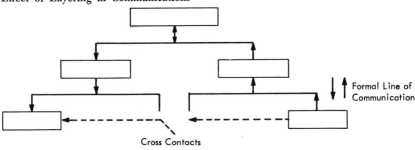

communication as indicated by the dotted line cannot be established, and all contacts must be made by way of all levels in the pyramid. Decisions will take longer to make, since information and coordination will be secured less expeditiously.

Layering is sometimes insisted upon in order to assure that the superior executive is kept informed of activities conducted below, as a control measure. However, when action at lower levels does not actually require the superior's advice or other participation, he can be kept informed by the subordinate of action taken, without actually becoming a link in the chain of communication.

Increasing the number of echelons in the firm lengthens the channel of communication. The more positions a communication must pass through, the greater the possibility that information may become distorted. Thus the danger that communications do not remain clear and understandable, and are not transmitted with a minimum of delay, is increased.

Supervisory expense may be increased because more levels of supervision are added with a narrow span of control. For example, if a span of 5 were maintained consistently throughout an organization comprising 6 levels, the number of managers would be significantly more than if the span were increased to 10 and the levels reduced accordingly.

It is said that when an executive administers through a narrow span of control, morale is often affected unfavorably. To the extent that layering and faulty communications develop, however, and possibly narrowness of promotion channels, there is danger of lower morale. In the next section we shall examine the hypothesis that morale is improved in a wide span.

4. Narrow versus Wide Span of Control. In recent years, questions have been raised by both the management theorist and the practitioner about the traditional views on span of control. These views generally hold that a span of three to eight or nine[3] subordinates is unrealistic. In practice, executives frequently exercise a larger span of control without difficulty. Some executives can supervise more than others, and the conditions under which they manage are different. Furthermore, a wide span of control permits decreasing the levels in the organization thus minimizing the problems resulting from numerous levels discussed above.

The desirability of minimizing levels cannot be denied. The span of control cannot, however, be widened indiscriminately. When a large number of subordinates are supervised by an executive, communication and coordination problems may develop. Although delays due to layering may not be present, problems within a unit may be increased.

Under what conditions, then, can widening the span of control be considered? When the subordinate executives are engaged in specialized and independent functions, a wider span is possible.

---

[3] The range of three to eight or nine subordinates has often been cited as representing generally the most effective span. Usually such citations recognize the possibility of exceptions. See, for example, R. C. Davis, *The Fundamentals of Top Management* (New York: Harper & Bros., 1951), p. 276.

An illustration of these two sets of conditions is shown in Figures 12–8 and 12–9.

FIGURE 12–8
Span of Control with Interdependent Subordinates

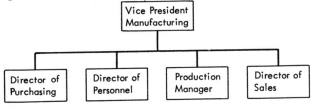

FIGURE 12–9
Span of Control with Relatively Independent Subordinates

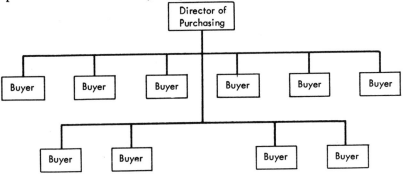

In Figure 12–8, the four directors must contact one another as well as the common superior frequently. In Figure 12–9, each buyer is a specialist in his particular field. Not only may contacts among buyers be infrequent, but contacts between individual buyers and the director of purchases may not occur often.

A number of other factors also determine the practical span of control. An executive who must himself perform certain duties such as public relations will have little time left for supervising immediate subordinates. His personal skill, knowledge, adaptability, and even physical fitness will figure in the number he can successfully manage. The rate of growth of an organization will also be a determinant, since rapidly changing business situations will influence the executive span. Then too, the extent to which an organization remains stable will decidedly influence the width of span.

Where subordinates are capable of exercising individual discretion and decision-making authority, and where the policy is one of considerable delegation of authority, a wider span of control is feasible. In certain instances, some of the duties of an executive can be assumed by an assistant or an "assistant to." With his assistant acting as a personal staff or aide, the executive has more released time and can devote more attention to subordinate unit executives, thus increasing his span of control.

Factors in Structural Design

The factors that determine the type and form of organization structure were discussed in Chapter 6, Organizing. Their significance is therefore recognized in brief review here. Such factors were the objectives of the enterprise, attitude and philosophy of top management, available personnel, size and location, and desirable characteristics of a structure.

Objectives, in stating the purpose of the enterprise, give an indication of what should be accomplished, which immediately suggests the question of how it should be accomplished. Thus, the organizational mechanism to be used must be decided upon, including the authority, responsibility, and communications relationships. The attitude and philosophy of top management will always be a motivating or a limiting factor in how the structure for carrying out the organization's work is built. Some adjustment to available personnel is always necessary. The size and location will be an influence in the development of an organization, also. More complex administrative problems, which invariably accompany growth and widespread location, must be met by structural design. Characteristics of a sound organization are always determining factors in that they serve as guides in the organizing process and also as criteria by which to judge the effectiveness of the developing organization. These characteristics serve also as tests of a sound organization and are described more fully in the following section which deals with control of the organization structure.

Control of Organization Structure

Provision for proper control is a necessary ingredient in the development and maintenance of sound organizational structure. This has three main aspects which are briefly discussed here: namely, (1) procedures for control, (2) organizational aspects of control, and (3) organization characteristics which act as criteria of soundness.

1. *Procedures for Control.* Procedures used to measure the effectiveness of the organizational structure include use of organizational audits, reports and records, and personal observation. Organizational audits may be made periodically and include an examination of the responsibilities and authority assigned to all jobs and units in the firm, and a review of lines of communication. Review of job titles and job content will help keep job descriptions and relationships current.

A study of the factors of structural design should be made. Objectives of the organization as a whole, and of each level and unit, may be undertaken. Examination of how functional differentiation meets present needs of the firm should be made. Whether available personnel have the qualifications specified for their position should be ascertained. Changes in size and location of the firm units may dictate modifications of the structure. Organization and procedural charts must be brought up to date; otherwise, they are worse than none at all.

Reports can also serve as effective control tools of management. Such reports as the status of manpower, personnel behavior and personnel costs, economic health and outlook of the firm, and other indications of effectiveness of a part or all of the organization are helpful in evaluating the organizational structure and relationships.

Personal observation should not be overlooked as a control procedure. Judgment based on personal observation is often a discerning control measure; bringing to light phenomena not apparent from formal written audits and reports. Also, personal observation is often one of the few techniques available for evaluating the informal organization and its effect on the formal structure.

2. *Organizational Aspects.* There is some tendency for larger companies to set up staff departments whose function is chiefly that of development and control of the organization proper. This is particularly true where the long-range importance of sound organization development is recognized. Such a staff department is almost always placed near the top executive and is concerned with both planning and control work. When such a staff department is not justified on the basis of organizational economy, other staff departments may assume some functions of organization planning and control. Usually, the personnel department is the most likely unit. It is, nevertheless, a responsibility of top line management and is becoming more and more a concern of the chief executive.

3. *Tests of a Sound Structure.* When the structure of the firm

has been built in accordance with good organizational principles and practices, it should be able to pass the following tests:

1. The structure should be related to organizational objectives and policy.
2. Stability, flexibility, balance, and simplicity should be chief characteristics of the organization.
3. Provision should be made for growth or contraction.
4. Logical grouping of functions into units and within units should be followed.
5. The structure of authority, responsibility, and relationships should be known and understood by all.

The design of the organization, or any part thereof, should be derived from the objectives for each level of organization, and from the policies that guide the effectuation of those objectives. Overall objectives serve as points of departure for planning subobjectives. In order to achieve subobjectives, objectives can be stated for each lower level unit and its jobs. Moreover, the objectives of jobs and units on the same level must be integrated with each other and must be consistent with the objectives of the next higher level. Similarly, the structures of each unit and level should be integrated and consistent with the next higher level.

To be stable, the organization must maintain its equilibrium despite losses of personnel on any level. Such quality calls for effective policies and ways of developing individuals, particularly key personnel. Flexibility refers to the ability of the organization to adjust to sudden changes in business conditions. Organizational balance refers to having the various functions and organizational units of a size proportional to their importance and also to the remaining units. Theoretically, a unit has reached its optimum size when any addition to it fails to yield maximum economy and effectiveness. An organization should remain as simple in structure as is consistent with work needs. This point is so fundamental that it may appear superfluous. Yet, too often, firms, especially in periods of rapid growth, evolve such complex frameworks that control is made difficult. Labor costs go up; stability, flexibility, and balance are all jeopardized by the resulting unwieldy mechanism.

A sound organization furthermore allows for growth or contraction over a long-run period. Many firms have expanded rapidly in an extended sellers' market, only to be confronted with insurmountable obstacles when an economic slowdown dictated retrenchment. The challenge is to provide for dynamic equilibrium—that is, to allow the organization to expand or contract, and still maintain a stable, flexible, balanced, and simple organization structure. Flexibility, of course, refers to ability to adjust to short-run conditions, as contrasted to adjustment to long-run conditions, of growth or contraction.

A sound organization will be marked by a logical grouping of functions within units. In other words, departmentation has been performed as discussed earlier, and jobs within units have been organized on the basis of suitable grouping of activities. Lastly, the objectives, policies, functions, authority, responsibility, and relationships that have been planned and organized into existence should be made known to, and understood by, all concerned.

Newer Concepts in Organization Structure

The increasing complexity of today's organization along with an advancing technology have created a need for more adaptable and flexible models of organization. Among these are (1) systems management, (2) project management, (3) matrix management, and (4) the office of the president.

1. *Systems Management.* Systems management is achieved by identifying all components necessary for organizational effectiveness and by designing a plan that will assure their optimum interaction.

In this context, then, the organization is regarded as a system containing a number of subsystems—for example, production or marketing or accounting—and surrounded by larger systems such as the industry as a whole or even society as a whole. The business organization system includes: (1) inputs of information, facilities, materials, and effort; (2) a systematic process whereby the inputs are combined into an orderly arrangement of interacting components; (3) outputs such as products, customer service, wages, and profits; and (4) a feedback process which reports the results of operations and corrects the input mix if necessary so that the output meets predetermined objectives and standards, as simply illustrated in Figure 12–10.

Advocates of the systems management concept point out that the conventional functional design of the organization with its line-staff format does not always permit optimum efficiency in the various departmental activities involved in specific project undertak-

FIGURE 12–10
Simplified Concept of a System

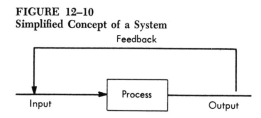

ings. The functional division of tasks, they argue, imposes barriers to smooth cooperation among the many different skills needed for completing any particular project. Systems management purports to achieve a smooth flow of activities under conditions which allow human effort to be fitted to the work process with high efficiency.

2. *Project Management.* Under project management a group of individuals possessing the required skills is organized into an autonomous unit for a particular task or project. Project management is an offshoot of the weapons systems concept applied by the aerospace industry in the development of ballistic missiles. The need for reduced lead time to develop an operational weapon system necessitated a different kind of organizational model. More recently it has been adapted to such large-scale projects as the building of a skyscraper to the construction of a nuclear reactor boiler vessel where a huge input of resources, manpower, materials, and equipment must be precisely integrated.

Project management is carried out by a project director appointed to motivate and coordinate the activities of engineering, marketing, production, accounting, and other personnel drawn from their respective departments or a separate pool to make up the project team for a particular project. Figure 12–11 illustrates the concept of project organization. Each project then has a complete line organization managed by the project manager who has full authority over all personnel, facilities, and operations required to complete the product.

The advocates of project management point to its clear visibility of project goals and to the team members understanding of their role and task. Responsibility for the project is definitely pinpointed, coordination is facilitated, and motivation and innovation increased. On the other hand, one of the strongest disadvantages of the pure project organization is that the cost in a multiproject company would be prohibitive because of the required duplication of effort and facilities among the projects.

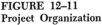

FIGURE 12–11
Project Organization

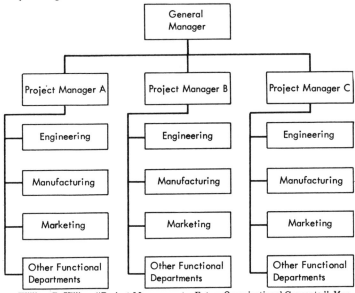

William P. Killian, "Project Management—Future Organizational Concepts," *Marquette Business Review* (Milwaukee, Wis.: Marquette University, College of Business Administration, Summer, 1971), p. 96.

3. *Matrix Management.* Matrix management is a form of organization that combines or mixes both the project structure and the traditional functional structure. It is desirable for producing large projects within desired cost, schedule, and performance standards. Figure 12–12 shows a simplified matrix organization chart.

In a matrix organization each of the functional groups is headed by a department manager who is responsible for his particular function. Coincidentally, a project manager is selected for project responsibility within each functional area of the division. Responsibility for the particular function remains with the functional manager while the project manager is fully responsible for project success. Similarly, individuals of each function may have project responsibility assigned to them, according to the needs of the project.

Advocates of the matrix form argue that it combines strengths of both the functional and project organizations. It also provides for specialized knowledge for carrying on a number of specific projects. And furthermore, it allows for quicker responsiveness of specialists by virtue of its established communication lines and its functional levels of decision making.

On the other hand, there are certain disadvantages of this type

FIGURE 12–12
Matrix Organization

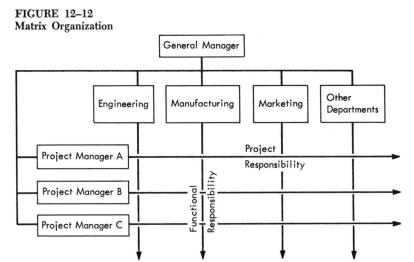

William P. Killian, "Project Management—Future Organizational Concepts," *Marquette Business Review* (Milwaukee, Wis.: Marquette University, College of Business Administration, Summer, 1971), p. 98.

organization. Possible problems may arise out of the dual accountability of personnel involved in the project. Then too, possible conflicts of objectives and purposes may exist between project and functional managers and also there is the possible difficulty of pinpointing profit and loss accountability for individual managers and groups in the project.

4. Office of the President. In the majority of corporations, the traditional chief executive is at the helm. However, within the last decade the pressures on the president have been so intensified that some firms have given him help by establishing an "office of the president." Diversification, decentralization, increasing technology, and product complexity are forcing some firms to set up a multiple chief executive function to ease the burden of the chief.

This concept is not unknown in Europe, and it may function under such various designations as "Office of the President," "Management Forum," or "Executive Committee." Whatever its name though, the idea behind the concept is not an alleviation of pressures through increased delegation and distribution of the president's functions. On the contrary, its basic purpose is to facilitate the president's office in executing all of its important tasks.

One large, southwestern bank which has implemented this approach emphasizes that their "Management Forum" does not function as a committee making committee decisions, but rather, the forum airs broad objectives and determines accountability for accomplishing these objectives. The individual forum members assume specific line and staff responsibilities. Three senior line officers, three staff officers, the president, and board chairman comprise the forum of this enterprising bank. Other firms, for example, that are operating with the team approach or variations of it are Caterpillar Tractor, General Electric, Borden, Scott Paper, Singer, Ampex, and Continental Can.[4]

The team approach appears to operate more effectively in those areas of the president's responsibilities which are generally more conducive to group consideration and decision making—responsibilities such as long-range planning, determining corporate objectives and policies, and the utilization of capital. However, the concept is less applicable in those areas where results are a direct function of the chief's singular skills and abilities such as in labor negotiations or the raising of capital.

The success of the team approach certainly is dependent on the personalities and strengths of the team members. Each member must be competent in his particular position. Communication among the members is most essential. Any major decisions by any team member are made with the full knowledge of the president who is still the ultimate officer.

For the broad-based internationalized firm there may be a real advantage in utilizing the team approach. With judicious use, it can multiply the effectiveness of the chief executive in a climate of continuing pressure.

QUESTIONS

1. What is included in the definition of organization structure?
2. What factors explain the origin of the concept of the functional organization at that particular time in history?
3. Why was the functional organization form not generally adopted by business firms?
4. What are the chief advantages of the line and staff type of organization?
5. What is included in functional analysis?
6. To what extent does the wide span of control eliminate the problems generally associated with the narrow span?

---

[4] *Business Week* (New York: McGraw-Hill Book Co., October 3, 1970), pp. 42–43.

7. What are the tests of a sound organization structure?
8. What type of needs does the systems concept of management appear to fill?
9. Identify the major differences among the project and matrix organizational forms and the traditional functional structure.
10. Discuss the advantages of the "office of the president" concept. Can you foresee any possible disadvantage to its use?

CASE 12–1

The Southeastern Department Store is a family-owned store which dates its founding back to the latter part of the 19th century. Southeastern has the reputation of being a full-line progressive department store that serves a three-county marketing area. It has grown substantially in both sales volume and size of staff and presently has a main downtown store and four suburban branch operations. It grosses approximately $50 million in sales annually, and its employees, including the branch stores, number approximately 900 full-time people. About 500 of these are employed in the six-story downtown building.

Original owner and founder, Mr. Samuel Horn, turned the store over to his two sons, Robert and Peter. Robert, the elder of the two, became president while Peter served as executive vice president. A growing southeast population and continued prosperity saw the store mushroom from a single store of a few dozen employees merchandising only clothing, to one that merchandises a broad range of both hard and soft goods. As the store expanded, the owners employed an accountant, who, as controller, expertly managed the store's finances. Later, in the late 50s, the son-in-law of the president was hired to be the store manager in charge of both the personnel and maintenance functions. However, the pressures of personnel management were too strenuous for the son-in-law who left after five years to try his hand at selling real estate. The personnel function was then left temporarily in the hands of a Mrs. Carbon, who had been the son-in-law's secretary.

The need for a full-time personnel director was apparent to the owners, Robert and Peter, who proceeded to hire Eric Brown, a business college graduate with about five years' experience as training supervisor with the local gas utility firm. During the employment interview with the president, Eric was informed he would report to either Robert, the president, or Peter, the executive vice president, depending on who was available at the time; and if neither was present, then he would report to the controller. "We share responsibility for each other's work," was the president's comment.

Furthermore, Eric was informed that the store's management desired a modern, up-to-date operation with the utmost attention given to the training of supervisors and sales personnel. "We want to be like Nieman-Marcus of Dallas, and training is our number one priority." Eric Brown was encouraged to work with the department heads of all functions and report back to the president if he encountered any problems of relationships with them.

After three months had gone by, the president called Eric into his office on the sixth floor and expressed dismay that the training program was not moving along as well as he had expected. In fact, he, the president, was disappointed in never having seen Eric in any of the selling departments working with the salespeople themselves. "The only way you can determine training needs is by watching and observing how a salesperson handles a customer right out there on the floor. As personnel director, it's your job to do this training. That's what you were hired for mostly; the other routines are incidental. Let your secretary handle them." Eric Brown, as he boarded the escalator to return to his office, pondered his next move as personnel director of the Southeastern Department Store.

1. What problem(s) of organization are evident at Southeastern?
2. How would you respond to the president's comment that "we share responsibility for each other's work here at Southeastern"?
3. If you were Eric, what would be your reaction to the president's order to determine training needs by floor watching?

CASE 12–2

George Warshaw is a market analyst in the marketing department of The Purless Manufacturing Company. His duties consist of performing market studies and research analyses for Walter Conrad, director of marketing research. As such, he is recognized organizationally for his sophisticated ability to use both the computer and advanced statistical techniques in solving marketing problems.

During the past six months, the vice president of marketing, Herman Schwartz, whose office is on the same floor, has occasionally dropped in on George to informally talk about some of the newer mathematical approaches to decision making. Walter Conrad, who is George's boss, guessed as to the nature of their conversations but never bothered to question either the vice president or George.

Presently, however, George, usually prompt, has been late in the submission of a major sales report for Walter. In fact, he was a week overdue when Walter called George into his office to determine the cause of delay. George responded by saying that the vice president had asked him to prepare some speech material on new sales forecasting techniques and it has taken much of his time. He was sure Walter would not mind since the work was for Walter's boss, the vice president of marketing.

1. What seems to be the problem(s) here?
2. If you were Walter, what would you say to George?
3. Do you think Walter should discuss this with his boss, the vice president? If so what should he say to Herman Schwartz?

13

Authority and Responsibility

Scope of Discussion

By THIS TIME, it should be apparent to the student of management that organizational effectiveness derives from the collective efforts of its people. The many technical, managerial, and operative groups cooperate to advance both the organizational and personal objectives. It is in this context then, the achievement of objectives, that the concepts of authority and responsibility should be examined. Because it is through the interrelationship of both elements, particularly the relationship of prescribed and delegated authority with resultant responsibility, that objectives are reached.

In this chapter we shall investigate the various aspects of authority and responsibility as they are related to management under the following headings:

1. The nature of authority.
2. Sources of authority.
3. Delegating authority.
4. Nature of responsibility.
5. Bilateral dimensions of responsibility.
6. Specifying authority limits.
7. Specifying responsibilities.

Nature of Authority

Authority is the right to do something. It may be the right to make decisions, to give orders and require compliance, or simply the right to perform a work assignment. Authority may also be de-

240

fined as "a relationship between two individuals, one 'superior' and the other 'subordinate.' The superior frames and transmits decisions with the expectation that they will be accepted by the subordinate. The subordinate expects such decisions and his conduct is determined by them."[1] Authority may also be defined as the power to command. Implicit in the word "power" is the ability to impose sanctions, grant rewards, and to exact compliance or obedience to the authoritative source. This logically brings us to a discussion of the sources of authority.

Sources of Authority

In academic circles there is considerable discussion about the source of managerial authority in the organization. Several main theories, however, seem to evolve from any investigation. These are the formal authority theory, the acceptance theory, and the competence theory. The formal source of authority derives from the institution of private property in our democratic society; it is the authority of ownership. Formal authority when delegated by the immediate line superior can be traced back up the line structure to the board of directors, the stockholders, and eventually to society itself. The extent of this authority is determined by the specific duties for which the job incumbent is responsible.

The acceptance theory of authority dilutes the power implications of management and emphasizes that the real authority rests with the subordinate who will "accept" the authority of management. This view, the acceptance theory, holds that any commands from an authoritative source become somewhat ineffectual unless those affected by those commands understand them, and find them consistent with their purpose. This view also presupposes the people affected are mentally and physically able to execute the command.[2]

The competence theory is an aspect of informal authority in which there is authority generated by the personal competence of the individual. It is developed by way of informal relationships among personnel and represents the authority ascribed to an individual by others. They do so voluntarily and out of deference for his status. His status in turn is built up as a result of personality

---

[1] Herbert A. Simon, *Administrative Behavior* (2d ed.; New York: The Free Press, 1957), p. 125.

[2] Chester I. Barnard, *The Functions of the Executive* (Cambridge, Mass.: Harvard University Press, 1938), p. 167.

characteristics, job importance and location, skill and knowledge, and similar recognition-gaining factors. Others thus subordinate themselves to his leadership and direction. This in a real sense is most similar to the acceptance theory—since it is "earned authority." It may serve to modify formal authority and help to effectuate it by determining how much formal authority will actually be accepted and acknowledged by subordinates.

In practice, however, all these theories—the formal, acceptance, and competency—have a basis for application. Formal authority envelops the entire structure of the organization within a societal framework while the acceptance and competency theories more narrowly relate to superior-subordinate relationships. These concepts are further discussed in this chapter under bilateral dimensions of responsibility and are also illustrated in Figure 13–1.

FIGURE 13–1
Sources of Authority

Type	*Description*
Formal	—is formal power; derives from institution of private property; it is authority of ownership; it is top down authority; it is imposed upon others.
Acceptance	—people subject to commands *voluntarily* accept them; real authority rests with subordinates who accept the authority of management; it is bottom top authority; it is self-imposed.
Competence	—authority is generated by the personal competence of the individual; authority is a derivitive of leader's personality characteristics, job position and location, knowledge and technical skills.

Delegating Authority

Delegation, in the business institution, occurs when certain of the executive's functions, responsibility, and authority are released and committed to designated subordinate positions. By delegating authority an executive turns over various aspects of his jurisdiction to his subordinates. He lets them do the work for which they were hired. But he is, nonetheless, responsible to his superiors for the success or failure of his subordinates. As a consequence, he may be reluctant to delegate authority as fully as he should. On the other hand, his subordinates may be equally reluctant to accept authority to proceed on their own. So this subject of delegating authority must be seen from the viewpoints of both (1) the delegator and (2) the recipient.

1. *The Delegator of Authority.* The first task of an executive in delegating authority is to overcome his reluctance to delegate, engendered by his own high sense of obligation. He recognizes his responsibility to his superior, and for this he should be commended. Indeed, this is a characteristic to be watched for in any candidate for a managerial position, for it is one that all successful executives have to a high degree.

Carrying this characteristic to an extreme, however, is undesirable. Refusing to delegate, for example, will eventually weaken the executive as well as his subordinates. He will be physically unable to keep up the pace of doing all that he attempts. And his subordinates will never develop to the point that they can carry on their legitimate tasks as competent people should.

The executive may also fail to delegate because he doesn't trust his subordinates. He is afraid they will fail him. But this is an indirect criticism of himself. If he had spent time on his managerial function of organizing, he would have selected and trained a dependable team with the technical ability to carry out assigned tasks.

Other executives refuse to delegate because it gives them a feeling of superiority to do technical jobs themselves. It bolsters their egos in front of their subordinates. It does not, however, give the latter a chance to grow, their self-respect is reduced, teamwork is weakened, and even the executive's own chances of success are ultimately minimized.

Finally, some executives refuse to delegate out of fear that the subordinates will replace them in their jobs. Worry won't help an executive protect his job, nor will such tactics prevent good subordinates from climbing over him—in some other company, if not in his own. If good subordinates leave, an executive is in an even poorer position because he has only inferior help left.

2. *Recipients of Authority.* Subordinates themselves may be reluctant to accept authority. Unless this reluctance is reduced, an executive will find himself doing the work of others whether he wants to or not. The initial step in removing reluctance of subordinates is to make sure that one is not surrounded by people who avoid authority because they are incapable of handling it.

Assuming that subordinates have the actual or potential ability to accept authority, why may they be reluctant, and how may the reluctance be overcome? Perhaps the major explanations are lack of confidence and fear of failure. The two go together. A subordinate thinks he cannot do the job expected and will have to pay the penalty of failure. So he finds some way of evading or ignoring the authority that is being bestowed on him. The boss must now do what should have been done earlier. The subordinate must be encouraged and coached with patience in actual situations. By doing, he will learn that he can do successfully. And at the same stroke the penalties of failure will recede beyond the point of being an obstruction to action.

Subordinates, particularly at lower levels, may refuse authority obligations because they do not wish to lose seniority privileges or the associations of present friends. Overcoming the argument against losing out with current associates is not easy. When a person moves from the rank of worker to that of supervisor, he will find that he now acquires a new set of characteristics as well as opportunities for further growth—professional, financial, and social.

Finally, subordinates may be unwilling to accept authority because they lack confidence in their superiors who may possibly issue ambiguous orders, play one subordinate executive against another, and look for scapegoats for their own mistakes. Under such circumstances, one would be hard pressed to take on authority delegations. The solution to such situations is difficult to find. Executives who indulge in such practices are neither likely to see the error of their ways nor to correct them even if aware of them. Ultimately the ambitious subordinate must seek other employment or hope that the guilty superiors depart the scene.

Nature of Responsibility[3]

Responsibility refers to the obligation of a subordinate to perform a duty or specific service for someone else. When an individual assumes an obligation he becomes accountable to the person who has assigned the responsibility. Part of the organizing function discussed in the previous chapter is to help insure that all necessary functions will be performed. This is done by seeing that each phase of work in each functional unit is made the responsibility of some organization member.

---

[3] Each person in an organization has an obligation for *something* to *someone*. Generally, and here too, the term "responsibility" is used to denote both dimensions of obligations. Some writers prefer to designate the obligation *for something* by the term "responsibility" and that of *to someone* by accountability.

This requirement of organizational development has important implications for the relationship of responsibility to formal authority. To discharge effectively the responsibilities of a job, the incumbent must have sufficient authority or right to carry out the obligation connected with it. Although authority is delegated from a higher line executive, the amount of responsibility for which the subordinate will be held accountable determines the amount of authority delegated. (See Figure 13–2.)

FIGURE 13–2
Visual Scope of Authority and Responsibility

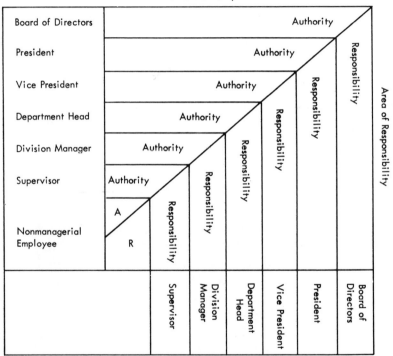

Area of Authority

Bilateral Dimensions of Responsibility

If an executive does delegate authority to others, he will not by that act alone become effective. He must hold his subordinates responsible for assigned delegations. And the subordinates, themselves, must not avoid the responsibilities for which they have accepted authority. So, an analysis of responsibility may be considered from the viewpoints of (1) the executive who is holding subordinates responsible, (2) the subordinate who accounts for his responsibilities, and (3) the distinct relationships of authority to responsibility.

1. *The Executive and Responsibility.* A large number of functions, factors, and forces can be applied in the task of holding subordinates responsible for their acts. Much pertinent material has been covered in earlier chapters on such subjects as managerial functions of planning, organizing, directing, and controlling. A few more comments will be made about them later in this section. For the present, however, it is desirable to concentrate attention upon the concepts of authority and responsibility as they relate to the matter of holding subordinates responsible for assigned tasks.

To begin with, getting results from subordinates—holding them responsible—is basically founded on the right that an executive himself has to exercise authority. This right is obtained in the first place by delegation from above. Every executive is acquainted with this source of authority, and great reliance is invariably placed upon it.

Thus, people are held responsible through the right to command obedience and to penalize the nonperformer. Up to the present time, authority by delegation still gets results, but not as effectively as it once did—and not with as much personal satisfaction to the user of such authority alone.

Were this the only source of authority, the right to command would be full of harsh and undesirable implications. Management would be not much more than a dictatorial process. But right to require compliance has a more pleasing facet because there is yet another source of delegation. Authority may be earned from below. Subordinates may willingly follow orders. They may willingly obey commands. Indeed, they may anticipate orders and cooperate in the performance of desired acts even without being told.

The wise executive, then, is the one who seeks to supplement the authority received by delegation with that earned from below. He seeks the willing cooperation of subordinates. He seeks to develop in others a willingness to follow orders. But how is authority earned from below? Several courses suggest themselves. An executive must possess competence in the technical field which he supervises; he must exhibit managerial skills; and he must be fair and alert to the problems and needs of his subordinates.

The first of these, technical competence, has an impressive value. Subordinates are impressed by the superior who knows the technical aspects of his job: of production, of accounting, of sales, of engineering, etc. The need for technical competence is particularly useful to an executive when he first takes over a new department. Then his past reputation will be a favorable force in the eyes of his new subordinates, who will be reserving judgment on him. Moreover, technical competence is something they can readily interpret for themselves. As time goes on, however, this factor of technical judgment will weigh less and less with subordinates. They will be concerned with an executive's managerial and human relations skills.

Subordinates sooner or later, and consciously or unconsciously, evaluate an executive on how he manages. They will be aware of the results of good management, if not of managerial performances which help cause the results. They will be aware of the absence of continuous emergencies, of controversy, of jurisdictional bickering, of shortages of materials and machine time, and of poor designs and procedures.

Respect and authority are earned also by the skill the executive has in dealing with the personal needs and problems of subordinates. Does he convince them by deeds as well as words that he has their best interests at heart? Does he procrastinate about employee wants and problems, or does he anticipate them and deal with them fairly and voluntarily? Does he function with an attitude of reluctance, or with an attitude revealing a sincere desire to be helpful?

Dealing with personal problems and needs is thus more than a question of being fair. An executive must also display an active, voluntary, interested, and sincere attitude in this connection. The loyalty of subordinates flows out to executives who are voluntarily interested in employees' concerns.

The human relations approach does not mean that an executive has to buy loyalty, or give up a share of what is really his own. The essence of good human relations is, instead, a prompt and fair recognition of the human problems of subordinates. By being alert and taking constructive action, the executive gives his subordinates convincing proof of his trustworthiness. They have confidence in him; they attach their loyalty to him; and they follow his commands willingly.

To summarize, earning authority from below depends upon a proper combination of technical, managerial, and human relations skills. There is no single right combination for all executives. Each must work out the emphasis that will work best for him. All too often, however, executives rely almost entirely upon technical competence to the exclusion of managerial and human relations skills in order to add earned authority to delegated authority.

2.   *The Subordinate and Responsibility.* A number of reasons may be advanced as to why subordinates do not carry out obligations as desired. They may, to begin with, not possess requisite capacities. Selection or training would be at the root of the problem. If the latter, it will be necessary either to shift the subordinate to a job which he is capable of handling or to remove him from the payroll, if possible.

Some subordinates shirk responsibilities because they are lazy and want to avoid work. Here is a problem in motivation. Is the laziness due to boredom, to lack of interest, or to the absence of a challenge in the job or in the total picture of life? If in the last, the cost of trying to awaken the individual may be too high unless one sees great potentialities for service. If the difficulty is in the job, the executive must figure out what, if anything, will remove the cause of the laziness. It may be that a job change is called for. It may be that the employee has not been shown the interesting facets or challenges in a job. It may be that he has never been asked to participate in analyzing his job and in making decisions about it.

Responsibilities may be shirked because it is "the thing to do." Some, if not all, employees may align themselves against management by agreeing among themselves as to how much work they will do. The quantity of work, the duties that will be performed, or the willingness to work overtime are examples of what may be fixed. Where such restrictions are imposed—and woe to the employee who breaks them—their removal depends upon the cause of this setting of restriction and the possibility of its removal.

Furthermore, the source of trouble may be in a negative reaction to managerial behavior. Employees may not like a particular supervisor and take their grudge out on all of management. Or they may not like the attitude of all management toward employees. They may have the feeling of being inferior to one or all of the management group.

To cite another group of reasons, subordinates may shirk responsibilities because they fear criticism for poor results. This fear may arise because of lack of confidence in themselves or because of negative leadership. A subordinate who is uncertain about doing a job well tends to hold off doing it. So, if this is the cause, he must be taught how to do it correctly.

On the other hand, negative leadership may be the source of trouble. Some executives use constant criticism as a tool to get results. They seldom compliment; they always find fault. So subordinates do as little as possible in order to minimize criticism. Somewhat similar to the negative leader is the one who wants to do things himself or in his own way. As a consequence, subordinates soon learn either to wait around until the "boss" shows up or to ask how things should be done, instead of acting on their own. Getting such nonmanagers of their own accord to see the light is difficult; it must be done by higher management, or it will in all likelihood not be done at all.

It should be apparent by this time, if it has not been noted before, that the foregoing discussion of why employees do not always execute responsibilities as desired invariably leads back to poor management techniques. Isn't the employee at fault, and wouldn't a good stiff dose of disciplinary action correct his faults? To a certain extent, under certain conditions, and with some employees, the answer is an unqualified "Yes!" The intent here has not been to discard fear, discipline, and negative leadership as management devices. They have their uses. Moreover, it is unlikely that they will be overlooked by many executives.

Rather, the intent has been to show that management itself is the cause of many shortcomings ascribed to labor or to subordinate executives. Perhaps even more importantly, the intent has been to provide enough evidence to make the following statement more convincing: the best way to change others is to first change oneself. When one improves his managerial behavior, he will soon find—perhaps to his own surprise—that great changes have "automatically" taken place in his subordinates.

3. *Relation of Authority to Responsibility.* It is now pertinent to examine the relation between authority and responsibility. Generally, the proposition is accepted that the two should be coequal. Under this proposition, the amount and kind of right to command should be equal to the amount and kind of obligations assigned to a given individual. Indeed, some interpret this proposition to mean that unless authority and responsibility are coequal in every position, a nonsensical relationship exists. Figure 13–3 represents the flow of coequal authority, responsibility, and accountability in a typical firm.

Without attempting an exhaustive analysis, some study of the proposition is in order. To begin with, is it equally easy to delegate authority as to assign responsibility? Anyone with practical experience in management knows that authority is relinquished with greater reluctance. The president may, for example, give the chief accountant the responsibility of keeping an accurate set of books. But he may reserve unto himself the right to decide what system of accounts to keep, who should be hired, and what kinds of accounting machines may be purchased.

Under these circumstances, some might argue that the chief accountant would be responsible for accuracy only within the limits of the personnel, equipment, and system supplied by the president. He will have the right to command the available resources and will be responsible for results obtained from them. Thus, if inaccuracies resulted from poor personnel, the chief accountant would not be responsible because he had no authority over their selection. Such an argument may possess theoretical soundness, but it is doubtful whether the chief accountant could use it in explaining inaccuracies to the president. So, for practical purposes, it is not uncommon for responsibilities to be assigned in greater amounts than authority. As the chief gains in experience, the president should gradually release increments of power until his total responsibilities are equaled by the total grants of authority.

Might it not be argued in this case that the president has more authority than responsibility and that these should be equated for him too? In one sense, it is as indefensible to have too much authority relative to responsibility as the reverse. But, in this case, is not the president responsible for the acts of the chief accountant? Or, to generalize the case, isn't every executive responsible for the acts of his subordinates, no matter how many levels removed? The answer is found in the generalization that an executive may delegate responsibility but never divest himself of it. In the present case, then, the president is still responsible for the accuracy of the books and, of course, he has the authority to take action to get it. His authority is not greater than his responsibilities.

This line of reasoning would seem to indicate that the total and ultimate authority and responsibility for an organization reside in its chief executive. Such a conclusion is practically and theoretically true. Certainly, the president may discharge a scapegoat and thereby seem to escape blame himself. But, in a sense, he is to blame for hiring the scapegoat, or for hiring inept assistants who hired the scapegoat.

What are the "authority" and "responsibility" of subordinates if ultimately all of these reside in the chief executive? In essence, authority is nothing more than the right to act in behalf of the president, or in behalf of one who is acting in behalf of the president; and responsibility is nothing more than a sharing of the obligations of another. As an example, when the chief accountant recognizes that the orders he issues are really those of his superior, and the responsibilities he shoulders are really those of his superior, he removes from himself one of the greatest dangers to teamwork—the egotistical feeling of independence. In its place comes the quintessence of teamwork—the recognition of being a sharer in the results, who must work with and for his associate and not as an independent agent.

Authority and responsibility are equated, therefore, not alone in a given position for particular duties but also to and through executive channels, as illustrated in Figure 13–3. In the accounting

FIGURE 13–3
The Flow of Authority, Responsibility, and Accountability in a Formal Organization

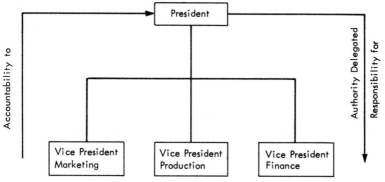

case again, to look solely at the job of the chief accountant in equating authority and responsibility is not enough. The authority and responsibility must be related to how much of each the president may desire to retain actively in order to best handle his ultimate authority and responsibility.

Specifying Authority Limits

The foregoing materials in this chapter have served to present a basic picture of authority and responsibility and the relation between them. It is now pertinent to make specific suggestions about prescribing limits of each. In this section concern will be with authority specifications, and in the next, with responsibility specifications.

As in most fields of human knowledge, it is one thing to grasp the theory of a subject and another to apply it. This is very true of the concept of authority. The following presents statements on how such authority rights may be defined, first, in relation to organizational and procedural jurisdictions and, second, in terms of specific delegations.

1. *Organizational and Procedural Authority.* Although provision is generally made for the organizational authority of executives, their procedural authority is often overlooked. Yet, due consideration for each is very important. Organizational authority has reference to the rights an executive has in connection with the organization unit he heads. The executive in charge of a traffic department is given the right to manage that department. The right would spell out his relation to his superior, to his subordinates, and to other departments with which he comes into contact or which come into contact with him. Thus, the traffic manager would, let us say, have line authority within the boundaries of his organization unit, and staff relationships with all other departments which he serves or which serve him.

Procedural authority has reference to the rights an executive is granted in connection with the portions of a procedure that pass through his organizational unit. Referring to the traffic manager, what rights does he have to reroute shipments as requested by the sales department or to hold up less-than-carload (l.c.l.) deliveries until a carload quantity can be accumulated? If he has no such rights, then he must merely perform whatever routine duties are necessary to ship each order as requested and to handle each l.c.l. order separately. In the latter event, his organizational authority indicates what rights he has and what duties to perform in connection with the projects that pass through his department. His procedural authority is limited to the areas or directions prescribed by those in the procedure who preceded him.

The relation between organization and procedure is illustrated in Figure 13–4. Here, the structure of the traffic department is shown in relation to a project that originates elsewhere, passes through this department, and is completed elsewhere. In this case, the traffic department is concerned with only one function in the project. This diagram in and of itself does not disclose what rights the traffic

FIGURE 13–4
Organizational and Procedural Relations

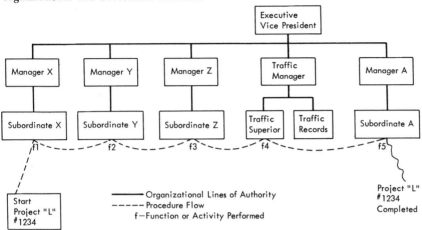

department has in connection with this function, but in some fashion or other (as suggested in a following paragraph), such rights should be delineated.

A striking example of procedural authority is seen in the work of police guards. Assume that in a given case they are instructed in the performance of their duties to allow no one to enter who does not have a security pass. Assume then that the president of the company arrives at the gate without his pass, and so the guard refuses him entry even though he recognizes the president. Organizationally, the president could discharge the guard, but that would serve only to wreck the procedure. It is through procedures that the work of the organization is accomplished. In the present case, procedural authority takes precedence over organizational authority.

Does this mean the president is subservient to the guard? Of course not. It is the organization structure, of which the president is in ultimate authority, that established the procedures. Once established, the procedures are to be followed until the organization structure through appropriate channels takes action to change, amend, install, or retract procedures. So, the president will have to get a pass by calling his secretary, let us say, and thereby abide by the procedures which he installed.

Since organization charts and procedural layouts, as illustrated very simply in Figure 13–4, do not give a good picture of authority limits, other means must be provided for this purpose. Simple devices of oral communication or learning by living together may be employed, but these have obvious weaknesses. Preferable are written statements in organization manuals, procedural manuals, job specifications, and standard practice instructions. It is important with such written methods to be sure that they are coordinated one with the other, and that they are kept up to date. If these precautions are not taken the manuals will be worse than useless.

2. Specific Delegations. Specific delegations of authority need to be made, and the wording of such delegations is important in making effective the individual's performance and in holding him accountable for attainment of standards set for his job. Delegated authority expresses the degree of freedom that a superior grants to a subordinate to take action in his organization unit or in a phase of a procedure. Such expressions may range from relatively complete freedom of action to almost complete restriction of freedom. Each company needs to work out a classification which will meet its particular needs. In the following, authority delegation has been classified into five general categories which have been found helpful in working out specific delegations for job descriptions and similar purposes. These are:

a)   Authority of full administrative discretion.
b)   Authority within established objectives and policies.
c)   Authority within general direction and procedure.
d)   Authority limited to standard practice instructions.
e)   Authority limited to acting when and as directed.

a)   *Authority of Full Administrative Discretion.* Wide administrative discretion involves the right to exercise a very high degree of initiative and freedom in the performance of managerial functions. This includes decision making within broad limits. It permits setting objectives and making policies in areas of major importance. Illustrative of this is the independent firm which becomes a subsidiary but is permitted to remain for most purposes an independent unit, carrying on nearly all the functions in the same way as it had prior to the merger.

b)   *Authority within Established Objectives and Policies.* This type of delegation of authority is more commonly found than the first level discussed above. Discretionary privileges are broad in scope, but conformity with general overall policies is expected. Even where broad administrative authority is delegated in some areas, the unit must still operate within established policies in such matters as finance, plant expansion, etc. Where a multiplant company is characterized by such decentralization, broad policy-making machinery may be operating at the top executive level, with the remainder of administrative processes being delegated to the next lower level. The branch manager has the assistance of expert administrative management from the top level, but is free to exercise his own initiative in matters below the broad policy level.

c) *Authority within General Direction and Procedure.* Delegation of authority limited by general direction and procedure is the third general level of decentralized authority. The right to make policy is almost nonexistent. Actual operating decisions are left to the manager within fairly wide limits. Broad general standards of time, expense, quality, and quantity are often given; control is secured by measuring performance against such standards, and by requiring reports periodically.

Such level of authority is particularly effective at middle management levels and lower levels of some firms. It permits exercise of initiative and thus furnishes a good basis for motivation of managers. It trains managers to assume responsibility and permits a relatively high degree of flexibility. Furthermore, higher executives, particularly at plant level, are still free to spend more time on administrative matters.

d) *Authority Limited to Standard Practice Instructions.* At the level of requiring conformity with standard practices, considerable initiative has been removed from subordinates. Objectives or quotas are determined quite exactly. Little or no discretion as to approach and method is left with the unit manager. Rather, procedures are planned in detail, and specific instructions for carrying them out step by step are developed.

Such limitation of delegated authority by standardization is often found on lower levels where repetitive work occurs, such as in an order-filling department. Examples may also be found in some garage service departments and in certain chain restaurants where simple and fixed menus are followed.

The manager must secure approval before taking action on any matter about which he is uncertain and must keep his superior regularly informed on results, and immediately informed on exceptions to standard practice.

Some disadvantages are cited for this limited decentralization of authority. It is said to stifle initiative and to be somewhat detrimental to morale. Although standardizing procedures may, in one sense, require little decision making on the lower level, a higher executive may nevertheless have to devote much time to details, because any matters for which there is no standard practice must be referred to him for decision. Furthermore, it is felt that such limited decentralization leaves little room for development of the managerial ability of individuals.

e) Authority Limited to Acting When and as Directed. The most restricted level of authority, where the most complete centralization possible exists, is where action can be taken only when and as instructions are specifically received. Theoretically, a complete absence of administrative discretion exists. Policies, procedures, and instructions are supplied for each instance. Obviously, this degree of delegation is not to be found frequently. There are organizational instances, however, where such limitation may be necessary because of the complicated and unrepetitive nature of work to be done, or because of the state of development of the individuals involved in exercise of authority. The manager in this situation makes decisions only when told, or the subordinate acts only when ordered.

With the above descriptions of authority levels as a basis, statements of authority can be drawn up for job descriptions, program assignments, and similar purposes, giving each executive a clear picture of his rights. If necessary, they should be explained so that any misconception of the printed word will be clarified.

Specifying Responsibilities

The obligations placed upon subordinates should be spelled out as precisely as are rights and privileges, and the coverage should be the same as in the case of authority. Thus, the organizational and procedural aspects of responsibility should be specified to balance the authority specifications. Since the relation between organization and procedure has been covered in the preceding sections, it will be unnecessary to repeat this material in connection with the matter of responsibility.

Attention shall be directed to the phraseology that should be used to describe the kind and degree of obligations placed upon subordinates. The phraseology suggested below does not imply that all users of these terms in various companies would agree upon their meaning. It is argued, however, that within a given company the same words should mean the same thing to all users.

Words alone are often used to define responsibilities. This is not enough. It is necessary to define the words. Some terms commonly used to specify responsibilities, and suggested definitions and explanations of them, are listed in the following:

1. *Conforms:* The person is expected to carry out his duties exactly as specified in procedures, manuals, blueprints, specifications, or oral instructions.

2. *Advises:* The person is expected at regular intervals, or as requested, to submit recommendations, or to advise, and counsel on specified matters or problems.

3. *Serves:* The person is expected to provide resources, facilities, personnel, or services to various parties either (*a*) as specified by the various parties and within their budgeted allotments, or (*b*) through his own budget, personnel, and resources.

4. *Inspects:* The person is expected to check products, services, processes, or equipment in conformance with preestablished standards therefor, and to report (*a*) deviations therefrom and/or (*b*) all conditions thereof to interested parties.

5. *Audits:* The person is expected to examine processes, services, or resources in conformance with such tests and standards as he deems necessary, and to report (*a*) deviations and/or (*b*) all conditions to interested parties.

6. *Appraises:* The person is expected to make current or periodical evaluations of personnel, organizational, or procedural performances not otherwise subject to quantitative measurements, and to report his findings to interested parties.

7. *Coordinates with:* The person is expected to work with and/or make contact with, for informational or consultative purposes, individuals designated by his superior, organizational or procedural manuals, or standard practice instructions.

8. *Reports to:* The person is expected to notify the stated superior, by designated means, of the results of his performances, and to be subject to the orders of the superior.

The foregoing are sufficient to illustrate what needs to be done in specifying responsibilities. It should be readily apparent from the foregoing that where this is not done, such words as "advise" or "consult with" would not of themselves be equally clear and equally meaningful to all concerned. The meanings of words should, therefore, be spelled out to the extent needed to make them clear; and, as was noted in relation to authority, the specifications should also be explained so that misconceptions will be minimized.

QUESTIONS

1. Discuss the various sources of authority.
2. How do you explain the failure of managers to delegate the proper amount of work to subordinates?
3. Why do subordinates avoid acceptance of responsibility? What are some remedies for such a situation?
4. How does procedural authority differ from organizational authority?
5. Discuss the different levels of authority as it may be delegated to lower levels.
6. How can management determine the degree of authority to delegate to a lower unit?
7. What is an example of authority delegated to act only when and as directed?

CASE 13-1

"Your chartered plane will be ready for takeoff at 11:00 this morning," said the secretary to Wilbur Cradley, vice president of marketing for Futuristic Office Machines in central Ohio.

Wilbur was most apprehensive about Len Wells, a sales representative in Grand Rapids. Len began as a sales trainee five years ago after transferring from Futuristic's production department. Personable, charming, and persuasive, he had convinced Wilbur (who was then field sales manager) of his potential as a salesman. During the first four years, Len's sales record was well above average.

However, during the past year, the present field sales manager has received numerous complaints about Len's personal habits. Several reports by customers revolved around Len's making sales calls while inebriated. Another complaint was that while not formally divorced, Len had left his wife and was living with an ex-girl friend. It seemed she was also his chauffeur at those times when he found navigation difficult. Already two large clients have transferred their business because of lack of service.

The field sales manager has talked repeatedly with Len about his personal behavior. "What I do off the job is my own business," Len always responded. But he promised several times to discontinue drinking on the job.

This morning, though, just as Wilbur Cradley entered his office, the field sales manager phoned from Detroit. It seemed that Len had neither been in his office nor out in the field for a full week. He wondered what he should do. Wilbur canceled all his activities for two days. He was on his way to counsel with Len about changing his behavior.

1. Is Wilbur properly exercising his authoritative role by flying to Grand Rapids? What is the responsibility of the field sales manager in this case?
2. If you were Wilbur what steps would you take in remedying the problem of Len?

CASE 13–2

President Jonathan Spring of the Sparkle Match Company daily made an inspection tour of the plant. The factory employed some 400 operative workers and produced both the old-fashioned strike match along with the safety paper match.

As the president moved through the various departments he would scatter comments, ideas, suggestions, and, at times, criticisms, to the machine operators and other employees. All departments were alert to his daily visitation, and there was evident a general feeling of excitation prior to his morning tour. Jonathan felt these trips were necessary—"Keeps everyone on their toes," he remarked, "and besides it gives them a chance to meet with top management."

On his most recent tour, a typical day, he:

a) Suggested that the supervisor of the mixing room (where sulphur and phosphorus are blended) hire an additional "clean-up man" to insure better compliance to safety standards.
b) Discussed the inventory status with the stock clerk and gave the supervisor a roughed-out new special order form for cartons and boxes.
c) Requested that idle machine operators, who were waiting for an equipment repair, clean up the area while waiting.
d) Listened to an employee's complaint about the quality of canned soup in the vending machines.

When one of the workers wondered why Mr. Spring takes time out to make these daily tours, his supervisor remarked, "Why shouldn't he? After all, he's top man of this outfit!"

1. What is your opinion of Mr. Spring's plant tours?
2. Evaluate the response, "After all, he's top man of this outfit!" to the question about the daily presidential tour.
3. As a consultant to the Sparkle Match Company, what advice would you offer the president about his authoritative role?

14

Line and Staff
Relationships

Introduction

THE DISTINCTIVE characteristics, advantages, and limitations of the line and staff organization structure were discussed in Chapter 12. Some attention was given there to the place of staff and its relationship to line organization. This relationship to the basic line structure is so vital to effective achievement of the company's objectives as to justify special consideration. For as an enterprise grows it relies more and more on services of specialized staff experts to maintain managerial efficiency.

An organization may grow in terms of (1) technical factors such as machines, processes, materials, and buildings; (2) specialization of technical factors such as particular people working exclusively on such tasks as purchasing, production control, or traffic; (3) absolute numbers of personnel; and (4) spatial coverage, that is, the geographical area expands either in one location or through branches.

To handle such kinds of growth, managerial specialization is required. Hence the discussion here will deal with the following phases of management specialization:

1. Effects of organizational growth.
2. Managerial solutions to problems of growth.
3. Kinds of staff.
4. Characteristics of staff personnel.
5. Staff specialists and their functions.
6. Aspects of staff authority.
7. Relationship of central staff to regional staffs.

Effects of Organizational Growth

As the small organization sees opportunity for increasing the volume of business, the means for doing so must be organized. Generally such increased activity will require more equipment or materials, more personnel, more space for operations, or a combination of these. For such additional factors to be integrated with the present organization requires additional managerial functions also.

Indeed, the management difficulty is increased by more than the equivalent of the mere addition of factors. The whole new organization is a more complex system of units, levels, and relationships. Thus, while technical, personnel, and space factors, for example, are added, the managerial functions are multiplied. That this is uniformly true has led to the recognition of the *law of functional growth*. This law states that as necessary functions are added to handle the increased volume of an organization, the number of relationships tends to increase in geometric ratio, although the actual functions may increase arithmetically.

So, as work expands, the organization expands both horizontally and vertically. To basic line technical functions are added differentiated staff technical functions, such as purchasing, engineering, and warehousing. Levels, as well as more units on the same level, are developed. Relationships become more complex at an accelerated rate, and assistance to the original managers of basic functions must be provided. To the management of operative work is now added another highly significant problem, namely, the management of other managers.

Managerial Solutions to Problems of Growth

The solutions to the problems of providing sufficient management for the growing organization are several. An obvious alternative is simply to multiply the number of line executives. As technical factors, personnel, and spatial coverage increase beyond the scope of present line executives, additional line officers, each with the same scope of responsibilities, are appointed. (See Figure 14–1.) In actual circumstances this solution would be applied in relatively few and limited instances. As soon as the firm expanded beyond the point of being very small, such a move would become a most uneconomical one.

More probably, another course of action would be followed to

FIGURE 14-1
Growth by Addition of Line Managers

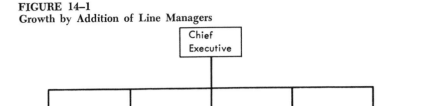

supply adequate management capacity. A manager, sensing the drag on his time caused by attending to many details, would probably employ a clerk to take over such detail and routine work as keeping time records of employees, distributing routine work instructions for the day, or making up a report on work progress.

Let us assume that the individual has been employed to assist the manager in the purchasing function. At first he will probably do the routine work of making out purchase orders, checking supply levels, and ascertaining that deliveries are made on time. As he learns about specifications, rate of use, sources of supply, and negotiations, he will assume the more responsible duties of purchasing. When the activities in this function rise to the point where the assisting clerk can no longer do all of them, he may be authorized to employ additional clerical help in order to free his own time for the more important part of the job. (See Figure 14-2.) He has

FIGURE 14-2
Adjustment to Growth by Adding Staff Units

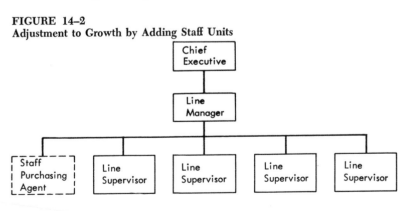

taken over at this point all or nearly all procurement duties, but still reports to the line manager who still has the responsibility for this function. The purchasing man, however, has assumed the role of staff specialist to the line manager. He has assumed the role of line manager with respect to his own clerical subordinates.

As the organization increases in volume a further development may take place. The potential advantages of having a common procurement function for all organizational units become apparent. The purchasing officer now is given authority and responsibility for organizationwide procurement. Commensurate with his new authority and responsibility, the purchasing agent moves up to a higher echelon in the organization. He may now be placed on the same level with his former superior, and both the purchasing agent and line manager may be responsible to a common line manager. (See Figure 14–3.) Thus, a staff unit may be elevated to a level where

FIGURE 14–3
Elevation of Staff Units

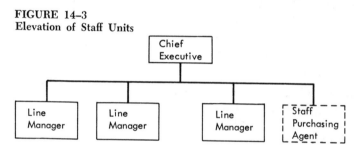

the executive in charge is responsible directly to the president. When a firm becomes multiplant in size we find frequently that a staff unit is set up at the home office level, while similar units operate at the plant level and below. This is generally called staff parallelism.

Kinds of Staff

Generally, there are two basic kinds of staff. These are *personal* staff and *specialized* staff.

1. *Personal Staff.* These are positions whose express purpose is to assist the manager in executing those aspects of his job which he cannot and does not wish to delegate to others. Personal staff mainly consists of three kinds of assistants: the line assistant, the staff assistant, and what is known as the general staff assistant.

The line assistant while in the direct chain of command is nevertheless staff to his superior because his job is to advise, counsel, and take over, when required, for his manager only. The line assistant has no responsibility separate from that of his immediate superior; consequently he has no powers of redelegation. Typical of the line assistants are the various "assistant managers" of production, marketing, and so on. The staff assistant is also known as an "assistant to," or "administrative assistant." More confined than the line assistant, he exercises no authority over other personnel, nor does he ever assume the responsibility of the line executive. Responsibilities of staff assistants differ widely. An assistant to the president may range in use from a personal valet in one firm to a presidential alter ego in another who sits in on board and other important meetings and may also handcraft important reports and speeches.[1]

The general staff assistant, who is an adaptation of military practice, serves as an advisor to top management in specific areas. He is generally a member of a staff group and is employed in addition to the regular corporate specialized staff.

2. *Specialized Staff.* This type of staff provides both advice and service to the line organization and other staff departments. Specialized staff departments restrict their activities to one specialized function or area. They may be called upon by all other line

FIGURE 14–4
Some Examples of Staff Positions

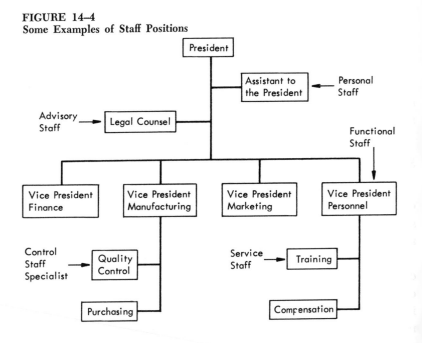

---

[1] Victor F. Phillips, Jr., *The Organizational Role of the Assistant-To* (New York: The American Management Association, 1971), p. 10.

and staff units of the firm. Personal staff, on the other hand, work primarily for one executive in helping him carry out his responsibilities. Figure 14–4 illustrates some typical staff positions.

Characteristics of Staff Personnel

Because of the very nature of his work, his inherent responsibilities and functions, the staff person assumes distinctly different characteristics than those of his line counterpart in the organization. What are some of these distinctive differences?

1. The staff man evidences certain comparative social differences. Generally he has more education and is younger than his line counterpart.

2. The staff man, moreover, sees himself as a professional with a sense of pride, obligation, and commitment to the profession itself. This may at times override his loyalty to the organization.

3. The staff man must rely heavily upon winning the voluntary cooperation of the line. Lacking formal authority, he must use effective influence and persuasion to win support of the line organization.

4. Irrespective of his personal ambition, the staff man must at times subordinate his own personality. Others, including his own boss, may receive credit and recognition for recommendations and suggestions which may have been reported previously by the staff specialist as a function of his staff work.

While these differences are recognized, they nevertheless should not impede the necessary and required integration of talents and synchronization of activities to achieve organizational efficiency.

Staff Specialists and Their Functions

The work of staff specialists can also be discussed on the basis of the functions of management which they help to perform. Some staff units devote the majority of their efforts to one function, such as planning, whereas others may be involved in several functions.

1. *Relation to Managerial Function of Planning.* The line executive is ultimately responsible for making decisions that will be carried out by his organizational subordinates. The work of planning is closely associated with the making of decisions. The decision maker must be thoroughly informed on the matter to be decided upon. Thus, the staff specialist may do virtually all the work except that of making the final decision to do something.

As a first step in the staff planning work, the staff specialist may help the line executive define clearly the problem to be solved or to formulate distinctly the goal to be achieved. The next step must be that of getting all available pertinent information about it. Following such inquiry and collecting of information, analysis and careful interpretation of data are in order. From the information that has been distilled so far, the planning staff draws up alternative solutions with a recommended course or courses of action. The recommendations are submitted to the chief for his consideration and approval.

The principle of completed staff work is often invoked here. It states that whenever possible the staff should prepare the complete report or plan to the point where only the superior's approval or disapproval is required.

An example of staff assistance in planning is the marketing research and planning department. The research unit of a coffee manufacturer may be directed to determine the cause of a drop in profitability. From its research, the marketing research department may suggest several alternative courses of action. It may recommend that the company process its own instant coffee, or that it purchase it from a current producer. In either event it will propose a recommended decision and a plan for carrying it out.

2. *Relation to Managerial Function of Organizing.* In the area of organizing, staff units have developed their contribution substantially. For the line manager in modern business to concern himself with providing all the necessary factors for operation would leave him little time for seeing that operations proper were performed adequately. Staff assists in procurement of the various technical factors and resources. An example is the work done by the purchasing department or the material storage department. These staff units not only do much of the planning for procuring equipment, materials, supplies, and services in cooperation with other departments; they also see to it that these requisites are brought together at their place of use at the right time, subject to approval by line personnel.

The procurement of personnel is another organizing function performed mostly by staff. Recruitment, selection, and assignment to jobs (subject to line manager's approval) are organizing functions that are the responsibility of personnel departments or their equivalent.

A third way in which organizing functions are assisted by staff is the installation of organizational units and procedures in the organization structure. In some firms organizational planning departments have been formed for the purpose of working out and installing such elements. In most firms such activities are done by the personnel management, office management, and industrial engineering staff departments.

The work of providing the various technical factors often requires that a staff department provide its services on a continuing and regular basis. An example is the maintenance departments. Such departments have come to be referred to as service departments and are at times distinguished from other staff units. The basis of distinction is the right assigned to them, to perform their services anywhere in the organization.

3. *Relation to Managerial Function of Direction.* By its work in such areas as training, development, and orientation of operative and managerial employees, staff assists in the direction function. These programs are intended to instruct personnel in the knowledge, skills, and attitudes required of an effective work force.

Staff may assist in the direction function in two other ways. The staff specialist may prepare written instructions or specifications which are released as authorizations to perform in a certain way or by a certain time. Staff specialists may also assist line management in the active supervision of work. The dispatcher who distributes work orders and schedules to individual operatives at machines, or the inspector who points out to employees ways of avoiding defective workmanship, are examples.

4. *Relation to Managerial Function of Controlling.* Finally, staffs may assist in the function of control. They are particularly helpful in comparing results with plans and in determining and recommending corrective action.

Measurement of results implies existence of standards against which to measure. Standards of material, quality, time, method, personnel, and service must first have been established. Ways and means of comparing performance against standards must be set.

Concurrent control, done at the point and time of performance, is generally the line supervisor's function. A certain amount of coordination, of adjustment among interrelated units while operations are proceeding, can be effected by the staff specialist. Postcontrol can be implemented largely by the staff. It involves actual determination of how well completed work conforms with standards or objectives. A report on satisfactory performance assures that control is effective. A report on unsatisfactory results suggests that the staff follow up its original finding with an investigation of the causes. Such finding should be the basis for (1) an explanation of why the deviation from planned performance was necessary or desirable, or (2) a recommended course for corrective action to remedy the "off course" performance. The actual decision, and the order, to initiate corrective action are, of course, the line superior's responsibility.

An example is the work done by the production control staff unit. Within the framework of overall production goals, it determines production quotas and time goals for various units. It constantly keeps in touch with operating units and, perhaps, such units as purchasing and stores, helping to coordinate needs and production of all interrelated units. It makes minor adjustments as necessary in order to keep all operations on time and in proper order of performance. At the end of a time period, a comparison is made with the quota originally planned. When there is a deviation, it is investigated and explained, and suggestions are made for improvement or adjustment.

Aspects of Staff Authority

The great variety of tasks performed by staff specialists gives rise to a significant question. How does the staff get and exercise authority to discharge its obligations? Whatever rights it has are delegated by a superior line officer. Staff is outside the basic line structure and is auxiliary to it. It must ordinarily carry out its responsibilities of assisting and facilitating through other than the formal line structure. The ramifications of the exercise of authority by staff will be discussed in this section.

1. *Authorization of Staff to Act for Line.* All formal authority that staff may exercise is received from a higher line executive. Consequently, the line may authorize staff to act in its behalf. The staff specialist is asked to assume certain responsibilities of the line unit; commensurate authority is delegated along with it. The ultimate authority over this action remains with the delegating line executive. This is so because the line retains its responsibility for performance of that action. Since it cannot delegate its responsibility or obligation to a higher level, it must also continue to have the right to change its authorization to the staff.

2. *Line Authority within Staff Unit.* While staff does not ordinarily exercise direct line authority toward other units, the executive

in the staff unit exercises direct authority over his subordinates. Direct supervision is needed in order to effectually produce the service for which the staff unit exists. As an example, the corps of inspectors in a plant may all be assigned to a quality control department and may act in a staff capacity to various production departments. They will have direct line accountability to the chief inspector, who will in turn have line accountability to the quality control manager. As a result, the principle of single accountability is maintained in a line and staff organization.

3. **Staff Assumption of Line Authority.** There are circumstances in which it may be desirable, even urgent, for staff to assume line authority. Such occasions should be kept to a minimum, but such a course is dictated at times.

a) *Emergencies.* Emergencies may arise when the combination of line authority and the staff's special talents should rest with a staff executive. For example, the medical department may refuse to permit a worker to continue at his present job because of an allergy, although the supervisor may wish to retain the worker.

b) *Technical Knowledge.* Other special situations may warrant delegating line authority to a specialized staff unit. The knowledge and skills demanded in the management of a technical function may be of such caliber that the staff specialist alone is capable of directing and controlling it, as well as planning and organizing it.

c) *Procedural Authority.* The work involved in machine maintenance may be such that only the department head and his subordinate managers can supervise maintenance and repair of machines. The authority of maintenance thus extends into the organization wherever its services are needed, and it exercises line authority over its function. The staff performs its work through procedures drawn up and approved as the accepted ways in which staff operation will be done. Thus, it actually exerts its authority by virtue of a procedure, that is, it exercises procedural authority.

d) *Professional Skill.* Even where no formal procedural authority exists, staff sometimes exercises influence that is almost indistinguishable from line authority. For example, after exploring alternatives the operations research staff may submit a recommendation, arrived at by involved and quantitative means, as to the most desirable product mix that a company should offer. The recommendation is then adopted with little question as to its validity simply because the line manager is not capable of evaluating the procedure from which it resulted.

Since placement of line authority in a staff position is not without organizational hazards, it should be justified. Every additional assumption of authority by staff is an inroad into the authority of the line organization, thus making placement of responsibility a nebulous thing. For this same reason the assumption of line authority by staff is often only a temporary condition.

Because the complexity of decision-making processes has increased, as in the case of the operations research group involvement mentioned above, it has been argued that distinctions between line and staff are superfluous. Organizational effectiveness, so the argument goes, will be increased by giving to each function decision-making rights with respect to its specialty. Such authority would extend to all others affected by the decision. For example, the purchasing agent would have line authority with respect to his function. The difficulty with this view is that there is no adequate placement of responsibility for results.

4. *Staff Influence without Line Authority.* For the staff unit to depend to a large extent on assumed line authority to exercise its duties would be to risk confusion and conflict among management. The effective staff specialist can use other alternatives to that of assuming line authority. He can engage in activities such as the following to further his staff influence.

a) Advisory Counsel. His job exists to advise and assist other units. By loyal and superior service to the interests of the organization, he can go far in earning respect for, and acceptance of, his services. Usually, the special skills and knowledge in themselves command the respect of those not directly involved in their execution. When these are applied so as to facilitate the discharge of the line manager's responsibilities, not only is the staff man sought after but his suggestions and directions are readily followed.

b) Consultative Skill. Ability to persuade other executives of its value is another helpful tool in the staff unit's kit for influencing others. Staff men often have the background and attitude that make them conscious of maintaining good personal relationships. Recognizing their lack of formal authority over other units, they may well realize the value of good salesmanship. Indeed, the personal popularity that the persuasive staff man generates is often a more potent force than the formal right to manage which is conferred through line channels. Such an individual combines the influence of personal relationship with the weight of his position. When such personal magnetism is combined with a tactful and logical presentation of the staff offerings, staff influence is well assured.

c) *Recourse to Higher Authority.* A third way available to staff in influencing other units is that of recourse to higher line authority. There may be occasions when the staff specialist feels it imperative that his recommendation be followed. Or, he may feel that his limited right is being unnecessarily challenged by another executive. A case in point is the salesman or sales supervisor who refuses to heed the admonition to restrict granting of credit to certain customers who are questionable credit risks. If the credit manager cannot directly take action to discourage such behavior, he may report the matter to the sales manager. It is then up to the latter to take remedial action. If the credit manager's position is justified, his influence will be felt through the sales manager.

5. **Adequate Use of Staff Services by Line Units.** The line organization is often reluctant to use the services of the staff. Line executives either may not understand the services available and applicable to their own problems, or they may be reluctant to use them because of hostility or fear of inroads on their own authority. If they are inclined to be independent, they may regard the need to consult staff as a sign of weakness. They may feel, too, that there is not always sufficient time to consult staff.

Some organizational philosophies stress avoiding the required use of staff advice by line units. This puts the staff man in the position of "selling" himself and his services, or being out of a job. On the other hand, there are firms in which the rule of compulsory staff advice is laid down for management. This, in effect, requires the line manager to consult appropriate staff units prior to making a significant decision. He is not under obligation to use the advice, but he must nevertheless listen to it before taking action. There are exceptions to this rule, but in general the level of significance of the decision can be specified.

Generally, good service should sell itself. Once quality service is rendered without adversely affecting the status or goodwill of the unit manager who has benefited, further requests for service can be expected. Line units less willing to avail themselves of staff help may be persuaded by the example of more enthusiastic ones who have been recipients of staff services.

If staff advice and facilitation are to be effective in content and really pertinent to the problem, they must be given with the assurance that the staff specialist himself will not suffer retribution because his ideas or recommendations may be in conflict with those of his superior. Staff advice is less than useless when it deteriorates to the level of merely seconding what the superior already has voiced, or if it attempts to give the answer which the boss is expected to want. It may help compound mistakes rather than avoid them, a situation to be deplored.

6. *Domination of Line by Staff.* At times line authority is assumed by staff under unfavorable organizational conditions. The line manager either may not be able or may not care to exercise all his management prerogatives. He may prefer to let the staff unit exercise line jurisdiction over certain of his responsibilities. While this abandonment of authority is a symptom of organizational weakness, it nevertheless exists.

The staff manager may, by development of informal authority, succeed in dominating line executives. His proximity and frequent access to the president's office may give him undue weight of influence. He may gradually broaden his procedural authority beyond its intended scope. Or, he may seize upon gaps in assignment of organizational responsibility and gradually build for himself additional responsibilities and authority, which may give the impression that he is headed for greater power in the firm, and he may thus command greater deference than is due him.

Review of organizational responsibilities and authority of all units, line and staff, and provision of training and education for management people of all units can help greatly to minimize such dangers to the line.

Relationship of Central Staff to Regional Staffs

A related question of line-staff relationships is that of relationship of the central office staff of multiunit companies to the regional staffs. Frequently, a parallel pattern of staff arrangement can be found; that is, the staff unit at the home office is duplicated at the plant level. This may not apply to all staff services, since central legal and public relations staff units, for example, may suffice for the whole organization.

Such duplication of staff is usually founded on good reason and is done to a greater extent where the organizational philosophy is that of decentralization. Here, the lower staff units are set up to help the regional plant manager exercise greater initiative in making decisions. The headquarters office is in a position to exercise staff help for the entire company. Its resources can help the regional staffs do their job better. Proper relationships can minimize time involved in, and maximize amount of, assistance given by headquarters to units.

1. *Authority and Performance.* Very rarely does the central staff unit have a line authority relationship to the staff at the plant level. This would interfere with the line authority of the plant chief executive. Unfortunately, there is some danger that lines of communication, because of weight of central staff influence, may come to be mistaken for lines of authority. A careful definition of the authority of staff functions, both at home and at the plant, can aid greatly in minimizing such danger. The central staff executive may contact the regional plant manager, but this also must be done in a staff manner. The latter has a direct obligation to the line superior at the home office, not to home office staff. Furthermore, if headquarters staff sends down a directive to lower staff, provision must be made for informing the latter unit's line superior.

The impact of authorizing central staffs to issue to branch managers directives having line authority can be understood upon brief reflection. Each time a headquarters staff unit becomes empowered to issue orders to a lower line executive, the decision-making rights of the latter are reduced. Decentralization moves more and more toward centralization because authority delegated from above is being reclaimed.

Generally, therefore, the authority of central staff lies in recommending to top management policies that affect the organization as a whole. In some instances, too, corporate or central staffs may perform certain services for the entire organization if economy and efficiency are served thereby. An example is centralizing in the home office the procurement of materials, supplies, or equipment used by all divisions or plants.

2. *Lines of Communication.* The lines of communication between central and regional staffs are usually direct. To channel all communications through the local unit manager would be to burden him unnecessarily and invite the dangers of layering. However, it is imperative that the line superior of the local staff be kept informed of matters transmitted which are pertinent to the discharge of his personal responsibilities.

3. *Surveillance.* In addition to dealing in the same services (but in a more comprehensive way), central staff exercises general

surveillance over unit staffs. Suggestions and assistance for improved functioning can develop from this relationship. Central staff can furnish valuable consultation service to lower units. Usually the central units have access to resources that lower staffs do not possess. Central staff has the benefit of working with all the company units. Not only can it apply experiences of one to problems of another, but it can be the focal point for coordinating ideas and interunit matters. It serves as the distributing center for staff reports.

An organizational pitfall that is sometimes encountered is related to the surveillance function. There is always the possibility that central staff may become overly critical of mistakes made by lower echelons, particularly in a decentralized firm. A staff specialist then writes up procedures in order to prevent this. Writing up procedures may, however, have the effect of harnessing lower units and giving them actually less authority than they had before. Then there begins the same centralizing process mentioned in the discussion of authority and performance.

4. Training. Central staff can assist in training division staff personnel and thereby insure that staff quality will be uniform and effective throughout the firm. It can even train lower echelon personnel by methods such as rotation among different company units, including headquarters. Of course central staff personnel must insure their own development by getting out to the regional units as often as necessary and in other ways remaining aware of the nature of current field problems which they presume to assist in solving.

The foregoing comments have attempted briefly to review the important aspects of the relationship of central and lower echelon staffs. With the growing complexity and size of decentralized firms, and with the development of widely dispersed companies (such as multinational firms), there is no doubt that parallel staff relationships will become even more involved. But such problems of complexity must be solved in order that coordination for the organizational units as a whole may be achieved.

QUESTIONS

1. What are some of the reasons why managerial specialization is not as prevalent in a small company as in a large company?
2. It has been said that the influence of the individual executive decreases as the size of the organization increases. Do you agree?

3. In what way does staff assist in the managerial function of planning? Of controlling?
4. Should staff units ever assume line authority? Under what circumstances?
5. Many firms follow the practice of cutting back or eliminating staff units at a considerably greater rate than the line personnel as the organization encounters economic difficulties. Does this seem to be a logical action on the part of the company?
6. Why are staff services resented or ignored by many line managers?
7. How does procedural authority effectuate the work of the staff department?

CASE 14–1

Before Max Wolfe was hired as personnel director of the Republic Department Store, a firm with approximately 400 employees, the function was ineptly handled by the recently terminated store manager. As a college-trained specialist, Max established a formalized office of personnel with its supporting subsets. He developed a formalized program with new personnel forms. He instituted procedures for reference checking and installed an extensive interviewing process. Both he and his equally skilled employment manager conducted intensive interviews in an attempt to secure qualified employees. Only after being thoroughly assured, would the personnel department refer applicants to the department heads for additional interviews and ultimate selection.

However, Max has discovered that the department managers were just cursorily interviewing applicants and almost immediately agreeing upon the recommendations of the personnel department. When Max questioned a department head about this, he answered, "In the past we never had the opportunity to approve of new employees. They were delivered to us by the store manager. But now we feel that since you're the personnel expert, and since we have been getting qualified people, if they are good enough for personnel, that's good enough for us."

1. What is wrong with the selection and placement procedures of the Republic company?
2. What has the content of this case to do with line and staff relationships?
3. Describe a process of relationships between the line department heads and personnel that would insure a proper delineation of responsibilities.

CASE 14–2

Recently, the Peerless Rubber and Plastics Company underwent a major reorganization. For the first time, it would follow a policy of decentralization. The major decision managers were to have complete authority over the entire division. The plastics division, for example, was to operate autonomously under the direction of the division manager, who was to function within established corporate policy. Several specialized staff functions were located at the headquarters level, and parallel units were located at the division level. Irrespective of the reorganization, the director of purchasing in headquarters began to issue detailed directives and procedures for the purchase of office equipment to the supervisor of purchasing in each of the divisions. The division purchasing supervisor, by the way, reported directly to the division manager. At a recent company meeting the plastics division manager questioned the director of purchasing as to whether he had heard about the firm's reorganization.

1. How did the policy of decentralization compare with the practice?
2. Should the director of purchasing have issued the directives and procedures to the division managers instead of lower staff units?

15

Informal Relationships

Scope of Informal Relationships

NOT ALL RELATIONS among people in an organization are of a formal nature. To be sure, charts of organization structure depict the channels through which authority and responsibility should formally flow. Layouts of procedures similarly depict the steps that should be taken in order to complete given projects. Such tools as standard practice instructions, commands, policies, rules, and regulations are formalized expressions of relations that should exist in an organization. Without the foregoing, an organization would be an ineffective grouping of specialists if, indeed, not a mob.

But even the most superficial acquaintance with any organized group reveals that many relations among people are of an informal nature. That is to say that channels of structure, steps taken in getting work done, and behavioral patterns do not always conform with specified conditions. There are innumerable informal relationships. Indeed, until one becomes fairly well acquainted with the informal ways, feelings, and expectations surrounding his job, results can be technically poor and personally frustrating. Hence, even an expert had better "learn the ropes" in his new environment if he wishes to get work done effectively and with personal satisfaction.

Such informal relations may occur in the organization structure of a business, in its procedures, and in the everyday contacts among various members of the group. This chapter is concerned with the following aspects of informal relations:

1. Nature of informal relations.
2. Lines of informal relations.

3. Sociological factors and forces.
4. Establishment of status and roles.
5. Operational aspects of informal relations.

Nature of Informal Relations

The nature of informal relations may be described by noting, first, the basic reasons for their development and, second, the fundamental forces in informal relations.

1. *Development of Informal Relations.* Informal relations develop for one of three basic reasons. First, they develop to attain business objectives for which formal structures have not been provided. Suppose a person is told to meet a given sales quota but is not told how. He will proceed on his own to figure out how to do the assigned task; that is, he sets an informal procedure into motion.

Such informality may be desirable or undesirable. It is desirable if formal plans would be too expensive to establish. It is undesirable if the executive could establish more effective plans in a more economical way.

Second, informal relations develop when there are forces and drives within people beyond those utilized by the technical needs of business. Were man simply a "commodity," his physical characteristics and skills could be handled much as are physical resources of materials and machines. His physical powers could be tapped to the extent needed, and any unneeded powers could be controlled and stored as desired.

Patently, man is much more than a physical factor of production. He is a composition of psychological, sociological, political, and ethical qualities. These qualities do not go into a "deep freeze" during working hours. The desire for recognition, for example, if not satisfied by the physical work situation, may seek an outlet through the formation of social gatherings on company time or through attachment to executives from whom reflected glory may be gained.

The third explanation for the existence of informal relations stems from the second. The informal structures provide outlets for the full nature of man. If the gregarious tendencies of employees are not satisfied by the job, they will be satisfied to some extent informally. For example, excuses will be found to gather together to "discuss" technical problems, groups will sneak off for a smoke, or grievances will be expounded during coffee breaks. Or jobs that do not challenge employees (and this also includes executive groups)—meaning a situation in which the resources of man exceed the job needs—are an ideal climate for the cultivation of informal relations.

Conversely, jobs that are "too big" for the incumbents may bring about informal relations. For example, a superior may distrust his immediate subordinates. So, he goes around them to those he can trust to get jobs done. Similarly, staff people may have no confidence in line executives with whom they should work. They therefore go directly to underlings in the line to get their ideas into operation before some executive blocks their adoption.

To sum up, people's physical powers not needed in work usually lie dormant or can be controlled with a minimum of effort. But psychological or sociological forces must be channeled, challenged, or drained off. If this is not done formally—and it never is fully—a variety of informal relations is the inevitable result.

2. *Fundamental Forces of Informal Relations.* Informal human relations are essentially expressions, therefore, of the psychological and sociological needs of man.

a) Psychological Aspects. The behavior of employees is explainable in part by their psychological makeup. That is to say, people behave as they do partly because of something within themselves—emotions, mind, attitude, needs—call it what you will; even psychologists disagree among themselves, as well as with other students of human behavior such as sociologists and anthropologists, about the exact nature of these forces. With due recognition of, and respect for, the disagreements among such specialists, and with an appreciation of the twilight zones that exist in all human studies, it will be simply stated here that "psychological" has reference to the egocentric phases of individuals.

To continue on a simplified plane, all individuals—employees— possess psychological needs which urge them to seek situations of satisfaction and to avoid the unpleasant. Strictly speaking, as egocentric individuals, employees want to satisfy their physiological needs or hungers—sex, food, and shelter. But once these are gained, the employees want other things to satisfy the urges of their egos—a feeling of physical well-being, mental peace, a good outlook, and pleasant stimuli for their senses.

Conversely, the search for the pleasant is paralleled by a campaign to avoid the unpleasant. Anything or any situation that brings about, or is likely to bring about, an unpleasant feeling in the body or mind is to be avoided, if possible.

Returning now to the matter of informal relations, these are explainable in part by psychological factors. When the psychological needs of an employee are not satisfied formally by the business situation—as far as business is capable of doing so—the employee will utilize the business situation informally, insofar as he can, to balance his psychological needs. Thus, an employee who does not get a sense of personal well-being from his job as outlined in a work order, let us say, will attempt either openly or in some subtle manner to do the job in his own way. Or, a supervisor may be giving his subordinates a rough time or even neglecting them. As a consequence, the employees turn to some individual other than the one specified by the formal organization chart to minimize the unpleasant feelings. These are simple examples of how psychological needs of employees lend themselves to the development of informal relations.

b) *Sociological Aspects.* Perhaps of equal, if not greater, import in explaining informal relations are sociological factors and forces. This refers to the needs of an individual that arise out of his associations with other individuals. Social drives are elemental to most individuals. Indeed, the psychological choices of most people are weighted heavily by sociological considerations. The two are actually intertwined beyond separation but for purposes of discussion are taken up separately.

Sociology deals with group relationships. It is concerned with behavior deriving from the interaction of people. It has an important bearing on behavior because most of us do what we do because of what others will think of us and our actions. This has long been recognized in the nonworking part of the lives of people. Only recently has there been a significant awakening to sociological importance in business and industry.

Such an awakening is desirable. Employees—like all individuals—are much concerned with what others are thinking about them. So, they do things and react to people in ways that will win the approval of those whose opinions they value. Thus, a given employee is willing to go out on a strike to retain the goodwill of his fellow workers, even though temporarily such action results in a heavy economic loss. Or, an employee may for the same reason loaf on the job or limit his output. These are manifestations of an "informal" nature that run counter to formal relations and standards.

A desire for prestige may motivate some persons to establish informal contacts. An individual may short-circuit his direct superior to bask in the limelight of associations with the "brass." Moreover, he can then brag to his colleagues about his intimacy with such levels. Presumably his status—the prestige accorded to him by his fellows—is thereby higher than that which his formal contacts would yield.

Some employees establish informal channels of communication to gain an otherwise unattained place in a group. Such commonplace activities as rumor spreading, gossiping, and office politicking are examples. Or, getting a strategic place in the "grapevine" serves the same purpose. In all of these instances, the employees obtain something from the group that is satisfying to themselves.

Informal developments, moreover, seldom parallel the objectives of the formal structure. Indeed, to gain group status at lower levels, it sometimes seems necessary to do things in opposition to formal relations. One must, for example, be "against the boss," be willing to reduce output, to waste materials, to express antagonism against company rules and regulations, and to act negatively in an undercover if not open manner. In these ways, proof is offered of one's allegiance to the group and therefore of his worthiness of group approval.

Curiously enough, the social pressures may run counter to the dictates of psychological needs or desires. Thus, an employee may take pleasure in doing a fair day's work in a craftsmanlike manner. That is, it would be inwardly satisfying to do so. But he refrains in order to avoid the censure and ostracism of his fellow workers. So, as in many other human actions, the group pressures are superior to internal, egocentric drives in reaching decisions as to what will be done. And this, in business, results in informal relations that run counter to the formal.

Lines of Informal Relationships

It is now appropriate to examine various lines of informal relations. These may be grouped as follows:

1. Superior-to-subordinate relations.
2. Subordinate-to-superior relations.
3. Horizontal relations.

4.   Procedural relations.
5.   External relations.

   1.   *Informal Superior-to-Subordinate Relations.* When one views the organization chart of any business, the lines from top superior to lowest subordinate seem to be unequivocal and clear-cut. Thus, the chart in Figure 15–1 seems to show, for example, that the pro-

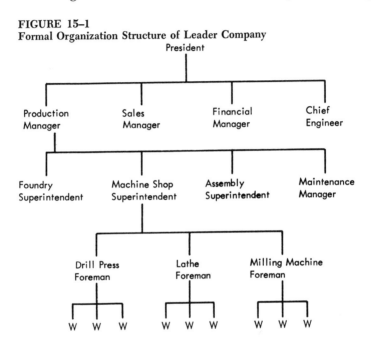

FIGURE 15–1
Formal Organization Structure of Leader Company

duction manager is the superior of the machine shop superintendent, and that the latter is the superior of the lathe foreman. Presumably, formal lines of authority run downward clearly through these men.

   The formal lines do run so. But the figure omits some informal lines. Were these included, the relationship between these men would be diagramed as shown in Figure 51–2. Here it will be noted that:

1.   The president prefers to go directly to the machine shop superintendent rather than through the production manager.
2.   The chief engineer bypasses the machine shop superintendent and works with the lathe foreman and even his workers.
3.   The production manager prefers to bypass the machine shop superintendent.

FIGURE 15–2
Informal Aspects of Selected Parts of Leader Company Organization

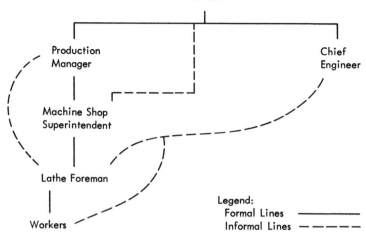

Hence, a number of informal channels from superiors downward have been established which do not show in the formal organization structure.

The reasons for such informal superior-to-subordinate relationships are varied. In the case of the Leader Company, investigation disclosed the following explanations:

1. In the case of the president, he was: (a) conducting himself in line with what he thought was his natural right to deal with anyone, anytime, on any subject; and (b) ignorant of the purpose of an organization structure.
2. In the case of the production manager, he was fearful for his own position, so he tried to protect himself by attempting to get the personal loyalty of the lower levels.
3. In the case of the chief engineer, he had a low opinion of the capacity of the machine shop superintendent to understand technical advice and preferred, therefore, to work directly with the shop.

The informal relations between superiors and subordinates made up, therefore, for the inadequacies, supposed or real, of the formal organization structure and its several incumbents.

   2. Informal Subordinate-to-Superior Relations. Looking upward, informal lines will be found to run in many directions other than those specified by the formal structure. Referring again to

Figure 15–1, it would seem that each person at every level reports to one, and only one, superior. Upon closer investigation, however, a selected sample of the organization revealed a number of additional lines of contact, as illustrated in Figure 15–3.

FIGURE 15–3
Informal Aspects of Selected Parts of Leader Company

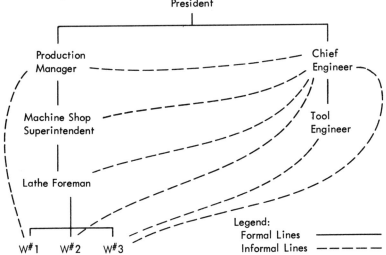

The dotted lines in this figure reveal the existence of a number of subordinate-to-superior contacts. Of special interest is the number of informal lines running to the chief engineer. Close study uncovered a variety of reasons for this condition, as follows:

1. The production manager went beyond the normal contacts of line and staff because:
    a) He thought the chief engineer was destined to be the next president, so he wanted to be on the right side of the heir apparent.
    b) He was fearful for his own position and tried to give the impression to the chief engineer that he saw the need for organizational cooperation.
2. The machine shop superintendent continually ran to the chief engineer because:
    a) He, too, sensed the likelihood of the chief engineer's promotion.
    b) He tried to offset the feeling that the chief engineer did not have too high an opinion of him.

      c) He did not like the production manager and tried to carry gossip about this superior to the chief engineer.

3. The lathe foreman sensed the chief engineer's desire to work with the shop directly, so he took every opportunity to work with him.

4. Worker No. 2, like the lathe foreman, was a favorite of the chief engineer because of his technical competence. He, too, felt free to go around the line directly to the chief engineer.

5. Worker No. 3 was playing a two-sided game:

      a) He was trying to worm into the chief engineer's good graces by running to him with any bit of information that would reveal his own technical skill.

      b) Yet he also was working on the tool engineer, feeling that this man would move up to the chief engineer's job if, as, and when the latter took the top job.

6. Worker No. 1, an old-timer who had grown up in the business with the production manager, felt a loyalty to him which resulted in his carrying information to the production manager of the politics that the others were playing.

Subordinates turn to superiors other than those to whom they are supposed to report, for a number of reasons. Their own superiors may actually have less authority than the formal structure would seem to indicate. They may be dealing in "futures," calculating that changes that are likely to take place are more significant to them than present advantages. They may gain a feeling of prestige by dealing with some highly placed individual. They may actually prefer personally to deal with someone other than their own superior. They may be "bucking" for a promotion in a way best calculated to achieve that result; and they like the feeling of getting the ear of a higher official by passing on gossip, rumors, and unfavorable reports on their direct superiors.

    3. *Informal Horizontal Relations.* Informal relations may also take place on a horizontal plane. Executives or employees of equal rank may contact each other informally, for good or bad reasons.

In the case of the Leader Company, Figure 15–1 would seem to indicate, for example, that the machine shop superintendent would have to go up to the production manager to deal with the maintenance manager. If "channels" were actually followed, such, to be sure, would be the case. But formalization to that extent would soon bring an organization to a standstill. Instead, the machine shop superintendent confers with, deals with, reaches decisions with, and handles various mutual problems with, the maintenance manager, with seldom a word to the production manager.

Informal contacts thus provide a desirable means of expediting the work of an organization. Various individuals can work out cooperative details without recourse to their respective superiors. Only reports of progress or exceptional cases need be brought to the attention of superiors. So long as subordinates use good judgment in what they do informally, the whole organization benefits, because the formal channels do not become clogged with everything that is happening.

On the other hand, some informal horizontal relations may not be so desirable. On occasions, horizontal cross contacts may be used to undermine or combat the formal. A not uncommon example is found at the worker level. Employees may, as a case in point, agree informally to restrict their output. No more than a given amount is produced by each worker. Any employee who exceeds the "standard" is ostracized—if not treated even worse—by the group. As a consequence, the output per employee is invariably at or below the level as established.

Another group of employee relations that may be termed undesirable includes instances of informal leadership. Here, employees turn to a fellow worker for leadership instead of to their formal leaders. An aggrieved employee, for example, seeks out a trusted fellow worker to pour out his complaints and to seek guidance on what to do. Similarly, workers may get informal leadership on a variety of matters of interest to them: how to organize a party; how to apply for a leave of absence; what to do if a machine breaks down; how to get materials or tools that are in short supply; how to deal with staff people who come into the department, etc.

In all these cases, employees presumably are not getting satisfactory leadership through formal channels. So they seek answers through informal contacts. The undesirability feature of these contacts is not necessarily a fault of the employees. Rather, the problem stems from poor formal management. If the formal executives did their work effectively and fairly, the need for most, if not all, of these informal contacts would disappear.

4. *Informal Procedural Relations.* Many informal relations take place in connection with established procedures. Indeed, this is a most fertile area for the development of informal relations. An interesting example, which will serve to initiate a discussion of such relations, is provided by the series of steps by which an employee

is supposed to get tools to complete a specific job. Let us assume
that the pertinent steps are as diagramed in Figure 15–4.

FIGURE 15–4
Selected Steps for Procuring Tools

1. Receive work order from supervisor.
2. Take work order to department clerk.
3. Department clerk makes out tool request.
4. Tool requests are taken to toolroom.
5. Toolroom issues needed tools.

These steps seem simple and clear enough. But at times—and,
as invariably happens, at crucial times—the worker finds that
needed tools are not available. The tool keeper informs the re-
quester that the tools asked for are out on another job or have not
been returned. This places the worker in a predicament which will
waste his time. After making his complaints to the tool keeper
(which will only put him at a disadvantage the next time he comes
in for tools), he returns to his supervisor for another assignment.
All the while he is not on piecework, let us say, but on day work—
which cuts down on his take-home earnings.

A few such instances and the employee will "learn the ropes."
This is an expression that means he will learn how to get tools informally. A number of lessons will be taught him by the school
of hard knocks. First, he will get on the good side of: (*a*) the supervisor, (*b*) the department clerk, and, (*c*) the tool keeper. The
supervisor can then tell him in advance on what jobs he is likely
to work. As a consequence, the worker can take early steps to: (*a*)
requisition tools early—if the departmental clerk will play ball with
him; (*b*) ask the tool keeper to inform him of hard-to-get tools;
or (*c*) actually hide tools until needed. Obviously, being on friendly
terms with the departmental clerk and the tool keeper can put the
worker in an advantageous position.

All of the foregoing informal steps are in addition to—and supplement or circumvent—the formal steps of the procedure for getting
tools. But if the formal procedure is inadequate for the purposes,
the worker can scarcely be blamed for establishing his own procedures. Indeed, working out personal procedures is one of the ways
by which employees add zest to otherwise routine and boring jobs.
It becomes a kind of game.

In playing the "game," various employees become adept at

different phases of it. Some become adept at getting the "umpires" to call plays in their favor. Thus, the employee who has a favorable relation with the tool keeper can invariably get what he needs while others starve for tools. Others become adept at forging or upgrading requisitions. Thus, tools in excess of current needs are acquired for future use. Other employees become adept at pilfering and storing tools. In such cases it is not uncommon to find a few employees who have a supply of selected tools that rivals, if indeed it does not exceed, that of the regular toolroom. And, finally, some are adept at learning what jobs are coming up in the future and then making advance provisions to meet the distant demands.

This may all sound somewhat unrealistic and rather ludicrous for a business operation. But it is far from an isolated case. What has been said about tools could be duplicated for the following:

1. Getting machines repaired and maintained.
2. Getting work through quality hurdles.
3. Obtaining trucks to move materials, tools, and parts.
4. Avoiding rush, emergency, or "hard" jobs.
5. Getting materials and supplies.
6. Working with various staff people such as engineers, accountants, training people, counselors, and auditors.

The informal procedural relations are by no means restricted to worker levels. Indeed, the higher one goes in an organization, the more likely one is to find such informal relations. The reason for this is simple. Formal procedures are much fewer in number and in completeness at the top than they are at the bottom. As a consequence, informal procedures are established to get the work of an organization done. So various line and staff personnel will have worked out informal procedures to do what the formal cannot. As a person moves up an organization structure, he will have to learn these unwritten, but nonetheless important, procedures.

5. Informal External Relations. It is also true that informal relations may develop between a company and a number of outside groups. Illustrative of major relations of this type are the following:

1. Unions.	3. Community agencies.
2. Governmental groups.	4. Public in general.

Although union-management relations may be governed by contract or legislative rules, much in this area transpires on an informal basis. Certainly, organizational structures and procedures here are at times not formalized to the degree that they are in internal operations. Even such matters as grievances, though supposedly in the realm of definite procedures, are often handled on an informal, let's settle-it-out-of-court basis. When it comes to collective-bargaining procedures, almost everything here is on an informal, personal basis. As time goes on, some formalization is taking place, but at present union-management relations can be fairly termed informal.

Relations with governmental agencies are also worthy of note in this connection. To be sure, contacts with, and reports to, various local, state, and federal groups are on a very formal basis through definite legal steps. But here, too, knowing the right people, how to work through various agencies, and what shortcuts can or should not be taken, is most helpful (all, of course, of an informal nature). Usually, such informal relations are best handled by those who have served in governmental agencies as administrators or legislators.

Community agencies of all kinds involve informal relations. Welfare and charitable groups may call for contributions or may actually help in business matters. On the one hand, a business may make contributions to such groups as the United Fund. On the other hand, it may obtain the services of such groups as Alcoholics Anonymous for some of its employees. Then, too, a company may work with various groups such as community improvement, church, educational, and social groups. The work relation may be very cursory or it may involve active participation by executives and employees.

Finally, every business has contacts with the public in general in varying degrees. Such relations are being viewed increasingly as very important. Through radio, television, and newspapers, more and more companies are trying to gain a favorable reaction from the public in general. This is desired not only to help sell products but also to gain support for its views when faced with unfavorable legislation or union opposition. In seeking such support through the channels of mass communications, business invariably relies upon those who are experts in public opinion and in communication channels.

Sociological Factors and Forces

Having explored the nature and types of informal relations in the preceding two sections, it is now appropriate to examine some of the basic forces in informality. Undoubtedly, the major area of interest here is the sociological. As already noted, an employee (worker or executive) is much more than an economic or technical factor of production. He is also a social creature. Hence, it is important to see how social manifestations affect informal relations. This is done by reviewing in this section the social aspects of business, and in the next section the establishment of social status and roles in business.

The term social as used here refers to how people act and interact because they are members of a group—in particular, a business group. Such interaction can be studied in terms of the following:

1. The social system of the community.
2. The social system of a particular business.
3. The status of particular positions and persons.
4. The roles of particular positions and persons.

1. *The Social System of the Community.* The term "society" has more meanings than that of a select group of party, industrial, or wealthy leaders. In any community, people are grouped according to how they make a living. Thus, factory workers have a milieu different from that of top executives or of top technical or professional employees. Even among factory workers, groupings take place between "common" laborer and craftsman. The social differences, if restricted solely to where one lived or with whom one associated after work, might be of little interest to business management. But the differences engender an attitude and reaction that carry over into the working situation. Anyone who has lived in a community in which there are marked social differences based largely on whether one is an employee or manager (or owner) is aware of the attitudes that carry over from the community to the business.

But the other elements in a community besides working positions may affect its social pattern and, in turn, business relations. There may be "old families," financial leaders, educational leaders, political leaders, etc., who may set the tone for a community. This tone may be democratic or autocratic; it may be for progress or for the good old days; it may be cooperative or narrowly selfish; or it may be forward looking or backward looking. Obviously, the place accorded labor in the community will be reflected in the working situation. The social structure, climate, and attitude in a community have an impact upon relations in the factory, office, or store.

2. *The Social System of a Particular Business.* Within an enterprise, social systems will be found to exist. Workers react to superiors as well as to one another because they "belong" to particular groups, or do not belong. Just being a worker places a person in a class apart from the manager class. In the worker class, one must therefore act in ways that do not injure his class. He perhaps must not work too hard, nor protect his tools, nor consider the supervisor his friend, nor do anything voluntarily to help the company make money. Managers, too, unconsciously if not consciously, take on a class coloration: they may think they are better than workers or have more significant and more worthwhile jobs.

But even within the worker class or the manager class, distinctions and groupings develop. Technical workers, like craft union members, may not care to associate with unskilled or semiskilled workers. Or, members of particular groups of workers such as foundrymen or machine operators may look askance at each other. Or, those who play on a particular softball team, or are "represented" by one, may set themselves apart from other team members or representatives. Executives similarly may establish subclass distinctions.

So, all through an enterprise social groupings of one kind and another, superimposed upon groupings of various shades, will be found to exist. Anyone who attempts to work without some consideration for existing social groupings is asking for trouble. Whether or not one likes them, they exist and they are not likely to disappear. When one steps into a new situation, this is one of the things he must include under the heading of "learning the ropes." But, old or new, the social system of a business is one of the most potent in the whole field of informal relations.

3. *The Status of Particular Positions and Persons.* Formally, each person in an organization holds a position to which are attached various rights and privileges. The amount of these rights and privileges places some persons higher than others. Thus, the president of a company has higher status than a vice president, and so on down to the worker level.

But the esteem in which various people are held seldom conforms with the level indicated by title. Informally, a given vice president, for example, may in the eyes of various people be ranked much higher than the president himself. Or, in the case of the Leader Company cited earlier in this chapter, the chief engineer certainly ranks much higher than the production manager. Yet, according to the formal organization chart they are of equal stature.

Thus, informal relations between people are based on, and activated in part by, the ranking each attributes to the other. And the informal ranking is perhaps of greater import here than the formal ranking. While lip service may be paid to formal titles, it is the prestige (or lack of it) that an executive or a worker earns from his various associates and subordinates that determines the cooperation he will receive. Moreover, informal status affects the kinds and degrees of contacts that will be made within an organization structure and throughout various operating procedures.

4. *The Roles of Particular Positions and Persons.* Also, every person formally has a given job to do. The factory supervisor, for example, presumably plans, organizes, directs, and controls the work of his particular department; and each of his crew is supposed to perform assigned tasks. Were this all, relationships between supervisor and worker would indeed be simple.

But there is much more to the job each holds than ever appears on any job specification. The supervisor, for example, does more than his managing job. Or, to use a popular expression, he plays several roles on his departmental stage. He is like an actor in a Gilbert and Sullivan operetta. One moment he is a departmental manager; another moment he may be a "stool pigeon" for higher management; another moment he is a father confessor to his troubled workers; another moment he is a self-pitying personage caught between a hardhearted management and uncooperative employees; another moment he is an opponent of unions; and another moment he is a blundering ignoramus, comically but tragically trying to act like an executive. (Figure 15–5 represents the various sources of role expectations of the manager.)

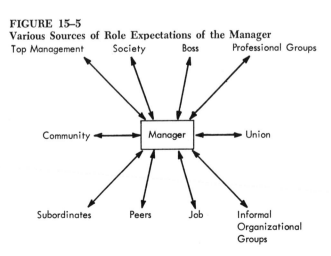

FIGURE 15–5
Various Sources of Role Expectations of the Manager

Moreover, the roles he plays may not be construed or perceived in the same way by all with whom he comes into contact. He himself may view his job as that of a first-line representative of management. But top management may view him simply as a communication or transmission center. Workers may view him as a natural enemy. Staff executives may view him as a dull obstruction.

And workers, too, become mixed up in a variety of roles. They may indeed be workers. But from various sides, they may be told that they are also partners in a business enterprise, loyal members of a union, citizens of their community, pawns in the hands of unscrupulous owners, participants in decision making, indispensable operators, and natural opponents of capital.

Since each person has several roles to play, none of them clearly defined, it is obvious that relations among people can be confusing. Indeed, the confusion sometimes is extended to such a degree that one sometimes feels the actors are fighting each other rather than putting on a cooperative play. When a given actor jumps from one role to another, he not only confuses the other actors but also frustrates himself. Yet, a director who can synchronize each player into a logical and accepted structure seldom appears. Indeed, the director himself (management at various levels) adds to the confusion by taking on conflicting roles.

Establishment of Status and Roles

If status and roles are so pervasive and influential, how do they become established and what, if anything, can be done about them? The first part of this question is answered in this section, and the second part in the next section.

Status and roles are established in a number of ways. Some forces are internal and some external to a business. Looking first at internal forces, differences in ability bring about differing status rankings or role assignments. In a sense, there is an element of hero worship here. The executive who has accomplished much, who has done big deeds, and who has overcome large obstacles is looked upon with awe. Or, the worker who knows his stuff and can do a superior job with finesse is respected by his fellow workers.

Somewhat similarly, a person who possesses rare skills stands apart from his fellows. He who has unusual knowledge or a knack for doing things is accorded a high measure of esteem and may be asked to do things that others are not. The knowledge or skill need not be related to the working situation. Thus, an employee may have an unusual memory for baseball or football data. Or another is skilled at cards, stock car racing, or bowling. As a consequence, these employees will be held in high esteem by their fellow workers. They may also be "elected" to represent the group in such matters as grievance handling, about which they may know very little.

Other internal factors determining status and roles may be such things as seniority, type of job, location of work, or equipment handled. By way of example, the old-timer may be accorded a ranking higher than that of a newcomer. Or a crane operator, let us say, may be held in higher esteem than a truck pusher. Again, a person who has a desk near the boss may seem to be better than those farther removed. Certainly, many office workers feel a superiority over factory workers for this reason. Finally, a person who can handle the intricacies of operating a cupola in a foundry will be ranked higher than someone who pushes a wheelbarrow around the foundry.

A number of external factors may explain the ranking given to people within the organization. Such things as the following may set off an individual favorably or unfavorably:

1. Race.
2. Religion.
3. National origin.
4. Family relationships.
5. Marital status.
6. Home location.
7. Education.
8. Knowledge of social amenities.
9. Club membership.

Whatever the reasons for the status or roles assigned to particular persons, recognition for them may be shown in a variety of ways. Formally, of course, such devices as titles, office furniture, parking assignments, and salary are common. Informally, recognition may be shown in a number of ways. Thus, people behave more politely toward those they respect; they are willing to do things for them beyond the normal standards, stand up for them when they are criticized, allow them privileges not accorded to others, and prefer to be near them. The converse is true when people do not respect their associates or superiors.

Operational Aspects of Informal Relations

Obviously, informal relations make up an area to which management should give much attention. But the most significant thing that can be said is that management had best go slowly in taking action in regard to informal relations. This is so because more is unknown than known about informal relations. Hence, if mistakes are made in dealing with informal relations, not only will undesirable repercussions result but also the relations will become even more informal and subtle. So caution is the keynote in dealing with informal relations.

Next in order of suggestions is that informal relations should be used, if possible, to reinforce the formal structures and procedures. If, for example, in the Leader Company, the production manager is supposed to be in charge of manufacturing, this formal setup should be buttressed by informal relations. The production manager should be trained to do his job so that he *earns* the respect of his subordinates; he should be given open support by top management so that various people will not want to short-circuit him; and he should be given insignia and perquisites of a top position so that he and others will respect the position no matter what happens, let us say, to the chief engineer. Of course, these things can only succeed if the production manager is the right person for the job to begin with.

This leads to other uses of informal relations. Formal selection, training, and motivation can be abetted by informal relations. Thus, the individual who has informally been assigned a high rank by his fellows should be given serious consideration for promotions. He has been "naturally" selected by the informal process. Or in training supervisors, it would be well to include subject matter or skills that make informal leaders successful. Thus, it would be as important to include attention to good manners, interest in the problems of others, and ability to listen patiently, as how to deal with technical aspects of production. Or, in motivating people, attention may be directed to the satisfactions that flow from gaining the respect of people as well as to the satisfactions of the paycheck.

Informal relations have a very important place in communications. If management could apply the "grapevine" to its own use, how much more effective could its own messages be? Yet the brochures, pamphlets, bulletin-board notices, letters, and talks of management do not seem to have the effectiveness of the rumor that spreads throughout an organization. Obviously the rumor, the grapevine, the gossip should be studied in order to learn how their effectiveness can be incorporated into the formal communication systems.

A significant area of usefulness, if it can be developed, lies in reducing conflict among classes, groups, echelons, and functional experts. Perhaps the first task here is to recognize that it is natural for line managers to suspect staff executives, for a worker to view the boss as an enemy, or for office workers to look down upon factory workers. But it is not necessary to let such interactions and attitudes continue. Find out then why various views are taken and work on them. Certainly, the office worker can get satisfaction from his job without looking down on the factory worker. Nor is it necessary for workers to consider the boss an enemy. Both are essential to a cooperative effort. Each can support the other without being considered an enemy to his class. But attention to the needs, views, and reactions of each must be sympathetic if the informal expressions of cooperation and partnership are to parallel the formal.

Above all, the informal relationships must be neither fought nor ignored. If a particular worker or executive is given a ranking higher than that assigned by the formal structure, the reasons therefor should be sought. The executive should not necessarily be viewed as an empire builder, or the worker as a trouble maker. Perhaps these people are exceptionally skilled and should be encouraged; perhaps other executives or workers are inept and should be trained.

Fighting informal relations only encourages the informal to fight the formal. When employees see that one of their informal leaders is picked on by management, they organize informally to take counteraction. If formal communications are misused to combat rumors, the rumors grow in intensity and falseness. If inadequate formal procedures are reinforced with dictatorial rules, even more ways are sought to circumvent the procedures and the commands.

This does not imply that the formal should give way to the informal. Rather, two points stand out. First, opposition to the informal will not destroy it; it will only drive it into subtler, more devious, and more formidable opposition. Second, by studying the informal—where it exists and why it is effective—the lessons can be applied to strengthen the formal and to join the two more effectively.

QUESTIONS

1. For what reasons may informal relations develop in a company?
2. Informal organizational relations essentially arise to serve what needs of people?

3. Do all needs of people reinforce each other or do they sometimes conflict with each other? What does this have to do with informal organizations?

4. For what reasons may vertical informal organizational lines differ from the formal vertical lines?

5. What is an informal procedure and why may one exist?

6. What is meant by the terms status and roles? Are these formal or informal manifestations?

7. In what ways may status and roles be established?

8. How may a company use informal organizations for its own purposes?

CASE 15–1

Whenever the employees of the repair department of the Meter Electric Company wanted to organize a social activity, they always turned to Joe Joyful; everywhere accepted as the top mechanic in the organization. Joe could organize a dance or a beer-bust, a children's picnic or a bowling tournament, so that it ran like clockwork. He figured out what had to be done, he lined up people to do the necessary chores; he saw to it that schedules and "logistics" were maintained, and he smoothed the inevitable ruffled feathers that developed in connection with such projects.

It seemed logical that management should decide that Joe had leadership skills and should be promoted to the supervisory position of the repair department when that job opened up. When the position was formally offered to Joe, he turned it down politely but firmly. When asked why, he said he wasn't the foreman type and didn't want the responsibility. The company pointed out that all of his party jobs had involved a great deal of foremanship and a great deal of responsibility. He nevertheless refused the offer saying he preferred to keep his mechanic's job.

1. Does managerial skill in one situation necessarily mean managerial success in another situation? Are informal and formal situations comparable?

2. What kinds of managerial responsibilities does Joe wish to avoid?

CASE 15–2

The Westonic Company had the reputation of being advanced in its policies and practices of personnel and human relations. On all areas of these matters, it was equal or better than neighboring companies or those in the industry. It was surprising, therefore, that in a random inspection of the company's premises one night, the company's security police ran across what amounted to a small-scale candy and tobacco shop. On being alerted of the find at once, the personnel director decided to keep the find a secret so that its operations could be observed.

Over the next several days, it was noted that this illegal shop, operated by a toolmaker whose work made it easy to carry on contacts with many people, was visited by operative employees, minor supervisors, and even a few middle managers. Even a credit and delivery service seemed to be operating. On making purchases, there were also conversations and gossiping.

What bothered the personnel director was to find this going on when the company had a well-distributed canteen system, scheduled coffee breaks, fine cafeteria, and a good grievance and counseling service. The total personnel program seemed to be well accepted in all of the morale surveys also.

1. Why do you suppose this informal setup existed?
2. What would you do about it if you were the personnel director?

16

Human Relations

Nature and Scope

THE TASK of management, as already noted, is to obtain coordination of the various factors in a business situation. Through such coordination, management in turn seeks to attain the various objectives of the business economically and effectively. Management refers not only to the executives at the top of an organization but also to the supervisors at the bottom. Each level of management has at its command a group of factors that must be coordinated into an effective team or machine, or part of a team or machine.

The factors may be grouped simply under the headings of men, machines, materials, and money. Each of the factors has a technical or mechanical aspect. The manager must, in a sense, possess the knowledge and skill to deal with the technicalities of these factors. His task would not be unduly complicated—at least not full of frustration—if each of the factors were solely composed of, and governed by, physical or technical laws and principles.

But one of these factors—man—is much, much more than a mechanical composite. To be sure, man has physical strength, attributes, and components similar to those of machines. Consequently, he is often referred to—and correctly so—as a factor of production. But to stop there would be far from correct. Man possesses many other attributes, which significantly affect his physical performance. He is also an ethical, social, political, economic, and psychological creature.

These dimensions of his personality are brought to the workplace whether management likes it or not. These may, indeed, interfere with his physical activities. Thus, workers may be emotionally upset, worried about marital relations, preoccupied with a political election, or concerned with a religious matter. In such instances, their physical behavior will be hindered and their cooperation difficult to obtain.

On the other hand, a well-balanced individual—one whose various life facets are harmoniously attuned—will enhance the effectiveness of the working situation. He himself will be more effective. He will favorably "infect" his fellow workers. And his superiors will be able to work with him with few difficulties, yet with the best of results.

It would be better for the organization if man would leave his nonbusiness characteristics at home. But man does not. He carries into the working situation a battery of forces which can bode good or evil. These nonbusiness phases and forces constitute the area known as human relations. How they are handled by management often has as much effort upon the success of a business as how technical phases are utilized. Management must, therefore, concern itself with human relations if it is to minimize their adverse potential and to maximize favorable possibilities.

To cover this subject adequately would require several volumes. Within the confines of this book, a more limited treatment must be undertaken. Yet, a reasonable and useful coverage of the subject, pertinent to the needs of management, is presented in the next few chapters under the following headings:

1. Human relations—a general discussion of the subject is the task of this chapter.
2. Morale—the factors and forces that determine the spirit of an organization and its members.
3. Motivation—the task of stimulating people to greater effort.

Specifics of Human Relations

Human relations is concerned with the sum total of human forces and effects other than the technical or physical. This concern is merited because of their impact upon technical utilization. And this concern encounters major challenges because of the constantly changing character of human feelings, attitudes, and interactions.

Management is thus dealing with a significant yet qualitative, changing, and abstract subject. But how does it relate to humans?

Is its work here esoteric, mysterious, and full of the occult? Much that one encounters under the heading of human relations inclines toward the personal touch, the either you're born with it or you're not, and the lay-it-on-thick idea. The fact that scientific knowledge is minimal about what makes people tick adds weight to the conclusion that human relations is extremely intangible. Yet enough is known so that managerial improvement is possible in dealing with the human factor. It is suggested here that the managerial approach to human relations should concern itself with the psychological, sociological, political, and ethical aspects of people through the following stages:

1. Procurement of desirable human relations.
2. Development of human relations potentials.
3. Maintenance of desirable human relations.
4. Utilization of human relations.

1. *Procurement of Desirable Human Relations.* Success in human relations is determined in large measure by the kind of people one has to deal with. In business, this in turn depends in no small part on the kind of people one has hired. So it is the better part of wisdom to start building good human relations with the selection process. This process may be divided into three parts: (*a*) specification of job needs, (*b*) attracting and screening candidates, and (*c*) induction and placement.

a) *Specification of Job Needs.* As the term implies, specification is concerned with definite descriptions of the personal characteristics required in particular jobs. Where written specifications are used, the descriptions are invariably limited to technical phases of work situations. Desirable as is this practice, concern here is not with these. Interest here is in the human relations phases of jobs. The problem is, as a consequence, to ascertain what personal interpersonal adjustments have to be made on each job.

The task of including human relations considerations in job specifications begins with a people-oriented analysis of each job. In particular, each job is studied in order to ascertain such things as the following:

a)   How many people are contacted on this job?
b)   Under what conditions do associations occur?
c)   What percentage of working time is spent with various classes of people?

d)   What authority and responsibility are involved in the various relationships?

e)   What kinds of status and role situations are present in the various interpersonal relations?

f)   What kinds of informal relations are likely to take place?

g)   What outside community, governmental, or union relations, if any, are part of the job makeup?

h)   What personal demands, if any, are made upon members of the employee's family?

If a job analysis discloses a large amount of personal interaction, a different type of person should be sought than for a job in which such interaction is at a minimum. Certainly, the interpersonal relations in a salesman's job are generally greater than in that of a night watchman. Even in sales work, the kinds of interaction are not all alike. Compare for a moment the interactions of the following:

1.   A salesman of diamonds in an exclusive shop.
2.   A salesman in the bargain basement of a large department store.
3.   A brush salesman canvassing house to house.
4.   A salesman in a used-car lot.

And even the interactions of each of these will vary from time to time according to prosperity-depression periods, and from area to area according to local social customs.

Perhaps the intangible and dynamic character of human relations adjustments has deterred many from making job analyses of this type. The feeling may be that these relations are too variable and too subtle to be worth careful study and specification. To a certain extent this is true. Yet anything that has a large impact upon company success deserves close attention. Certainly human relations falls within this category. Though the task is difficult, making job specifications that provide a useful picture of human relations content is something no intelligent executive will shirk; and successful executives do not. Perhaps they may not seem to make such studies, nor put their findings down on paper, but certainly opinions of this nature are available and are put to daily use.

Having made such a job analysis, the next step is to convert the findings into terms of human characteristics. Simply stated, this means defining the kind of person it takes to meet the specific interpersonal relations involved in a particular job. What kind of person does it take, for example, to be a research chemist? We are not interested here in his professional talents. But to what extent must we seek an introvert and to what extent an extrovert? The former would be personally happy in his isolated work; and the latter would be in balance with those he does meet. And since the chemist comes into contact with others who are very sensitive, highly attuned to the logical, and quite touchy about their professional status, can we locate a scientist who has an appropriate balance of respect for the opinions of others, yet has confidence in his own opinions and the judgment to know when to push his own ideas or to compromise? So on, through all jobs, the specifications should be expressed in personal, as well as technical, terms. It is not enough to say a job involves, for example, frequent social contacts with people of equal organizational status. This job statement must be converted, even though approximately and roughly, into such personal definitions as the following:

1. Be able to speak in public gatherings of from 5 to 15 individuals.
2. Practice common courtesies and good manners.
3. Refrain from "blowing up" over trivial matters.
4. Like to deal in person with other persons in solving technical problems.
5. Show preference for social contacts rather than "lone-wolf" behavior in individual working situations.
6. Possess a personality that is characterized as being "well liked."
7. Have a favorable appearance, dress, voice, mannerisms, and other personal habits.

General and crude though these statements are, at least they give some conscious expression to what is wanted in an individual. Perhaps, as scientific study increases, we may get social, personality, and human relations "quotients" that are as meaningful as the intelligence quotient. But, until that time, it is better to express human characteristics in qualitative, word-descriptive terms than not at all. There will be differences in interpretation, but not as wide as those when no specifications exist at all.

b) *Attracting and Screening Candidates.* With a picture in mind of the kind of person to be sought, the next step is to attract and screen candidates.

Attraction of candidates suitable from a human relations point of view is at present largely a matter of luck. Particularly is this true when good technical candidates are scarce. Then the practice is to take what you can get and hope that they work out. But when one studies the results of this policy, one wonders if it is very desirable. For under this policy we find the following happens too often:

1. Hiring almost anyone who turns up brings many psychological and sociological incompetents into the payroll.
2. The newcomers infect the staff with their own dissatisfactions.
3. The regular staff wonders what the company is up to in (a) hiring such incompetents and (b) paying them as much as, or more than, incumbents.
4. The supervisors have a hard time (a) breaking in and dealing with the newcomers and (b) reconciling and bringing together the old and the new.
5. Turnover among the new, and sometimes among the old, employees is high or increases.

If management didn't fear that a shortage of labor would interfere with output schedules, they might find that careful screening would be better than haphazard hiring. This means taking time to find candidates who will stick and do a good job. In the first place, study should be made of where good employees came from in the past. Present personnel—executives and employees—should be graded according to their human relations qualities: which are superior, which good, and which fair or poor. To be sure, some errors in rating will be made. But the errors are of minor importance compared to no grading. Then the records should be checked to see where the good and bad came from. Trends in such classifications as the following will soon appear: schooling, extracurricular and working activities while in school, how one's extra time is spent, and personal associations and hobbies. Having gathered such information, decisions as to where to look for people can be made with greater assurance of success.

After candidates have been attracted, the next step is to screen them. Screening involves adaptation of the devices and techniques used in the usual selection process. These include application blanks, reference letters, interviews, and psychological tests. In their present state of development, application blanks leave little room for optimism regarding their direct usefulness in screening for human-relations qualities. But they can serve as a basis for implementing good interviewing. The good interviewer, as will be noted more fully later, can seek to determine the "why's" of the historical incidents of a candidate's career. Why did he quit a given job? Why did he work his way through school? Why does he have certain hobbies? Why does he own his own home? The answers to these questions, not the bare facts on the application blank, will provide clues to a person's human relations qualities.

Reference letters, too, as usually constructed, contribute little to evaluating a candidate. Writing to a former employer may yield a check on a candidate's accuracy and perhaps on his veracity. One may also get a very general evaluation as to whether he was a good or bad employee. But, to be really useful, a reference letter would have to request specific information about the candidate's relations with fellow workers, superiors, colleagues, and union representatives, and about nonworking-hour associations. It is doubtful whether such could be obtained without an exhaustive personal contact, which is made only in very vital cases or for security purposes.

We come now to a device—the interview—which has very useful proportions in this connection. Wisely used, the interview is the best available device for most companies. A few basic rules can bring very handsome results. The first rule of good interviewing is to discard the notion that one is born with a knack for it and can get by with a few tricks.

The next rule of interviewing is to give both attention and sufficient time. People tell us a lot about themselves, not only by what they say but also by what they do. And it takes time to watch them and listen to them.

Another rule of interviewing relates to the questions asked and the direction given to the interview. To ask a candidate what his hobby is will serve little good. But to find out why he has that hobby is another matter. Much can be learned about the human relations side of a person who likes to sail, for example, if he will tell us why and how he got started, how he keeps up that study, what kind of sailing he likes to do, with what types of people he likes to sail, and what particularly intrigues him about it, or gives him the most satisfaction. A similar line of questions must be raised on all activities of a person.

Good interviewing also involves careful observance of a number of technical suggestions. Interviews should be conducted in favorable surroundings. They should be started and closed with finesse. The interviewee should be put at ease. The interviewer should talk as little as possible and not direct answers into desired channels. Information should be fully and fairly exchanged; and the individuality, answers, and confidence of the interviewee should be fully respected.

Finally, psychological tests are being used increasingly to disclose human relations characteristics. Because it is somewhat experimental and requires the services of skilled professionals, their use is rather limited at present but holds promise for the future. Even now, however, a few companies have had success in the human relations field with psychological tests. Personality, emotional stability, social awareness, introvert-extrovert patterns, interests, likes, and dislikes have been usefully measured in screening processes. When such tests have been combined with interviewing and validated in the firm or industry, a reasonable degree of success has attended efforts to screen out undesirable human-relations risks.[1]

c) Induction and Placement. The proper procurement of desirable human relations characteristics calls for careful induction and placement of candidates. It is not enough to hire good employees. They must be inducted into their new working environment with a minimum of disturbance or dissatisfaction to themselves or their fellow workers.

The successful candidate is generally touchy and ill at ease in his new surroundings. He notices things that old-timers do not even know exist. He is affected by everything he sees or hears. He is primarily operating in a human relations atmosphere and not a technical atmosphere.

He should therefore be inducted with this in mind—not with emphasis only on the technical factors, as is usually the case. Union leaders know this. When a new man appears, the union steward doesn't add to his confusion and sensitivity by telling him about processes, machines, policies, rules, and regulations. On the contrary, the steward has one message to get across—what a good friend the union is and can be to him—no technicalities, just "we're your friend." But the company, from personnel director to supervisor, may induct with do's and don'ts, rules and regulations, costs and output, processes and products, etc. The one method relaxes and the other tenses. The one creates a favorable human relations atmosphere and the other does not.

Certainly, management is responsible for output. Certainly, management hired the person to help get out production. Certainly, the man must fit himself into the machine procedures and the working setup. But management's induction policies and procedures

---

[1] To be sure, some critics charge that such techniques lead to conformity. What they mean is conformity to undesirable standards of human behavior. Certainly no one could condemn conformity to desirable standards, difficult though it may be to get agreement on what are desirable standards.

should lay stress upon reducing the feelings of tenseness, sensitivity, overawareness, and uncertainty. By being interested in the employee's personal reactions, management can gain his loyalty and confidence. Then attention can be directed to the technical phases of the work situation.

2. *Development of Human Relations Potentials.* Once employees with good human relations characteristics have been hired, the next step is to develop such characteristics to their fullest potential. Here, in general, industry has made little progress. While much is being done to develop the technical knowledge and skill of employees and executives, practically nothing is being done about human relations needs. What development is taking place here is incidental to other training and education programs, or to the normal give and take of daily activities. But much is lost through such neglect. Moreover, unions take advantage of opportunities and attract loyalties that otherwise might accrue to management. If management desires to promote a program of human relations development, it must take the following three steps:

a) Measure current status of human relations.
b) Establish desired standards of human relations.
c) Prepare a program to raise actual to desired standards.

a) *Current Status of Human Relations.* The task of measuring current human relations has two major phases. One has to do with the reactions of employees to the company, its executives, and its programs. The other has to do with the human relations impact of the company, its programs, and its executives upon the employees. A clear picture of these sentiments, expectations, feelings, and perceptions must be derived before anything constructive in the way of change or development can be attempted.

Measurement can be made in a number of ways. Observation is a very simple method. The reactions of employees can be observed by supervisors, staff executives, or outside consultants. Interviews can also be conducted to determine how employees feel about their working relations. Questionnaires can be sent to employees or their wives, or can be completed at the workplace. Records of output, quality, absenteeism, and accidents can be studied to provide a clue to human relations. None of these will be absolutely precise and above suspicion. But careful usage of any of these can provide valuable information. More will be said on this problem of measurement later in connection with morale measurement.

b) Standards of Human Relations. What if current human relations are known? How much better should they be? Here, the answers must be very general. Moreover, desired levels will change with time, and from place to place. Nevertheless, management must seek answers here, else it will continue to be accused of being behind the times.

With due appreciation of the difficulties involved, at least a few suggestions in the form of questions will be made. Management could well ask itself such questions as the following:

1. What kinds of religious facilities should be provided on the working premises?
2. What help of a psychological or psychiatric nature should be made available to employees and executives?
3. What steps should be taken in regard to employee alcoholism and drug addiction?
4. What should be done for employees who are having marital difficulties?
5. What can be done on the job, or after working hours, to give employees opportunities to utilize all of their psychological, sociological, and emotional capacities?
6. In what ways can people be helped to help themselves in these matters?

Such questions will never be satisfactorily answered. But seeking answers to them will do two things. First, it will remove the feeling of guilt when nothing is done. Second, it will serve to provide more accurate answers as time goes on.

c) Raising Actual to Desired Standards. By comparing actual human relations levels to desired levels, a determination of what needs to be developed can be determined. Then a developmental program can be undertaken. This would have to give attention to four phases: content of program, methods of instruction, organization for development, and staff of instructors.

The content of a program would depend upon human relations needs. Supervisors perhaps would have to be taught the human relations tasks in dealing with subordinates. Employees may need help in how to gain self-satisfaction out of the working situation. Or, they might take courses in psychology, sociology, history, literature, public speaking, etc., just for the good that would come out of such courses themselves. Executives at all levels might have their eyes opened to the need for giving consideration to human relations needs as well as to technical factors.

Methods of instruction can also be varied. Some human relations training can and should be undertaken on the job. In the case of executives, this would well be true. Formal courses can be offered on company premises or in conjunction with local schools, colleges, or correspondence schools. Special lectures may be arranged. Visits to cultural institutions may be encouraged. Or clubs, such as a great-books series, can be organized.

The organization for a development program also has numerous possibilities. Some programs may be organized on a voluntary employee basis or through an employee association, if one exists. Some may be tied in with community agencies such as the YMCA, churches, or schools. Some may be operated through the company's training or personnel department. In any event, it would be well to appoint some one individual as a coordinator, channel of information, or center of advice and assistance. In that way, help can be directed to those in need of assistance, loose ends and duplication can be avoided, and expert and sympathetic guidance can be provided.

Staffing of a developmental program can be handled in a number of ways. First and foremost, every executive in a company should consider it a part of his everyday job to cultivate better human relations. But other help will also be needed. Special courses, conferences, and "schools" will need either regular, full-time staffs or personnel drafted from other assignments for temporary duty. Then, too, help may be obtained from consulting firms, community agencies, schools, and the like. Of course, the nature and extent of the program will determine the staff requirements and how they will have to be met.

3. Maintenance of Desirable Human Relations. Assuming that a company has procured employees with good human relations characteristics and has taken steps to develop potentials, there exists also a need to maintain desirable human relations. To do this, human relations programs must be operated with a view to the following:

a) Removal of undesirable situations.
b) Improvement of desired situations.
c) Cultivation of assisting situations.

a) *Removal of Undesirable Situations.* Good human relations cannot be maintained if situations are allowed to exist that bring about dissatisfactions among employees or management. Thus, employees for one reason or another may be dissatisfied with management. This is a grievance. On the other hand, management may be dissatisfied with certain workers. This is a disciplinary situation. Unless the situations that cause these dissatisfactions are found and removed, human relations in the given company cannot be maintained at desired levels.

Grievances, actual or potential, are a grave menace to good human relations. If employees are aggrieved, they must be placated. If employees are apt to become aggrieved, steps of prevention must be taken. In either event, grievance handling—by cure or prevention—calls for adequate and fair procedures and policies.

To cure grievances, management must adopt and follow an acceptable grievance procedure. In too many cases this has not been done until a union has forced such an adoption. In such instances, the grievance machinery appears as a reflection upon management. No matter how fair a company thinks it is, it won't appear so unless it voluntarily establishes a grievance system upon which the employees can rely for impartial and complete justice. Thus, to the machinery of handling grievances must be added a willingness—indeed, an eagerness—to see that all complaints of employees are given full, sincere, and sympathetic treatment.

Disciplinary action has reference to dissatisfactions of management. Here, human relations are disturbed because employees are not doing things according to, or doing them contrary to, management's wishes. Here again, cure or prevention may be called for. If employees are breaking rules, not conforming to instructions or regulations, or failing to meet production standards, management must "cure" the situation. Since disciplinary action is to be taken, this implies some form of penalty. Something negative of sufficient weight is to be brought into play to cure the wrongdoers. The negative action may be a reprimand, a temporary loss of wages or privileges, or a discharge. In such instances good human relations are maintained by, first, disciplining the culprit so that his behavior improves and, second, warning others to behave, lest they suffer punishment, too.

But whether discipline is achieved by curative or preventive methods, management should follow good principles in either case. In the first place, penalties should be defined in advance for specific types of violations and for each repetition thereof. Penalties should be uniform through an organization so that favored treatment is not accorded in particular areas. Opportunity should be provided for full hearings if employees feel that their penalties are too severe.

And management should always incorporate some form of constructive suggestions for improvement along with whatever negative action may be taken.

b) *Improvement of Desired Situations.* Where relations between management and employees are characterized as good, steps should also be taken to protect and enhance the good relations. This can be done through good motivational and morale practices. These are explored more fully in later chapters, but a few comments about them are in order here.

Perhaps the most constructive job any executive can do—in addition to his technical managerial functions—is that relating to motivation. As time goes on, stimulation of employees seems to become an even more important phase of an executive's work. It would seem that employees should be self-motivating. Getting ahead ought to be a desirable goal of every employee. But too often such seems not to be the case. Management must seek to "press the right buttons" to get people to work more effectively.

Though financial motivators may be important, nonfinancial motivators are also available. To begin with, a deep, personal interest in the problems and ideas of subordinates is a powerful motivational tool. Or, words of encouragement, of praise, of commendation can do wonders with employees. Or, doing things voluntarily for employees—without always seeming to be forced to do so—brings about a motivational force for good. Finally, understanding how to use the psychological, emotional, and sociological drives in people constitutes a whole area from which motivational pressures of a positive nature may be selected.

To further underline the importance of the superior in enhancing human relations, research bears out that those superiors who have the most favorable and cooperative attitude in their work groups are perceived by their subordinates as having certain characteristics. Superiors are perceived as being supportive, friendly, and helpful rather than hostile. They show confidence in the integrity, ability, and motivations of the subordinate rather than suspicion or distrust. They see that each subordinate is well trained for his specific responsibility. They, furthermore, coach and assist those employees whose work is below standard.[2]

Another large area of human relations enhancement is that of morale building. Employees (and executives are included here, too)

---

[2] Rensis Likert, *New Patterns of Management* (New York: McGraw-Hill Book Co., 1961), p. 101.

have attitudes that make for willingness or unwillingness to work. The attitudes, or state of mind, may develop for a variety of reasons. Hence, management must be on the alert constantly to see that nothing within the company engenders a poor state of mind. Attitude surveys, questionnaires, interviewing, and observation are examples of methods by which morale attitudes and factors affecting morale may be determined. Then appropriate steps may be taken to retain situations conducive to good morale, to remove morale-destroying situations, and to communicate with employees what actions management is taking in regard to morale building.

c) *Cultivation of Assisting Programs.* Desirable human relations may also be maintained by cultivating a variety of contributory services and plans. For example, recreational and social programs can contribute to better human relations. Social gatherings, athletic teams, hobby clubs, and musical programs can provide for human relations needs not served by the working situation itself. They provide an outlet for energies, desires, and skills that otherwise may be neglected or poorly channeled.

Of a somewhat similar nature are various employee-service programs. A company may provide legal or medical services which can be most helpful to particular employees. In addition, employees who do not need such services but see the good they are doing develop a better appreciation of their company. Help may also be provided for those who may need psychological or psychiatric aid, marital counseling, or various types of guidance. All of these serve to minimize the tensions that make for poor human relations. To be sure, help here is largely in regard to noncompany situations. But more and more companies are moving toward providing help even in these instances.

The application of a variety of security programs is also helpful in maintaining good human relations. By relieving the fear that flows from loss of job, loss of health, or accidents, much good can be done. Of course, such undertakings cost money. Many persons are opposed to such extensions of interest by private enterprise. But the trend seems to be in that direction. If such extensions do result in greater productivity, it is difficult to criticize them. If they are mere gift giving, then it is a questionable practice. Only time can tell how effective are such things as income-guarantee plans, hospitalization and insurance plans, pension plans, and the like. But many feel that they are an indispensable part of a total program of developing better human relations.

4.   *Utilization of Human Relations.*   The final phase of a good program of human relations is concerned with what goes on in the actual working situation. This phase is taken up last only because what happens here is affected so much by what has gone before. It is simply impossible to have good human relations on the job if poor labor has been hired, if workers and executives have not been adequately developed in regard to good human relations, and if good motivation and morale-building programs are neglected. But if all the preliminaries have been properly handled, then attention to on-the-job factors can be the capstone to a complete program of good human relations.

Utilization of good human relations in the working situation involves attention to the following:

a)   Human relations and the job.
b)   Responsibilities of line and staff.
c)   Communication factors.
d)   Motivational factors.

a)   *Human Relations and the Job.*   American ingenuity has been unsurpassed in developing and designing efficient job situations. Employees are provided with the finest materials, the best machines, and the most streamlined methods of doing their work. The designs have been so fine engineer-wise, however, that the employees are made to feel that they have been engineered into a machinelike condition. The technical results have been good, but they undoubtedly would have been much better had some thought been given to human reactions in the design of the working situation.

A simple approach here would be to give attention to the ideas of workers. If employees are asked to offer suggestions about designs before the designs are made or have been tentatively made, their reactions are better than when they are not asked. The ultimate design may be the same whether employees have been asked or not. But in one case the employees will have a better feeling about the working situation than in the other. So, in addition to developing a better human relations atmosphere on the job itself, the company may also obtain useful technical advice and ideas.

On-the-job human relations are improved, too, if employees have been previously trained in how to improve the job itself. Such programs as work simplification training, motion and time study principles, company product and process lectures, and explanations of customer requirements are very useful. They give an employee an attitude and approach to his job which brings into play more than just the routine physical or mental skills. They make him a more complete partner in the business enterprise. Again, they serve to utilize energies and skills that would otherwise be misdirected or go unused.

On-the-job relations can also be improved by showing channels of promotion and improvement. An employee who knows how one job leads to another, and what a particular job can contribute to doing well on the next, takes a viewpoint that is more wholesome than that of an employee who is in a "blind alley" situation. The future is thereby tied into the present. The current job takes on a fuller meaning. And so, current relations inwardly and outwardly are improved.

b) *Responsibilities of Line and Staff.* On-the-job relations are closely affected by line and staff executives. Of course, one's immediate supervisor has a powerful effect here. His attitude and behavior can be an influence for good or evil. If he hopes to be a good influence, he must take the following major steps:

1. He must be alert to, and know, the wants, needs, and reactions of his subordinates.
2. He must know how and to what extent he can satisfy and reconcile these needs and reactions.
3. He must know how to relate human relations forces to company objectives, and vice versa.

More will be said on these matters in Chapter 17 on employee morale. But it is noteworthy that the foregoing emphasizes the fact that an executive must be as much a human relations expert as he is a managerial or technical expert.

Staff experts also can have profound influence on the working situation. This becomes increasingly so since most organizations are mainly integrated combinations of line and staff units. Access to, and direct contact with, such units as engineering, research, accounting, auditing, financial, personnel, maintenance, and inventory are so common as to go unnoticed. Yet, how these contacts are made affects the attitudes and reactions of various employees and executives.

But staff people may try to impose their will and line people may resent the superior attitude taken by staff people. As a consequence, relations between them—human relations—become strained and unwholesome.

Staff units have a responsibility to provide useful advice, service, plans, and resources. Such provisions should lead to good relations because those served are relieved of performing the service tasks themselves. But line people sometimes resist staff people because the latter assume they have superior skill or knowledge. And staff people sometimes become resentful when the line refuses their services. As a consequence, on-the-job human relations deteriorate. Improvement thus depends upon good service rendered in an understanding manner.

c) Communication Factors. Good utilization of human relations is also significantly affected by communications. How much information is exchanged between employees and executives? How fast and freely do the exchanges take place? What attitude is reflected in such interchanges?

Favorable answers to these questions will indicate a much higher level of human relations than occurs when the reverse is true. How well a man works on his job depends in part on how much he thinks he knows about what is going on and thinks his boss knows about his interests and problems. Given a good two-way flow, up and down, the man will perform more effectively than without it.

It may be argued that some of the information in which the employee is interested is none of his business. Perhaps in the strictest sense this is true. But what if his productivity is hurt if he doesn't know? And what if no one is hurt because he does get secret information? Under these circumstances, it would indeed be foolish not to communicate more-or-less fully with employees.

Sharing, as noted, is a two-way street. The downward flow can make the employee feel good for a number of reasons. He becomes a part of the business; his fears about the unknown are reduced; and he can better understand what is going on. The upward flow can relieve his tensions; make him feel powerful enough to talk to the president, if necessary; or give him the impression that his ideas are significant and sought for. In either event, communications add to his psychological and sociological satisfactions.

d) Motivational Factors. The utilization phase of human relations is significantly affected by motivational factors. It is on the job itself that any employee or executive can determine with some degree of accuracy whether he is getting paid fairly.

The pay as stated earlier may be financial or nonfinancial. But as he works away, the person thinks from time to time about his compensation in dollars or other forms. Is he getting enough dollars, is the satisfaction worth the effort, what do others think of his status, and what will the future disclose? As he thinks about these matters, he reaches certain conclusions, which in turn affect his relations with his fellows, his superiors, and others with whom he associates. Thus, he is motivated toward good or bad human relations.[3]

Obviously, management has a heavy burden here to get its thinking on the right track. Its motivational plans and techniques must be good. But, in addition, they must be understood and accepted by the employees (and various levels of executives). Then, as a consequence—in the actual utilization phase—human relations will be favorably affected.

QUESTIONS

1. What constitutes the human part of human relations?
2. What can a job specification contribute to better human relations?
3. What devices would be most useful in screening applicants in terms of human relations elements or requirements?
4. Where should emphasis be placed during the induction process insofar as human relations are concerned?
5. What steps must management follow if it desires to undertake a program of human relations development?
6. What methods are available as aids in measuring the current status of human relations?
7. To what subject areas must attention be directed in order that the utilization phase of human relations may be most successful?
8. How much and what kinds of information would it be desirable to communicate to employees?

CASE 16–1

After a successful career as a professional golfer, Bill Star decided to go into the business of making and distributing a golfing game which he had invented. The business was a challenging one besides being of vital personal interest to him.

In short time, he saw his little business grow—as he took in a few related sidelines—to the point where he had 16 people working for him in the home office and shop and about a dozen more in the field selling and promoting his wares.

[3] See Chapter 18 for a more extensive discussion of the subject of motivation.

With such a small company, it was necessary for Bill to work alongside the men frequently. So he was as much a worker as a manager. Moreover, Bill, as an extrovert, mixed well with people all his life, and he enjoyed the camaraderie and give-and-take of friendly banter. As a result, Bill was well liked by his men. Communications between them were on a most informal basis, and all kinds of problems (company as well as personal) were discussed freely. Indeed, at times it would have been hard for a visitor to identify the boss upon entering the premises.

For the first five or six years of the company's existence, the interpersonal relationships and the company's business moved along on a fine upward trend line. Then Bill began to notice changes. Employees tended to come to work late, coffee breaks were more frequent, customer service seemed more ragged, and attention to business and to Bill's orders was not as sharp. Business seemed to be slowing down while customer complaints were rising.

1. What role should Bill play in this organization?
2. Would his role be any different if the company were a very large one?

CASE 16–2

During a session on human relations in an executive development program, one of the executives complained that practically all that he had heard in the conference amounted to little more than theory. First, he pointed out, that in his own experience, he had often inherited a number of "cases" upon taking over a new department which even a psychiatrist couldn't have handled. Second, he doubted that he—or anybody—could have foreseen the kind of human relations problems some of his subordinates had turned into. He cited as an example a man who had been a top-notcher, a real "ball of fire" for six years, then overnight became a noncooperator, without any company loyalty, whose work record went way off the beam. And, third, he argued that the way young people act nowadays, to them human relations is all one-sided—their side. They want everything and are irritated when one suggests that they should work as their fathers did.

1. Is there nothing this executive can learn from his present staff that would be helpful now or in the future in a human relations way?
2. What is your opinion of his point about the impracticality of dealing with new conditions?

17

Morale

Nature and Scope

MANAGEMENT's task is to operate an effective, coordinated team. This result is obtainable in part, as already described, by the skill of management in performing managerial, technical, and human relations functions. It is obtainable in part by the technical skill of the team members and in part by the willingness of members, first, to utilize their skills individually to the maximum and, second, to cooperate with others in combining their individual skills.

The last of these factors—willingness to work and to cooperate—is by no means the least. Indeed, in many cases willingness seems to be the greatest. Particularly is this noticeable when willingness is lacking. For example, a company may have excellent buildings, well-designed products and processes, and high-quality materials. Yet production is low. The missing ingredient is willingness to work. Conversely, employees with a willing spirit overcome the handicaps of poor layout, crowded conditions, and poor tools and materials. Not only is output high, but a friendly, cooperative, and enthusiastic spirit pervades the whole atmosphere.

Morale, through the centuries and in all types of organizations, has been recognized as a significant factor in explaining the degree of success of a group. It is desirable, therefore, that every executive apply available practices and principles of morale development. To do this, he must be aware of the following phases of the subject:

1. Meaning of morale.
2. Theory of morale development.

3. Factors of morale development.
4. Determination of current morale.
5. Plans of improving current morale.
6. Morale follow-up.

Meaning of Morale

Definitions of morale are many. A review of them all would show that it is composed of the following:

1. What it is—an attitude of mind, an *esprit de corps*, a state of well-being, and an emotional force of individuals as members of a group.
2. What it does—affects output, quality, costs, cooperation, enthusiasm, discipline, initiative, and other aspects of success.
3. Whom it affects—immediately, employees and executives in their interactions; ultimately, the customer and the community.
4. How it operates—through willingness to work and to cooperate in the best interests of the organization and, in turn, of the individuals themselves.

A simple definition is used here merely to provide a quick clue to the foregoing details. Morale, then, is a state of mind and emotions affecting willingness to work, which in turn affects individual and organizational objectives. Morale, in and of itself, does not necessarily connote the existence of a good state. The attitude of employees may be very poor, in which case morale is poor. Hence, the definition outlines morale in all its possible degrees from low to high. Determining what morale is in a given case is a problem in measurement.

In talking about morale, it is important to note that it is a group dimension. A particular individual may have a favorable attitude toward his own department and supervisor. He may, as a member of a union, however, take a very unfavorable stand along with his fellows against certain company policies. Management must seek, therefore, to develop favorable attitudes not only at the individual level but also at the group level, a morale task.

One more point about this definition: It is of importance to organizational success. Yet it also refers to individual satisfaction. An employee has as much at stake in the state of morale and its results as does management. When the employees' morale is low, evidently they have been driven to this sad state by some serious mistake or wrong interpretation. To develop good morale, management should not assume that employees have a built-in inclination toward poor morale. On the contrary, labor is just as interested in good morale as is management; perhaps more so, because labor not only suffers from the results of poor morale but also must suffer the mood of poor morale as well.

Theory of Morale Development

In undertaking any program, it is desirable to have a good theory—a sound explanation—of how the program works. A morale development program is no exception. It is suggested here that such a theory should give consideration to the following:

1. Logical sequence of development.
2. The essence of morale.
3. Effects of good morale.

1.   *Logical Sequence of Development.*   If morale is a state of mind, to use this brief phrase for its other facets, how does it come about? What causes this state of mind? It might be stated simply that management, environment, or what the company does cause it. But, to continue the questioning, why might these cause it?

At first blush it would seem that management, for example, only does what is logical when it runs a company. It seeks to earn a profit by producing a product or service at a reasonable price. This it hopes to do through the proper utilization of labor, tools, materials, machines, and other resources. So, it hires enough labor at going rates and expects from it the skills and talents that labor possesses. No more of labor does it ask—so it seems—than of the materials that are purchased. The materials have certain qualities that are needed, and so does labor.

But of all the resources management buys, labor has a set of characteristics peculiar and unique unto itself. It is "used," to be sure, as are the other factors of production. But it in addition thinks and feels how it is being used, why it is being used, whether its compensation is satisfactory, and, particularly, how it compares with other factors and with its own members. It, in short, reacts to, as well as acts in, its environment.

In the ultimate analysis labor wonders whether it is getting enough out of the group effort for what it contributes. And this thinking becomes immensely critical when labor measures its limited time and resources against the fact that compensation must be adequate and fair "here and now," or is forever lost.

To reemphasize, compensation need not be in money. Assuredly, money is a pervasive standard of expressing the value placed upon an employee. It is something that others as well as the employee himself can see. But there are other forms of compensation: opportunities for advancement, doing a job that brings personal satisfaction and group or community approbation, recognition as a significant technical contributor while retaining respect as an individual human being, and a variety of job privileges and perquisites.

But is the compensation in all its forms commensurate with the contributions of the employees? If it is, the employees feel good and are willing to work hard. If it is not—or if the employees feel it is not—they feel bad and are unwilling to work hard. Thus, understanding of personal success as related to company success which the employees helped to create, determines the attitude of mind, which for the sake of convenience, goes by the name of morale.

Ideally, factual economic proof for each person's exact compensation should be the basis of such an understanding. But this is seldom, if ever, the case. Who can explain in a company of 40,000, let us say, why a particular person deserves to get $6 an hour? Unfortunately, the answer is negative if one should try to convince each of the 40,000.

So, much understanding is based upon other factors. Employees "feel" that compensation is right or wrong by the—

a)   Gossip they hear from other workers.
b)   Profit reports they read in the papers.
c)   Salaries of executives they read about.
d)   Treatment they get from superiors.
e)   Claims and arguments of union representatives.
f)   Working conditions, in particular and in general.
g)   Intelligence or education they themselves possess.
h)   How they feel about their fellow workers.

Obviously, then, almost anything, foolish as it may seem, may affect understanding and, in turn, attitude of mind. There is no subject, therefore, that can be considered by management to be without morale implications.

2.   *The Essence of Morale.* The state of mind termed morale is in essence, then, determined by a balancing of personal and company interests. The employees who conclude that their own interests are being served fairly when they contribute to the organization's objectives develop a favorable attitude of mind as illustrated in Figure 17–1. Conversely, their attitudes are poor if they conclude that their interests are being served unfairly in relation to their contributions.

The sequence of attainment of company goals and personal goals is also significant as far as morale is concerned. In cases of good morale, the employees work for the company first, and then get their reward. In cases of poor morale, the employees want assurances of pay first, and then the work is rendered as illustrated in Figure 17–2. While the interests of both parties are intertwined, in the former case, the logical sequence for effective relationships is in effect; but this is not so in the latter case. When people mistrust each other, however, they cannot be blamed for trying to protect themselves.

FIGURE 17–1
Balance of Interests and Morale

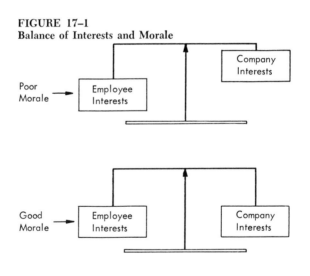

FIGURE 17–2
Sequence of Morale Development

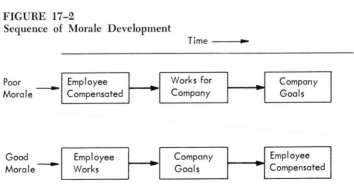

To sum up, morale develops out of a mutual satisfaction of, and expectations of continued satisfaction of, interests. Each party understands the need for the other. Each party understands that his interests depend upon the fulfillment of the other's interests. In the case of labor, it understands that to gain its own goals it must help the company achieve its goals. Labor must also believe that the share it gets is fair in relation to what it, as well as others, contributes. If the interests of all parties to a group endeavor are, in their respective minds, fairly served, then their morale will be high. The accomplishment of this result has taken place through the process of successfully integrating interests.

3. *Effects of Good Morale.* The subject of theory of morale must contain evidence of desirable effects of good morale. These effects may be classified as immediate and ultimate.

Immediately, good morale has some very important results for management and for employees. Management finds that subordinates are willing to follow its requests and commands with enthusiasm and respect. Indeed, work is done with a minimum of commands or supervision. This is a very pleasant condition for the executive. Moreover, he will find that employees will work hard in the face of difficulties. If emergency orders must be processed or work completed without adequate tools or materials, again the employees will respond with willingness. Most of all, employees show openly a respect for, and confidence in, their leaders that is satisfying to the leaders themselves.

Good morale has immediate effects upon employees, too. They work with satisfaction and pleasure. The hours of work go by in an atmosphere of relaxed effort. Nothing seems to drag, the days are not empty and boring, and a feeling of insignificance is absent. It is, in short, good to be at work and in association with one's fellows and one's superiors. Work—as much as it can be—is a pleasure and not a misery. Since one spends so much of his waking life at work, the immediate effects of good morale are greatly to be desired by the worker himself.

These immediate effects cause some desirable, ultimate effects. For management, there are higher output of better products at lower costs, and more consistent, higher profits. For labor, there are higher wages, more secure employment, and a higher standard of living. For society in general, there are more goods and services obtained more effectively from its limited supply of resources.

These effects do not all flow from morale itself. Morale should not be looked upon as the only source of success. Even the best employee cannot "make bricks without straw." But the best employee can do much, much better with what he has than the worker whose morale is low.

Factors of Morale Development

It is now pertinent to note the factors that have an effect upon employee morale. As a broad statement, the factors are anything that can influence the attitude of employees; they are infinite. A more useful approach to this matter of factors is to classify the factors according to their sources, as follows:

1. Employee factors.
2. Management practices.
3. Extracompany forces and factors.

1. *Employee Factors.* The quality of morale is definitely influenced by the type of employees. If the ability of employees to understand reasonable explanations is low, try as it might, management will not be able to get its message across. Thus, in its policies of hiring, a company should seek not only people who are capable of doing their jobs but also those who can grasp the logical relationships and rewards involved in group effort.

The status and roles of employees have a bearing upon the possibilities of morale development. Employees may be members of a union. In that case, they will invariably take on attitudes and reactions because of their membership. This does not mean that such attitudes will necessarily be negative. But it does mean that management will have to deal with a group that is not easy to convince of the views management considers correct. Even when not organized, labor may take on particular attitudes because of such things as the labor-management history in a given community or the degree of class consciousness of labor and of management.

2. *Management Practices.* Of course, an important group of factors affecting morale is that falling within the province of management. Included here would be, first, the various subjects regarding which management normally makes decisions and, second, the manner in which management acts in carrying out its various duties.

In regard to the first of these categories, a brief outline is sufficient to indicate the significance of the various subjects to the morale of employees. Few employees indeed would be unaware of or uninterested in how the following were decided:

1. Objectives—to what extent the goals of stockholders, customers, and labor are to be served.
2. Policies—the basic guides established in a company relating to such questions as wage levels, seniority versus merit, promotional channels, working conditions, and union-management relations.
3. Procedures—steps to be taken in handling such matters as grievances, disciplinary action, employee services, and counseling.
4. Communications—the extent to which, and the channels through which, information is to flow back and forth between organizational levels.

These listings are sufficient to illustrate the impact such decisions can have upon the morale of employees. Any one of these areas has more than enough powder to blow up relations between labor and management. Conversely, they can be the source of great good.

But morale is affected not only by what management does but also by how it does what it does. Thus, an executive may be absolutely fair in his decision in selecting a particular man for promotion. But to other interested candidates, the selection may appear the rankest kind of favoritism. This happens when the executive is secretive about the standards used to evaluate the various candidates, when he gives his preferred choice special privileges or opportunities to gain needed experience, or when he refuses to discuss the matter with those passed over. Or, an executive may be absolutely fair in an offer of a wage increase. But to the recipients, the offer may seem unfair. Here again, this is so when the executive cannot clearly explain how he arrived at his offering figure, issues it as a take-it-or-leave-it proposition, or has been niggardly in the past.

The behavior of executives is particularly significant as a morale factor. Some executives are autocratic in their attitude toward subordinates. Others convey a feeling that they are better than their subordinates—that the latter are second-class citizens. Others are suspicious of the motives and actions of employees and openly indicate their lack of confidence. Others avoid, if not despise, the company of their workers. Still others are contemptuous of the intelligence of employees. Such attitudes are quickly noted. Obviously, it is natural for employees to return a negative attitude of mind. To reverse this behavior, as many other executives do, serves to enhance the morale of employees.

3. *Extracompany Forces and Factors.* Morale may also be affected by forces and factors outside the company itself. The union is a significant example, and various community and family relationships are another.

The union is so closely intertwined with company affairs, and increasingly so, that it may be incorrect to classify it as an extracompany agency. But legally it is. Certainly it is a potent morale factor. How employees feel toward their company is significantly determined by the indoctrination they receive from their unions. And at times—such as during a strike—their attitude seems to be totally swayed by this force.

This is not intended to imply that the union is to be viewed as an implacable foe of management, that it inevitably is opposed to whatever management stands for. There is no doubt that there are those in management—and those in labor—who take this position. A fairer view seems to lie elsewhere. The union, in its best role, is a guardian of the fair interests of labor. It should be concerned with a fair share for labor, not an unfair share. It should seek logical, factual, and scientific answers to labor-management problems, not dogmatic, prejudiced, or expedient answers. In its rightful role, a union need not be construed as a negative morale factor. It can well contribute to the willingness of employees to work hard and to cooperate effectively. This the union can do by helping to remove unfair or ignorant practices. Many companies have been forced by unions to seek the right paths as have done so voluntarily.

Various community and family dimensions also affect employee morale. More and more employee attitudes toward their work are being influenced by how their company concerns itself with community affairs. They are influenced by the degree of attention which a company gives to educational facilities, inner city affairs, air and water contamination, and welfare institutions in the community. Whether or not this should be so is beside the point; yet as long as employees react to this area of company relationships, it is something management must take into consideration.

It might seem a herculean task to cope with such an infinite variety of morale factors. This is not so. Not all are effective at the same time. But to work with any of them, management should be able to determine which ones are effective at particular times. To do this it must be able to isolate the significant ones. A check list, expanded from the list of factors suggested above, will be helpful in that connection.

Nor should a manager be pessimistic because some of the morale factors seem to be out of his jurisdiction. Perhaps an executive cannot make a direct attack upon such morale factors as unions or community relations. But something can be done. Education can be a powerful tool to help an employee make a better appraisal of the arguments presented by his union, and counseling aid may help him solve his marital problems. Efforts in such directions are time-consuming and divert executive time and resources from company business. But if ultimately they result in higher productivity and better cooperation, who can really argue that they are not company business?

Determination of Current Morale

With this background of the meaning and theory of morale, it is now appropriate to discuss ways and means of working toward morale development and improvement. The action to be taken can be simply expressed by the following formula:

Desired morale less current morale equals
    a)   deficit to be made up or
    b)   excess to be protected.

Before plans can be developed, it is significant to determine the current state of morale. The present section is devoted to a description of how this may be done by taking up, first, measures of morale and, second, methods of measurement.

1. *Measures of Morale.* Unlike temperature or distance, morale cannot be measured directly. It is as yet impossible, for all practical purposes, to delve into the mind in order to ascertain its particular state. Physiologically, it is possible to study the brain, but this has little at present to offer in determining what an employee thinks or how that thinking affects his feelings. As a consequence, morale measurement must be based upon indirect units or interpretations.

Indirect measures of mental attitudes are of three types: experimental, personal, and practical. The first of these has to do with psychological attempts to measure attitudes. Clinical studies are made in a variety of ways to get a person's reactions, his outlook, physiological changes, and ideas. From measurements of mental, emotional, and physical differences, variations in reactions of different people to the same situations or stimuli are noted. Such measures are useful at present only in particularly difficult situations, where the high cost may be offset by important results.

More useful measures may be obtained from personal manifestations of various types. For example, the behavior of employees is very revealing. Are employees surly or cheerful, despondent or happy, listless or enthusiastic, dull or alert? These overt actions can be excellent, though qualitative, measures of morale. Another group of personal measures is that of verbal expressions. Employees express opinions or attitudes concerning such things as company policies, executive behavior, working conditions, or other matters. Whether or not their expressions really reflect their true morale is something that must be carefully checked by management in one way or another. This problem of methods will be touched on in the next few pages. A third group of personal measures is obtained through noting their complaints or expression of unwillingness to work. Records of such things as grievances, disciplinary cases, absenteeism, tardiness, and refusal to work overtime will quickly reveal trends in morale changes.

Actual results of one kind or another constitute practical and useful, if indirect, measures of morale. What is the trend in individual productivity, group productivity, quality of work, unit costs, machine breakdowns, tool losses, material usage, and the like? To be sure, trends here may be due to factors other than morale. But it is possible to reach reasonable conclusions as to the existence of morale in these results. Assume, for example, that productivity in a given department has fallen 10 percent during a particular month. An investigation is made. It is found that no technical changes have taken place during the period in question. The only change has been the assignment of an engineer to the position of assistant supervisor. Upon further investigation, it is found that the employees are fearful that the appointment was made to establish tighter output standards and to check the liberal attitude of the well-liked supervisor. Whether their fears are justified is, for the moment, beside the point. The fact is that the output figures did indicate a lowering of morale.

2. *Methods of Measurement.* A number of methods are available by which measures of morale may be obtained. The major ones are observation, interviews, questionnaires, and record keeping.

a) Observation. Observation can be one of the best methods by which to measure morale. Every executive has this tool at his command. All he has to do is look at his subordinates. Perhaps the very simplicity of this method lulls executives into ineptitude. They look but they do not see. Or they are so overloaded with details, or important tasks, or an overextended span of control, that they have no time to look. Or they may foolishly pride themselves on an ability to size up individuals with the merest glance. Or they may be afraid to look lest they find something ·wrong. An executive with these failings will get no benefit from observation; he may, indeed, get actual misinformation from it. Moreover, he is forced to expend funds on other methods of measurement, which might well have been avoided had he used direct observation.

To use observation, an executive must practice observing, and then do it consciously and systematically. He will be aware of employee morale and morale changes if only he will watch the employee's behavior, listen to their talk, and note their actions. People "tell" us constantly how they feel. They tell us by a shrug of the shoulder, a change of facial expression, shuffling of feet, nervous fluttering of hands, tonal expression, a change in work habits, or avoiding our company. An observant executive will make note of these. Any departures or deviations from "normal" will put him on immediate notice that something may be wrong.

Herein lies a possible shortcoming of observation. How soon can an executive detect that an unfavorable change is taking place? How far from normal must an employee deviate before the deviation is noted? May not the damage be done before its occurrence is detected? Answers will be unfavorable when executives are not good observers. But when an executive is a good observer, he should be able to detect deviations faster than by any other method, except in the occasional case of an employee who registers a complaint about something unfavorable that he anticipates may happen.

b) Interviews. Interviewing is another useful method of morale measurement. And, again, it is a tool any manager could learn to apply with great profit to himself. Interviewing provides for a face-to-face, personal, and verbal exchange of information, ideas, and points of view. But it is not something that will be satisfactory if done in a casual, unplanned, or careless manner.

But interviewing can be very effective. To make it effective, the interviewer must adhere to a few basic rules. Some were reviewed in the preceding chapter, but a few other ideas are in order here. Employees either must be made to feel free about coming in for interviews or must be sought out at times that will give a good sampling of their attitudes.

One seldom encounters a successful plan of employee-initiated interviews. Assuredly, many companies announce an "open door" policy. A count of those employees who come voluntarily through the doors would reveal few takers. A few may go to the top, but more to their own superior or to the personnel department if they are burned up about something. But as a method of measuring morale, particularly in initial stages of change, such interviews have little to commend them. Of course, they should not be discouraged, else this safety valve will be removed.

Employer-initiated interviews are to be preferred if interviews are to be relied upon as a method of measuring morale. In such instances some plan for sampling opinions is desirable. Thus, an executive may plan to talk informally to a given number of employees every week or month. Or he may use some anniversary such as hiring date to contact conveniently his subordinates. If staff members such as personnel department representatives or counselors participate in the interviewing, they may schedule interviews in particular departments or for particular types of workers. In this way, trends in particular areas may be determined and compared with other areas or past periods.

c) Questionnaires. A popular method of measuring morale is that of the questionnaire. On a printed form, employees are asked to express their opinions on specific or open-end questions. In the first type an employee may be asked such questions as the following: Do you get a satisfactory answer from your supervisor when you ask him about wages? A specific list of answers is provided from which a choice can be made as follows:

Always   Usually   Sometimes   Seldom   Never

This type of questionnaire makes it easy for the employee to answer and for management to collate and compare answers. But it does restrict the employee, or may cause him to supply answers to questions about which he has never thought. (See Figure 17–3 for a sample section of this type questionnaire.)

An open-end question has no terminal limitations. Of this type is the following question: What do you dislike most about your work? Here, the employee is restricted neither in what he may say nor in how much he says. It is difficult, however, for management to collate and compare the answers. And many employees do not like to take the time to write out full answers or cannot express themselves satisfactorily.

FIGURE 17-3

Section of Morale Questionnaire with Specific Questions in the Area of Supervision and the Distribution of Employee Response

... ABOUT SUPERVISION			
1. How do you feel about your supervisor's knowledge of what is going on in your section?	Very Dissatisfied 9%	Fairly Satisfied 22%	Very Satisfied 69%
2. How do you feel about how often your supervisor checks on your work?	Very Dissatisfied 10%	Fairly Satisfied 26%	Very Satisfied 65%
3. In your opinion how well does your supervisor organize the work in your section?	Very Poorly 16%	Average 28%	Very Well 56%
4. How do you feel about the training your supervisor has given you as far as helping you to do the best job you are capable of doing in your present job?	Very Poor 19%	Average 27%	Very Good 54%
5. How do you feel about your supervisor's abilities and knowledge of the jobs he supervises?	Very Poor 8%	Average 17%	Very Good 75%
6. Do you feel that you know exactly what is expected of you?	Rarely 9%	Sometimes 24%	Always 67%
7. How is your supervisor about keeping you informed on how well you're doing?	Very Poor 24%	Average 34%	Very Good 42%
8. How often do sudden rush jobs occur in your work?	Always 46%	Sometimes 38%	Rarely 16%

Reprinted with Permission of the Nationwide Insurance Companies, Columbus, Ohio.

In either type, the questionnaire may cover either only selected subjects or the "waterfront." The latter type suffers from excessive length but is useful in isolating particular subjects that may be causing discontent. The former can serve to obtain quickly the views of employees on particular topics. Then, from time to time, the questionnaire can be repeated to determine what the trend is on the particular subjects.

This subject of trend is especially significant in morale measurement. To go to another field for a moment, no manager would be satisfied to use, year in and year out, an inventory of materials which he had once taken. Nor should he be satisfied to rely continuously upon a single inventory of employee attitudes. For morale changes just as material stocks do. It is desirable, therefore, to take continuous samples of attitudes. Such samples are more useful if made upon a comparable basis from time to time.

d) Record Keeping. It is also desirable to design and operate a good system of record keeping if such results as output, quality, and costs are to be used to measure morale. Output and quality records should be kept by individuals and departments. Absenteeism and tardiness should be recorded on personnel summary cards and recapitulated on departmental record sheets. Similarly, records should be kept on any other measures that may denote morale changes, such as grievances, disciplinary action, suggestions made, and merit ratings.

Plans of Improving Current Morale

Once the current state of morale has been ascertained, steps may then be taken to improve morale—if a deficit exists. A deficit may be readily apparent when something is obviously wrong. When negative morale is written all over the attitudes or actions of particular individuals or departments, there is no problem of where action must be taken. But when it is simply desired to raise morale, what will constitute a reasonable increase becomes a matter of judgment or guesswork. Suggestions for improvement will be classed according to whether something is obviously wrong or general improvement is desired.

1. *Apparent Negative Morale.* When a study of current morale reveals that the state of mind is unsatisfactory, it is necessary to analyze the reason for this condition. As far as company-centered causes are concerned, three major explanations are possible. First, some policy or practice of the company or of an executive is wrong. Second, the low-morale individuals may be misinformed about something or somebody. Third, the low-morale individuals hold views irreconcilably at odds with those of the company or of some executive.

Where the first of these holds true, the course of action is obvious.

The company policy or executive action causing the trouble should be corrected at once. This suggestion is easier to state than to follow. Most of us will go a long way to justify our actions, no matter how mistaken we may sometimes be. Yet, we thereby dig ourselves deeper into holes from which it is even more difficult to extricate ourselves. Employees do not, however, lose respect for a boss who admits a mistake. They cannot, of course, respect a boss who makes too many mistakes; but they will have contempt for one who refuses to admit an error when it is perfectly obvious to all concerned that such is the case.

When employees hold on to misconceptions, another plan of attack is called for. The difficulty in such cases may well be with management's ineptness at communicating ideas properly. For example, ask any executive to explain to a particular worker why he should receive a certain hourly wage, no more, no less. In just a few minutes confusion will be thick, and the executive himself will be more than anxious to run for fresh air.

Indeed, it is surprising that we as managers do as well as we do in explaining these things when we ourselves are very uncertain about them. Management often struggles for months to cut through the mysteries of some such program as job evaluation. Then the executives expect employees to understand it just because the plan is printed in a nice pamphlet. Time and again this happens—months of thought for one group, but minutes or hours for another.

But what if employees hold views that are opposed to those of management? A reasonable attempt should be made to educate the employees. This might be termed propaganda or indoctrination by some. The unfavorable implications of these terms are deserved if management is attempting to get across biased, untruthful, and unfair information. But the negative charges are not warranted if management is fairly presenting its views on particular problems or topics.

2. *General Improvement.* When morale is generally good, another plan of action is called for. This would include the following three broad stages:

a) Organizational placement of morale responsibilities.
b) Determination of morale relationships.
c) Specification of morale plans.

First, a very important part of any morale-building plan is to determine who in an organization is to be responsible for its execution. Obviously, every executive is a morale factor. To leave it in such terms, however, is not enough. Each executive should be told, preferably in writing, what he should be doing about morale, the extent of his jurisdictional responsibility and authority, and his relationship to other departments. As a very simple example, a supervisor of salesmen should have more than an inkling of how he should work with the personnel division in such an area as counseling employees who have complaints.

Second, a morale-building program should be based upon a clear conception of the theory that underlies it. Again, a written statement should be prepared on the relation of company objectives and personal objectives, the process of integrating interests, the factors that cause good morale, and the results of good morale. This statement is best prepared through the medium of conferences and then should be discussed thoroughly with various levels of executives individually and in groups. Thus the theory, through its developmental and transmittal stages, will become a vital part of every executive's actions.

Finally, specific morale duties should be prepared for every executive. Thus, all, or selected, executives may be told to inform employees on new contracts the company has signed. At another time, information on expansion programs may be passed on. Later, each executive may be told to have a friendly dinner meeting with all, or selected, subordinates. Then, some form of social or recreational activity may be undertaken. And so, on and on, constructive programs of a specific nature are sponsored. This serves to keep up the morale-building program. It also serves to keep the executives conscious of this vital phase of their work.

Morale Follow-up

Morale programs, like any other plans, must be followed up to see how they are working. This is very difficult to do because morale effects may be brought about by factors other than that of a specific morale-building effort. For example, suppose a company puts in an educational program intended to increase economic understanding and, thereby, morale. Suppose that attitudes of employees subsequently are better. Would it be reasonable to conclude that the educational program was responsible if, during the same period—

1. A substantial wage increase had been granted.
2. Additional amounts had been earned in overtime work.

3. The supervisors had shown a more constructive interest in the problems of employees.
4. A new parking lot had been opened, which greatly eased a congested situation.

Obviously, it is difficult, if not impossible, to allocate credit for the morale increase in this case.

Nevertheless, an effort should always be made to check on a program. If other things are not equal at the time a particular program is in effect, the task of evaluation will not be easy, but it should be done, nonetheless. Besides checking on morale, before and after, records can be kept of what happened to such things as grievances, output, absenteeism, and suggestions. Facts of this nature will throw additional light on the effectiveness of a specific morale program. Even getting opinions from those affected by a program is helpful. For example, the mere fact that employees like the economic educational program cited above is a helpful sign, even though it is impossible to determine how much the program has changed their fundamental thinking.

Follow-up, even of the most uncertain type, has value in keeping executives on their toes and in gathering lessons for future planning. Advance knowledge to the effect that his work in counseling—let us say—is to be checked will make any executive more careful. He will plan, organize, and carry out his tasks with more precision. Moreover, once his task is completed, he will be better prepared to suggest future improvements. He will be aware of shortcomings. He will be thinking about needed corrections, and will undoubtedly develop constructive suggestions.

A good follow-up program should also place responsibility for follow-up upon specific individuals. Before a counseling program, for example, is put into effect, it is desirable to state who is going to be responsible for checking it. When the checks are to be made should also be indicated; and how the checks are to be made should be stated, if possible. Such advance planning reduces future misunderstandings and fear of negative spying.

To conclude this discussion of morale, the variety and detail of suggestions made here would seem to imply the need for a rather thorough and costly program. This deduction is correct. But, to make sense, a particular cost must always be weighed against possible losses and gains. In the case of morale, a company without a good program will incur great losses (in production, for example) and great expenses (in grievance handling, for example). A company with a good program will have to spend goodly sums for its programs. But it will invariably offset this by reducing losses and other expenses. Moreover, it will be a much more pleasant place both for the workers and for the managers.

QUESTIONS

1. What ideas must be encompassed in the concept of morale?
2. What is the relationship among company objectives, employee self-interest, and morale?
3. What are some of the immediate and ultimate effects of morale?
4. Give examples of managerial factors or practices which have an important impact upon morale.
5. How would you compare observation and questionnaires as methods of morale measurement?
6. By what methods may the level of morale be ascertained?
7. If morale in a company is good, what would you suggest that management do about morale, if anything?
8. In what ways can programs of morale follow-up be useful?

CASE 17–1

One of the branch stores of a midwestern chain store system had expanded largely because of the growth of the city in which it was located. Volume expansion, increases in store hours per day, and a change to a seven-day sales week had brought about the need for more personnel as well as double-shift staffs.

Despite the increase in volume of business, central office management was dissatisfied with the percentage of the market potential obtained by this branch and particularly with the profits and costs of the branch. Top management scheduled, therefore, a series of meetings with the branch office staff to discuss the various problems.

A variety of opinions came out of the meetings. The branch manager blamed lack of success on inexperienced help and inadequate training. He also questioned the purchasing done by the central purchasing division. The personnel division claimed that it seemed impossible to schedule satisfactory training sessions what with split shifts and high turnover. And the advertising and sales promotion manager claimed that there was inadequate coordinative planning on the scheduling of special sales.

After mulling over the results of these meetings, the executives decided that it would be best to transfer the branch manager to a small outlet (one within his capabilities, it was said). A new manager would come in and sweep clean the mess. No sooner was this done than serious dissatisfactions were expressed by the old branch manager over his transfer, by his old subordinates who considered him the "best boss we ever had," and by a number of other branch managers who felt that there was little security in the organization.

1. What do you think of the decision by top management?
2. When a solution is decided upon, to what extent is top management obligated in selling it to the various parties concerned with it?

CASE 17–2

The personnel director of a given company had always proceeded on the assumption that morale and productivity were correlated positively. He believed that high morale meant high productivity and low morale, low productivity. But in reading a research report on this subject, he was surprised to find that in a couple of companies, low morale was associated with better results and that high morale was associated with poorer productivity.

Wondering about this, he decided to discuss the report with the executive vice president, a real old-timer. The latter burst out in full agreement with the report saying, "I could have told you that without a lot of fiddle-faddle research. The only time I've ever made any progress or really achieved anything was when I was unhappy with myself and with conditions. Then I buckled down. But every time I get smug or satisfied, I start to slide downhill. What's more every time I've pampered myself or anybody else, things went from good to bad. Yes sir, progress is based on unhappiness; let's make employees dissatisfied in the right ways, then you'll see the fur fly."

1. What is your opinion of these views on morale and productivity?
2. Would you lower morale in the hope of raising productivity?

18

Motivation

Nature and Scope

IN THE FOREGOING chapters it has been stressed that an executive is supposed to get work done through others by exercising skill in management. The executive is expected to concern himself with planning, organizing, directing, and controlling the work of others. This emphasis upon the functions of management is occasioned by the conviction that few executives can long be successful without effectiveness in that direction. Yet, on every hand, successful executives are noted who seem to violate every principle of good management or go on blissfully unaware of their existence.

What brings them such success? Sometimes technical skill; sometimes an uncanny ability to foretell the future; and sometimes a great talent for motivating people. The first two are indeed worthy of cultivation and analysis, but the last is of greatest interest here. If executives can be successful with motivation skill alone, how much more successful could they be if to it were added managerial skill? In other words, although great stress has been placed on managerial functions, this does not imply blindness to the contributions of such devices as motivation.

Attention is, therefore, now directed to practices and principles of motivation that an executive can adopt. It is advisable to repeat that motivation should not be considered as a tool to be used in isolation. It is best used in a context of a full program of managerial functions, skills, and behavior.

In this chapter, motivation will be discussed under the following headings:

1. Basic aspects of motivation.
2. Kinds of motivators.
3. Steps in motivating.
4. Rules of motivating.

Basic Aspects of Motivation

The manager who hopes to add motivation to his arsenal of executive tools must have a clear comprehension of this device. He must be fully aware of its meaning, the theory of its operation, and the various parts of which it is composed. Attention is now directed to each of these.

1. *Meaning of Motivation.* Motivation, simply defined, is the act of stimulating someone, or oneself, to take a course of action which will result in the attainment of some goal or the satisfaction of some need. Thus, to the manager there is the very important idea that subordinates can be made to do some things that they might otherwise not do; do more than they might otherwise do; do work with greater economy, less supervision, and more cooperatively; and thereby help the company attain its goals of higher profits. And to the employee, there is the idea that by working harder, he may thereby earn more money, make his standard of living more secure, and gain prestige at work and in the community.

2. *Theory of Motivation.* Motivation is thus seen to be an interacting system of stimuli, courses of action, and results.

a) Stimuli. In business, the sources of stimuli may be, and usually are, of various kinds. The stimulus may be in the manager himself, as he exhorts, let us say, a clerk to do a more accurate job. The stimulus may be in the clerk himself, whereas the manager is a mere catalyst, the opportunities for personal gain may be pointed out by the manager to the previously unconcerned clerk. The stimulus may be in the words of fellow workers who expect the clerk to maintain group norms, whatever they may be. Or the stimulus may be in the expectations of one's family or friends.

As to the kinds of stimuli which may be employed, their variety is innumerable. More is said about this later in the chapter. For the moment, it will suffice to say that stimuli may be abstract or concrete, direct or indirect, individual or group, economic or personal, psychological or social, and company or noncompany. There is no one stimulus that serves for all people and all occasions.

b) Courses of Action. Through the application of stimuli, it is expected that some course of action will be taken. To the company, this invariably means that employees will do their assigned jobs more productively, economically, and cooperatively. To the employee, this means that he will apply his talents more effectively to his tasks, cooperate with his fellow workers, and contribute more creatively to the growth of the organization. In short, the stimuli prod people to action.

c) Results. The purpose of motivational efforts is results. This is an involved and often an involuted aspect of the motivational system. It might seem that the basic result to the company is profits and to the employee better pay and more security. But to each there invariably are many more and intertwining results.

To the company, the ultimate goal of profits, certainly depends on a variety of intermediate, preliminary, and interdependent results. Better workmanship, on-time performance, better quality, lower costs, better cooperation—and so on—the list is unending. All this points to the fact that motivation has an impact upon all levels and all areas of the company.

To the employee, motivational results are an even more intriguing subject. For example, is money the result of motivation, or the things that money can buy? What is the result he is working for—personal or family satisfaction, reduction in insecurity, increase in prestige, personal fulfillment, higher status? Obviously there may be any number of goals. This deserves, therefore, fuller attention in later sections of this chapter.

But before proceeding further in this discussion, it is well to note that it is far easier to talk about motivation than it is to carry out a program of motivation. To begin with, there are stimuli beyond number that might be applied and they all seem unequal in power. Which should be used in a given case—a smile, a dollar raise, a compliment, a promise of a raise, or a preferred desk location? The theory of motivation does not provide a clue as to which will prove the best spur under given circumstances. Moreover, a particular stimulus may actuate one individual but fail with another. Or it may work with a given individual one time and fail with him the next. Again, how hard should the stimuli be applied. Sometimes a light touch is enough, and sometimes a heavy hand is needed. Finally, there is the problem of conflicting stimuli being applied at the same time. Thus, the company may be using one set of stimuli, a union another, and the employee himself a third set. Theories of motivation are indeed weak in answering such questions and problems as yet.

3. **Factors of Motivation.** To employ motivation with some hope of success, one must also take note of some basic factors of motivation. These can be classified according to the manager when motivating, the person being motivated, and the situation or circumstances.

Many people believe that the full force of motivation lies in the person doing the motivating. In the case of the executive, it is presumably his magnetic personality, which induces undying loyalty and high production. Lacking this quality, an executive presumably can count but little on motivation. Such a belief has little to substantiate it, but it does point up the importance of the motivator. Perhaps a magnetic personality can charm one's subordinates. But most executives should seek to cultivate other devices. In particular, thought should be given to the matter of how an executive can himself, through motivation, serve others rather than simply himself. He then assumes the responsibility of developing worthwhile plans of motivation.

The second group of factors pertains to the person or persons being motivated. Here, close study must be made of individual and group composition. Differences in such as the following must be considered in establishing motivating plans:

1. Personal background.
2. Education.
3. Age.
4. Marital status.
5. Financial status.
6. Health.
7. Political affiliations.
8. Religious beliefs.
9. Social relationships.
10. Psychological makeup.
11. Union affiliations.
12. Company experiences.

This approach to motivation essentially is a recognition of the fact that there must be a capacity or potential for motivation within a person. One cannot, to use an example from another field, stimulate a seed of corn to grow into a rose bush. No more can one expect a person to become something for which he has no potential within himself. Hence, for an executive to act with wisdom in motivating his subordinates, he must have information on the qualities they possess.

Finally, motivation must be concerned with particular circumstances and environment. What might work in a company with a long history of union relations would, doubtless, be questionable in one with a long history of no unionization. Or, the motivating plans would have to be adjusted to given conditions of background, nationality, or creed of a particular area of the community or country. Again, the general attitudes of management toward labor and of labor toward management would be pertinent factors in laying plans of motivation. To cite one more example, the economic conditions—past, present, and future—of a particular company, community, or area would have considerable effect upon motivational plans.

To summarize this section, there is need for a word of warning and of optimism. The warning lies in the statement that motivation requires close, detailed attention to motivator, "motivatee," devices, and circumstances. But optimism is found in the fact that executive motivation is far from solely dependent upon personality. With these words in mind it is now appropriate to examine particular groups of motivating devices.

Kinds of Motivators

Having provided a varied picture of the system or model of motivation, it is now appropriate to describe specific kinds of motivators. This is done under the headings of (1) basic needs and wants of people, (2) individual motivators, (3) group motivators, (4) company motivators, and (5) financial motivators.

1. *Needs and Wants of People.* The foundation on which all motivational plans must be built is the satisfaction of human needs and wants. Patently, the acts of all normal human beings are for the purpose of satisfying as far as one can those ends (means, needs, wants, or values) which sustain and give meaning to life. We live, act, and function—to begin with—to maintain life through food, shelter, clothing, etc. We need to protect ourselves from various risks of living, so various security needs must be sought. We are emotional and gregarious beings, so feeling good individually and socially are obvious needs. We are growing and mental beings, so creativity, challenges, and self-fulfillment are basic needs.

Some students of human activity and motivation have arranged such basic needs into a so-called hierarchy of needs.[1] This implies that some needs such as physiological or security must be relatively satisfied before higher order needs such as creativity or self-fulfill-

---

[1] See Figure 18–1 for a representation of the five levels of need priority as established by Abraham H. Maslow, *Motivation and Personality* (2d ed.; New York: Harper & Row, 1970), pp. 35–51.

ment can be sought effectively. Such in general may be the case. But it is not easy to specify what order of priority particular individuals will establish for themselves. For example, a given individual may well prefer to concentrate his activities on creative risk-taking at the expense of insuring himself of basic food needs. Since a manager often has to deal with people on a one-to-one basis in contrast with employees in general, this difference should be recognized.

It would be unrealistic to deny that people, generally speaking, have certain basic needs which motivate them to action. Fundamentally, all people have such basic needs and wants. But as yet we cannot specify with any precision to what degree or in what order particular individuals are motivated by these wants. Moreover, these basic classes of wants are seldom attained directly in business. Rather, intermediate goals must first be attained in order to achieve the basic needs. For example, if a given worker wants the esteem of his fellow workers or friends, he must first attain such goals as higher organizational positions, more salary, or special privileges. Such intermediate goals are the steps to the more basic needs. Granted the existence and potency of basic human needs, the manager must use their motivational force in dealing with both individuals or groups.

2. *Individual Motivators.* It is obvious that as human beings, people have certain basic needs. Unless these are satisfied, life may either be lost or lose its significance. So, people in various ways and in varying degrees strive to satisfy them. Food, shelter, clothing, and sex come immediately to mind. But soon thoughts turn to such needs as religion, creativity, understanding, peace of mind, and security. Again, the student is referred to Maslow's need hierarchy in Figure 18–1.

Have these any connection with the business world? To ask the question is to answer it immediately with a resounding "yes." Most of the foregoing needs are directly served through work. We earn through work the resources to purchase particular commodities and services that will satisfy our material needs. Moreover, the work itself may satisfy personal needs through such things as craftsmanship, artistic expression, creation, and feelings of significance and accomplishment.

It must be the task of every executive to determine how such individual motivators can be employed to stimulate desired business results. Plans should be developed to utilize these drives in increas-

According to Maslow human needs exist in a hierarchy that consists of five categories. (See Figure 18–1.) Theoretically, a person moves through the levels of this hierarchy in order. After the first level needs are satisfied, the individual proceeds to the next level. Each individual varies to the extent of his progress along this hierarchy, and it becomes increasingly difficult to reach the ultimate goal of self-actualization, which means to become all one is capable of becoming.

SOURCE: Abraham H. Maslow, *Motivation and Personality* (2d. ed; New York: Harper & Row, 1970), pp 35–51.

ing production, quality of work, loyalty, and good discipline. As a simple example, when an employee is given a job to do, he should be told on occasion how the job affects his pay, standard of living, job security, and opportunities for promotion.

3. *Group Motivators.* No less potent as motivators are the stimuli that arise out of social interactions. Without doubt, we are very strongly affected by what people think of us and our actions. Even our actions in satisfying our basic wants—food, shelter, religion—are often affected by what we feel will gain group approval. Why do we want to live in certain areas of a city, wear certain kinds of clothes, trade our cars long before they wear out, and prefer certain professions? In many instances, the deciding factor is group opinion—our families, neighbors, or working associates.

In this area, business executives have not done as well as might be expected. Indeed, business has fallen far behind unions, for example. Employees are influenced more by what their union associates will think of their actions than by what might happen to their pay. This is seen sometimes when employees go out on strike and remain out for months. After the eventual settlement, someone calculates that it will take "20 years to make up through the increase in pay what was lost in wages during the strike." The thought being conveyed by such a calculation is that employees made a foolish mistake. Perhaps so, but they valued group opinion more highly than economic earnings.

As life becomes more civilized, the power of group motivators grows. One may argue that group pressures result in dull uniformity and a nonthinking conformance. But these pressures are not likely to be decreased as time goes on. If executives are smart they will, in the first place, utilize group pressure and, in the second place, seek to improve their quality and standards.

FIGURE 18–1
Hierarchy of Needs (adapted)

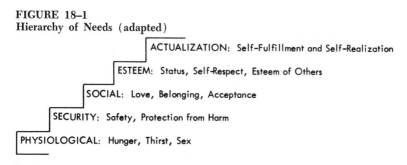

ACTUALIZATION: Self-Fulfillment and Self-Realization

ESTEEM: Status, Self-Respect, Esteem of Others

SOCIAL: Love, Belonging, Acceptance

SECURITY: Safety, Protection from Harm

PHYSIOLOGICAL: Hunger, Thirst, Sex

Sociological influence is gradually taking its place alongside the psychological and economic as a recognized motivating force. Unfortunately, knowledge of the "society" of business is as yet rather slim. But current research indicates that social or group relations are powerful forces for good or evil in the business institution. It is imperative, therefore, to accept this challenge as a constructive opportunity in motivation. (Figure 18–2 illustrates the various determinants of the need hierarchy for an individual.)

FIGURE 18–2
Determinants of the Need Hierarchy for an Individual

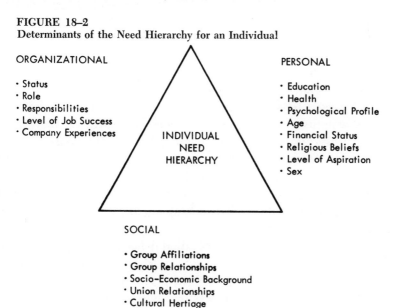

ORGANIZATIONAL

· Status
· Role
· Responsibilities
· Level of Job Success
· Company Experiences

INDIVIDUAL
NEED
HIERARCHY

PERSONAL

· Education
· Health
· Psychological Profile
· Age
· Financial Status
· Religious Beliefs
· Level of Aspiration
· Sex

SOCIAL

· Group Affiliations
· Group Relationships
· Socio-Economic Background
· Union Relationships
· Cultural Hertiage

4. Company Motivators. Further attention should be given to the relation of nonfinancial motivators to the business situation. It may seem that what people want out of life is inconsistent with the needs of business. After all, doesn't a man have to give up a large part of his life to the company? Doesn't he have to do many things he would prefer not to do? Doesn't he have to work when he would rather loaf and play?

Many people think that answers to those questions make a business enterprise seem to be the enemy rather than the friend of man. At this point, it is interesting to review the work of Frederick Herzberg in identifying certain organizational factors of motivation.[2] A little thought would show that business is not necessarily inimical to human needs. But the fact remains that many people feel otherwise and act negatively toward the companies that employ them and the executives who direct them. Managers should take the initiative in dispelling such adverse notions and their accompanying reactions.

To begin with, no matter where he works, man must ordinarily "earn his bread by the sweat of his brow." If a man does not work for a business enterprise, he, nonetheless, will have to work somewhere. He must, therefore, give up part of his life to earning a livelihood. He must do this though he might prefer to loaf and play. So, the point is not whether he should work or play; the point is where and how he should work. After he has worked, perhaps he'll have time to play.

Viewed in this way, the favorable light that can be played upon business is obvious. Management should be able to show that business provides people with the best opportunity to gain what they want. Warranted, people have to work in business. Warranted, they must give up loafing and playing. But work in business is so effective and productive that people are thereby free to enjoy other activities. In no other type of productive enterprise is the relation between working hours and leisure hours so favorable. Yet, this advantage is seldom stressed by management in its communications to labor.

In addition, if man must work, should he not seek the environment in which work would be most satisfying in itself? This does not imply that work, like play, will ever be pleasurable in all ways. But it does imply that work has potentialities for deep satisfaction, creativity, and self-fulfillment. Through the centuries, philosophers have argued that work—yes, hard work—brings the deepest satis-

---

[2] See Figure 18–3 for a comparison of job satisfiers and dissatisfiers in the business firm as researched by Frederick Herzberg, Bernard Mausner, and Barbara Block Snyderman, *The Motivation to Work* (New York: John Wiley & Sons, Inc., 1959), p. 81.

faction and contentment. This thought has been echoed by those whose lives have run the gamut of human activities and found this out through personal experience.

Yet here, again, many executives have failed to bring out this salient thought to employees at all levels. This failure is unacceptable. In the first place, business has innumerable jobs that can challenge the imagination, skill, and aims of anyone. Just to go through a modern factory is to be struck by the complexities and technicalities that are abundantly present. But some persons may retort that for every challenging job in industry, there are hundreds, if not thousands, of boring and monotonous jobs. True, but here, again, industry can show how it is attempting to turn these jobs over to machines. Moreover, employees are challenged both to help develop new ways of working better and to run the machines so developed. Unfortunately, we seldom stress these possible ways of making even the most monotonous job more satisfactory.

5. Financial Motivators. Employees—at all levels of an organization from top to bottom—may not be inspired by money alone. But dollars certainly are important motivators. Moreover, pay is a concrete and general summation of all other motivators. Perhaps a person works hard because he likes his work or his boss, because he is bucking for a promotion, or because he wants to gain personal or group significance. But, in the final analysis, what he takes home on payday summarizes in one package much of everything else. So, without underestimating nonfinancial motivators, it is well first to give thought to financial devices of motivation.

In taking up financial motivators, thoughts may turn immediately to some form of wage or salary incentive plan. Examples that might come to mind are piecework, bonus plans, commission plans, and profit sharing. All of these must seek a fair relationship between pay and effort.

But there is much, much more to the problem of devising a good financial motivator than that of relating reward to effort, difficult though that may be. Full treatment of all the areas needing study would require several volumes, but attention is here briefly called to these areas, which are:

1. Factors of financial compensation: such as time, effort, output, dependability, loyalty, willingness to assume responsibility, scarcity value, and bargaining strength.
2. Form of compensation: that is, the "package" in which the

Herzberg's theory is based on a study of 200 engineers and accountants. He concluded that some job conditions operate to dissatisfy employees when the conditions are not present, but their presence, on the other hand, does not strongly motivate employees. These strong dissatisfiers are known as maintenance or hygiene factors since they support satisfaction of a reasonable level. Maintenance factors are concerned with the job context or environment. They are: company policy and administration, supervision-technical, salary, interpersonal relations—supervision, and working conditions. These are mostly to the left side of the scale.

Motivational factors are concerned with the job content and the satisfaction gained from performance on it. They lie mostly on the right side of the scale. They are: achievement, recognition, the work itself, and responsibility.

As shown in Figure 18-3, the width of the boxes represents the duration of motivated or dissatisfied feelings while the length of each block shows the frequency with which each factor appeared in the sequence of events reported as a motivator or a dissatisfier.

financial compensation is paid, such as profit-sharing or commission plans.

3. Understanding of plans: that is, careful attention should be given to gaining a clear understanding of how the chosen plan works.

4. Mechanics of payment: such as, calendar day of payment, payment in cash or by check, location at which payment is made, and frequency of payment periods.

5. Relativity: that is, attention must be directed to how much must be paid for different jobs and to different people on the same job.

6. Programming: that is, attention must be directed to the proper placement of financial payment in the total program of motivation, human relations, and personnel management.

Steps in Motivating

It is now appropriate to see how an executive may actually proceed to motivate his subordinates. This activity divides itself into two parts: first, what he does; and, second, how and why he does it. The former involves steps in motivation and the latter involves rules governing the steps. Both are performed, of course, simultaneously. But for purposes of discussion it is preferable to

FIGURE 18–3
A Comparison of Satisfiers and Dissatisfiers

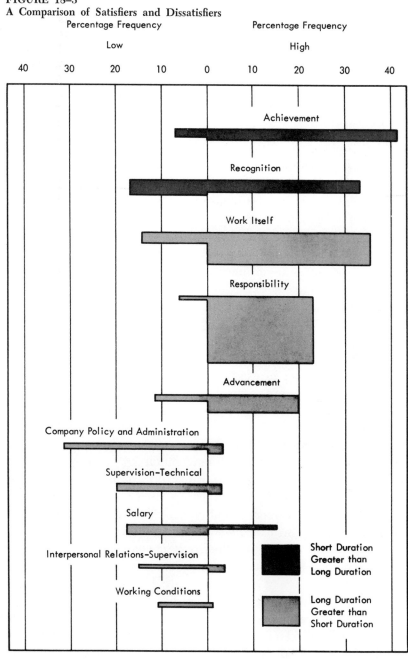

take them up separately. This section is devoted, therefore, to steps of motivation. The next is devoted to rules of motivation.

The major steps of motivation include the following:

1. Sizing up the situation.
2. Preparing a set of motivating tools.
3. Selecting and applying motivational plans.
4. Follow-up.

1. *Sizing up the Situation.* The first stage of motivation is to determine motivational needs. Which employees need motivation? All of them, of course, to some degree. So, determination of motivational needs is not a matter of absolutes but rather of relatives—how much and what kind of motivation is needed when, and by which individuals or groups of individuals? Notice that "size up" has a number of facets besides the mere question of kind of motivation. An executive must determine the quantity of motivation, as well as the kind, for each individual or group. Not the least of these facets is timing. For a compliment, let us say, which might have motivated a particular employee when he was a young man is an empty gesture if he receives it only at a retirement banquet.

Much stress in sizing up must be laid upon individual differences. Not all people react in exactly the same way to the same stimuli. Guaranteed, people are more alike than they are different. One can be too concerned with the psychological study of individual differences. Hence, it is well to start with the premise that people are basically alike. Keeping this in mind, the skilled executive seeks an answer to the question of how much "A" and "B," who are alike, differ. For example, "A" and "B" are alike because both are interested in getting ahead. To "A" that means, let us say, the same job with more money, but to "B" it means moving from the technical ranks to an executive position. The fundamental drive in each case is the same, but the specific goal of each is different.

Differences in individuals or groups must be viewed as influences affecting the attainment of specific goals. All men need food; in that, they are alike. But whereas one may desire champagne and caviar, another wants only beer and pretzels. One worries about providing a college education for his children, another is more than satisfied if his children get through high school. Or, one takes great pride in the quality of work he turns out, and another is interested in seeing the time clock reach the quitting hour. The determinants are how much an individual wants from life—either of the things for which he must pay, or of the satisfactions from work itself.

So, the executive must be an astute student of his subordinates. He must tune into their aims, hopes, ambitions, and desires. And, he must be aware that each subordinate is both an individual and a group member. Hence, he must determine what group-engendered differences exist in them as well as what egocentric differences exist in them.

This job of sizing up can be one of the most rewarding and satisfying that any executive can do. It is a difficult one, certainly. But next to the mystery of oneself, there is the equal mystery of one's fellowman. If the philosophers tell us to "Know thyself," they include also in that, "Know thy fellowman." The highest study of man, so the philosophers have said, is man himself. All this means that an executive who does his job in this respect—and he will have to apply himself diligently to this task—may serve not only his company but also his fellowman; and, above all, he will bring great satisfaction and meaning to his own life.

2. *Preparing a Set of Motivating Tools.* Having determined the motivational needs of a particular person or group, an executive must then be ready to select and apply specific tools of motivation. But this means that previously he must have prepared a list of such tools, from which appropriate choices may be made. The wise executive collects in advance information on motivational devices. In his own experience, but, perhaps better still, from the experiences of others, he can distill a list of what devices seem to work, with what types of people, and under what conditions.

Such a listing has the merit of any preliminary, advance planning. The executive can include, reject, and cull various motivational tools. Moreover, by actually developing a list, he can minimize possibilities of overlooking useful devices and of wasting time repeatedly mulling over his ideas of motivation as occasions arise for their employment. He will, in addition, gain confidence in his motivational skills because he will retain on the list only those devices that seem to work well for him.

3. *Selecting and Applying Motivational Plans.* The critical stage in motivation is, of course, the application. This involves selection of the appropriate plan, the method of application, and the timing and location of the application.

Which specific plan of motivation from his list should an executive decide to apply in a given case? Obviously, an answer to this involves a number of decisions. Who is the individual involved? What has worked, or not worked, in the past? Are any precedents or other employees involved? What does the selected motivational device involve in terms of executive skill, time, and resources?

Having selected a motivational device, an executive must give thought to how he will apply it. It is not enough to decide, for example, that a given employee is to be approached through compliments on his craftsmanship. An executive should think through the words he will use, and intonations of the words, and his own gestures, in paying the compliment. He should rehearse his contemplated behavior. For in such situations he is an actor; and preacting—as through role playing—will make his performance smoother and more effective.

And, finally, an executive should carefully consider where and when motivation is going to be applied. Taking the compliment as an example, some employees like to be told in public of their good deeds. But some prefer to avoid the spotlight. Timing, too, is most significant. How soon after a good deed has been done should an employee be told of management's appreciation? This is a most interesting question in the stimulus-response area. If that question is incorrectly answered, a compliment may be worse than useless. Conversely, correct timing can add to motivational effectiveness.

4. *Follow-up.*   The final stage of motivation is follow-up, or feedback. Here the primary purpose is to determine whether an individual has been motivated. If he has not, an executive must seek to apply some other device. For motivation was intended to achieve some result—such as higher output, lower costs, greater loyalty—that as yet is not attained.

In addition, follow-up serves to increase the effectiveness of future motivational acts. An executive learns what succeeded, what failed, and most importantly, he learns the "why" of success or failure, if at all possible. Then he can adjust accordingly his plans and actions in the future.

Follow-up has another advantage. If one knows in advance that his actions are to be checked, he is invariably more careful to begin with. Thus, his current motivational plans and actions are probably performed much better. Such checking does not necessarily imply a negative attitude. On the contrary, a plan of self-criticism is one of the most positive and constructive forces for good, whether in private or professional life.

Rules of Motivating

In the performance of the steps of motivation, the executive should be guided by some fundamental rules or bench marks. Such basics are not laws; we do not as yet know enough about motivation to be that certain. But past experience has taught us some useful lessons. As time goes on, we should add to our store of knowledge. The following suggestions provide a basis for building one's own list of guides; it is by no means intended as a final or conclusive statement.

1. *Self-Interest and Motivation.* Without doubt, motivation is largely built upon selfishness. This may seem to be an undesirable foundation. To the extent that selfishness tends toward greediness, the undesirability cannot be denied. But selfishness may be "intelligent." This is so when a person realizes that his own purposes are best served when he helps others, too, to attain their purposes. For example, an employee may be ambitious to climb the executive ladder. He can try to accomplish this by climbing over other people. Or he can try to climb by helping other people be effective team members. Both methods are selfish, but one is intelligent.

Moreover, selfishness is simply a fundamental part of life. To deny this would be unrealistic. To seek some other basis of motivation would be to deny all that we know of human life. The aim should be, instead, to learn more about selfishness. At what point does selfishness turn from good to bad? How can we ourselves determine whether we are being wise or unwise in our selfishness? How can we judge when short-run selfishness is long-run foolishness? How can we be sure that our personal goals do not harm others and thereby harm ourselves, sooner or later? Answers to these questions would help to make our motivational efforts fair, effective, and personally satisfying.

2. *Attainability.* It may seem too obvious to mention, but motivation must establish attainable goals. What we hold out for a particular person must be attainable by him. This does not mean easily or at once. Obviously, such goals as a better job or a supervisory position may take years to attain. But they must be attainable.

There are enough goals to hold out without offering every employee a vice presidency, or store managership, or a laboratory of his own. These goals are, of course, available, but they are attainable by only a few. It would be far better to stress the difficulty of attainability than to seek the short-run gains of making their attainability look easy to one and all, if only they would work hard; far better to concentrate motivation on those goals which most employees can attain.

Attainability must be related to time as well as type of reward. Profit sharing, for example, loses much of its punch because effort on a hot day in July will not be rewarded until a distant, cold day in January, if at all. Similarly, whether it be in pay, promotion, or privilege, the compensation must come within a reasonable time after effort is expended. Otherwise, the motivation will be ineffective currently or in the future.

3.   *Proportioning Rewards.* Good motivation is dependent also upon proper proportioning of rewards among people, and for the same person at different times. A uniform plan of compensation for salesmen, for example, loses its zest after a while. That is why various types of contests with different rewards should be set from time to time. One contest may be based on sales of new products, another on percentage of increase, another on number of new customers, and another on service calls made. And the rewards may be trips to different resort areas from year to year, desired products such as automobiles or mink coats for wives, or college scholarships for the children of winners.

Or, looking at a particular person, an executive must determine what he should do from time to time to change motivational appeals. One time the appeal may be money, another time the chance for promotion, and another some special privilege such as going to a seminar. Such decisions involve careful study and thought on the part of every executive.

4.   *The Human Element.* It is well to refer again to the idea that people are swayed as much by intangible concepts and appeals as by concrete goals, if not more. This all goes back to the fact that we are feeling, as well as thinking, bodies. Indeed, some students of human life go so far as to conclude that people ordinarily think far less than they think they do. In the opinion of these students, emotions are the directors of human activity.

To what extent this is true is debatable. One would be brave to deny the importance of feelings in human relations. One needs only to work with people to see how quickly their actions can turn into undesirable channels if their feelings are hurt, their egos or personalities insulted, or their ideas slighted. The executive may have been absolutely right in his logic and facts and decisions; but because a person was offended, everything went wrong.

5. *Individual-Group Relationship.* Motivation must be based upon group- as well as individual-centered stimuli. For a long time management acted as if subordinates were solely and simply egocentric creatures. If action was wanted, attention had only to be paid to the individual drives and needs of people. There is some basic truth in this. Each of us is to a large extent an island unto himself.

But more recently management has learned the terrific impact that groups have upon individuals. What we do as individuals is greatly influenced by what others think of our actions. As a consequence, management must in its motivational efforts recognize group pressures. Can a wage incentive plan succeed if the group is against company-operated programs? Can a promotional plan be effective if the group considers promotion to a supervisory position a traitorous act?

There is no intention here to deride the ideas of the group. If management does not like the ideas or pressures of the group, derision or disagreement will do no good. Motivational efforts that run counter to group ideas are bound to be ineffective. This does not mean that management must take a pessimistic point of view, admit failure, and give up. It has two courses of action: first, to utilize motivational plans that do not run counter to group forces; and, second, to seek to change the ideas of the group.

6. *Managerial Theory.* Finally, management must base its motivational efforts on a sound theory. Here it is interesting to review McGregor's Theory X and Theory Y approach to motivation. McGregor refers to Theory X as the "carrot and stick" theory of motivation. It works well just as long as the "means" for satisfying man's physiological and (within limits) safety needs can be offered or withheld by management. Work itself, wages, working conditions and benefits are examples of "means." "By these 'means' the individual can be controlled so long as he is struggling for subsistence. Man tends to live for bread alone when there is little bread."[3]

On the other hand, cites McGregor, the "carrot and stick" theory of motivation does not succeed once man has attained a satisfactory subsistence level and is motivated primarily by higher needs such as self-respect or self-fulfillment.[4] Instead he proposes a different management strategy based upon Theory Y (see Figure 18–4).

---

[3] Douglas McGregor, *The Human Side of the Enterprise* (New York: McGraw-Hill Book Co., 1960), p. 41.

[4] Ibid., p. 42.

FIGURE 18–4
McGregor's Theory X and Theory Y Assumptions of Motivation

THEORY X ASSUMPTIONS

1. "The average human being has an inherent dislike of work and will avoid it if he can. . . .
2. Because of this human characteristic of dislike of work, most people must be coerced, controlled, directed, threatened with punishment to get them to put forth adequate effort toward the achievement of organizational objectives. . . .
3. The average human being prefers to be directed, wishes to avoid responsibility, has relatively little ambition, wants security above all. . . ."*

THEORY Y ASSUMPTIONS

1. "The expenditure of physical and mental effort in work is as natural as play or rest. . . .
2. External control and the threat of punishment are not the only means for bringing about effort toward organizational objectives. Man will exercise self-direction and self-control in the service of objectives to which he is committed. . . .
3. Commitment to objectives is a function of the rewards associated with their achievement. . . .
4. The average human being learns, under proper conditions not only to accept but to seek responsibility. . . .
5. The capacity to exercise a relatively high degree of imagination, ingenuity and creativity in the solution of organizational problems is widely, not narrowly, distributed in the population. . . .
6. Under the conditions of modern industrial life, the intellectual potentialities of the average human being are only partially utilized."†

* Douglas McGregor, *The Human Side of the Enterprise* (New York: McGraw-Hill Book Co., 1960) pp. 33–34.
† Ibid., pp. 47–48.

The assumptions of Theory Y stress that the limits of individual collaboration toward organizational goal achievement are not limits of human nature but of management in not discovering how to extract the potential represented by its human resources. Theory Y places the problem of motivation upon the shoulders of management in that "if employees are lazy, indifferent, unwilling to take responsibility, intransigent, uncreative, uncooperative, Theory Y implies that the causes lie in management's methods of organization and control."[5]

By this time the student should appreciate that motivation is far from being an expression of the manager's magnetic personality. All of the foregoing chapter has been a negation of this idea. Certainly, an executive who has an appealing and forceful personality should use it to inspire his subordinates. But motivation is far, far more than this. It involves practices that run from careful selection of good subordinates through thoughtful study of the needs and characteristics of people. It involves careful planning, good organization, effective direction, and detailed controls.

Motivation, in short, is a field in which hard work and study will pay big dividends. It still is largely an art. But it is an art that can be practiced with reasonably satisfying success by all who are willing to expend the time, the thought, and the effort, and who have the right attitude.

QUESTIONS

1. What are some of the important obstacles that must be overcome in motivating employees?
2. What factors have an impact upon motivation?
3. What aspects or areas need study in connection with financial motivators?
4. In what respects do individual motivators differ from group motivators? Give examples of each.
5. What motivation, beyond the purely economic, does the business enterprise have to offer?
6. What is the relationship between steps of motivation and rules of motivation? Why are both necessary?
7. What is your opinion of self-interest as an element in motivation?
8. What is meant by proportioning rewards in the process of motivation? Why is it desirable?

CASE 18–1

The newly appointed supervisor of the tool-making department has been reviewing the records of the tool makers as a means of getting better acquainted with his men. He is using every possible

---

[5] Ibid., p. 48.

means to get thoroughly acquainted because he has been told that this department has been falling down and needs to be motivated.

He has paused at the record of Joe Strate because Joe already has impressed him as one of the below-par men. The record surprises him because in education, psychological tests, and preceding ratings, Joe was among the top 10 percent. So he decided to have a conference with Joe that afternoon before quitting time.

The discussion has proceeded for only a few minutes when Joe invites the supervisor to stop at his house that afternoon on the way home to see some of his hobby work. There, Joe shows the supervisor some of the finest parts for miniature racing cars he has ever seen. And Mrs. Strate points out that her husband can hardly be dragged out of his workshop to get a good night's sleep.

1. Does Joe have a motivational potential and can it be exploited? How?

2. How do you account for his lack of motivation on the job?

CASE 18–2

The following is a message, among a variety of others, that was communicated to the employees of a company whose employees were out on strike:

The first month of the strike is over. So now you have lost a month's earnings. How much more are you going to lose? No more if you return to work now!

Figure your loss so far. Fill out the spaces below:

$$\left(\frac{}{\text{Your Hourly Rate}} + \frac{\$0.30}{\text{Our Offer}} \right) \text{Times 160 Hours} = \frac{}{\text{Wage Loss}}.$$

This is based on the company's fair offer.

We have heard that we are accused of forcing you out on strike. Nothing could be further from the truth. We welcome you to return to work.

We are told that someone sent congratulations to the union for taking a militant stand against the repressive company. We question the use of militancy in our relations and you know that we are not repressive.

It has been said that you must struggle against the company to get justice. Our offer is fair and retroactive. Does that sound like you need to struggle?

It is said that a strike is necessary to get an honorable settlement. We have faith in the honor of our employees and we, ourselves have always dealt honorably. We dispute that a strike creates honor.

Return to work without further loss of wages or bargaining rights. Remember, each week's wage loss is roughly equivalent to fifteen cents an hour for a whole year. This strike increases your losses and hours. Return now.

THE MANAGEMENT

1. Is this a good communication on the part of the company?
2. What is needed for the reader to have confidence in the arguments set forth in this communication?

19

The Executive
and Ethics

Scope of Discussion

THE PRECEDING chapter has been concerned with the importance
of interests in motivation. Yet, it has avoided the question of the
degree to which the interests of the manager and employee are
alike or different, and this question is important to all parties in
or affected by a business organization.

Indeed, the interests of managers and employees—their purposes,
goals, needs, and values—are often seemingly opposed. Stockholders, for example, usually expect the highest returns on their
investments. Labor desires higher wages, increased security, and
other benefits. Customers want highest quality at lowest possible
prices. Suppliers desire the best prices for their goods and services;
and the public in general wants business operations to be without
deleterious and polluting effects. All these parties cannot get the
"most" of their particular wishes. The basic question then is, "How
is some degree of balance to these demands achieved or sought?"

To begin with an answer, assuredly each interested party attempts to justify its own demands. Stockholders, labor, customers,
suppliers, and governmental agencies exert various types of influences and supply supporting evidence and arguments. But it is beyond the scope of this text to take up a study of all these forces.
It is pertinent here, however, to examine the role of the business
in this matter of reconciling or balancing opposing interests.

In this aspect of his responsibilities, the manager must give careful attention to the subject of ethics. He must give due consideration
to the rights of others besides those of his employer—the stockholders. In part, he is helped in his decision making by the quantitative forces in the competitive markets—whether of goods, finances,

or labor. But in large part, he must arrive at fairness of opposing interests by the qualitative standards of ethics.

It is the purpose of this chapter, therefore, to discuss the factor of ethics in relation to executive decision making and the business environment. The subject is taken up under the following major headings:

1. Nature and significance of ethics.
2. Role of value systems.
3. Ethical behavior in the organization.
4. General public and business ethics.
5. Plan for business ethics.

Nature and Significance of Ethics

In an open society, such as ours, the unethical practices sometimes associated with business make interesting copy for the news media. In fact, it is commonplace to find examples in the daily press of some kind of ethical wrong doing in the business community. Within recent years, for example, major scandals have occurred in the auto industry, where a president is forced to resign because of conflict of interest, and the electrical equipment field, where several vice presidents of a major manufacturer were convicted of conspiracy to fix prices.

These and other unethical practices are, of course, immoral and unconscionable. While unethical practices are not representative of business behavior, nevertheless, they are symptoms of some corruption in the business community. In our open society any excesses of executive behavior become readily visible to the public irrespective of the innumerable business transactions conducted every day in an atmosphere of honesty and integrity.

To be sure, the American business community has come a long way since the era of the individualistic, antisocial, profit-seeking capitalists described in *The Robber Barons*.[1] Today through a combination of self-regulation and federal legislation, the firm evidences increasing interest and concern for its ethical behavior. It recognizes a responsibility to the society which permits it to exist and function. It recognizes, too, that the unrestrained use of economic power to the detriment of the public good can only result in increased government intervention and control.

---

[1] This book by Matthew Josephson (New York: Harcourt, Brace & World, Inc., 1962) is a classic exposé of big business in the 19th century.

1.   *Definition of Ethics.* A basic problem in any discussion of business ethics is common agreement as to the meaning of a term which lends itself to subjective interpretation. Ethics has variously been defined by some sources as:

—"due regard for other people"
—"conforming to moral standards"
—"the determination of rightness or wrongness in situations"
—"what the law requires"
—"the science of moral duty"
—"what my conscience allows"

This basic lack of uniform agreement compounds the problem for the executive in his perception of ethics. Consequently, a definition of commonly used terms is necessary. For our purpose, ethics then is the science of morals. It is the study of the morality of human conduct and the standards for that conduct. Ethics strives to delineate what conduct is good and what is bad or what conduct is to be acceptable and what is unacceptable. A code of ethics consists of a standard of ideal, and acceptable behavior in society and organizations.

2.   *Sources of a Code of Ethics.* Just how does an executive go about developing his own personal code of ethics? From what sources does it spring? As mentioned, a person's code of ethical behavior is largely shaped by certain standards against which his individual conduct is framed. These standards are identified as:[2]

1. *The Subjective Standard.* The executive's morality is viewed subjectively. If the behavior of others is similar to his, it is considered moral. If the behavior of others is sufficiently different from his own, in terms of patterns of action and belief, then he is likely to consider it ethically unsound.

2. *The Normative Standard.* Morality is that standard approved by the greatest number of people. This is the voice of society, the culture, and the group. Legal standards are the legal criteria of morality and are. but the norms of the past society, so to speak. The question here is, "to what degree does the normative behavior of others influence the behavior of the executive?"

3. *The Objective Standard.* This is the religious criteria of morality. It is that behavior espoused by the precepts of the Judeo-Christian religious faiths. It is a more objective and permanent

---

[2] Adapted from V. Clayton Sherman, "Business Ethics: Analysis and Philosophy," *Personnel Journal* (Swarthmore, Pa.: Personnel Journal, Inc., April, 1968).

basis for establishing one's behavior. While executives will use the Judeo-Christian ethic in varying degrees of application, it, nonetheless, does constitute another framework within which managers function ethically.

4. *Influence Agents.* A fourth standard or criterion for the manager's ethical behavior is the exemplary influence of certain people who through close personal contact exert a significant effect upon his life. In this class and in recognized rank order of importance are: father, boss, mother, teachers, clergy, wife, and business associates.[3] Again the question arises as to the significant effect of these sources in determining the executive's behavior. Certain sources, it appears, like one's superior exert a more profound influence on the job than say one's business associates or peers. (See Figure 19–1, for a descriptive model of influential factors in the determination of ethical behavior).

FIGURE 19–1
Influential Determinants of Ethical Behavior

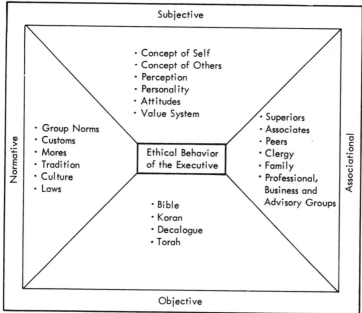

Summarily, the behavior of an executive is a composite reflection of beliefs and attitudes from different sources of influence. Each

---

[3] Raymond Baumhart, *Ethics in Business* (New York: Holt, Rinehart & Winston, Inc., 1968), p. 68.

364 Elements of Managerial Action

manager evidences a peculiar, ethical profile; and while his resultant behavior may be similar to that of other managers, the basis for his actions may be distinctly different.

Role of Value Systems

Any discussion about business ethics, about "what is" versus the "what ought to be" in terms of executive behavior, must concern itself with the manager's value system. By definition, a manager's value system is a composite of beliefs, expectations, and motivations. A value system is intrinsic, highly perceptual and reasonably permanent. "It provides a framework that influences individual behavior and social expectations. It provides the basis for making value judgments. Values which are internalized and exert the greatest influence on behavior might be called *operational;* those which are outwardly professed, but not fully accepted internally, might be termed *adoptive.*"[4]

What this means is that many people function in organizational life with a dual value system that is seemingly inconsistent. Examples of this would be a personnel director who is primarily a service-oriented individual who works for a firm that is devoid of humanistic feelings in its approach to employees and views the personnel function as "the office to hire and fire the rank and file," or a salesman, highly moralistic, who has a superior with little ethics, less morals, along with a high propensity for women and liquor.

Eventually, however, one's value system determines one's actions. The personnel director and the salesman must either change their value systems—or leave the firm. Understandably, the value system of the manager is important because it influences:

1. A manager's perception of situations and problems he faces;
2. A manager's decisions and solutions to problems;
3. The way in which a manager looks at other individuals and groups of individuals—thus influencing interpersonal relationships;
4. The perception of individual and organizational success as well as its achievement;
5. The limits for the determination of what is and what is not ethical behavior by a manager;
6. The extent to which a manager will accept or resist organizational pressures and goals.[5]

[4] Clarence C. Walton, *Ethos and the Executive* (Englewood Cliffs, N.J.: Prentice-Hall, Inc., 1969), p. 33.
[5] George W. England, as quoted in Walton, *Ethos and the Executive,* p. 34.

Ethical Behavior in the Organization

1. *Self-Perception of Ethical Behavior.* Any discussion of the executive's ethical behavior must begin from the viewpoint of the executive himself. How, then, does the average modern manager view or perceive his own behavior in terms of relationships with his firm, client, and society?

The average executive, various studies show, feels that he is more ethical than the average businessman and also that extensions of himself (his department, company, industry and country) are more ethical than their counterparts. He also feels that good ethics is good business in the long run, especially in employee and customer relations. The golden rule, most executives believe, while useful as a starting point, is inadequate as a norm for solving most ethical problems in business. Furthermore, studies bear out that the executive who does not attend church or synagogue appears to have attitudes just as ethical as those of the church-affiliated manager.[6] Again, and to reemphasize, more than any other singular influence on the job is the influence of one's boss. The executive's behavior is profoundly influenced by the behavior of his superiors in the making of decisions both ethical and unethical. This points up, of course, that improvement of standards of conduct in the organization rests with the manager himself. Consequently, any expected change in ethical behavior must stem from the conscious actions of the organization's leadership.

2. *Ethical Practices in Business.* In the Baumhart study cited previously, the executives themselves were asked to identify what they considered to be "the one practice I would most like to see eliminated." Of 1,512 executives surveyed, 791 responded accordingly:[7]

Unethical Practice	*Percent Specifying This Practice*
Price discrimination, unfair pricing, price collusion	25.6
Bribes, excessive gifts and favors, call girls	22.5
Dishonest advertising	14.4
Unfair competitive practices, e.g., pirating employees or ideas	13.2
Cheating customers, overselling, unfair credit practices	8.8
Dishonesty in making or fulfilling contracts	7.0
Other	8.5

---

[6] Baumhart, *Ethics in Business*, pp. 4–5.

[7] Ibid., p. 27.

3.   *A Basis for Professional Conduct.* A major frustration encountered by the executive is his relative inability to place the ethical issues in clear-cut categories. There are many gray areas where
issues are indeterminant and borderline or applicable rules are difficult to find. It is hollow logic to assume that all executives instinc-
tively know what guidelines to follow. If the executive predicates
his ethical behavior on the law alone, then this supports the idea
that anything not in the law is permissible behavior. This, of course,
is questionable thinking. "While our system of laws provides a substantial basis for ethical conduct, ethics is much more comprehensive. Law deals with man as he is, setting a minimum standard
of conduct. Ethics seeks to lead man to what he ought to be and
do; it establishes a maximum standard."[8] Business ethics concerns
itself with the *is* of business behavior versus the *ought to be.* The
ought to be needs to be defined more clearly. What the executive
needs is an "informed conscience." Or as an editor of *Fortune*
observed:

Consciences come free; *informed* consciences require the output of some
mental and moral energy. A company president who is worried about
the present ethical challenge to the U.S.—and there are many such—can
start by clarifying some of the fuzzy orders of his own corporation.[9]

Many organizations are doing just that—indicating required behavior in the firm. Increasingly, business is spelling out in policy
terms both its definition and interpretation of business conduct. The
Celanese Corporation, as an example, in an especially prepared and
published policy booklet on business conduct offers guidelines of
compliance with both Celanese policy and the federal laws and
regulations as they relate to conflict of interest, antitrust compliance,
the use of inside information, and trading in securities.

In addition to self-initiated statements by the firm on required
ethical behavior, there are strong influences by other external
groups and organizations which interact with the firm. These organizations may be classified as professional associations, public advisory groups, and business associations.[10]

---

[8] Stephen C. O'Connell, "Ethics in Business," *The Appraisal Journal* (Chicago:
The American Institute of Real Estate Appraisers, July, 1966), p. 359.

[9] Editorial, "Business Ethics—Too Much Gray Area," *Fortune* (New York: Time
Incorporated, September 1966).

[10] Adapted from Keith Davis and Robert L. Blomstrom, *Business Society and
Environment* (New York: McGraw-Hill Book Co., 1971), pp. 143–45.

1. *Professional Associations.* This group offers codes of conduct which support, among other things, fairness, full disclosure, and decisions free of influence. These codes govern the conduct of their members in business.

    Standards for buying and selling which are sponsored by the National Association of Purchasing Management, for example, are influential in the development of companywide policies on gift giving and acceptance.

2. *Advisory Groups.* Codes of behavior are also offered by foundations, religious action groups, and minority groups. As Davis points out, however, "there is this difference with professional groups. The professional groups are self-generating a code for their own self-control both in business and out of it. Advisory groups, on the other hand, offer to raise the standards of *others.*"[11]

3. *Business Associations.* In this category are the many business associations representing specific groups such as florists, retail druggists, and grocers. The National Retail Druggists Association, the National Merchants Association, and the National Grocers Association are some examples. While these groups primarily serve their own interests, they also set ethical standards for dealing with consumers and others. In this way they control unscrupulous members, maintain a public image, and expel offenders who consequently are denied the values of membership.

General Public and Business Ethics

What is the public's estimation of the ethical values of the businessman, particularly when he is compared to other occupational groups?

In a recent study[12] of public perceptions of business, it was determined that industries, business firms, and occupations do reveal substantial differences when appraised by the public. It was observed that certain professionals such as medical doctors and clergymen are viewed as highly ethical, whereas other professionals such as advertising men and political figures are held in low esteem by opini-

---

[11] Ibid., p. 344.

[12] John Hess, "Public Policy as a Function of Perception of Business Ethics," *Economic and Business Bulletin,* School of Business Administration, Temple University, Vol. 20, No. 3 (Spring, 1966), pp. 29–36.

ion leaders.[13] Figure 19–2 presents a composite profile of the opinion leaders' perception of the ethical level of various occupations.

FIGURE 19–2
Opinion Leaders' Views of Occupational Relationships (composite profile)

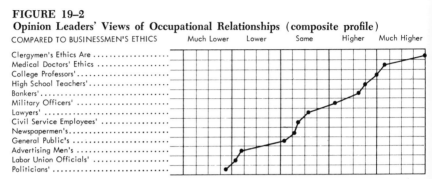

Source: John Hess, "Public Policy as a Function of Business Ethics," *Economic and Business Bulletin*, School of Business Administration, Temple University, Vol. 20, No. 3 (Spring, 1966), p. 31. Used with permission.

Figure 19–3 reflects perceptual discriminations among business occupations in response to the question, "In your opinion what is the general ethical level of businessmen in each of the following professions or jobs?" The self-explanatory profile is a composite picture.

FIGURE 19–3
Opinion Leaders' Views of the General Ethical Level of Businessmen in Various Positions or Professions (composite profile)

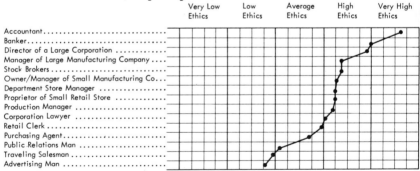

Source: John Hess, "Public Policy as a Function of Business Ethics," *Economic and Business Bulletin*, School of Business Administration, Temple University, Vol. 20, No. 3 (Spring 1966), p. 32. Used with permission.

[13] Opinion leaders are defined as individuals who by virtue of their position or profession are able to influence significantly the opinion of more than a close group of people. The group surveyed for this study are: newspaper editors, Protestant clergymen, bank presidents, history professors, and business professors. Business school seniors representing a sixth group were included to facilitate a comparison between the views of potential opinion leaders with those of more established leadership groups.

Important implications in this study indicate that "while the groups studied do not think too highly of the ethics of his class, they do not desire to substitute governmental control of business for the free market system, except in extreme circumstances."[14] Also, "it appears that the behavior of business is viewed more sympathetically as the problems of business are better understood."[15] A lesson to business from this study is the need for improved communications with opinion leaders and also the need for improvement in helping the public understand how the American business system operates.

Plan for Business Ethics

So far, the subject of ethics has been taken from the vantage point of theory. Now it is desirable to consider an approach to the development of a relevant and realistic code of business ethics as a basis for decision making.

1. *Test for Personal Ethics.* This is now done by discussing tests for personal ethics, development of professionalism, and a corporate program for ethical behavior. Developing a test of ethical practices for today's executive goes well beyond both the law and the application of the golden rule. A practical suggestion for the manager in the ethical aspects of decision making would be the self-administration of an ethics test designed to cover the widest range of possible executive behavior:

1. Does the contemplated activity violate the tenets of either of the Judeo-Christian beliefs (the Ten Commandments or the Torah)?
2. Would my wife and family (including parents) approve of my proposed decision or behavior in this case?
3. In the event your action will *not* be audited by your manager or company would it be the same as if it were?
4. How would the contemplated action appear to the public if all the facts, interests, motives, and profits were divulged?[16]
5. If uneasy about a proposed act, you find yourself arguing that it is a familiar practice in which almost everyone indulges, then test your position by assuming that yours is the sole instance

---

[14] Hess, *Economic and Business Bulletin*, p. 36.

[15] Ibid., p. 36.

[16] Edmund Cahn as quoted in Walton, *Ethos and the Executive*, p. 91.

and you *alone* have committed it. What do you think of it in this light?[17]

6. If you have never been in . . . office, how would the contemplated act appear to you as an ordinary member of the community whose authority made it possible?[18]

7. How would you characterize the act if it had been done by your most detested . . . [business] adversary?[19]

2. *Development of Professionalism.* Definitely, at this stage of our discussion, it can be concluded that ethics, as acceptable behavior permitted by the law, is not enough for the businessman. Nor is a code of ethics built upon the golden rule enough to form a basis for ethical decisions. Nor is business behavior predicated exclusively on religious principles enough. All these assist, of course, in establishing a code of behavior, but what is also needed is a constructive support that functions as another standard along with the law and religion in postulating a basis of conduct for the businessman.

What is suggested, then, is an increasing dedication to the concept that management is an emerging, true profession. There is nothing new about the concern for professional management and with it a definite code of ethical behavior. However, what is different, is the increased focus and attention it is receiving today in both business and academic circles.

What are distinct operational ground rules of professional ethical behavior for the manager? These are offered for the manager's consideration:

1. The professional business manager affirms that he will place the interest of the business for which he works before his own private interests.

2. The professional business manager affirms that he will place his duty to society above his duty to his company and above his private interests.

3. The professional business manager affirms that he has a duty to reveal the facts in any situation where a) his private interests are involved with those of his company, or b) where the interests of his company are involved with those of the society in which it operates.

4. The professional business manager affirms that when business man-

---

[17] Ibid., p. 91.

[18] Ibid., p. 91.

[19] Ibid., p. 91.

agers follow this code of conduct, the profit motive is the best incentive for the development of a sound, expanding and dynamic economy.[20]

3. *A Corporate Program for Ethical Behavior.* Finally, what can the executive himself do that is both supportive of his individual professionalism and conducive to maintaining an atmosphere of ethical corporate behavior?

First of all, the executive can manifest a personal example of ethical behavior for others to emulate. By exhibiting a positive code of ethics he establishes a climate within his department that encourages and supports the positive ethical business practices of his subordinates.

Also, the effective manager will support a corporate policy of *expected* ethical behavior in his business relationships—a policy that is clearly delineated, communicated, and enforced by management through regular audits of management performance.

Moreover, in pursuit of more substantive action for the advancement of corporate ethics, the manager will encourage and support the codes of conduct espoused by professional groups for industry in general and specifically for functional groups of which he is a member such as marketing, personnel, finance, and so on.

There is one final action the manager can undertake, and it's most vital. He can support, rather than circumvent, legislation that is already enacted. Recognizing the fact that unrestrained business behavior leads only to more regulation by government through its many enforcing agencies, he will exercise vigilance in interpreting and applying the law to himself and his organization.

QUESTIONS

1. Discuss the reasons for the increased concern for ethics in business.
2. Describe how an individual develops his code of ethics for use in relationships with people and groups.
3. In what way does one's value system influence behavior?
4. To what degree have associations and social groups modified questionable business practices? Cite examples.
5. How is the concept of managerial professionalism related to a positive code of business behavior?

---

[20] Robert Austin, "Code of Conduct for Executives," *Harvard Business Review,* Vol. 39 (September–October 1961), pp. 53–61. As quoted in Walton, *Ethos and the Executive,* p. 90.

CASE 19-1

Louis Smith was a highly skilled pension actuary for a West Coast life insurance company with its home office in Los Angeles. Now in his early forties, he had worked hard and long in achieving professional competence. His contribution was significant to the success of the department. Moreover, besides being extremely qualified, Louis exhibited exemplary personal conduct. He neither smoked nor drank; he was a model husband and a paragon of ethical behavior in his relationships with clients, the firm, and its personnel. He reported directly to the director of pension sales who in turn answered to the vice president of marketing.

When the director of pension sales recently retired, the vice president decided that his replacement should be hired from an outside source; since, in his opinion, neither the department nor the present staff contained an adequate successor.

After several interviews of candidates recommended by an employment agency, the vice president hired Jack Jones, a pension specialist whom he met at a recent insurance seminar. Jack offhandedly indicated that while he never actually managed a full-blown pension sales department, his years of experience and professional acumen more than qualified him for the post. Furthermore, he had voiced in glowing terms his past successes and accomplishments. He seemed ecstatic about the future of the pension market and the role he would occupy in helping the firm achieve success. The vice president had been most impressed.

During the first two years in his new post, Jack failed to produce any measurable increase in pension sales for the firm. The results were contradictory to Jack's promised "innovative marketing techniques." More disturbing though to Louis Smith was Jack's penchant for extended luncheons prefaced by at least two vodka martinis. Louis was unsuccessful in evading Jack on his invitations to join him for lunch. "You should have a drink or two," he used to say to Louis, "makes the afternoons more tolerable." Louis, however, was resolute in his determination to avoid drink, even upon the insistence of Jack, who was his boss.

The overall situation subsequently seemed to deteriorate. Sales were off, and the pension sales force suffered considerable turnover in the field. Coincidentally, Jack's luncheons became longer and Louis was more distraught than ever at having to accompany Jack. The climax occurred late one Friday afternoon when both Louis and Jack, arm-in-arm, stumbled out of the Wrangler Cafe directly opposite the main office. Louis had finally succumbed to Jack's invitation to drink.

Coincidentally, the director of underwriting observed all this as he glanced out his window while dictating correspondence. Generously he placed both in a cab and gave money and directions to the cab driver to take them home. The following Monday, Louis submitted his resignation and began looking for a new actuarial position. By the end of the week he had found an excellent position with a major competitor in San Francisco.

1. Discuss the basic problems that arose out of employing Jack Jones as pension sales manager.
2. What approach would you have recommended for filling the vacancy created by retirement of the director of pension sales?
3. Do you think Jack Jones was guilty of unethical behavior? In what respect?
4. Why do you suppose Louis Smith resigned?

CASE 19–2

John Green, branch manager for the Northern National Bank, learned that the bank personnel department was interviewing and hiring college candidates for a management trainee program. He remembered that Floyd Brown, son of one of his largest commercial borrowers, had just graduated from the college of business of the state university and wanted employment in his hometown.

The branch manager discussed the situation with Mr. Ramsey, the personnel officer, and then phoned Mr. Brown to suggest that his son, Floyd, contact Mr. Ramsey for an interview. Immediately after the interview with Mr. Ramsey, Floyd Brown was hired as a management trainee and placed under the supervision of John Green for a six-month training program in commercial bank operations at the branch location.

John Green was impressed by Floyd's performance. Floyd seemed enthusiastic and readily assumed responsibility. Mr. Green eagerly communicated this information to Floyd's father and assured him of the bank's satisfaction with his son's progress. It is uncertain whether or not the association of bank and son influenced the decision of Mr. Brown, but at any rate, several days later Mr. Brown transferred from a competitor bank his personal checking account, savings account, and also a sizable company payroll account. All these were in addition to his existing loan business with the bank.

About four months after Floyd was hired, his performance lagged, his enthusiasm waned, and long periods of unexplained absence from his work became routine. Mr. Green notified the personnel director of the problem, and both hoped the situation would improve.

Both Mr. Green and the personnel director, Mr. Ramsey, talked to Floyd, who now felt that he needed increased responsibility along with added salary for more job satisfaction.

Several weeks later Mr. Green phoned Mr. Ramsey and requested that Floyd be terminated since he had missed the last four days without giving any excuse. Mr. Green suggested that the personnel director phone Floyd's father and apprise him of the situation.

1. Discuss whether or not there is a question of unethical behavior on the part of Mr. Green.
2. Do you feel that the Northern National Bank exercised sound recruitment and selection principles in hiring Floyd Brown?

CASE 19-3

"Furthermore," said Joseph Smith, presently a stockbroker for the Eureka Company, "in the event I am hired by Gold Star Brokerage I will bring along, I promise, a copy of each client's file now in our office. I guarantee you, I will be able to transfer about 80 percent of their business to your company because of my persuasive influence with the clients."

Mr. Earl Black, director of Gold Star Brokerage, mulled over Mr. Smith's statement.

1. Is there a question of ethics in Mr. Smith's promise, irrespective of his ability to deliver the goods?
2. As director of Gold Star, how would you evaluate Smith's promise?

20

Communications

THE MANAGERIAL functions of planning, organizing, directing, and controlling the activities and work of others are not self-communicating. They do not transmit themselves automatically between management and its many groups. Some kind of interconnecting system of networks and channels must be established to transmit information, ideas, and directions, and to exchange understandings of problems, viewpoints, and need areas. Figure 20–1 is a model of the basic flow of a communication system.

FIGURE 20–1
A Communication Model

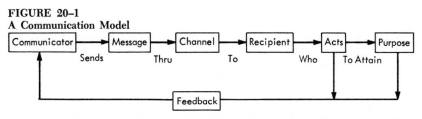

Reproduced (adapted) with permission from Michael J. Jucius, *Personnel Management* (7th ed.; Homewood, Ill.: Richard D. Irwin, Inc., 1971), p. 305.

Nature and Scope

In fact, no organized activity can take place without communications. But communication, itself, is a complex function involving the senses, experiences, feelings, attitudes, and interests and other factors which cause us to perceive the phenomena of actions, activities, and words in specific ways, as illustrated in Figure 20–2.

Consequently, it is a subject that deserves particular attention

FIGURE 20–2
Variables in the Communication Process

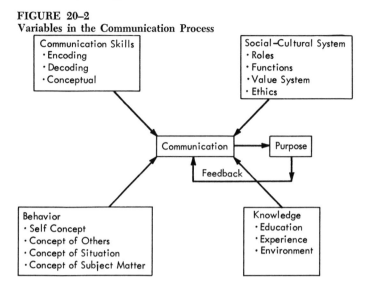

by the manager. It is taken up in this chapter under the following headings:

1. Lines of communication.
2. Purposes of communication.
3. Barriers to communication.
4. Principles of communication.

Lines of Communication

If a diagram of all lines of communication in use at a particular time would be drawn, it would show an incomprehensible maze. But, after careful study, definite patterns would emerge, revealing four distinct formal channels plus an informal one. These are:

1. Superior to subordinate.
2. Subordinate to superior.
3. Intramanagement—across organizational levels.
4. Extraorganizational—to outside groups.
5. Informal lines—underlying the formal organizational structure.

1. *Superior to Subordinate.* This line between superior and subordinate is so well known and accepted, at least formally, that it may seem to require little attention. Everyone expects the "boss" to communicate with his subordinates. He is supposed to issue orders and directives—to announce his expectations and wishes. Furthermore, it is hoped that he will explain his orders and wishes.

But, a general expectation is not enough. The line from an executive to his immediate subordinates should be clear and explicit. Each person should know from whom he is to receive commands and information. If more than one supervisor is to be allowed the right to communicate with a particular subordinate, this, too, should be made known to the subordinate. Though it might be argued that a subordinate should not have to report to more than one superior, particular exceptions to this rule are often made. However, it is desirable to clarify which executives have channels of communication to particular individuals and under what conditions and purposes.

Rightly or wrongly, executives other than those who have been granted a formal channel may informally contact subordinates. It was mentioned in an earlier chapter that such informal channels develop because of inadequacies in the formal structure or because sometimes it is the most flexible thing to do. In such instances, the formal structure needs to be corrected. At other times, political-minded or unaware executives may be communicating on their own lines of informal communication. Such situations should be prevented where possible. In any event, informal downward lines are invariably found in every organization. This subject of communications will be touched on again later in this chapter.

2. Subordinate to Superior. Channels upward between subordinate and superior are also an obvious part of any organization. One of the first things any person wants to know about his job is, who is my boss? Yet, while each subordinate may be informed that he is responsible to a particular individual, he may find it necessary to report to more than one superior.

In fact, for various reasons he may find it desirable to circumvent or supplement the contacts with his immediate superior. A salesman may direct some reports to the district sales manager as well as to his immediate supervisor. He may communicate certain messages—such as grievances—to the personnel manager; or he may have a "friend in court"—perhaps the marketing research manager—to whom it is desirable to communicate certain facts, opinions, and rumors relating to sales.

Whether all these lines should be allowed to exist is problematical. Some of the informal lines could be eliminated if the formal ones functioned properly. On the other hand, certain informal lines because of their effectiveness will flourish indefinitely. Again, whatever their merit, such lines do exist in the upward direction.

3. ***Intramanagement Across Organizational Levels.*** Numerous horizontal lines of communication may be established across the vertical organizational lines. Some of these are for organizational purposes, while others are for procedural purposes. In the former case, communications may be necessary between line departments or between line and staff departments. For example, jurisdictional problems or areas of cooperation or conflict may have to be resolved between manufacturing units or between some of these units and the personnel division. Or, it may be necessary to designate to what extent manufacturing and personnel divisions will participate jointly in such areas as collective bargaining, safety activities, and employee training and development.

Communication links must also be formally inserted between the steps of procedures. In a hiring procedure, for example, an office supervisor may initiate a hiring requisition; the personnel division is supposed to fill that requisition; and the payroll section is responsible for maintaining payroll records of the person hired. These steps must be integrated through some specific method of communication. Indeed, procedural communications undoubtedly constitute a very large, and sometimes involved, part of any organization's communications. If these communications are not provided for adequately by formal channels, then the informal lines of various design and of varying degrees of intensity and subtlety will be established by the employees and executives themselves.

4. ***Extraorganizational to Outside Groups.*** Lines of communication are also found running to various external groups. Among such groups are governmental offices, both local and national, customers and suppliers, advertising agencies, unions, community agencies, schools and universities, homes of employees, and the public in general. Some of these contacts may be highly formalized, as in the case of certain governmental or union relationships. Most, however, are made in an informal manner. Their purpose may be either informational, instructional, or persuasive in nature. It's only in recent years that business has improved its extraorganizational channels of communication.

5. ***Informal Lines Underlying the Formal Organizational Structure.*** One of the most interesting phenomenon of organizational communication is the informal channel of communication. The informal communication system underlies the formal system with its own personnel subsystems and networks just as the informal organization underlies the formal organization. The grapevine, both the written and oral, constitutes the medium of the informal organization and has a variety of purposes and features. It is a normal consequence or outgrowth of human relationships in the organization. It satisfies the needs to socialize, to converse, and to gossip. It helps develop group integration and a feeling of identity among the individual employees. It assists in orienting new personnel to work routines, and it supplements the flow of information from upper levels of management.

The features of the grapevine are these. It has a tremendous capacity to carry information, both helpful and harmful to the organization. Helpfully, it provides a manager with much needed feedback about employees and their work experience. Negatively, it can be used to spread inaccurate and unauthenticated rumors. Another feature of the grapevine is its rapidity of transmission. At times, it appears to function more quickly than the formal management system. It is a known fact, too, that in many instances, management will use the grapevine to transmit information which the formal system does not wish to carry and purposely leaves unsaid. One final feature of the grapevine is its ability to infiltrate the toughest organizational defenses for both reception and transmission of data. Implicit, here, of course, is the message that if management is to minimize the grapevine, then it must do an effective job of supplying accurate and immediate information to employees on matters of importance to them.

Purposes of Communication

Once the various channels of communications have been identified, it is appropriate to describe their purposes. Perhaps this can best be done by following the same pattern as in the foregoing; that is, downward, upward, crosswise, extraorganizational, and the informal.

1. *Downward Flows—Management Communications to Employees.* The major purposes of the downward channel are to provide instructions, information, and to increase understanding. More concretely, these purposes are sometimes translated into the following specific intentions of communication programs:

a) To gain understanding and support of company plans, objectives, and policies so employees will support all actions essential to success of the operation.

b) To inform about the organization, its history, progress, and its prospects for business and growth.

c) To convey information about the day-to-day activities and operations of the company and its personnel.

d) To explain reasoning and thinking behind management decisions and actions and particularly behind changes as they affect the employee.

e) To discuss personnel and labor relations objectives, policies, practices, and decisions.

f) To make its views known on economic, political, and community affairs.[1]

2.   *Upward Flows—Employee Communications to Management.* The primary purpose of upward flows is to report on the results of one's stewardship; to describe progress (or the lack of it) in reaching objectives; or to account for the use of assigned resources, human, financial, and material. This entails the technical aspects of a subordinate's position.

But, there are other—and sometimes more important purposes to be served by the upward flow from employees. Some of these purposes are:

a) To keep management informed of attitudes, trends, and reactions among employees as an aid to decision making and control.

b) To allow for the expression of personal opinions, grievances, or complaints.

c) To permit the employee to contribute his ideas and suggestions as they affect him and his work.

d) To allow for worker participation in the decision-making process in areas of mutual interest and concern.

e) To confirm worker acceptance of individual and group goals and obligations.

The upward flow is the reciprocal of management's downward flow in a communications system. Such a free-flowing two-way channel is absolutely necessary if understanding is to be achieved.

3.   *Crosswise Flows.* The purpose of cross organizational flows is to integrate the effort of otherwise separated units. If the work of the production department, for example, is to be coordinated with that of the marketing department, cross contacts are necessary.

---

[1] "Adapted from Employee Communication: Policy and Tools," *Studies in Personnel Policy*, No. 200 (New York: National Industrial Conference Board, Inc., 1966), pp. 15–19.

The plans of each must be synchronized in terms of such elements as quantities, qualities, production scheduling and distribution, cost and pricing factors, and promotion and advertising. Coordination is the purpose that must be served.

But, crosswise flows also have other purposes similar to those of vertical flows. Information, clarification, instructions, and persuasions may be transmitted and exchanged to either reduce misunderstanding about, or to support or reinforce positions taken, on various subjects. Indeed, a most significant function of crosswise channels is to reconcile differences and resolve conflict that may arise out of normal relationships between functional departments and line and staff units. Sometimes, and unfortunately, this kind of activity preempts the major work to be accomplished. But anyone who has observed the differences that build up among, for instance, production, engineering, and budgetary control realizes the necessity of such horizontal communications.

4. Extraorganizational Flows. Formerly, extraorganizational flows were limited since a company's contacts of a business nature were primarily with customer and supplier. With the exception of incorporation procedures and a few simple reports to governmental agencies, formal contacts with government were few. And, business contacts with unions were minimal because of the relative insignificance of unionism.

Increasingly, though, organizations have enlarged their extraorganizational flows of communication. The reasons for this lie in the growing regulation of business by government; the intensified competition of rival businesses; pressure from community, social, and ethnic groups; the accelerated trend of consumerism in the marketplace; and the growing impact of unionism.

More specifically, companies may interest themselves in extraorganizational flows for a variety of reasons:

a) To promote favorable legislation on such subjects as taxes, labor, and corporate practices.
b) To remove unfavorable consumer attitudes toward the company, industry, or the company's products.
c) To win understanding, approval, and support of the organization's position on vital economic, political, and social issues.
d) To establish and enhance a positive image of the industry, the company, and its products or services.
e) To explain and clarify its position in labor disputes.

Because of the increased extraorganizational flows and because of the importance of such communications, many companies have found it desirable to place responsibility for them in a specialized area such as the public relations department.

5. *Informal Flows.* As described previously, informal communications originate spontaneously outside the formal channels. Its medium of expression, the grapevine, evidences no predetermined pattern or direction of flow but is rather kaleidoscopic in both content and direction. It is a normal concomitant of group behavior. Management, therefore, should neither ignore the grapevine nor deny it exists, nor attempt to obliterate it. Rather, it should utilize the grapevine's personnel and networks for these purposes:

a) To serve as a barometer of employee feelings, attitudes, and sensitivities.

b) To allow employees the opportunity to verbally ventilate their feelings.

c) To keep the lines of communication open between the executive group and the employees.

d) To minimize rumor or to offset unauthentic information already being carried by the grapevine.

Barriers to Communications

From all that has been said thus far, it might seem that good communications are easy to achieve. Effective attention to lines, purposes, content, and media of communications seemingly should insure success. Were this totally true, then it would be difficult to see why communications in organizations fail so often.

But there are a number of obstacles, some difficult and complex, that impair the communication process. Among these are the following:

1. Organizational barriers.
2. Individual barriers.
3. Semantic barriers.

1. *Organizational Barriers.* This type of barrier arises from the fact that the structure and parts of an organization tend to obstruct communication flows. To begin with, the boss, himself, may be unwilling to communicate. He may feel that communications and meetings are needless. Important to remember is that the attitude of the boss strongly determines the kind of organizational climate in which communication takes place.

Communication flows are sometimes blocked by lack of policies. Policies, in many cases, are a reflection of management's intentions. Therefore, a lack of policy may be interpreted by employees as a lack of desire to communicate.

The immediate supervisor may act as a filter of vertical communications. He may purposely block communications with subordinates by avoiding interpersonal dialogue or by failure to listen. This can be disastrous since to the group he supervises, he, the supervisor, represents the organization. Furthermore, negative communication practices carry over and directly influence his personal effectiveness in such responsibilities as motivating, counseling and coaching, performance appraisal, and so on.

A major corporate barrier may be the organization structure itself. The structure has built-in principles that should facilitate communication. For example, the principle of unity of command states that a person should report to only one supervisor. Orders and instructions from several different supervisors obviate this principle. Another principle, the span of control, indicates there is a limit as to the number of subordinates a supervisor can manage effectively. Too many subordinates obviously will either prevent or seriously dilute communication dialogue between the two parties.

Another barrier, one that is structural in origin, is excessive layering of authority levels. This refers to the number of hierarchical organizational levels that can cause eventual filtering of communication both upward and downward. Since the chain of command is cluttered with many superiors, it's more difficult for communication to move freely. A natural consequence of such blockage is the subsequent reinforcement of the grapevine which then conveniently "bypasses" the obstructed formal channel.

2. Individual Barriers. Obstacles in this category are largely psychological in character and stem from the individual differences in people.[2] Some of these are:

a) *Human Perception.* A person's perception is a complex of beliefs, judgments, truths and principles, biases and prejudices that help him determine or assess his personal estimation of situations and circumstances. If management's communications

---

[2] Reproduced (adapted) with permission from William V. Haney, *Communication and Organizational Behavior, Text and Cases* (3d ed., Homewood, Ill.: Richard D. Irwin, Inc., 1973), pp. 55–56 and 334–36.

are consonant with the employees, then there is reception. Another way of saying this is that people will often tend to hear and be impressed with those statements which are in accord with what they already believe and will tend to give less consideration to those things with which they do not agree. Figure 20–3 represents the complexities involved in the communication process.

FIGURE 20–3
Complexities of a Communication System

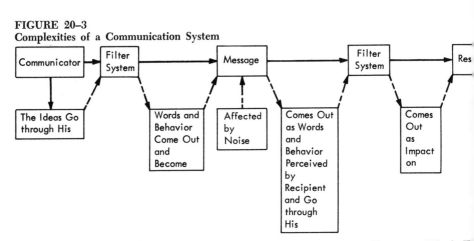

Source: Reproduced (adapted) with permission from Michael J. Jucius, *Personnel Management* (7th ed.; H wood, Ill.: Richard D. Irwin, Inc., 1971), p. 305.

b) *Insincerity and Lack of Confidence.* By insincerity is meant a manager's superficial concern about employee opinion when really he does not care. Or employee views may be solicited after the answer is already decided upon. Repeated insincerity becomes apparent and consequently forestalls further communication.

c) *Stereotyping.* This barrier may arise out of a person's preconceived ideas about what individual people and groups of people mean. It is a form of indiscrimination in which once an image or impression is determined, it is universally applied to any individual, irrespective of any differences or distinctions that person may have which differentiate him from the stereotyped group.

Thus, we hear what we expect to hear about or from a person of a particular group. This fault spills over into group versus group or class versus class stereotyping. Some workers feel, as a class opposed to management, they must refrain from accepting the views expressed by management. Such typing of classes occurs in the executive levels, too. Staff people may categorize line executives as production oriented, parochial, and mostly noncooperative individuals. Line returns the compliment by classifying staff people as impractical visionaries who constantly scheme to control that which is line's function. Upper levels of management may be suspicious of lower level supervisors, feeling the latter are not company-minded enough. Front-line supervision, on the other hand, may view management as a group, simply profit and cost-minded, with little regard for the daily problems of either work or human relations in the shop.

3. Semantic Barriers.   The purpose of language is to convey meaning. Words do not mean anything but are simply vessels or containers of meaning. Meaning is in the people using the words, not in the words themselves. Furthermore, the same words may have different "meanings" to different people or groups of people. Words have what is known as denotative and connotative meanings. The denotative meaning of words is the dictionary definition of the word. The connotative meaning, on the other hand, is the result of the emotional aura or atmosphere surrounding the word in its usage. "Collective bargaining" and "unions," for example, are words that infuriate some executives but make workers feel good. Conversely, the words "Taft-Hartley" engender ill will in the minds of many employees but are balm to the feelings of employers. Somewhat similar, but perhaps not so violent, reactions would be caused by such words as "security," "automation," "management prerogatives," and "right to work."

Principles of Communication

By this time, it should be apparent that communicating is a vital function in organizational activity. Some writers take the position that good management *is* communication. But if this vital function is to be carried on effectively, its practices must conform to sound rules and principles. Some suggestions along these lines are represented by the following:

1.   Management's actions should fit its words. In the final analysis, it is what the communicator does that really matters. Actions

that are opposite the communicated purposes or intentions result in subsequent distrust and disaffection by the receiver.

2. The purpose of each communication should be isolated. The target, person, or group should be identified and the communication adjusted to the intellectual and interest level of the target.

3. Two-way communications should be predicated on a basis of mutual trust between people. Reasonable openness should characterize the climate of communications in the firm.

4. Management should attempt to cultivate feedback on a voluntary and regular basis to insure a proper goodness of fit between the communicator and the recipient. Figure 20–4 is a model

FIGURE 20–4
Feedback in the Communication System

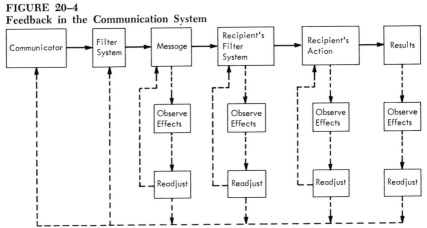

Source: Reproduced (adapted) with permission from Michael J. Jucius, *Personnel Management* (7th ed.; Homewood Ill.: Richard D. Irwin, Inc., 1971), p. 306.

of the feedback principle in the communication system. In fact, communication does not exist until the original communicator has received feedback from the recipient of the original message. *No* feedback is telling.

5. Management should listen to all groups—middle management, supervisors, employees, and the public as well. It should listen as a technique for feedback on reactions, attitudes, feelings, moods, and humor. This also means that management needs to listen to the results of employee morale surveys, consumer opinion surveys, community polls, and so on, in addition to the more immediate expressions of its subordinate management and employees.

6. Management should use understandable language. Communicate, not to impress, but to convey something of value. This does not mean a "speaking down" or "writing down," but it means utilizing language levels that are commensurate with the intellectual levels of the group. There are indeed enough potential barriers to effective communications without the added imposition of so-called "gobbledegook" or unintelligible language that prevents understanding. The sheer usage of such language by management may be considered by the employees, labor groups, and the public as self-evidence of an avowed intention to avoid communicating.

In summary, effective communication between management and its many groups, particularly employee, is possible if the organization really aspires to work at it. Research proves that employees evidence the desire for upward communications (one that would probably grow under proper encouragement and removal of frustration and obstacles).[3] In this, there is both economic and social payoff in terms of profitable ideas, better ways of doing things, and increased personal satisfaction in the environment of the enterprise.

QUESTIONS

1. Are there differences among channels of communication and lines of authority and responsibility? Explain.
2. What is meant by the statement that communication downwards "takes the elevator" while communication upwards generally "takes the stairs"?
3. What are the purposes of communication channels from subordinate to superior? Give several illustrations.
4. Discuss the possible corporate barriers to effective organization communications.
5. Discuss the possible individual barriers to communication.
6. Define what is meant by feedback. How can management be certain it is getting proper feedback from the groups to which it has communicated?
7. How does semantics affect communication? Give examples from your own experience.
8. First, identify and then discuss the basic principles of communication.

---

[3] See Alfred Vogel, "Why Don't Employees Speak Up," *Personnel Administration,* May–June 1967.

9. Why is increasing importance being ascribed to extraorganizational flows of communication?

CASE 20–1

In April 1971, when the Fair Credit Rating Act came into effect, the branch manager of Northern Savings and Loan called a general meeting (omitting the company lawyer) to tell (1) of a change in company policy to accept sums of $100 or more to a savings certificate without changing the maturity date, and (2) to generally explain the Fair Credit Rating law. He gave broad generalities and implications of the law and stated, "We cannot be too careful in dealing with this." When the teller in charge of giving out credit ratings from the company files asked, "What specific information should be given out?" she was told, "I'll talk with you later." A week after the law went into effect and the branch manager had not approached her on the subject, the teller asked the manager for a conference regarding the new credit law. It was granted that afternoon. During the conference the teller was given the exact same information that was given at the general meeting and no more. When the teller asked for specific information as to "what exactly should be given?" the manager said, "Well, you decide, but don't forget that our loan department sometimes needs information from these people you give ratings to." The teller went to her supervisor for clarification of this statement. "He's funny. Just do what you think is all right," she was told.

When the teller waited on the company lawyer several days later, she asked about the law and what should be given out. The lawyer explained the law, how it could affect the business, and what information could be safely given out. The manager, overhearing the conversation, interrupted and apologized to the lawyer for the teller asking "dumb questions," and then reprimanded the teller for "going over her supervisor's head in getting answers to questions he had already answered."

The savings and loan auditors came in several weeks later and during their examination, questioned the policy of accepting sums of less than $1,000 and lack of maturity date changes. Both the branch manager and the savings officer denied knowing of "anyone even mentioning such an absurd thing." The accounting department individuals were all reprimanded for this action.

After talking with the savings officer and the branch manager, the accounting supervisor called the home office which confirmed the trial policy put into effect as of the general meeting, and the following day, the accounting department received a written memo from the home office on the policy changes.

The supervisor was reprimanded by the branch manager for his actions that made him "look like the company fool."

1. What are the policy problems facing Northern Savings in this case?
2. Why do you suppose that the branch manager and the savings officer denied knowledge of a factual circumstance?
3. If you were president, what course(s) of action relevant to policy would you prescribe for this savings association and its management?

CASE 20–2

The Jones Manufacturing Company manufactured and distributed a full line of insulation materials for both industrial and residential use. It marketed its products through local sales representatives who worked out of district sales offices throughout the country. Each office consisted of an order processing division and a sales division.

Paul Miller was a sales correspondent with several years of experience. A college graduate, 25 years of age, and a marketing major, he was still a bachelor who lived at home with his parents. Knowledgeable, extremely qualified, handsome and personable, he was very popular in the office division because of his knowledge of both the firm's products and its pricing policies. At the time he was one of only two single men who worked with eight eligible young women in the sales order processing division. The two men along with the eight women reported to Otto Smith, office manager, who in turn reported to the district manager.

Through sheer coincidence, Paul's desk in the open-style office layout was flanked by the desks of women on all sides. Consequently, his desk was a kind of communications and social center. Frequently during the day, the girls, even though they reported to Otto Smith, would stop by Paul's desk, both genuinely and ostensibly, for information and help on processing company sales orders.

Paul Miller enjoyed his work and the social benefits that accrued from it. He worked diligently, and his section functioned most efficiently. Merit pay raises came to him regularly because of his valuable contribution.

However, Otto, the office manager, was having a problem of space allocation. The growing volume of business necessitated hiring two new salesmen. Since the sales division had no additional space, Otto was in a dilemma. One Saturday morning, he called in the maintenance supervisor and gave him orders to rearrange the office. They proceeded to expand the sales division to accommodate the desks of the two new salesmen. In so doing they were forced to physically move Paul's desk and files to a far corner, an alcove of the office where he was now actually flanked with a wall to front and right sides and a row of files to his rear. To his left was the desk of the only other (and confirmed) bachelor, age 55, in the office.

When Paul arrived for work on Monday morning he was absolutely dismayed to find a new salesman's desk in his original workplace. Still wearing his hat and coat he barreled into Otto's office and yelled, "What the devil's going on around here? Where's my desk?"

Otto Smith quickly tried to explain the space problem and hesitatingly proceeded to show Paul his new location in the alcove. By this time, the office was transfixed—all work stopped. Even the district manager emerged from his private office to see what was causing the commotion.

All eyes were on Paul and Otto. When Paul saw the location of his desk, he fumed in utter disbelief. "Look here, Otto," he growled, "I'm going downstairs to the coffee shop to cool off. I'll be back up in a half hour, and if my desk isn't where it was Friday night when I left here, then you know darn well what you can do with my job!" With that he walked away.

Otto Smith meekly phoned the maintenance supervisor and gave new orders to reposition Paul's desk in its original position. "I just can't afford to lose a good man," he explained to the district manager.

1. Identify and discuss the communication problem evidenced at the Jones Manufacturing Company. How could these problems have been prevented?

2. What other problems besides those of communication do you see here? What solutions would you propose?

21

Managerial Manpower Procurement

Scope of Discussion

HAVING EXAMINED the nature of management and the managers' relations to people, it is now appropriate to look at the manager himself. In this chapter and those that follow, attention is directed, therefore, to managerial procurement, development, appraisal, compensation, behavior, and trends.

Procuring the executive team—or staffing as it sometimes is termed—assumes an important role in the organization today. Business firms are aware that not only their present competitive success but also survival of the firm itself depends largely on effective executive procurement. So urgent is this need for insuring the growth and stability of the company that the executive staffing function is often assigned to a specialized staff unit located at a high level in the company.

Management manpower procurement in past years was mostly a function of selecting the most technically skilled in a unit as the replacement for a management vacancy or failing in that, to recruit from the current external employment market. For example, the best salesman became the new sales manager; the best machinist became the new shop supervisor.

But the concept of management manpower procurement has undergone an evolution over the years as new forces have made their impact upon the organization. These forces primarily relate to the effects of the managerial knowledge explosion, the application of new technologies, and with this a present shortage of specialized administrative and professional talent.

Moreover, as management has grown to be recognized as consisting of specialized skills, knowledges, and attitudes, the emphasis has shifted to more carefully prepared plans to insure the availability of management personnel when the need occurs. Increasingly, technical and managerial manpower needs are being consciously predetermined. In our highly competitive and complex age, waiting for vacancies to occur before seeking replacements—particularly for higher level employees—is a luxury few can afford.

In this discussion of managerial manpower procurement, consideration will be given to the following topics:

1. Nature of managerial manpower procurement.
2. Management manpower procurement defined.
3. Responsibility for managerial manpower procurement.
4. A rationale for managerial manpower planning.
5. Determining executive needs.
6. Management manpower planning process.
7. Determining quantitative needs.
8. Sources of executives.
9. Responsibility for selection.

Nature of Managerial Manpower Procurement

Managerial procurement must concern itself with providing adequate manpower to meet changing organizational needs. Thus, recruiting, selecting, planning, forecasting, and scheduling for management needs must be integrated into such future trends or with such short- and long-range goals as:

—Diversification of product line
—Degree of market dominance
—New product development
—Implementation of new technologies including the computer
—Desire for new markets
—Expansion of physical facilities

In addition to the above internally generated influences, management manpower procurement is also measurably affected by external economic, political, and social changes impinging on the firm. For example, changes, or even anticipated changes in such following fields would be of considerable significance:

—Competition both domestic and foreign
—Manufacturing and distribution technology

—Governmental posture regarding policies toward and regulation of business

—Social legislation

—Demographic composition of the labor force

Consequently, then the challenge to management is to isolate and identify the range and character of its future requirements in the light of these and other possible influences. Obviously what is needed and suggested is a consciously planned and integrated program built and managed by competent personnel around predetermined objectives, supporting policy, and procedures.

Management Manpower Procurement Defined

Managerial manpower staffing includes the overall procurement, compensation, development, and appraisal of the executive group. Management manpower procurement is a further subdivision of the staffing function and is concerned with the recruitment, selection, and placement of management talent.

Management manpower procurement may be further described as a complex of interrelated activities in which those responsible for this strategic function:

1. Recruit and select qualified management personnel for both present and future needs.
2. Develop plans for the overall future managerial requirements of the organization.
3. Forecast in quantitative terms the present and future needs of the executive group.
4. Assess the present capability of its executive resources in terms of future needs.

Responsibility for Managerial Manpower Procurement

Usually the personnel department of a firm is charged with the duties involved in procuring lower management personnel, but it is not always the agency which fills upper executive positions. The higher the level in the organization, the more executive staffing becomes the province of the directors, the president, and other top management. The stability, flexibility, vitality, and capacity for growth of a sound and continuing organization are dependent upon the presence of capable executives. Assessing the qualifications of top executives, for both the present and future, is oftentimes a main concern of the president and his top aides.

So it often happens that a special staff unit is created at the top level of the organization to manage the procurement, development, appraisal, and compensation of the executive group. Such a staff may initially perform analyses of the overall organization, specific jobs, and groupings of jobs. It may then carry out the duties of seeing that the executive posts are staffed with competent people. Such a staff unit is sometimes identified by the title of organizational planning and development or one similar to this. Moreover, some organizations, more recently and innovatively, have set up a new specialized staff unit of manpower planning that serves alongside the other operative functions of personnel such as training, compensation, employee benefits, and so on.

Generally, it is the larger growth-oriented firm that evidences interest in managerial manpower planning. While in the smaller firm, the manpower planning responsibility may be relegated to other more immediate and pressing concerns of the personnel department. The work of the specialized staff department, however, is to assist the line executive in obtaining and maintaining the optimum team. In the final analysis, though, it must be remembered that the line executive himself makes the final decision regarding the selection, development, appraisal, and promotion of the subordinate.

A Rationale for Managerial Manpower Planning

There are several compelling pressures which have caused an increased awareness for a deliberate and consistent approach to the strategic acquisition and use of management talent.[1]

1. There has been an absolute increase in the number of top management jobs. Many of these jobs are in such fields as new products administration, research and development, management information systems, and computer technology. A higher order of professional, technical, and social skills will be required in the future.

2. Population forecasts predict a critical shortage of managers in

---

[1] Adapted from H. Monroe Willys, "Strategy in the Management of Executives," *Business Horizons* (Bloomington, Ind.: University of Indiana, Spring 1963), Vol. 6, No. 1, pp. 35–44.

the age brackets of 30–44. This shortage will continue through the seventies.

3. There has been a steady increase in the sheer size of corporations. This itself requires additional numbers of management.
4. Increased size, new product emphasis, broader geographic coverage, including global, and the trend toward decentralization has multiplied the need for general managers to head up divisions and more divisional managers to head up functions.
5. The normal aging processes that lead to turnover for reasons of illness, death, early retirement, or poor performance.
6. The rapid obsolescence of knowledge and skills of executives will require not only intensified developmental programs but also planned shifts and transfers of management personnel in keeping with needs of the organization and its personnel.

Because of these pressures, careful plans of determining executive needs as noted in the following section are increasingly being adopted. (Figure 12–1, by the way, illustrates the relationship of manpower objectives, plans, and programs to organizational objectives.)

Determining Executive Needs

A logical and simple formula for selection of qualified executives may be stated as follows:

1. Perform the job analysis.
2. Prepare job descriptions.
3. Prepare man specifications.
4. Select qualified candidate.

How this formula can be applied is discussed in the following paragraphs. The determination of executive needs involves essentially finding answers to the questions of what kind of executives are or will be required, and how many will be needed.

A basic tool used in answering the first question is the job analysis. Having information on all aspects of the job is a prerequisite for selecting a person who will fill the job capably, or who can be trained to do so. An orderly and planned program of job analysis will make such information readily available whenever it is needed. Job analyses can also be helpful for such personnel activities as executive development, promotions, executive appraisal, compensa-

FIGURE · 21–1
Model of Relationship of Manpower Objectives, Plans, and
Programs to Organizational Objectives

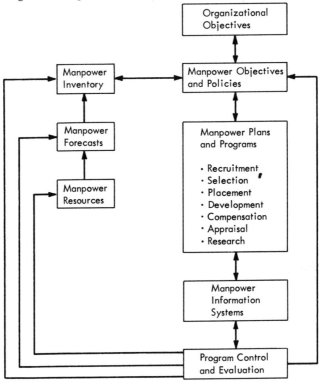

tion, and organizational analysis and planning. It is thus a good
idea to strive for comprehensiveness in making the analysis. The
greater the detail and completeness, the more its utility.

1. *Perform the Job Analysis.* A policy decision must also be
made as to whether the job analysis will be performed by company
personnel or by outside consultants. When the analysis is performed
within the organization, the executive in charge should be relatively
high in the organization. Often such responsibility is at the vice
presidential level. A planning committee may be appointed to give
overall guidance. The actual work of analysis may be done by the
personnel department or by a staff organization planning department. In .a large multiplant organization experienced assistance
often may be obtained from a specialized headquarters staff.

When outside consultants are utilized, they may be employed
for consultation and advice only, or they may assume responsibility

for carrying out all the steps in the procedure. When the company has available staff but lacks the experience, the first alternative may be followed; the second may be a solution to the problem when the firm is too small, or for other reasons decides not to do the work itself. Such other reasons may be to add prestige to the program or to gain acceptance by managerial personnel who may tend to show more confidence in an outside agency.

It is a cardinal principle that whether an outside consultant is used or the program is carried out by company personnel, in order to be effective it must have the wholehearted support of top management. Probably the best way in which such support can be exhibited is through a statement of intention by the chief executive that all positions eventually will be analyzed and accounted for by job descriptions.

2. Prepare Job Descriptions.   The preparation of job descriptions requires the analysis and write-up of the job under headings similar to the following:

a)	Job-identification data.	*c*)	Responsibility areas.
b)	Duties and functions performed.	*d*)	Authority relationships.
		e)	Performance criteria.

a)   *Job Identification Data.*   Necessary identifying information about the job will consist of the job title or titles, whether alternate titles exist; code name, if such is used; organizational unit and level of job; and, perhaps, current holder of job.

b)   *Duties and Functions Performed.*   The objectives of the job and the activities that are performed in their achievement are analyzed in some detail. Informational items that might be covered are:

(1)   Percentage of time spent on each activity.
(2)   Regularity with which activity occurs.
(3)   Rating of importance of each activity.
(4)   When and how it is performed.
(5)   Reports, and other communications or devices used.
(6)   Where performed.

Reasons why activities are performed, when not clearly evident in the description of duties, should also be included whenever possible.

c) *Responsibility Areas.* Areas of responsibility for which the manager is accountable to his superior should also be recognized in the job description. These constitute the framework within which duties are performed and might include the following:

(1) Subordinates—performance, behavior, and attitude.
(2) Resources—proper utilization.
(3) Materials—maintenance of adequate supply and condition.
(4) Public relations—matters to be covered.
(5) Communications—contacts to be made.

d) *Authority Relationships.* Statements of authority relationships may include:

(1) From whom authority is received for this position.
(2) To whom orders and instructions are given.
(3) The authority relationships that exist horizontally with equal managers and also with staff units.
(4) Lines of promotion that are most logical for the incumbent of the position.

e) *Performance Criteria.* Here might be listed factors which are basic guides to evaluating performance of duties and functions in the position. Such factors might be:

(1) Development of personnel.
(2) Soundness of organization.
(3) Cost per unit of product.
(4) Attitude and morale of subordinates.
(5) Reputation of company in the market or community.
(6) Contribution to profit.
(7) Operation within budget.

3. *Prepare Man Specifications.* Some firms prefer to let the job description be the sole means for stipulating what type of person should be selected for a job. Others have gone a step further and translated the requirements of the job into the personal characteristics which the incumbent should possess in order to do satisfactory work. This is, of course, a difficult task requiring not only thorough knowledge of the job but good judgment, so that the man specifications will be neither too lenient nor too demanding for a particular job. Where such man specifications for minimum satisfactory performance are available, they afford a more direct and effective means of evaluating the prospective manager or manager trainee. They may be classified into groups similar to the following:

a) Formal training requirements.
b) Experience requirements.
c) Physical qualities.
d) Mental qualities.
e) Emotional and personal characteristics.
f) Social characteristics.

a) *Formal Training Requirements.* Many managerial positions are sufficiently complex that a certain amount of formal training is necessary for minimum satisfactory performance. Thus, a job description may indicate that the type of work involved demands at least four years of college or the equivalent. When this is included in the man specification, a large number of those who would not qualify are immediately eliminated from consideration.

b) *Experience Requirements.* Some executive jobs require the maturity, knowledge, and skill that can only come with time actually spent doing work of similar nature. For example, the position of director of training and education may require that the aspirant to this job have not only a college degree but also two years' experience on the staff of a secondary school or college.

c) *Physical Qualities.* Not always are physical factors included in man specifications. The importance of physical ability should not be underestimated. Such factors as the state of a person's hearing or eyesight may be important to effective discharge of executive duties. A job requiring considerable travel and contact work in various locations may indicate a need for the executive to be in an excellent state of health and to maintain a high degree of physical stamina. In fact, it may be said that these qualities generally are needed for the kind of leadership performance which we expect from major executives.

d) *Mental Qualities.* Mental qualities that must be exercised on the job may be stated in terms of general intelligence level or learning ability, but it is much more helpful to define mental requirements in a specific way. Thus, it might be specified that a prospective manager should have ability to:

—Write effectively.
—Speak extemporaneously.
—Exercise sound judgment.

—Become familiar easily with scientific terminology.
—Visualize things in perspective.
—Analyze and evaluate.

Thus, a fairly satisfactory statement of mental characteristics can be formulated.

   e) Emotional and Personal Characteristics.   The emotional and personal characteristics that an executive needs are among those more difficult to define. Because individuals differ by degree in their emotional makeup, it becomes a question of defining the degree of emotional stability that one must possess. Describing the kind of situations demanding varying degrees of emotional stability may be attempted to give some basis for describing emotional makeup. Personal characteristics, too, are not always easy to spell out. Factors such as interest, appearance, mannerisms, ambition, initiative, and ability to speak before groups may be used to specify personal characteristics sought in an executive.

   Although it is difficult to describe emotional and personal characteristics precisely, those performing the selection function nevertheless tend to make some judgments regarding the degree in which a candidate possesses characteristics consistent with the nature of the job. Considerably more research needs to be done in determining job requirements and man specifications in this area. Many an executive has proven emotionally incapable of withstanding the tension of job responsibilities, even though he possessed good mental qualities and experience.

   f) Social Characteristics.   As a supervisor of others, the manager necessarily is involved in a variety of contacts with subordinates, superiors, and other individuals in the organization, and also with people outside the organization. The ability to meet people at various levels, to be able to socialize, to work as a member of a group, to participate in extraorganizational activities in the community—these all require social qualities which, while difficult to define in a quantitative and accurate fashion, still must be considered. An estimate must be made of the kinds and degrees of social demands that are found in the performance of a particular job, and an attempt must be made to determine whether a candidate could meet these. In this field behavioral scientists have been instrumental in pioneering methods of analysis and description.

   In earlier chapters it was pointed out that authority is effective not only because it is delegated from above but also because it is "earned" from subordinates. The kinds of personal relationships which the manager develops with his subordinates are an important factor in the authority and leadership accorded him by his employees. Therefore attention to the social characteristics which an executive possesses can be justified.

Management Manpower Planning Process

There are two times at which to determine the number of personnel needed: (*a*) after a vacancy occurs, or (*b*) before a vacancy occurs. Recognizing the need for a replacement after occurrence of a vacancy requires no advance planning, but neither does it assure organizational stability. It results in necessarily hasty judgments as to the fitness of replacements and often requires bringing in a replacement from outside the firm. This, in turn, may damage morale of those in the organization, particularly when personnel are present who have the managerial potential but no opportunity to be recognized. In short, recognizing managerial needs after a vacancy occurs and then taking action is shortsighted and costly. Even so, it is still a common approach to meeting personnel needs.

Consequently, much more desirable is a formalized planning process which may be simply defined as having the required quality and quantity of management personnel at the required location and time. The manpower planning process consists of the performance of certain related activities which include: (1) perpetual unit appraisals, (2) individual management appraisals, (3) formal recruitment activities, and (4) continuous developmental programming.

1. *Unit Appraisal.* The organization has an ongoing systematic program that regularly assesses the current organization, department by department, in terms of present executive talent and capability. The computer helps make this activity possible.[2]
2. *Individual Management Appraisal.* There is a formalized and instrumented appraisal program with regular appraisal of the manager's achievement of responsibilities and measurable accomplishments. (Chapter 23 discusses this subject in more detail.)
3. *Formal Recruitment.* There is a formal program of recruitment, selection, and placement not only for the college graduate but

---

[2] For an interesting and analytical study of the utilization of the computer in the executive procurement process see: Lawrence L. Ferguson, "Better Management of Manager's Careers," *Harvard Business Review,* March–April 1966, p. 140.

also various specialists and technicians for whom there is a need that cannot be filled from within. The computer itself, for example, has also resulted in the creation of new technical specializations arising out of computerized systems in the firm. The project director, systems analysts, programmers, and operations research people are newly created positions requiring sophisticated training in such areas as mathematics, statistical analysis, engineering, information retrieval, and so on. Increasingly it is being recognized that the need for qualified computer personnel extends beyond the present and available market and will require the organization to anticipate broad future needs by establishing current programs and policies in advance of these needs.[3]

4. *Continuous Development.* There is a perpetual ongoing and coordinated organizational development program that assists in the personal and professional growth of the individual manager. (Incidentally, Chapter 22 treats the topic of development.) As the organization moves forward toward more complex and sophisticated kinds of activities and problems, its management is simultaneously being developed to meet the challenges.

Determining Quantitative Needs

Determining needs before vacancies occur requires the commitment of personnel and resources toward advanced planning activities. But the payoff is in terms of the proper quantity and quality of managerial personnel. The most common device employed by industry is the management replacement inventory. This instrument was first employed by organizations during World War II to insure a satisfactory complement of personnel under conditions of rapid turnover caused by military personnel needs and the rapid movement of individuals from one firm to another.

Such tables or replacement inventories can be prepared using job descriptions and man specifications, appraisals of individuals, and a sound projection of future growth expectations of the company. For each position, information can be gathered that will show: (1) its relative importance; (2) age of occupant and period until retirement; (3) possible time before promotion or transfer;

---

[3] An adaptation of material taken from William J. Wasmuth, Rollin H. Simonds, Raymond L. Hilgert, and Hak Chong Lee, *Human Resources Administration* (Boston: Houghton Mifflin Co., 1970), p. 417.

(4) possible replacements and the degree to which such replacements need more training, education, or experience; or (5) whether any qualified replacement is available now or in the near future. Figures 21–2, 21–3, and 21–4 represent an organizational approach to the development of a systematic managerial manpower inventory.

FIGURE 21–2

MANAGERIAL BACK-UP SYSTEM

One variation of the manpower inventory technique employed by the Power Generation Division of the Babcock and Wilcox Company (a major international manufacturer of power generation equipment for utilities and industry) is entitled a "Managerial Back-Up System." Undertaken by the Manpower Planning Group of the Personnel Section it consists of four distinct procedures:

1. Key management positions within the major departments and profit centers are identified.
2. A corporate skills search is conducted for each selected managerial position using skill descriptions along with data from the appropriate manager. Searches are made to identify only those employees who currently have the required: a) technical skills; b) managerial experience; c) present performance; and d) promotability rating; to be considered as immediate "back-up."
3. Accumulated point values are awarded to each prospective back-up manager on the basis of available skill, education, and performance-promotability data. Points are awarded on a one-hundred point scale. The numerical grades [see Figure 21–3] narrow the field of selection to the better prospects.
4. *Managerial Back-Up Charts.* The three best-suited prospective managers are then entered on back-up charts with a maximum of three for each position, and are shown in rank order of preference. As a ready reference, pertinent data is also shown on the back-up chart (e.g., age, present department, total point value rating, education, salary grade, and seniority). The "back-up" charts are then given to the Head of the Department for approval.

Figures 21–2, 21–3, and 21–4 are reprinted here with the permission of The Babcock and Wilcox Company, Corporate Headquarters, New York.

Consequently, top management can be prepared to know what action to take if a position vacancy should occur suddenly, and what

FIGURE 21-3
Managerial Backup System: Awarding Points (100 points total [or maximum] possible)

1. *On Basis of Skills:*
   16 points—management experience[1]
   14 points—1st ranked skill[2]
   10 points—2nd
   8 points—3rd
   6 points—4th
   4 points—5th
   2 points—6th

   60 points maximum
2. *On Basis of Education:*
   10 points—having a degree
   10 points—having a degree with the correct major[3]

   20 points maximum
3. *On Basis of Performance:*[4]
   10 excellent
   6 very high
   0 good
   —6 satisfactory
   0 not evaluated

   10 points maximum
4. *On Basis of Promotability:*[5]
   6 promotable at present
   4 promotable in the future

   10 points maximum

[1] Refers to the field, number, and type of subordinates previously supervised; for example, engineering—4 years—7 employees.
[2] Candidates proficiency in required technical or administrative skills identified as necessary by the present job incumbent.
[3] Refers to the matching of candidate's specific major field with that field more critically identified in the position.
[4] Candidate is rated on present performance.
[5] Candidate receives maximum point value if he meets both tests.

plans are necessary to prepare someone to succeed to each position in the future. Both long-range and short-range planning can be effected with elimination of present and potential weak spots in the organization. When a determination of present and future needs has been made, steps can be taken to explore sources of executive talent.

FIGURE 21-4

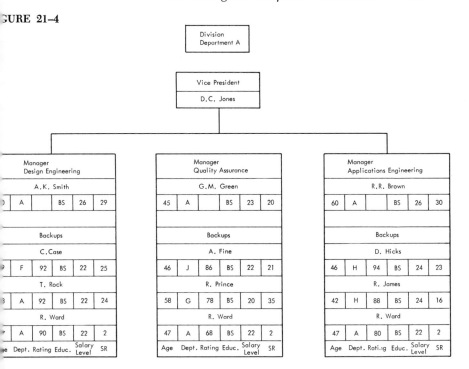

Sources of Executives

There are basically two sources of managerial personnel, internal and external. There are advantages to the use of each, and a well-balanced program for assuring a supply of managers will provide for both.

1. Internal Sources. When detailed records are kept of individuals presently in the organization, the potential of each can be considered for his eligibility to succeed to another position, either with or without additional development. Thus, a management inventory can be a very helpful device for organizing such information. It indicates possible sources of individuals for a position, how long it will probably be before they can be promoted, and how much additional experience or training they should have before they are ready for the change.

A position may also at times be filled by transfer. Interests of a manager may be such that he prefers another position, even though a promotion may not be involved. This sometimes occurs under a rotation system of executive development, when an individual may find a managerial position in another department more to his liking.

Certainly it is sound policy not to overlook internal sources. Some such individuals may not have had an opportunity to attain a high level of formal education, but they nevertheless may have qualities that fit them for responsible executive leadership. Also, they may have acquired diversified experience and would thus not need as much training as an outside prospect. To allow such talent to go unused is costly and inefficient. A second advantage is that a policy of filling positions from within has the effect of improving morale. The knowledge that qualifications are periodically surveyed to discover manager talent is a motivating influence toward self-development and willingness to advance the organizational objectives. A third advantage is that the firm's reputation, and attraction for applicants, will be enhanced when its policies toward present personnel become known.

Obviously, a company should rarely follow an exclusive policy of using internal sources. Not only would an insufficient number of candidates be available but inbreeding would result, with consequent loss of new ideas and experiences. Then, too, if outside sources were not used, persons in the organization might become too sure of job succession to exert sufficient effort. The firm could not be assured of getting the most suitable candidates. Thus, reliance on outside sources is a necessity in all but the rare instances.

2. *External Sources.* Companies will go to outside sources for several reasons. The chief one, of course, is that no qualified candidate is to be found in the organization. Another reason may be to avoid a disagreeable situation which may result when each of several aspirants feels he should be selected for a position vacancy. The choice of any one may leave the others extremely dissatisfied and uncooperative. A third reason may be that even though qualified men may be found within, an outstanding executive with a highly successful record may be available, and it is desired to take advantage of his talent.

The most common external sources for managerial candidates are colleges and universities, other firms, private and public employment agencies, advertisements, and individual applications.

Colleges and universities are the most common sources for junior management trainees. Recruiters have the assurance that prospects have advanced formal training. A relatively large pool of prospects is available. Furthermore, recruiting specialists may specify what backgrounds candidates should have in order to be considered. Finally, many college graduates already have acquired some experience in business through part-time work while attending school or through temporary summer employment.

Mobility of employment is relatively high in managerial ranks, and often firms attract good management timber from *other companies*. Excellent executives with proven capabilities are thus acquired without the lengthy developing period required to achieve high performance levels. During some periods of economic prosperity, or when particular kinds of executives are in short supply, the competition among firms for managerial talent may become so intense that it may result in "pirating" of executives.

Private employment agencies have for many years rendered services as brokers for executive jobs. A reflection of the growth in the executive job market is the fact that some agencies specialize in finding executives for top organizational-level jobs only. The distinctive characteristic of this type of activity is that very seldom does the candidate come to the agency. The caliber of executive sought in this kind of recruitment is usually already in high demand by firms. Private employment agencies dealing in managerial recruitment are frequently staffed with experts professionally trained in selection and placement techniques, who can assist in diagnosing a firm's management needs.

Public employment agencies in earlier years did not enjoy the same popularity with firms seeking managers as did private agencies. The improvements made in public agencies since the beginning of World War II, however, have increased their level of service and made them worthy of consideration. Professional staffs capable of doing effective and tactful employment procedures have been developed. Furthermore, there is no charge for the services of public employment agencies (although, indirectly, business helps support them through taxes, of course). Thus, management feels that it may as well avail itself of benefits that derive from the use of these agencies.

Individuals contacted by *advertising* are a frequent source of management talent. Advertising is often criticized because of the work involved in screening large numbers of respondents who obviously will not be suitable. This criticism can be minimized by wording the ad so as to clearly exclude such persons. Also, advertising in specialized publications will come to the attention of those in whom the firm is most interested. Examination of the Sunday editions of large metropolitan newspapers will give evidence that firms are not discouraged by the considerable screening required by using the usual newspaper advertisements.

Finally, there are always a considerable number of *individually initiated applications* that are worth considering. In a time when mobility of executives is taken for granted, it is not unusual for a manager to be on the alert for better opportunities elsewhere, even though he may hold a well-regarded position and be contented with present compensation, managerial duties, and other conditions. The general value of this source may change with the economic cycle, since the better executives may be less likely to search for other jobs during low business activity or when there will be fewer opportunities beckoning to them. There is always the possibility of making some excellent finds among applications initiated by individuals, however, and this source of management candidates should not be disregarded.

Responsibility for Selection

Both line superiors and staff units have a responsibility for effectively screening managerial candidates. The line superior must assume the ultimate responsibility for satisfactory performance of subordinate managers in his unit. Therefore, he should have the right and obligation to make the final choice. This implies that he must be fully knowledgeable concerning the jobs under him and their man specifications. He must also have adequate information about the individual under consideration. He should have a final interview with the applicant, which in turn suggests that he have some skill in conducting interviews.

Much of the selection procedure prior to the final decision is carried out by the personnel staff or its equivalent. It is responsible for making initial contacts and screening the obviously unsuitable. It prepares pertinent information on the remaining prospects for the benefit of the line officials. It gives assistance and advice in other matters at the request of the line. The staff thus acts in its proper role of technical expert. Staff personnel should be fully equipped by training, experience, and facilities to render a high level of service. Only in rare cases should the staff have the authority to make final selection of executive personnel.

Some firms use a committee or selection board to determine the fitness of an aspirant to a managerial post. In such a case the candidate may be interviewed by a group of executives, usually a combination of line and staff. A pooled judgment is in such cases considered more reliable than decisions made singly. Committee members may interview the candidate individually and convene to weigh his qualifications and decide, or the applicant may be asked to appear before the several executives acting as a board.

Finally, outside consultants are being utilized more for procuring specialized types of managerial personnel whose selection requires contacts and methods unavailable to the employer. In some cases, a consultant firm may also be retained to select most of the management complement from either internal or external sources. This aspect of selection as well as all processes of executive procurement must, of course, be in full compliance with the various civil rights regulations regarding equal employment opportunities.

QUESTIONS

1. Do environmental factors affect managerial manpower procurement? Give examples.
2. What, in your opinion, is justification for a formal approach to executive manpower planning?
3. Where should organizational responsibility for the executive staffing function be located?
4. Why should an executive job analysis be made in considerable detail when such jobs are broad-gauge in nature?
5. In your opinion, should desired emotional and personal characteristics be specified for a particular executive position? Why?
6. What are advantages of using internal sources for procuring executive personnel? Are there any significant disadvantages?
7. How can management determine the number of executives it will need to obtain over a certain time period?
8. Is induction for an executive necessary? Why? If so, what do you think it should consist of?
9. What is the role of the line executive in making the selection decision about a management prospect?

CASE 21–1

The Eastern Electric Company is a nationally known electrical equipment manufacturer. Over the years it has followed a policy of "promotion-from-within-only" for the more highly skilled operatives and management personnel. Only in exceptional circumstances are outsiders employed for these positions. Top management frequently voiced the attitude of the company toward promotion from within by saying that when a top executive retired the firm hired a new office boy. In fact, this policy became so much of a fetish that Eastern would discourage applicants, including college graduates, for management posts. "We don't want our people to think we are soliciting applications from outsiders."

1. What do you think of such an unequivocal policy of "promotion-from-within-only" for a company like Eastern?

2. How can management determine whether its present personnel are adequate to fill future management manpower needs?

CASE 21–2

J. Donaldson Peabody, president of the Midwest Hardware Supply Company, is the last of the old-time entrepreneurs. As founder and owner, he has seen his company mushroom from a one-floor warehousing operation with a handful of employees and a small line of agricultural tools, to an all-line hardware operation with a multistory central warehouse and an employee force of 500.

Marketing a full line of hardware, the field sales force is comprised of 30 salesmen and three district sales managers who report to the sales director. Just last week, they held a retirement party for one of the district sales managers during which J. D. Peabody was heard remarking to his sales director, "I've just finished interviewing a man recommended by his boss who is a personal friend of mine. I think the candidate will make a fine replacement. I have invited him and his wife to my house for dinner. Just as soon as I find out what *she's* like, I'll tell you whether we're going to hire *him* or not."

1. Evaluate the president's approach to selecting a managerial replacement.

2. What do you think about the president's intention to "interview the wife" as a managerial assessment technique?

22

Developing the Managerial Team

Scope of Discussion

IN TODAY'S progressive enterprise much emphasis is being placed on the training and development of management personnel. It is estimated that American industry spends approximately $3 billion on formal training programs alone each year. About $600 million are directed specifically to management development programs, while the total annual expenditure on training of all kinds is considered to be above $10 billion.[1] In one company, for example, up to 35,000 employees have enrolled as students, at an internal education and training expenditure of over $40 million. In fact, this company is half-jokingly referred to as an "educational institution with a manufacturing subsidiary."

Such emphasis applies not only to management in business firms but also, and increasingly, to such diverse organizations as hospitals, governmental agencies, social welfare units, and educational institutions. The ultimate purposes of development programs are dual: first, to insure the continuity of qualified leadership; and, second, to maximize the contribution of sound management to the success of the organization.

Implicit in formalized plans of management development is the contention that development cannot be left to chance or to random experiences. This means that careful consideration must be given to all dimensions of development. What must be considered is taken up in this chapter under the following headings:

---

[1] Adapted with permission from Rolf P. Lynton and Udai Pareek, *Training for Development* (Homewood, Ill.: Richard D. Irwin, Inc., 1967), p. 7.

411

1. Purposes of manager development.
2. Reasons for development of managers.
3. Some concepts of manager development.
4. Content of developmental programming.
5. On-the-job developmental methods.
6. Off-the-job developmental methods.
7. Training and developmental techniques.
8. Evaluation of developmental programs.

Purposes of Manager Development

What should be the purposes of a formal system of training and development? Succinctly, these are:

1. To raise the present level of managerial performance to its highest achievable level.
2. To develop the latent potential of individual managers for ultimate broader assumptions of responsibility.
3. To insure a reservoir of qualified manpower to satisfy the organization's present and future needs.
4. To satisfy the manager's personal need for professional growth and career progress.
5. To provide a favorable climate that encourages and sustains individual development and professional achievement.

Management development includes both training and education. "Training" as used here refers to the acquisition or increase of skills and knowledge required to perform the specific tasks in a management job. "Education," on the other hand, has a broader connotation. Its purpose is to enhance the decision-making aspects of management. It also refers to developing an individual, morally and mentally, so that he acquires a greater understanding of and adaptability to his total environment.

When a person's understanding of the factors that affect him is increased, a better adjustment to his role in the organization is expected to result. Similarly, understanding the relationship of his firm to the total business environment and even to the broad economic, political, and social environment should help develop in him the value judgments, attitudes, and the vision of a leader. Ultimately, the result of sound training and education should be the acquisition of effective knowledge, skills, and attitudes in the manager who aspires to the role of leadership.

Reasons for Development of Managers

Why could not those purposes of manager development mentioned above be served by normal in-service experiences? In many companies—smaller ones particularly—maybe they can. But even a brief review of economic, technological, social, and demographic changes that have occurred in our society is enough to record the need for better plans of executive development.

1. *Increasing Complexity.* Today's organization is much more complex and complicated to manage. The manager must not only be concerned with the management of production but also with other disciplines and concerns such as marketing, finance, taxation, human relations, government, and law. Complexity also requires more advanced knowledge and skills in new and emerging fields, examples of which are computerization, automation, logistics and international management.

2. *Technological Change.* The applications of new technologies will demand more sophisticated training and development. Technological advances while primarily replacing lower level workers will require more qualified managers thus compounding the managerial shortage.

3. *Executive Obsolescence.* Changing technologies and a changing environment outdate the knowledge and skills of management, particularly those in the scientific and professional fields. This requires constant updating not only to keep abreast of the current developments in one's areas of expertise but also to prepare for future ones as well.

4. *Occupational Shifts.* Over the years, there has been a persistent increase in the number of professional and technical people with a corresponding decline in the number of unskilled. From 1930 to 1966, there has been a proportionate increase of 117 percent in the professional class and 86 percent in service occupations.[2] Increased management development activities must be consistent with this shift and growth of occupations.

5. *Company Growth.* Among *Fortune's* 500 largest companies, for

---

[2] Orme W. Phelps, *Introduction to Labor Economics* (4th ed.; New York: McGraw-Hill Book Co., 1967), p. 38.

example, total employment increased by 31 percent between 1955 and 1965. Sheer growth in numbers requires more line management and more corporate staff management personnel as well. In fact, between 1955 and 1965 there was a 28 percent increase in the average number of corporate officers employed in the nation's 100 largest companies.[3]

6. *Increased Professionalism.* Management is recognized as a distinct and professional kind of work with professional status, an established body of knowledge, principles, functions, and techniques which can be learned and taught. Professionalism requires continued dedication toward individual improvement and progress.

7. *Broader Social Consciousness.* Within recent years, business had evidenced a deepening social responsibility for the development of its employees. There is an increasing reliance upon the organization to assist the employee. This social responsibility is not only the result of societal influences and external pressure such as laws but also arises out of the organization's recognition to assist people in dealing with the problems that are associated with an advancing technology and the many changes resulting therefrom.

Some Concepts of Manager Development

Earlier attempts at developmental programs in business were often a heterogeneous collection of phases, fads, gimmicks, and unrelated methods and techniques. Many so-called programs were sheer experiments. However, out of much confusion, there has gradually evolved, through combined experience and research activities of business and the university, some fundamental principles of development. Whereas 20 years ago only the larger, well-financed and staffed firm could afford a training and development specialist in their ranks, today even smaller organizations have these specialists. Indeed, training which was formerly a subfunction of minor consequence to the personnel director now is capstoned with its own professional association and an official publication.[4]

---

[3] Arch Patton, "The Coming Scramble for Executive Talent," *Harvard Business Review,* May–June 1967, p. 156.

[4] Known as The American Society for Training and Development (ASTD). Formed in 1945, it presently (1967 figures) has 70 regional chapters and 5,500 official members. Source: Robert L. Craig and Lester R. Bittel (eds.), *Training and Development Handbook,* (New York: McGraw-Hill Book Co., 1967).

The following concepts or guidelines are generally accepted as being relevant to manager development in the enterprise:[5]

1. All development is self-development. This accepted truism is pivotal to all other principles. It means that development is not something done to a man. The results of training and development should be change—change in knowledge, attitudes, and skills. This change cannot be imposed by some other person but, contrastly, must be self-induced, voluntarily accepted and assimilated by the individual. The motivation, the effort, the obligation, and the responsibility for development lies within the man himself.

2. Manager development must be for *all* managers in the organization. Its objective should be to challenge all to increased personal growth and progress. This means that programming opportunities should be geared to all levels, not necessarily a selected few "crown princes" arbitrarily predestined for top management positions. Otherwise, the effect would be to discourage those not selected.

3. Responsibility belongs to the line. It is impossible for the manager to delegate the development process. While he can delegate certain activities, this responsibility belongs to him. The General Electric Company feels this responsibility is an essential part of the boss's job. In fact, he is evaluated on the degree to which he facilitates subordinate development.

4. Development requires action. By this is meant that if a person is to develop, he must change. Yet, nothing changes by itself; change is produced by some influencing agent or stimulus. Development occurs because of some action or reaction on the part of the learner. New knowledges, new behavior patterns, and skills require involvement by the learner. Involvement is necessary to learning. Increasingly, company developmental programs provide actual practice in applying management knowledge and actual use of skills required on the job.

5. Emphasis is on the present job. Current thinking stresses a manager's development on his present assignment rather than on possible future ones. While promotion is an important motivator, undue emphasis diverts the manager's attention to excessive looking ahead. The developmental process should be interfaced

---

[5] Largely adapted from Walter S. Wikstrom, "Developing Managers: Underlying Principles," *Management Record*, November 1962, pp. 15–18.

with the present job and its improvement. Simultaneously, the manager is helped and encouraged to prepare for future and sometimes unknown responsibilities.

Content of Developmental Programming

Essentially, all management developmental activities should have as fundamental objectives an increase in the executives' knowledge, or an acquisition or improvement in managerial skills, or a fundamental change in attitude or belief. More directly, the actual agenda and instrumentation to achieve such objectives varies widely with the different and particular needs of organizations and individuals. For illustrative purposes, however, the following are typical areas and topics of concern in developmental programming:

—Ongoing growth and development in the manager's technical field. Improvement of functional expertise and skill in the fields of production, personnel, marketing, finance, etc.
—Improvement of skills and techniques both qualitative and quantitative for more effective decision making.
—Understanding and application of the computer sciences. Using the computer as another language.
—Better conceptual and pragmatic understanding of the process of management and its functions and elements. Development in planning, directing, and controlling.
—Development in the behavioral sciences. An understanding of the variables in individual and group behavior, of motivation and morale.
—Development of interpersonal skills. The ability to communicate more effectively, to interview, and to lead conferences. Learning the techniques of coaching and counseling. Figure 22–1 illustrates a conceptual approach to management development.

On-the-Job Developmental Methods

On-the-job methods are considered important because of their relationship to the principles of development mentioned earlier. While on the job it is easier to diagnose the person's individual strengths and weaknesses. Through recognizing and assuming responsibility for job performance and results as he must, the manager is motivated to continual self-development. Guided on-the-job training permits direct application of the person's new knowledge and

FIGURE 22–1
Model of Approach to Management Development

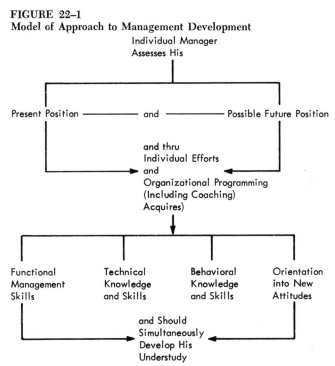

Individual Manager
Assesses His

Present Position ———————— and ———————— Possible Future Position

and thru
Individual Efforts
and
Organizational Programming
(Including Coaching)
Acquires)

| Functional Management Skills | Technical Knowledge and Skills | Behavioral Knowledge and Skills | Orientation into New Attitudes |

and Should
Simultaneously
Develop His
Understudy

Reprinted and adapted by permission of the publisher from *The Development of Executive Talent* edited by M. Joseph Dooher and Vivienne Marquis © 1952 by the American Management Association, Inc.

skills. There is concurrent responsibility for work performance and, also, direct and continuous feedback of results for evaluation purposes by the persons's superior. The superior then can coach, counsel, and advise the subordinate on actual performance in order to adjust it to performance standards.

The success of on-the-job methods is predicated however on two important organizational principles. First, responsibility and accountability must be clearly and distinctly identified, preferably through written position descriptions. Second, there must be a program for systematically evaluating the individual's performance and progress. Management appraisal, by the way, is the subject of Chapter 23.

Some of the more common on-the-job methods are as follows:

1. *Job Rotation.* Consists of transferring managers from job to job, department to department, or branch to branch in a deliberately planned program to broaden their knowledge and acquire diversified skills. Assignments may be either short or long range in

time—anywhere from several months to several years depending on the assignment. The benefits of job rotation, as a method, are that it permits managers to develop a generalized rather than a specialized base necessary for top executive positions. It permits cross pollination of personnel concepts and ideas. It assists in breaking down barriers that arise out of misunderstanding between line and staff or between functional departments.

On the other hand, job rotation does entail certain limitations. The value received from short-term rotational assignments is oftentimes questionable. Frequent relocation can also affect the manager's morale and that of his family. There is, also, less pressure to perform if the trainee is rotated on short-term assignments in an "observer" capacity. The trainee should be in a position long enough for him to assume and perform functional responsibility. Otherwise, his understanding of the assignment is a topical rather than an integrative experience.

2. *Planned Progression.* Whereas one of the objectives of job rotation is generalized knowledge of the organization, the objective of planned progression is to program the manager for the acquisition of specific knowledge and skills within a specific functional area. It is directed toward a developmental need area as revealed by an audit of the manager's capabilities. It consists of assignments which fill in or complete certain needed aspects of development.

3. *Management Trainee Programs.* In many organizations, there are special training programs for recent college graduates. This type of program has a variety of names, but its purpose is to give the college graduate a general orientation to the firm and its operations prior to his definite assignment. Many times, the specific assignment is unknown, until after the company has had the opportunity to assess the individual. Generally, placement is a function of mutual agreement between trainee and the firm. The program's length may vary from a few weeks to two years, and usually the trainees are directly controlled by a staff man from the staff personnel or management development department.

4. *Special Projects.* This is a widely acclaimed method utilized by firms to provide challenge to the manager. The promising manager may need broader experiences or exposure in a particular need area; or, conversely, the organization has a specialized problem to solve or undertake. It may be a production problem, or research on a new product, or a distribution method. While the nature of assignments may vary, generally it is a temporary or part-time re-

sponsibility in addition to the man's regular duties. While doing so, he is observed and guided by his boss.

If special projects are just additional work in the field of the manager's competency, then they are just added work. On the other hand, challenging assignments outside his scope can help "stretch" a manager. If he is required to develop new perspectives, learn new knowledge, use new skills or methods, become familiar with the unfamiliar, then true development will transpire.

5. *Understudy Assignments.* The understudy plan provides the conditions under which the manager learns the job of his superior so that he is able to either substitute for or replace him if the position is vacated. The superior is responsible for coaching and instructing the understudy who is sometimes designated as "assistant to" or "staff assistant."

Advantages to this method are these. It allows the "trainee" to familiarize himself with the job's requirements before assuming its responsibilities. Relatively little time is needed by the successor to make the transition, thus assuring continuity of effective management. The boss is free to disengage himself for extended periods of time without fear of significant loss of departmental effectiveness. And when the boss is ready for promotion, it need not be delayed because of a lack of replacement for his own position.

Some disadvantages of this method are these. Effectiveness of the method depends solely on the superior since the understudy's development is largely related to his experiences with the boss. Faults, as well as positive strengths, may be perpetuated. The understudy may become a replication of the boss. Furthermore, this method requires a conscious process of delegation by the superior. The superior may hesitate to delegate for several reasons: he lacks confidence in the understudy; sees the understudy as a threat to his security; or he may not know how to delegate.

6. *Group on-the-Job Developmental Methods.* A common practice of development is to assign special jobs or problems to a group of managers known as a task force. Its assignments span the organization, and its members come from different functions or locations within the firm. An assignment to a task force allows the manager the broadening experience of cooperating with managers of different backgrounds. This is conducive not only to a broader based understanding of the organization but also to better interdepartmental communications that result from the knowledge and awareness of the other managers and their units.

Multiple management is a practice similar to the task force. Sometimes known as junior executive boards, its members are generally drawn from middle management ranks. These boards are purely advisory. Their purpose is to investigate, analyze, and offer recommendations to the board of directors or to the top officer of the function they serve, such as production or marketing.

7. *Miscellaneous Methods.* Some varied, and sometimes overlooked, methods of on-the-job development are also recommended, such as:

1. Substitute assignments. Assigning a potential manager to fill the temporary vacancy created when the present manager is away for extended periods such as vacations.
2. Participation in company training programs. Allowing a manager to conduct training sessions in his field of competency can be extremely developmental to the growing executive.
3. Staff meetings. Permitting junior managers to attend or to sit in for the boss at relevant staff meetings can provide an added dimension of development.

Off-the-Job Developmental Methods

There are a wide variety of off-the-job methods employable by an organization. Off the job, by the way, does not necessarily mean "outside the company," since many activities of this type are conducted by company personnel either somewhere on the premises or away at some designated site, such as a hotel or conference center. Most commonly accepted, by definition, "off-the-job" development means those training activities that are not considered part of the manager's day-to-day work. Instead, more formal in character, these activities are additive or supplemental to the experiences gained on the job. An advantage, too, is this: the participant can devote full attention to the program in an atmosphere without the pressure of job responsibility.

1. *Company Training Programs.* In this category are an endless variety of activities administered by the unit responsible for corporate development and training. Sessions are generally held in company conference rooms or training centers. The faculty for this type of program is usually company personnel with occasional use of the outside consultant.

2. *Seminars, Conferences, Institutes.* These are generally of a specialized character, sponsored off the premises by professional

training associations or management groups. Their purpose is to augment development through participation in seminars conducted by professional learners in a field of expertise.

3. *University Courses and Programs.* Participation by universities in corporate executive development has been along two different lines. The first is illustrated by enrollment of managers in courses that are part of the regular curriculum offering. The second is represented by what is known as university development programs. These are generally designed for management at the middle and/or senior levels. There are approximately 45 major university development programs in existence.[6]

Most of the growth in university-sponsored programs has occurred since 1950. Such programs range in length from two to three weeks and may require on-campus residency by the participant. These programs should not be confused with the infinite number of shorter programs offered on the campus and often sponsored in conjunction with professional and trade associations.

An advantage claimed for university programs is that they encourage cross-fertilization of ideas among executives who represent different company experiences and viewpoints. Furthermore, executives feel more free to discuss their own weaknesses or to voice their opinions without fear of criticism or review by company colleagues or superiors. Then, too, executives can enjoy a learning environment free from the pressures of their daily tasks.

Training and Developmental Techniques

There are many useful techniques employable in developmental programs. The proper techniques depend upon the objective of the program or conference, its content, and for whom and by whom the program is conducted. In certain cases, a combination of techniques might be appropriate. The choice of technique is generally at the discretion of the company trainer or program leader. It must be remembered that the specific technique is really an instrument for helping effect change in the individual within a learning environment. Consequently, it must be chosen carefully for effects commensurate to its cost.

1. *Lecture Technique.* The lecture technique or the traditional classroom approach is by no means obsolete in management devel-

---

[6] "Executive Development Programs in Universities," *Studies in Personnel Policy*, No. 215 (New York: National Industrial Conference Board, Inc., 1969), p. 1.

opment programs. It consists of a verbal presentation with the learners engaging in a listening role. There is little interaction or feedback between the trainer and participant. While there are obvious limitations to this technique, it generally is applicable for large groups while conveying new information in a sequential, logical pattern of development. To enhance learner motivation, this technique should be employed in conjunction with other types of participative techniques, such as small group discussions, workshops, or panel discussions.

2. *Role Playing.* As the name implies, this is a technique of simulating situations, generally of a conflict nature between individuals and then having participants enact the part or role of the personalities. In management training programs, the emphasis is placed upon developing empathy into the attitudes and feelings of others and awareness of their reactions to one's own behavior. In addition, there is often an opportunity to practice the acquired human relations skills in specific problem situations. Sometimes, though, in sales training programs, for example, the emphasis is upon practice and delivery of sales presentations for eventual critique by the trainer.

3. *Conferences.* As a training technique, the conference is widely used in management development circles. It may be used in several ways—as a training vehicle in solving specific management problems, or it may be used to acquire knowledge and understanding of concepts.

As a problem solving technique, the conference enlists the participation of group members. A situation is offered for decisional consideration, and the conference leader actuates and coordinates the group discussion so that individuals contribute their thinking to the logical solution. Simultaneously, they learn the information and skills contributed by the leader and the others. When necessary information is not available from anyone in the group, individuals may still be made responsible for obtaining it. The entire group can be guided through the logical steps in problem solving.

As an informational or instructional conference, the conference combines the desired features of the lecture while allowing for ample discussion and feedback. Thus the conference technique has a number of advantages. It provides a learning atmosphere in which individual members benefit by sharing of experiences and ideas. Understanding is measurable through immediate feedback, and creative thinking is often stimulated through interpersonal exchange. It allows for suggestions and opinions and is conducive to improved motivation and morale. Because a sense of participation is present, group members tend to assume greater responsibility for the decision and generally cooperate more willingly in effecting the solution.

To be successful, the conference technique requires a qualified leader skilled in discussion leading techniques; and a planned agenda with clearly stated objectives that identify the conference as either problem solving, instructional, or informative in character. It requires a properly equipped conference room and able conferees. Generally, a group should be limited to 15 to 20 members. Members should be selected on the basis of some interest and knowledge they already possess. This permits not only some useful contribution to the solution of the problem but also provides knowledge, skill, and an attitudinal framework for benefiting from the discussion experience. One word of caution, though—the interchange so essential to efficient conferences should not be hampered by unreasonable differences in the rank, status, age, or experience levels among the participants.

Finally, this technique of development requires time for progress and cannot be precisely scheduled. On the other hand, if the program is not carefully planned, the conference can readily degenerate into an unproductive "bull session."

4. Case Study. The case is a written description of a realistic situation in the business enterprise. It can be general or specific in its nature and approach. With considerable descriptive detail, it is presented for analysis and discussion. Usually, advance preparation by participants is required for the discussion. Practice is obtained in analyzing factual data, applying basic principles, separating symptoms from causes of behavior, evaluating alternative causes of action, and then deciding upon a definite course of action. For managers with experience, cases furnish a manner of weighing personal judgment and analysis against that of other participants.

5. Business Games. A business game is a form of business simulation that actively involves the participants in decision-making roles. A descriptive model of a firm is constructed. Participants are usually divided into management teams and then given various kinds of information about company operations, including data on investments, production capacity, sales, inventory, pricing, advertising, and other pertinent data. Decisions are then made in these functional areas with management teams competing with each other to see which one can most effectively improve its market position or its profitability in relationship to the other teams. Participants have the opportunity to observe how a decision in one area, for example, sales, will affect the other areas of the company in a competitive market.

The model is often programmed on a computer; and, consequently, results of decisions are processed and made available almost immediately. Some business games are quite simple in design with a few variables as inputs for decisions; but, increasingly, a higher degree of sophistication involving many variables is being achieved so that the game more nearly approximates actual business situations.

6. T-Group Training. The T stands for training. It is also known as laboratory training and is sometimes equated with sensitivity training. However, there is a real distinction since sensitivity training is more related to group psychotherapy. The T-group technique focuses on the development of a laboratory environment in which participants have the opportunity to learn about themselves, about interpersonal relationships, about groups and group behavior, and about larger social problems.[7] Its origin dates back to the National Training Laboratory (NTL) of the National Education Association which held its first laboratory session at Bethel, Maine in 1947.[8] Presently, many kinds of institutions—business, education, services, as well as government—employ this technique, oftentimes using qualified consultants as group trainers.

The objectives of laboratory training are to assist the learner in achieving self-awareness and social effectiveness in interpersonal relationships. As managers develop new insight into individual effectiveness, they are expected to develop desirable changes in attitudes and behavior.

One suggested criticism of T-group training however is this: The target for change is essentially the individual and not the organization. When the participants return to their old structures, they step back in the same definition of their roles.

The returning participant may have changed, but his superiors, colleagues, and subordinates more than likely have not. Nor has the organization changed. Critics say this aggravates any existing frustration and tension.[9] Within recent years, though, there has been

[7] Leland P. Bradford, Jack R. Gibb, Kenneth D. Benne, *T-Group Theory and Laboratory Method: Innovation in Re-education* (New York: John Wiley & Sons, Inc., 1964), p. vii.

[8] Ibid., p. 8.

[9] Daniel Katz and Robert Kahn, *Social Psychology of Organizations* (New York: John Wiley & Sons, Inc., 1966), pp. 390–91.

an expansion of laboratory programs, and innovations have been introduced and evaluated. One of these is the closer linking of the T-group to the realities of specific organizations. This is accomplished in part by dealing specifically with problems of organizational change in the organizational setting involving members of that same organization who are ultimately responsible for implementing change.[10]

The results of T-group training, like all training, are difficult to measure. But, research seems to indicate that T-group training improves job performance for some people, but not all. The degree of benefit appears to be related to the extent people are willing to engage in "unfrozen" participation and their willingness to accept feedback.[11]

Tangible results from applied research, the newer forms of innovation, and a growing corps of qualified trainers along with an evident interest by corporations seem to make T-group training an increasingly popular and acceptable form of development.

Evaluation of Developmental Programs

Some control activities must be exercised in the interest of effective management development. The effectiveness should be measured or appraised. Yet, this is most difficult since the identifiable results of managerial development programs cannot always be readily traced to certain causal factors in the program. Other causal and nonrelated factors may influence favorable change on the manager. Moreover, the work of a manager is such that changes in performance may transpire only over a protracted time period. Nevertheless, some assessment of developmental efforts is desirable, not only because of corporate cost and time factors involved but also because of the critical essentiality of the commitment to development.

Although no single method achieves complete satisfaction, several evaluative methods may be used to conclusively measure the impact of developmental efforts. Among these are: (1) measurement of changes in operational results, (2) measurement of change in behavior, (3) assessment of participants, and (4) evaluation of the program by participants.

---

[10] Ibid., p. 558.

[11] George Strauss and Leonard R. Sayles, *Personnel: The Human Problems of Management* (Englewood Cliffs, N.J.: Prentice-Hall, Inc., 1967), p. 583.

1. *Changes in Results of Operations.* Since one chief objective of management development is improvement of current performance, changes in results of operations might be one index of effectiveness. Such information might be found in production or sales figures, budget and other financial data, profit figures, turnover figures, morale indices, and similar quantitative information.

2. *Changes in Personal Behavior.* Actually, there should be less concern with measuring the accumulation of knowledge and more with measuring the character and quality of attitude and action as they relate to improved job performance. Periodic appraisals will assist the superior in comparing personality and behavior traits, including attitudes, with ratings given the manager before training.

3. *Examination of Participants.* Sometimes an examination may be given to participants after certain phases of, or at the conclusion of, a program. In this way, some measurement is made of the degree to which program knowledge and understanding has been obtained. Such examinations, however, fall short in attempts to evaluate the effect of training on job performance. This method is perhaps more useful in motivating participants during the program rather than a post-program appraisal method. Furthermore, examinations of this type, with an academic flavor, are apt to incur the resentment of many executives.

4. *Evaluation by Participants.* The participants themselves are frequently asked to evaluate a program. While it is difficult to achieve the participant's objectivity in assessing the effects of training on his job performance, nonetheless, there is merit to this method. The participant's attitudes and his subjective opinion are important since these indicate the degree of influence exerted by the program. This method can offer constructive criticism with respect to program content, its applicability, method and quality of instruction, physical facilities, and similar topics.

5. *Need for Better Evaluation Methods.* Unquestionably, much can yet be done to improve evaluation methods. More precise methods need to be developed through research and continual experimentation. Often, measurement is difficult because of ill-defined objectives and standards for developmental activities. Unless specific objectives are established, then measurement techniques are useless. While it is recognized that certain programs do not lend themselves to evaluation, top management should nevertheless continue to support research using those techniques and instruments for the quantitative as well as qualitative measurement of programs. The purpose

of development should be perceptible change in the behavior of the participants. This is the most significant function of training; and if organizations are to spend their money wisely, then continuous evaluation attempts are necessary.

QUESTIONS

1. What accounts for the high degree of interest in executive development programs since World War II?
2. Why do training and development programs not always achieve desired effectiveness?
3. Evaluate the statement that manager development processes are for the larger firm only.
4. What are the significant values of role playing as a means of manager development?
5. Discuss the arguments for and against the use of sensitivity training as a developmental technique.
6. How can executive development programs be evaluated? Are there any shortcomings to present methods of evaluation?

CASE 22–1

In a certain service-oriented industry, all management training program activities are of the in-house type designed for use only by firms within this particular industry. Central to these programs is the educational facility of the national association. Its purpose is to develop, package, and promote the use of these programs for employees of members of the association. The programs themselves, however, are conducted by managers who evidence an interest in teaching. The student groups are a mix of management from within the member companies.

Typical courses offered cover a range of topics such as the principles of management, economics, finance, communications, and basic courses in the behavioral sciences. There are courses in the technical areas of the business also. There appears to be little interest or participation in university related programs. "We have our own college right here in the company," the president proudly admitted.

1. Discuss the advantages of in-house training programs as described above.
2. What limitations or weaknesses do you visualize in such programs?

CASE 22-2

"We have had managerial training programs and seminars now for the last 10 years here at Great Lakes Mutual Insurance Company," said President Neal Neffers, "but no one has ever yet proved to me that these activities truly produce desired results. Oh, I know all about how interesting and stimulating they are," he went on, "but what I'm talking about is definite proof of improvement in management performance."

Sales management development director, Bernard Hager, thought about this challenge as he developed his agenda for a sales management seminar for new district sales managers. The normal week-long program consisted of lectures and discussions by experienced staff people in such responsibilities as recruiting and selecting of new salesmen; training salesmen in not only essential product information but also training in prospecting for policyholders; and closing sales. The new managers also had sessions in managerial planning, directing, and controlling, and in motivation and leadership.

Bernard Hager intuitively felt these programs produced results. This was the first time he had to account concretely for results.

1. Assuming you had the latitude, what measures or techniques would you employ in determining the effectiveness of this sales management development program?

CASE 22-3

The vice president of production of a basic steel producer remarked to his training director, "Management development programs are not really instrumental as change agents in the development of managers. The only real development activity in the making of an executive is the day-to-day experience of actually managing people and making decisions about important matters. That's how I learned to become an executive, and that's what I think this company should do—focus on gaining experience as the main method in development."

1. What is your evaluation of this executive's remark?
2. If you were training director, how would you respond?

23

Appraisal of Manager Performance

Scope of Discussion

THE SUCCESS of a business organization is largely dependent upon the effectiveness of its management personnel. Hence, it is highly desirable, if indeed not imperative, to assess managerial performance. Such assessment is best done by appraising managerial contributions to the attainment of organizational goals. Moreover the contributions must be measured in both qualitative and quantitative terms.

As a process of measuring executive personnel, appraisal falls mainly in the area of the staffing function. But it also has pertinence to the functions of planning and controlling. It is through planning that the goals are established against which management performance is evaluated. And it is through controlling that managerial performance is evaluated and redirected if adjustments are deemed necessary. These aspects of appraisal are pertinent to all managerial echelons. Hence programs for their operational execution must be established throughout the organization. Appraisal programs call for careful design and execution. To gain insight into how this may be done, the subject of appraisal is discussed in this chapter under the following headings:

1. Purposes of manager appraisal.
2. Dimensions of measurement.
3. Methods of appraisal.
4. Procedure for appraisal.

Purposes of Manager Appraisal

Organizations employ a system of management appraisal for a variety of reasons. First of all, it is used to assess the current performance of each manager against established criteria. Plans and programs for improvement should evolve out of the discussions between the manager and his superior. Consequently, an increase in the performance level of the manager should result.

Appraisals can also identify strengths and deficiencies; they can assist in identifying individual as well as group developmental need areas. The need areas subsequently become targets for developmental action. Another value is that a formal and periodic appraisal program encourages superiors to regularly observe the behavior of their subordinates. In this respect, properly conducted appraisals implemented with effective counseling and coaching can enhance mutual understanding between the executive and his subordinates.

There is also the desirable benefit that accrues from an objective assessment of one's own worth and contribution. The performance appraisal itself can serve as an influential and persuasive agent on the individual's future performance. Additionally, many firms use the appraisal program as a basis for both salary adjustments and promotion purposes, And, furthermore, when appraisals are conducted on a regular basis over a period of time, they are useful in job transfers and possible terminations.

Dimensions of Measurement

What dimensions of a manager should be measured if the purposes of appraisal are to be attained? Included among those which have been used are: (1) managerial skills, (2) personal skills, (3) quantitative factors, (4) character trait factors, and (5) management by objectives. These dimensions of measurement must be considered with relevance to the organization and the job in which and for which they will be used and, therefore, should be selected by knowledgeable executives and technical staff. Moreover, selected factors should represent significant and key aspects of job performance and should be clearly defined so there is maximum agreement as to their meaning.

1. *Managerial Skills.* A logical approach to appraising performance is to identify the basic skills involved in satisfactory management and to develop statements which describe them. For example, the following managerial skills and qualifications might be used:

a)   Technical job knowledge.
b)   Ability to plan departmental operations.
c)   Ability to organize, including assignment of responsibility, delegation of authority, and arranging of communication channels.
d)   Ability to direct work of subordinates.
e)   Ability to motivate subordinates.
f)   Ability to control, including coordination and follow-up.

What constitutes the mastery of each of these skills can then be determined. For example, it may be agreed that effective performance in planning by the department manager is indicated by the following key conditions:

a)   A plan for the department is submitted in writing for the coming year.
b)   Goals are set for weekly and monthly production results.
c)   Projects assigned are defined accurately, and time requirements are spelled out clearly.
d)   Budget proposals are submitted on time.
e)   Manpower shortage never occurs except in extreme emergency.
f)   A plan for personnel training is drawn up and kept current.
g)   Policies and procedures for the department exist in writing and are reviewed regularly.

Similar statements could be developed for the other listed skills required for successful performance of management functions.

   2.   **Personal Skills.**   Personal skills were referred to in the preceding chapter. They are utilized in performing the managerial functions effectively; thus they are personal "tools" in managing. Top management may feel it worthwhile to appraise proficiency in personal skills. Such appraisal, however, must usually be done in terms of how these skills are used in performing the managerial functions. Personal skills possessed by an executive might be:

a)   Analytical skills.
b)   Teaching and coaching skills.
c)   Decision-making skills.
d)   Human relations skills.
e)   Communications skills.
f)   Conceptual skills.

   3.   **Quantitative Factors.**   Another approach to evaluation of actual performance has been to establish quantitative measuring sticks

for gauging managerial behavior. It is not always easy to justify the precision which a quantitative standard represents. When it is accepted as a fair standard, however, it permits an objective approach to measurement. (There is the question, though, of how readily standards are changed when job conditions change.) Such measurements, when used, are usually applied against technical-function areas, such as sales, maintenance, or personnel. Thus an executive in charge of a major department or division might be measured on the basis of performance in these and other responsibility areas.[1] To further illustrate, his performance in one area of responsibility might be measured as follows:

Managerial performance in personnel relations is satisfactory when, in his department:

a) Employee grievances submitted through formal channels number fewer than six per month.
b) Employee turnover is less than 6 percent.
c) Time paid for but not worked by employees is less than 18 per 1,000 man-hours (excluding vacations).
d) Transfers to other departments for other than production reasons are less than three per month.
e) Amount of quality defects due to improper methods or lack of attention is less than 3 percent.

Other criteria could be included in the above lists, and similar lists could be composed for fields such as sales, production, maintenance, and inspection. Most important though, in the use of such standards is that they be reasonable and accepted by all concerned. Obviously, their construction should involve the assistance of the executive who is being evaluated as well as that of his boss and others who are qualified to make a contribution.

Figures 23–1 and 23–2 are an appraisal instrument utilized by a major rubber company. Notice, particularly, this firm's emphasis on developing a program for manager improvement that includes specific action steps within a definite time frame.

4. *Character Trait Factors.* The use of character or personality traits as factors in evaluation was widely employed in the past, but more recently has been depreciated because of the difficulty of measuring the impact of traits upon the individual's performance.

---

[1] For a discussion of quantitative standards and their use, see: AMA Research Study No. 42, *Setting Standards for Executive Performance* (New York: American Management Association, 1960), pp. 19–22.

FIGURE 23–1

```
┌─────────────────────────────────────────────────────────────────────┐
```

G GENERAL TIRE   **PERFORMANCE REVIEW**   DATE COMPLETED:_____

EMPLOYEE'S NAME   JOB TITLE   LOCATION/STORE/TERRITORY

AGE   NO. YEARS WITH COMPANY   NO. YEARS AND MONTHS ON PRESENT JOB   NO. EMPLOYEES HE SUPERVISES   DISTRICT/PLANT/DEPARTMENT

OVERALL PERFORMANCE: CHECK BOX WHICH BEST DESCRIBES THE EMPLOYEE'S WORK DURING THE PAST YEAR OR SINCE THE LAST REVIEW.

☐ OUTSTANDING   ☐ GOOD–SATISFACTORY   ☐ MARGINAL   ☐ OTHER:_____

A. STRONG POINTS AND ACHIEVEMENTS (LIST SPECIFIC POSITIVE ACCOMPLISHMENTS OR SUCCESSFUL AREAS OF GROWTH AND INDICATE ACTION TO BE TAKEN TO CONTINUE GROWTH.)

B. AREAS NEEDING IMPROVEMENT AND ACTION TO BE TAKEN TO CAUSE IMPROVEMENT (LIST SPECIFIC ACTIONS OR ACTIVITIES THAT WILL LEAD TO IMPROVEMENT ON THE JOB AND/OR PREPARATION FOR PROMOTION OR TRANSFER, ETC., BETWEEN NOW AND THE NEXT REVIEW OR SOME OTHER AGREED UPON DATE.)

EMPLOYEE SIGNATURE_____   I HAVE SEEN THIS REVIEW AND HAVE BEEN COUNSELED ON MY PERFORMANCE.

DATE COUNSELED_____

IMMEDIATE SUPERVISOR_____
     NAME AND TITLE

TO THE RATER: Use Reverse Side For Company Private Statements on Employee Potential.

7082 Rev. 3–72

Highly central to this approach is a dependency upon the evaluator's subjective opinion of predetermined personal characteristics that were assumed to be associated with successful performance of the job. The focus here is on personality traits rather than on identifiable and measurable factors of achievement.

Consequently, such subjectively indefinable and immeasurable characteristics as "initiative," "aggressiveness," dependability,"

FIGURE 23–2

EVALUATION OF POTENTIAL - COMPANY PRIVATE

THIS PAGE REFLECTS THE OPINIONS OF YOU AND YOUR EXECUTIVES REGARDING THIS EMPLOYEE'S PROMOTABILITY AND GROWTH. IF IT IS DISCUSSED WITH THE EMPLOYEE (AND IT IS NOT NECESSARY THAT THIS BE DONE), DO NOT REVEAL YOUR RATING UNTIL YOU HAVE COMPLETED REVIEWS WITH YOUR EXECUTIVES ACCORDING TO DIVISION PRACTICE AND PROCEDURE. REMEMBER, PROMOTION DEPENDS UPON COMPANY NEED AND THE AVAILABILITY OF OPPORTUNITY. YOU SHOULD NOT MARK AN EMPLOYEE PROMOTABLE UNLESS YOU KNOW TO WHAT HE CAN BE PROMOTED.

IN MY OPINION THIS EMPLOYEE IS: CHECK AND COMPLETE THE MOST APPROPRIATE BOX.

☐ ABLE TO GROW IN PRESENT POSITION:
ACTION REQUIRED TO CONTINUE THIS GROWTH.

_____
_____
_____

☐ POTENTIALLY PROMOTABLE IN _____ (INDICATE WHEN) AS FOLLOWS:
INDICATE NECESSARY TRAINING/EXPERIENCE, GOALS SET TO MEET THESE REQUIREMENTS, ETC.

_____
_____
_____
_____

☐ PROMOTABLE AS SOON AS PRACTICAL:
LIST POSITION(S) AND SUGGESTED REPLACEMENT(S).

_____
_____
_____
_____

☐ OTHER, EXPLAIN:

_____
_____
_____

OTHER MANAGEMENT OPINIONS:

NAME AND TITLE _____
        ☐ AGREE   ☐ DISAGREE   COMMENT: _____
NAME AND TITLE _____
        ☐ AGREE   ☐ DISAGREE   COMMENT: _____
NAME AND TITLE _____
        ☐ AGREE   ☐ DISAGREE   COMMENT: _____

DO NOT WRITE BELOW THIS LINE

Printed here with the permission of the General Tire and Rubber Company, Akron, Ohio.

"loyalty," to name but a few, constitute some of the criteria for evaluation.

A major criticism of the trait method of rating, however, is that not only are the standards unclear but also that it is predicated on the assumption there is a psychological constellation of traits that make the best executive. On the other hand, it should be recognized that individual performance or behavior is the cumulative result of personality traits however difficult those traits are to measure.

Perhaps social scientists sometime in the future will be able to measure traits more definitively, but presently there are these distinct disadvantages:

The ambiguity of such descriptive terms leads to judgments which are biased by the rater's subjectivity and which, therefore, are usually unreliable and invalid.

The judgments generated by this approach are often difficult to communicate to the employee who is likely to believe that he possesses such traits to a high degree.

A rating of traits does not provide an employee with adequate guidance for improving his performance.[2]

5. Management by Objectives. A fifth approach that deserves special recognition is known as management by objectives. It is also referred to frequently as appraisal by results. A management by objectives (MBO) approach represents a departure from traditional methods of appraisal in that the emphasis shifts to the evaluation of results, of objective achievement—of what the manager *does* more so than what he *is*.

Explicit in this approach are two concepts that state (1) the clearer the idea the manager has about what he is trying to accomplish, the greater the chances of accomplishing it; and (2) progress can only be measured in terms of what one is trying to make progress toward.[3]

While management by objective programs may differ in methodology, essentially, there are these stages to the program:[4]

1. Superior and subordinate at all organizational levels jointly agree upon the specific and precise results that are to be accomplished by the subordinate. Time constraints are also established for completion of expected results.
2. Both superior and subordinate agree upon the criteria for measuring and evaluating performance.

---

[2] Stanley Sloan and Alton C. Johnson, "New Context of Personnel Appraisal," *Harvard Business Review,* November–December 1968, p. 14.

[3] For a survey of corporate practices in MBO see: "Managing by and with Objectives," *Studies in Personnel Policy* No. 212 (2d ed.; New York: National Industrial Conference Board, Inc., 1970), p. 2.

[4] See Figure 23–3, a diagram which represents the different sequential stages in implementing the MBO program.

FIGURE 23–3
The Process of Management by Objectives

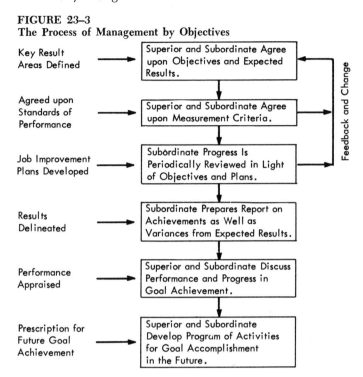

3. Periodically, the superior and subordinate review the degree of progress toward the predetermined and agreed-upon goals. Objectives and plans are revised or updated as required.

4. The superior functions as a coach and counselor in assisting the subordinate to achieve his objectives. Emphasis is on mutual planning and problem solving. The role of the superior is primarily supportive rather than coercive.

5. At the conclusion of the reporting period the subordinate prepares an achievement report which lists all major accomplishments and indicates variances between the expected and actual results.

6. In an interview setting, superior and subordinate discuss the variance in goal achievement and then develop subsequent objectives for the ensuing time period.

Advantages of Management by Objectives. The proponents of the MBO approach stress that goal setting and not criticism should be used to improve a manager's performance. Superior results are observed when the supervisor and subordinate together set specific goals to be achieved, rather than merely discussing needed improvement. Moreover, it is felt that frequent reviews revolving around presently occurring needs are more productive and less threatening to the subordinate than the usual annual appraisal discussion.

Second, personality does not exert a strong influence in evaluation since the emphasis is more on objective evaluation of what the man has substantively accomplished rather than on what is subjectively thought of him.

Third, this approach is conducive to an integrative relationship—a less unilateral and more a bilateral exchange—between superior and subordinate. It tends to increase commitment; commitment tends to heighten motivation; and motivation which is job oriented tends to make managers more productive.

Finally, management by objectives is increasingly accepted because it lends itself better to evaluating the efforts of professional managers whose work may be creative rather than functional.

Figure 23–4 represents a typical instrument used where a manage-

FIGURE 23–4

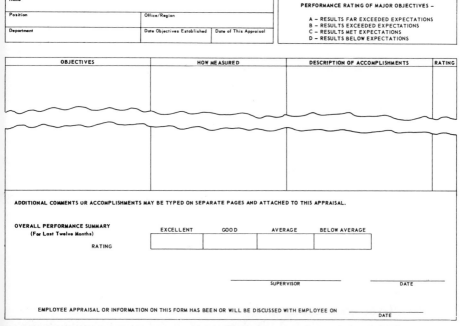

Reprinted here through the courtesy of the Nationwide Insurance Companies, Columbus, Ohio.

ment by objectives program is adopted by a major all-line insurance organization. In this firm it is employed only with middle and upper management levels. The superior (1) lists the preestablished objectives mutually agreed upon for the appraisal period; (2) indicates the basis on which performance is measured (this will involve both a scheduling for completion and quality of performance); (3) indicates the rating for each objective or accomplishment, using the scale shown on the form; (4) supplements the evaluation with any additional comments or accomplishments; and (5) summarizes the overall performance for the 12-month period.

Methods of Appraisal

In view of the authority relationship, the immediate superior executive should always be the chief appraiser; however, other individuals, such as the superior's supervisor or peers of the executive may also be involved. The organization furthermore, depending on its needs and preferences, may elect to use one or various methods by which the appraisal factors can be considered. Some of these methods are:

1. Ranking method.
2. Graphic rating methods.
3. Forced-choice method.
4. Group appraisal method.
5. Assessment center method.
6. The clinical interview.
7. Critical incident method.

1. *Ranking Method.* This approach requires the superior to evaluate the subordinate on his performance and value to the organization when compared to others in the firm. There are several varieties of this method. The simple ranking technique permits the evaluator to array his subordinates from the most valuable to the least. It is an overall rating, and usually without consideration of specific factors. As such, it is of little value in deciding the developmental needs of an executive. Furthermore, it is of little value because almost every management position is different from every other one.

2. *Graphic Rating Methods.* This method provides for evaluating the executive on the basis of individual factors. For each factor, a range of measurement is provided by breaking down the factor into degrees such as superior, above average, average, below average, poor. To assure accuracy and uniformity of measurement it is important that each factor and the degrees of each factor be quite clearly defined for the rater and a common understanding of their meanings needs to be resolved. Many rating forms also require written statements which further describe the ratee in the light of the factor, or give examples from his job behavior which substantiate the rating. A rating scale which uses defined degrees would look like this:

Ability to Motivate

[   ] Inspires subordinates to superior, consistent, and willing effort.

[   ] Usually gets employees to give very willing and above-average effort.

[   ] Gets employees to respond in an average manner to his supervision.

[   ] Frequently fails to get cooperation and adequate effort from subordinates.

[   ] Consistently fails to get subordinates to produce in a satisfactory manner.

3. *Forced-Choice Method.* This is considered an improvement in accuracy over other systems in that it reduces the effects of rater bias. The rater is provided with sets of statements, each set consisting of both favorable and unfavorable descriptions. The rater must check what he considers the most applicable favorable statement and the most applicable unfavorable one. He, however, does not know which statements actually are counted and which are meaningless for purposes of the evaluation. Thus the superior cannot evidence favoritism either voluntarily or unknowingly. Here is an example:

    ————— Anticipates problems
    ————— Lacks drive and initiative
    ————— Possesses social maturity
    ————— Tends to be tactless with subordinates

Obviously, the construction of a set of statements, properly discriminating, is a complex and difficult task. Also, since the rater does not know how he is rating the subordinate, the rating is of little value for an appraisal interview. There is also the question of effort lag in such a program where the feeling may prevail that a randomly selected judgment is as good as a carefully selected one.

4. *Group Appraisal Method.* As generally administered, this method combines the ratings of several supervisors in the firm. The appraisal group usually is composed of the subordinate's supervisor as well as several other supervisors who have knowledge, through work contact, of the person's performance.

Group ratings may be conducted in the form of a conference among the raters, or such ratings may be made independently by each appraiser, then combined for discussion purposes. Although the former appears to have an advantage because lack of information by one rater about some aspect can be supplied by another who happens to have such information, there is danger of constructing a compromise appraisal rather than one incorporating the true judgment of each appraiser. It is preferable, therefore, to have each appraiser work independently and then have a discussion to compare the results.

The theory underlying group rating is that a better coverage of the individual's strong and weak points will result. Also possible bias on the part of the superior may be modified by other, more impartial, ratings. This rating method has merit, but it must be remembered that no one is in a more advantageous position than the immediate superior for evaluating the performance of a subordinate.

5. *Assessment Center Method.* A recent innovative adaptation of the group approach used by some large corporations is the use of assessment centers to formally assess corporate talent. An assessment center is simply an off-job site where managerial assessments take place.

Military assessment techniques were originally employed by the Office of Strategic Services for officer selection during World War II. Since then, The American Telephone and Telegraph Company has been a pioneer in using the assessment center approach for management selection.

Assessments of managers at the centers are a combination of data gathering techniques such as personal questionnaires, projective tests, an intensive personal interview, along with the collective evaluations of several trained specialists who observe the manager's actual performance in simulated situations. These simulated situations are constructed so as to elicit specific dimensions of management performance such as planning and organizing, leadership and communications skills, and decision making.

Among the various techniques employed during these simulated exercises are the in-basket technique, role playing, and the business game. At the conclusion of all tests and situational exercises which last several days, each member of the evaluation staff independently prepares an individual assessment which is further synthesized into a summary report that includes an overall assessment of the individual's strengths and weaknesses as well as his potential to the organization.[5]

6. The Clinical Interview.[6] This type of interview is conducted by clinical psychologists, usually consultants, who are trained and skilled in interviewing and in administering and interpreting certain standard tests including the so-called "projective techniques." These are tests in which a person responds verbally or in writing to relatively unstructured or ambiguous material such as ink blots, pictures, or partial sentences. Generally, the psychologist familiarizes himself with the position for which the person is being assessed and has established the criteria of personality characteristics important to success or failure in this particular job. He evaluates the test responses, the interview responses, and conduct of the man being assessed and then balances these against the personality patterns and characteristics known to the psychologist by virtue of his training and experience. He then prepares a report of the personality and potential of the man being assessed relative to the position in question.

Some companies use this kind of assessment technique for several purposes: to supplement the regular appraisal program; to interview candidates for management posts; or as a counseling medium by a trained expert.

Advantages of this approach, according to its proponents, are that it permits the clinical psychologist to apply his professional expertise to a particular situation; and it is suited for bringing out personality characteristics that are closely related to success and failure in jobs.

Disadvantages of this technique, on the other hand, are that its accuracy depends largely on the degree of expertise of the psychologist; and it also takes more time and is somewhat more costly than conventional techniques.

7. Critical Incident Method. This method focuses on the predetermined critical requirements of a job. The requirements are those crucial behaviors that determine whether a job is being done effec-

---

[5] For a more detailed analysis of this concept see Walter S. Wikstrom, "Assessing Managerial Talent," *The Conference Board Record* (New York: National Industrial Conference Board, Inc., March, 1967).

[6] For a more thoroughly delineated description and evaluation of the clinical interview, see Robert B. Finkle and William S. Jones, *Assessing Corporate Talent* (New York: Wiley-Interscience, Division of John Wiley & Sons, Inc., 1970), pp. 28–30.

tively or ineffectively. Critical incidents of both effective and ineffective behavior are obtained from managers, the incumbent himself, and others close to the job being analyzed.

The incidents are then analyzed and refined into a composite picture of the required essentials in a particular job. From this, a checklist is developed which forms the framework against which the manager is eventually evaluated.

Procedure for Appraisal

At this juncture in our discussion, it should be recognized that when the appraisal process is divided into a logical sequence of steps, the result can be a more accurate measurement of the individual's value to the organization. Furthermore, the results of appraisal constitute a sound basis for judging his future possibilities with the firm. The steps in the appraisal process may be summarized as follows:

1. Determination of job needs.
2. Appraisal of performance—present and potential.
3. Appraisal interview and determination of individual needs.
4. Suggesting a developmental program.
5. Putting the program into action.
6. Follow-up.
7. Benefits of appraisals.

1. *Determination of Job Needs.* The job duties, responsibilities, authority relationships, and other information included in the job description, form the basis for developing criteria to be used in the measurement. The criteria selection and their development was discussed, as you will recall, in the preceding section.

2. *Appraisal of Performance—Present and Potential.* The actual appraisal consists of measuring the individual's performance and the characteristics that influence his performance in terms of the appraisal factors which have been developed for the particular position or organization.

A distinction should be made between appraisal of the executive's *current performance* and of the *potential* which he may show through his performance. Figure 23–5 illustrates a form employed for appraising the potential of management personnel. Current performance should be the first concern in evaluation—how does he discharge the actual job responsibilities for which he is presently

FIGURE 23-5

ESTIMATE OF PROMOTABILITY

1	SOC. SEC. NO.	2	NAME (LAST)	(INITIALS)	COST CENTER	DEPARTMENT
			POSITION TITLE	SECTION	JOB CLASS	AGE	YRS. SERVICE

3 ACCOMPLISHMENTS: *(List significant accomplishments during past year - BE SPECIFIC)*

_____

_____

_____

_____

_____

4 PRESENT PERFORMANCE   *(Enter corresponding code in the box to the left)*

CODE
☐
E   EXCELLENT *(Top 10% of those with similar responsibilities)*
G   GOOD   *(Next highest 40% of those with similar responsibilities)*
S   SATISFACTORY   *(Next lowest 40% of those with similar responsibilities)*
L   LESS THAN SATISFACTORY   *(Lowest 10% of those with similar responsibilities)*

5 EVALUATION   *(Complete only one section - A, B or C)*

A. ☐   **PROMOTABLE**

LIST BELOW SPECIFIC POSITIONS OF GREATER RESPONSIBILITY TO WHICH THE PERSON IS PROMOTABLE EITHER NOW OR WITHIN 1-3 YEARS. *(For each position of greater responsibility chosen, enter in the box to the left a zero (0) if the individual is promotable "now" or enter the number of "years" you estimate his promotability to be - DO NOT USE HALF YEARS.)*

☐   _____
☐   _____
☐   _____

INDICATE BELOW ANY POSITION(S) OF SIGNIFICANTLY GREATER RESPONSIBILITY THAN THOSE LISTED ABOVE TO WHICH THE PERSON MIGHT BE PROMOTABLE BEYOND THREE YEARS: *(Enter years estimate in box at left.)*

☐   _____
☐   _____

IF APPLICABLE, INDICATE BELOW, FUNCTION, DEPARTMENTS AND SECTION TO WHICH THE PERSON MAY BE TRANSFERABLE. *(Enter (T) in box at left if the individual is transferable.)*

☐   _____

B. NOT PROMOTABLE   *(Enter corresponding code in the box to the left)*

CODE
☐
T   LIMITED TIME REMAINING FOR DEVELOPMENT OF CAPABILITIES
H   HEALTH   *(Please explain under "other")*
U   ABILITIES NOW CLOSE TO FULL UTILIZATION
O   OTHER *(Explain):* _____

C. NOT EVALUATED   *(Enter corresponding code in the box to the left)*

CODE
☐
A   ON ASSIGNMENT LESS THAN 6 MONTHS   *(Insufficient knowledge of person.)*
O   OTHER *(Explain):* _____

6 ☐   ENTER X IN THE BOX TO LEFT ONLY IF THE MAN IS AN EXTRAORDINARY INDIVIDUAL CONSIDERED TO BE EVENTUALLY PROMOTABLE TO A TOP LEVEL DECISION MAKING POSITION. *(Could be considered in top 3% of Division work force.)*

7

ESTIMATE OF POTENTIAL BY: _____
IMMEDIATE SUPERVISOR   TITLE   DATE

REVIEWED BY: _____
NEXT-HIGHER SUPERVISOR   TITLE   DATE

Source: The Babcock and Wilcox Company, Group Headquarters, Power Generation Group, Barberton, Ohio. Used with permission.

accountable? Following this there should be a considered judgment as to his aptitude for future development and promotability. For obvious reasons, the appraisal of current performance should be discussed with the individual being rated. Beyond this, the appraisal of his potential should be of great interest to higher management, especially for such purposes as long-range organizational planning.

3. *Appraisal Interview and Determination of Individual Needs.*
The manager who has been evaluated will normally want to know
where he stands. An appraisal interview, well planned and conducted, besides divulging results can assist him in developing his
promising attributes and in taking corrective action regarding those
areas in which he is deficient. Thus, the superior should determine
in advance the points to be discussed with the individual in terms
of his strengths and weaknesses, and simultaneously develop suggestions for improvement. When these are constructively covered in
a bilateral discussion, it is much more likely that the subordinate
will welcome evaluation of his performance, will make additional
suggestions for improvement, and will cooperate in taking subsequent action. Usually it is more effective to discuss the positive
points of the evaluation at the onset of the interview in order to
convince the subordinate of the constructive purpose of the process.
Weaknesses and suggestions for improvement can then be taken
up.

The appraisal of the individual's potential may include judgment
as to his qualification for further responsibility, the approximate
length of time for qualification, and also the type of development
to be prescribed. The determination of individual needs can often
be made in conjunction with the appraisal interview.

Sufficient time, of course, should be allowed for the appraisal
interview, and a friendly atmosphere should prevail. Privacy should
be assured even if it means getting away from the work scene.
Whenever possible the subordinate should be encouraged to talk
about his own performance. He will be more likely to bring out
his own weaknesses and suggest ways of overcoming them.

4. *Suggesting a Developmental Program.* When a clear understanding has been arrived at with the subordinate manager as to
individual needs, then a program of development can be evolved.
Some firms follow a policy of having the individual develop his
own program of self-improvement and then submit it to his superior
(and perhaps, the staff director of management development) for
approval. The help of a staff man is usually sought at this point
so that means of improvement can be matched as closely as possible
with needs. Certain courses may be prescribed to increase technical
knowledge in an area. It may be that a variety of work experience
is indicated in order to give the executive a companywide point
of view and a better knowledge of relationships existing among or-

ganizational units. Or plans may be made to develop needed human relations skills. Possibly, present methods of learning need to be augmented by more teaching to accelerate the process of development, and a system of coaching may need to be initiated.

5. *Putting the Program into Action.* Plans for development as a result of the appraisal should include time, place, content, and type of development. When programs of the understudy, coaching, or on-the-job type are prescribed, particular care should be taken to see that sufficient time is set aside for instruction, discussion, and counseling. Otherwise this important phase may be neglected. Definite procedures should be established so that training or education is carried out in a systematic manner and adequate control can be exercised.

6. *Follow-up.* No program of appraisal is complete without a follow-up to assure that development is actually taking place. The methods of follow-up differ little from regular methods of appraisal—the results of development should, after all, show up in performance. Some specific review of the proposed development program itself and of the manager's participation in it may be in order. Superiors and others may analyze the executive's progress, and he should be encouraged to analyze his own progress. Counseling interviews with the manager can be scheduled at appropriate intervals to discuss his progress and perhaps to modify the development program so as to coordinate it more closely with his needs.

7. *Benefits of Appraisals.* Methods of appraising managers are still far from being perfect, but there are few functions that can have a more impressive impact upon managerial climate and organizational effectiveness. When the superior recognizes the importance of evaluation and is willing to take the time and effort to do a conscientious job, when there is mutual understanding between the boss and the subordinate of what is expected and what is important in the job, and when evaluation is not viewed by the subordinate as a disciplinary measure, the benefits can indeed be great. The manager is given an opportunity to learn how he stands with his boss and with his company. He is given the chance to state both his own feelings about his performance and his reaction to the appraisal of his work. Invariably the principle of participation is invoked.

The appraising executive stands to benefit from the process, too. He is encouraged to analyze the responsibilities which his subordinates bear and which after all are part of his own broader function.

This may lead him to greater self-analysis, which will produce better bases for his pay-increase and promotion recommendations, better control generally, and in short, better executive performance.

QUESTIONS

1. Discuss the overall value of executive appraisal to both the organization and its management.
2. To what extent do quantitative performance standards meet the need for effective evaluation criteria?
3. What activities should be covered in a comprehensive appraisal process?
4. Identify and discuss the chief reasons for the popularity of management-by-objectives type appraisal programs.
5. Discuss the chief principles of conducting the post-appraisal interview.
6. Why is it important to distinguish between current performance and potential performance in making the appraisal?
7. How can management utilize the results that derive from management appraisals?

CASE 23–1

Felix (Rocky) Rogano was a rough-and-tumble kind of executive, who, as a one-time truck driver, had worked himself up through the ranks of the Interstate Motor Express Company. Self-taught and successful, "Rocky" had been an Army infantry officer during World War II. He believed in experience as the major method of development. "It's when you're under fire, that you really prove yourself," was one of his favorite expressions.

Rocky felt that in the main, the company's young management trainees were too soft and needed further tempering. However nonmalicious—he believed that a periodic "chewing out" was therapeutic to another's progress. "It worked damn good in the Army," he used to say. "Good guys always benefit from it."

Patrick Doyle, originally recruited as management trainee, had been previously assigned for about six months as a supervisor in Rogano's traffic division. Patrick's interim appraisals as a trainee were extremely complimentary, and Patrick himself felt he was making genuine progress. In fact, "Rocky" had already tentatively identified him as his own potential successor.

One morning "Rocky" strode by Doyle's desk and almost shouted, "Hey Pat, come on into my office now and let's talk about your performance." After Doyle followed Rocky into his office, he sat down and for the next half hour was in the state of traumatic shock as Rocky excoriated him endlessly for minor mistakes and unimportant peccadilloes that Doyle committed during the last six months.

In a kind of appraisal summary, Rogano reminded Doyle that his performance was "just average—you see, just average" and that it would have to improve "significantly" to meet the standards of successful supervisors. He further promised to again review Doyle's performance in another six months.

Felix "Rocky" Rogano thought to himself as he put away Doyle's file, "A real fine prospect. With some experience he'll be one of our best. Sure as hell glad we got Doyle."

As he walked back to his section, Patrick Doyle was very much perplexed. For the first time since joining Interstate he thought about looking for a new job.

1. How do you feel about Rogano's approach to supervisory evaluations?
2. What suggestions would you offer Rogano for improving his techniques for appraising performance?

CASE 23-2

The Supreme Manufacturing Company, makers of world-renowned quality control equipment, decided for the very first time to install an appraisal program. It was to be for its engineering personnel only. Top management believed that engineers were a different class of people. So, after reviewing various type programs it decided to opt for a self-appraisal kind of program—"one that is for professionals."

In a bulletin to the engineering department the president outlined the self-appraisal program that excluded both engineering clerical and stenographic employees. The procedure for appraisal was to consist of these steps:

a) Draw up a set of objectives for your position.
b) Develop both plans and methods for improving your job and technical skills.
c) Evaluate success in achieving your goals.

d) Submit your self-appraisal form within two weeks to your immediate manager.

When the managers began to analyze the submitted self-appraisal forms, they were dismayed to find little, if any, correlation between their identification of job objectives and those of the engineers. Secondly, the plans and methods for development of skills were, in many cases, prohibitive because of cost factors. Some plans included attendance, with extensive time off, at far-flung collegiate programs, seminars, and conferences. Finally, the majority of managers considered their performance to be superior in every respect.

1. Do you agree that engineers are "a different class of people" requiring a distinctly different type of appraisal program? Why or why not?
2. Evaluate this firm's procedure for self-appraisal. What are the inherent disadvantages of such a program? Are there any advantages here as you see them?
3. What, if any, are possible basic problems existing here that may preclude the success of a self-appraisal program?

24

Compensation

Introduction

DISCUSSION of executive staffing of an organization would be incomplete without giving attention to financial compensation. While managers, as individuals, respond to a variety of stimuli, just as do nonmanagerial employees, financial compensation is of significant importance for executive morale and effectiveness. Designing and operating a sound compensation plan requires considerable effort in dealing with a complex of problems. Hence this chapter is devoted to a discussion of executive compensation under the following headings:

1. Nature of the compensation problem.
2. Financial evaluation of managerial jobs.
3. Base-salary levels and differentials.
4. Salary increases.
5. Incentive plans for higher management levels.
6. Nonfinancial compensation.
7. Trends in executive compensation.

Nature of the Compensation Problem

Compensation of executives is not a simple matter of dollars and cents. A number of qualitative characteristics complicate compensation decisions. To begin with, compensation of managers is traditionally considered a highly personal matter. The amount of executive pay, except that of certain corporate officials, is usually confidential. Thus, it is more difficult to discuss and evaluate propriety of salaries for particular positions, or to establish salary levels that will have some reasonable relationship to individual jobs.

Moreover, financial motivations have more than just monetary incentive value. Frequently, executive job income may be well in excess of an amount necessary to meet apparent needs of the individual. The size of the paycheck and other financial emoluments, nevertheless, are so significant that an executive will take a position with another firm in order to "better" himself. In other words, the rate at which his financial compensation increases often indicates to the ambitious executive how fast he is rising in the organization.

Another characteristic of financial compensation is the difficulty of analyzing the executive job. The higher the organizational level, the more the job is made up of intangible factors such as creative thinking, long-range planning, or decision making, or of immeasurables such as the public relations aspect of an executive's job. It is difficult to subject the executive job to close scrutiny and to quantify its elements. Therefore, putting a dollar valuation on each element of the job and then adding up the elemental values to get a total summation may become somewhat difficult to justify as a method for determining the basic worth of the position. Yet, without making an analysis of the executive job, can the salary paid for its performance ever be more than an inexact approximation of its worth?

A fourth characteristic is the lack of comparability that exists among executive jobs. There are relatively few of the same management jobs in any one organization. Therefore, it is difficult to set up standard management job descriptions such as exist for an assembler or a class A electrician, for example. A division manager for one area may have duties and responsibilities considerably different in nature, scope, and magnitude from those of the manager of another division. Moreover, a comparison between two similarly titled jobs in different firms frequently is of little assistance in gauging the relative worth of such jobs. The duties may vary considerably, or the philosophy of the two managements may be responsible for an otherwise unaccountable pay differential. Other peculiar characteristics could be mentioned to illustrate the problems to be solved in the administration of an equitable and effective salary system.

As a consequence of these characteristics, compensation planning calls for considerable thought and expertise. Perhaps the most fundamental basis for such planning is that of a sound scheme for evaluating managerial jobs. It is to this subject that attention is now directed.

Financial Evaluation of Managerial Jobs

Evaluation is essentially a process of measurement. Hence, in this section, consideration will be given to, first, the extent of evaluation of executive jobs and, second, the methods of job evaluation.

1. *Extent of Evaluation of Executive Jobs.* Job evaluation is a procedure for measuring a job in order to determine its worth in the organization relative to all other jobs. Prior to a determination of its relative worth, a base salary is usually arrived at which represents compensation paid for minimum satisfactory performance. Increments in an individual's compensation are then subsequently based on factors such as improvement in performance beyond the minimum acceptable.

Evaluation of higher management jobs has progressed at a less rapid rate than for lower management or supervisory jobs. This has been largely due to the increasingly complex nature of management jobs as the organizational hierarchy is ascended. The difficulty of analyzing executive positions has in past years, therefore, resulted in less enthusiasm for job descriptions and evaluations. Indeed, there are some who argue that it is not worthwhile to draw up elaborate job descriptions and evaluations, because top managerial positions cannot be broken down into significant factors for measurement of a job's worth. Some firms are redesigning evaluation programs with more focus on fitting the job to the man and his proficiencies instead of fitting the man into the job.

Notwithstanding such objections to systematic job analysis, it is also true that more and more firms are attempting to analyze, describe, and evaluate managerial jobs, often up to and including that of the chief executive. Whether executives are satisfied with the pay plan is, in part, dependent upon their compensational relationship with other executives in the organization.

It should be obvious, too, that the effectiveness of an executive compensation program will be largely dependent upon its acceptance by all those executives whose positions are involved. This means that any job-analysis and evaluation program should be thoroughly communicated to and understood by the executive group. Preferably, too, the responsibility for executive compensation planning should rest with a high-ranking committee usually chaired by a top-level officer of the firm.

2.   Methods of Executive Job Evaluation. The methods used in job evaluation for managerial positions need not differ in essence from those used in measuring the worth of operative jobs. If job descriptions have been developed in connection with recruitment and selection of managerial personnel, then this provides the basis for evaluation. However, since the nature of the jobs differ, the criteria selected for use will also differ. The method can be chosen according to whether it is desired to measure specific and critical factors that reflect the job's value, or to measure the job as a whole. Whichever approach is followed will depend upon whether the firm has sufficient detailed information about the job and/or whether the philosophy of the firm advocates an analytical or holistic evaluation.

In the following paragraphs, methods of systematically evaluating jobs are briefly discussed. First to be discussed will be the point system, because of its prominence in salary evaluation. Other methods that have been employed are the ranking system, and adaptations of the factor-comparison system. These will be taken up subsequently.

a) Point System. The point system is the most frequently used system for job evaluation of operative and clerical jobs. Its application to executive jobs has followed at an increasing rate. In this system measurement or evaluation is made in point units. It is alleged that maximum objectivity in measurement is thus gained. Several significant factors that are common to all jobs being evaluated are first identified. Such factors may be education, knowledge, experience, responsibility, decision making, and so on. A maximum number of possible points is determined for each factor relative to other factors being used. Gradations or degrees for each factor generally are developed also. Definitions for each factor, and grades for that factor, should be clearly spelled out so that all those participating in the evaluation may have a common understanding of them.

Jobs are then broken down into component factors and evaluated, factor by factor. Each factor of each job is assigned a point value in relation to the maximum points allotted to that factor generally. When all factors of a job have been rated, their allotted points are totaled, and the result is the total point value of the job. When all jobs have been thus evaluated and their total points ascertained, a relative standing for each job is achieved. The dollar value for each job is determined by converting the points into monetary units. A conversion scale is usually set up which equates a definite number of points with a predetermined dollar amount. The scale generally will already have taken into account the community or industry level of salaries.

b) Ranking System. In the ranking system, jobs are aligned in order of relative importance. Jobs are not broken down into elements but rather are examined as wholes. Often a top-level committee, which is acquainted with the duties and responsibilities of each position, performs the ranking. The assumption here is that committee members doing the ranking not only will be able to give each job its relative rank but also will be able to determine the amount of spread between jobs accurately enough to bring about equitable base salaries reflecting such spread.

c) Factor-Comparison Systems. As in the point system, so in the basic-factor-comparison system jobs are measured on the basis of individual factors. Factors are measured on a monetary scale instead of a point scale, however. Factors in those jobs being evaluated are compared with factors in key jobs, which serve as measuring standards. Such key jobs are selected beforehand because the base rates for these are already considered to reflect accurately the worth of the job to the organization, and are in line with the market rates. Factors in these key jobs are evaluated, and their proportion of the total monetary worth of the job is determined. The key jobs are ranked factor by factor, and a portion of the base pay is allocated to each factor. The jobs to be evaluated are then compared with this key-job scale, one factor at a time. Since the scale (key jobs) is already in monetary units, no conversion need be made, as in the point system.

Base-Salary Levels and Differentials

1. *Lower Management Jobs.* Supervisory, or lower management, jobs are usually evaluated separately from operative jobs but are sufficiently different from higher executive jobs to warrant separate treatment. Concern for industry levels is necessary to assure not only that base salaries are consistent within the organizational structure but that there is consistency with similar firms in the community or in the industry.

Frequently it has been found that supervisory salary levels are too close to the salary levels of subordinate operative jobs. A good evaluation system will minimize this. (It is only fair to state, however, that sometimes skilled-operative-earnings levels bear close proximity to supervisory levels because of high overtime or incentive earnings.)

When a major change is made in the compensation level of one group, the levels of other groups should be adjusted accordingly. Thus, a proper differential in levels is maintained. Some students of compensation methods charge that such differentials have not been maintained. They allege that operative levels have moved steadily upward, but that there has been a reluctance to raise levels at the top echelons accordingly. Consequently, the percentage differential between any two managerial levels has gradually decreased. Another factor that operates against consistent salary levels is the tendency to make salary adjustments on an individual basis in management ranks. Such individual salary adjustments do not refer to increases made on the basis of a sound merit-appraisal system, of course; these increases are usually made within a predetermined range. A proper job and salary structure will minimize the existence of out-of-line salaries.

2. Higher Management Jobs. Uniform salary levels for higher executive jobs are not easy to achieve. Differences in responsibilities and compensation philosophy of the company, as well as bargaining power of individual executives, account for this. Base salary levels in one firm may be appreciably lower than in another similar firm; however, compensation policies in the first firm may emphasize fringe benefits or stock-purchase plans to a much greater extent.

Generally speaking, however, executive compensation is directly related to the size of the company in terms of sales volume, and also the type of industry. For example, the average chief executive officer in the air transport industry whose firm has a sales volume of $40 million was paid $97,000 while his counterpart in a $400 million business was allowed $114,000.[1] It also varies between different industries irrespective of their sales volume. The average top officer among firms in the drug and cosmetics industry with $100 million in sales received $108,000 while the chief in the foods industry with the same volume earned $72,000.[2]

---

[1] Arch Patton, "Top Executive Pay: New Facts and Figures," *Harvard Business Review*, Vol. 44, No. 5 (September–October 1966), p. 96.

[2] Ibid., p. 96.

Salary Increases

Policies on making pay increases will vary from company to company, depending sometimes even on company philosophy, among other factors. Initial increases may also be made on the basis of length of service. In this case the assumption is that the manager is learning and improving his performance during his first six months or year on the job. That he has the aptitude to improve has been concluded in considering him for the job in the first place. The expectation that he will receive the increase should also act as a spur to his learning the job as rapidly and effectively as possible.

Increases based on length of service are generally used only during the very early periods of an executive's performance. It is usually felt that increases should be the result of actual demonstration of commendable performance; thus management tends to look to executive appraisal or rating as a basis for deciding on pay raises. But for some firms a problem presents itself here. Some companies consciously avoid using performance appraisal, as discussed in Chapter 23, to determine pay increases. They reason that appraisal may lose some of its value for analyzing performance and encouraging personal development when the emphasis is on measuring the performance for salary increases. In such a case, they point out, the incumbent executive and the rating executive may give disproportionate attention to justifying the evaluation which is in line with their salary judgments. Yet, it is difficult to argue that salary increases should not be based on a sound consideration of the manager's performance as evidenced by key criteria.

Incentive Plans for Higher Management Levels

Among incentive plans for higher executives is found a greater variation than for any other personnel group. The premium that has been put upon motivation of higher executives reflects their influence on the competitive effectiveness of the firm, and also indicates the scarcity of effective top-level executive talent. Among the kinds of incentive most frequently provided for higher executives are the following:

1. Profit sharing.
2. Incentive bonus plans.
3. Stock options.
4. Tax-savings plans.
5. Deferred compensation.
6. Pensions.
7. Certain nonfinancial benefits.

1. *Profit Sharing.* Bonuses based on the amount of profits made by the firm are a popular type of incentive. Criteria for determining the amount of such reward may be corporate profits (the most common criteria), dividends, sales, or some other element. Bonuses may be in cash or in stock. The company may execute a contract with the individual executive, designating that such compensation will be a certain percent of net earnings, for example. Often, however, a maximum dollar limit is set.

Instead of arrangements with individual executives, a group bonus plan may be effectuated which will embrace a number of executives. This may have an additional advantage of rewarding executives as a team. Such plans may provide in advance for a definite percentage of profit to be divided in cash among designated executives. Other such plans may state that a given percentage of profits will be divided among executives named at the time by the directors or an executive committee. A third arrangement is to establish a trust into which is paid a determined portion of the profits for the benefit of either a specified group of executives or a group to be named later by official action. Payment of money placed in such trust fund is usually deferred until a later time, rather than paid on a cash basis, and may be paid out later as retirement or severance pay.

2. *Incentive Bonus Plans.* These are money bonuses given for extra results that are noticeably different from the executive's normal or typical productivity. However, the bonus plan, as an incentive to generate extra effort and productivity, is being questioned. Bonuses, it is claimed, are ineffective when:[3]

1. Almost all those eligible get a bonus—thus rewarding the inefficient performance of the below-average producer.
2. Ineffective amounts are rewarded—awards, it is believed, should not be less than 20 percent of salary, otherwise its impact of recognition or incentive is short-lived.
3. Performance is inadequately appraised—where there is little or no direct relationship between the award and quality of performance.
4. Timing is schedulized and annualized—the bonus becomes expected in January and forgotten in February.

---

[3] Adapted largely from N. B. Winstanley, "Management 'Incentive' Bonus Plan Realities," *The Conference Board Review* (New York: National Industrial Conference Board, Inc., January, 1970), pp. 35–36.

5. Bonuses are used to make up salary deficiencies—it may engender the attitude of "I got it coming to me."
6. Secrecy prevails—and only a few in the bonus-eligible group know how awards are determined.

3. Stock Options. Options to buy stock, usually at less than the market price (but not below a certain minimum), may also be offered to executives. The executive is not obligated to buy stock but may exercise an option to do so. Conditions attendant to the exercise of the option have to do with length of employment with the firm and holding the stock for a minimum period after exercising the option. Tax advantages (capital gains as against ordinary income tax) are a chief reason for offering stock options.

Stock options have been criticized on the ground that they give an executive an unfair advantage for making a personal profit. He may exercise his option to purchase stock if the price trend is upward; he is not required to purchase, however, if the price is unfavorable. He can acquire considerable gain if he sells the appreciated stock after a minimum holding period (and pays only capital gains tax).

However, the Tax Reform Act of 1969 has affected options in several ways, as *Business Week* reported:[4]

Under the old law, an executive paid no tax until he sold his stock, then paid a capital gains tax of no more than 25 percent on the difference between his option price and selling price.

Beginning in 1972, the old rate will go up to a 35 percent maximum for all capital gains of more than $50,000. But what really takes the heart out of the qualified option is a brand-new provision. Now, in the year he exercises a qualified option an executive must report the paper gain between the option price and market price as tax preference income, even though he still has to wait three years to sell it for capital gains.

The figures begin to hurt when they get big enough to reduce the "earned income" sheltered by the new 50 percent maximum tax, thus shoving more of that income into the ordinary 70 percent tax bracket. The net effect is that the higher the paper gain from exercising stock options, the bigger the tax bill on salary and bonuses . . . Despite its fall from grace, however, . . . for those . . . making less than $75,000

---
[4] *Business Week* (New York: McGraw-Hill Book Co., October 3, 1970), p. 80.

it is perfectly acceptable and is likely to continue to be the backbone of most compensation plans for years to come.

Consequently, it appears the Tax Reform Act has forced many companies to reevaluate their stock option plans. Present thinking is to install plans which "are tied more to long-term company profits over which the performance of key executives can have a real influence rather than compensation devices pegged to the stock price, over which managers have little direct control."[5]

Those who argue for stock options contend that such opportunities only reward top executives in line with their contribution to the company. They provide an incentive for the executive who has been with the firm for a long period of time and may not expect many more increases in salary. For the younger executive they may be a stimulus to advance to a position where he will be eligible for options. Another advantage cited for stock options is that they can be used with effectiveness in a small or weak company just as in a large firm. The attractive potential in stock options may draw and hold managerial talent where other compensation methods could not. Thus, advocates of this type of incentive contend that the organization benefits from high-management effort to make the firm a success and that competition for top executive posts makes such a potential-reward system a necessary element in executive compensation.

4. Tax-Savings Plans. Besides plans such as the stock option, compensating devices are in effect that are designed to minimize the tax burden attached to executive compensation. The employer may agree to reimburse the executive in the amount of tax that has been paid on his compensation. Another less obvious arrangement may provide for payment of a sum calculated to leave for the executive a predetermined after-tax income. Such plans are not regarded with favor by many, since they give the rather obvious impression of discriminating in favor of the executive who already is in high-pay brackets, while all others must pay their taxes in the normal manner.

---

[5] Ibid., p. 80. (Note: This trend appears evident in a later *Business Week* survey of 126 of the largest firms in 30 industries. The survey shows that the salaries of their chief executives climbed 7 percent against a 15 percent rise in corporate profits. This contrasts with a 3.5 percent increase in 1970 in the face of a 12 percent profit decline. At the same time, overall compensation, including bonuses and incentive payments, and profit sharing rose 9.3 percent in 1971 compared with a gain of only 2 percent in 1970. *Business Week*, May 6, 1972, p. 41.

5. Deferred Compensation. The trust fund for profit sharing referred to earlier is one means of deferring compensation until some time after it is earned. In recent years, arrangements have been developed whereby an executive may be paid during the latter years before retirement at a rate less than he ordinarily would receive. Upon retirement, however, his pay is continued at a substantially higher level than what his mere retirement pay would amount to. This tends to level out his income before and after retirement. Deferring compensation until retirement has the effect of easing the tax burden on the high income ordinarily paid during the time the executive is active. Usually, some consideration is provided in return for such deferred compensation, such as the agreement by the executive to make himself available for consulting service to the company, or not to enter employment with a competitor.

6. Pensions. Executive pensions also come under the heading of incentives, since they are often quite liberal in amount, and thus can be considered an inducement to stay with the organization until retirement. Table 24–1 projects estimated annual pensions by type of business.

TABLE 24–1
Estimated Annual Pension at Age 65, by Type of Business

Types of Business	Number of Executives	Estimated Annual Pension		
		Medium	*Mid-50%*	*Range*
Retail trade	116	$32,000	$24,000–	$48,000
Manufacturing	1,545	30,000	19,000–	46,000
Gas and electric utilities	293	26,000	18,000–	40,000
Commercial banks	548	22,000	15,000–	33,000
Insurance	581	18,000	13,000–	30,000

Harland Fox, *"Top Executive Pensions—1969," The Conference Board Record,* Vol. 8, No. 1 (New York: National Industrial Conference Board, Inc., January, 1971), p. 39.
Note: These pension estimates were obtained for most of the three highest paid executives in some 1,000 companies in five major types of business.

This, however, does not prove that manufacturers provide better pension benefits. The pension dollar is the result of three factors: (1) an executive's credited service at age 65; (2) his salary over some or all of the years of credited service; and (3) the pension plan formula which links salary and service.[6]

[6] Harland Fox, "Top Executive Pensions—1969," *The Conference Board Record,* Vol. 8, No. 1 (New York: National Industrial Conference Board, Inc., January, 1971), p. 40.

Table 24–2 reflects estimated pension as a percentage of salary by type of business. The difference in the estimated pension as a

TABLE 24–2
Estimated Pension as a Percentage of Salary, by Type of Business

Type of Business	Number of Executives	Pension as Percent of Salary		
		Median	Mid-50%	Range
Commercial banks	548	47%	36%–	56%
Insurance	581	45	35 –	53
Gas and electric utilities.....	293	44	37 –	51
Manufacturing	1,467	38	28 –	49
Retail trade	110	31	24 –	40

percentage of salary may also reflect differences in the amount of credited service the group of executives in each type of business will have upon reaching age 65.[7]

Nonfinancial Compensation

Noneconomic inducements cannot be ignored, since they may have the effect of providing status for executives or indirectly supplying benefits for which the executive otherwise would have to expend his own resources or do without. Among such nonfinancial emoluments are the use of company automobiles or specialized staff services for personal purposes, access to company-owned recreational facilities, or the provision of liberal vacation arrangements. Within the company facilities, such advantages as exclusive dining rooms or elegantly furnished offices may be supplied.

Nonfinancial benefits such as these provide two values important to the executive. Some are the equivalent of additional financial remuneration. More important, though, is that they give him status, clearly indicating his role as a respected and influential organizational leader. Thus as conditions which help to fill psychological and sociological needs of an individual, they act as powerful incentives. We may properly conclude that the sound planning of nonfinancial benefits can be an effective auxiliary incentive to supplement financial incentives.

---

[7] Ibid., p. 40.

Trends in Executive Compensation

In more recent times, there appears to be developing certain distinct trends in the field of executive compensation. There seems to be, first of all, the increasing recognition that even at executive levels differentiated salary changes are a major indicator of performance. Salary is indeed an accurate measure of how the executive is getting along. Directly related to this earlier statement is the increased awareness that pay at the higher paid echelons will be more recognized as a significant motivator of good job performance when it is seen by the managers themselves to be tied to their job performance.

An additional development seems to be taking place in many executive compensation plans and this is the tendency toward offering present salary or bonus dollars rather than deferring compensation or issuing stock options. The tax law changes of 1969 have forced companies to strongly consider compensation programs that focus on the "cash now" approach.

Finally, more firms seem to be reformulating executive compensation programs with more flexibility, with built-in, "cafeteria-style" packaging, that is, allowing the individual executive the opportunity to select those compensation options that he values most and feels more conducive to satisfying his personal financial needs without adding to the compensation costs of the firm.

QUESTIONS

1. What are some distinctive characteristics of executive compensation?
2. Why is it difficult to compare executive positions bearing the same title in different industries or in different firms in the same industry?
3. What difficulties might you expect to encounter in using the point system for establishing base-salary levels of managers?
4. What are the advantages of profit sharing bonuses for executives?
5. Cite certain disadvantages which are related to the use of incentive bonuses.
6. What accounts for the use of stock options as executive incentives?
7. How do deferred compensation plans operate?
8. "If monetary incentives are high enough, management need not be concerned about nonfinancial benefits." Do you agree? Explain.

CASE 24-1

A national foods corporation recently hired a consultant to develop and install a job evaluation program. The president of the firm instructed the consultant to develop a program that would envelop "all levels of the firm."

When the consultant presented his completed job evaluation program, it was actually three different programs using different factors for operating employees, for basic supervisory personnel, and for middle management. However, there was no job evaluation program for top executives. The president was dismayed. The consultant explained that such a program for top management positions was impractical for several main reasons. First, top management jobs are far too complex and intangible to be evaluated objectively and quantitatively. Secondly, he said, even if it were possible to evaluate their positions, such evaluation would not adequately reflect the worth of their jobs because bonus plans and stock options were part of the executive compensation program at the foods company.

1. Do you agree with the opinions of the consultant?
2. How would you react to these contentions of the consultant if you were the president?

CASE 24-2

The salary evaluation committee is at an impasse about the relative importance of longevity, or length of employment, in the determination of managerial salary increases. Several members of the committee feel the length of service reflects a manager's interest, loyalty, and concern for contribution and should be a factor in determining increases. Others feel that the manager is entitled to an increase only if he is making a significant contribution or in the event of a promotion, but they do not feel that it, length of service, should be instrumental in granting a salary increase.

1. With which argument do you agree?
2. To what extent should length of service influence managerial salary increases?

25

Executive Behavior in a Changing Environment

Scope of Discussion

MANAGING in today's organization which is surrounded by an ever-changing environment is not without its risks. Organizational growth, product complexity, and technological progress may produce certain problems and challenges to management. The first is the possibility of obsolescence to the manager himself and the second is the problem of managing change. The purpose of this chapter is, first, to examine the subject of managerial obsolescence, to determine its causes, and to offer a possible solution. Second, the nature of change and its effects upon both manager and the firm are discussed. And third, some practical suggestions will be offered for introducing change into the organization with minimal resistance to those changes.

To accomplish these purposes, the discussion in this chapter will be grouped as follows:

1. The manager and obsolescence.
2. Need for continual self-development.
3. A test for personal growth.
4. The manager and change.
5. Minimizing resistance to change.

The Manager and Obsolescence

1. *Obsolescence Defined.* Obsolescence literally means no longer being current—having become outmoded, or losing utility in application. Managerial obsolescence, in this case, refers to the

manager being out of date in his position or in his fields of competency. More directly then, obsolescence may be considered as the difference between what the practicing manager knows and what he should know of the current state of knowledge and practice in the field of professional management.

2. Reasons for Obsolescence. There are several possible and different reasons why an executive may become out of date in the business environment. A main causal factor is sheer physiological deterioration of the body and mind. While this is normal in the process of aging, it may be accelerated by the quickened pace at which some managers travel. Furthermore, required new knowledges and their application will make such weaknesses discernible much earlier in the person's career.

Another major reason is obsolescence of the function and its processes with which the manager works. In this instance, the need for the work itself is displaced due to improved technology or replaced processes. Managerial jobs in existence for years may suddenly become extinct. If the manager has talent, he can be readily transferred to another function and subsequently retrained in new systems or processes. However, irrespective of talent, if the executive is immune to change, or has not concerned himself with self-development and improvement, he may not have the necessary foundation for adjustment to the new system or process.

A third contributing cause of obsolescence may be the manager's mental inflexibility. While many dynamic managers have sought out and incorporated new knowledges, skills, and techniques, others have been merely content to gravitate upwards in the organization without plans or strategy for the future. They attempt to impose a style of management acquired years ago and one suited to a different time and era long since past. Knowledges and attitudes acquired 15 or 20 years ago are truly inapplicable to the shifting events and circumstances of a present environment.

Consequently, there is a definite, if not imperative, need for the manager to keep current in both his conceptual and technical development. Essential to the intellectual growth, maturity, and progress of the manager is the necessity for a strict adherence to a concept of continuous self-development.

Need for Continual Self-Development

To the student of management, perhaps presently immersed in a course of study, the argument for continuous self-development may appear quite redundant. Yet, at the risk of being labeled repetitious it must be mentioned that the forces compelling the need for development are increasingly apparent. There are these extrinsic reasons for a program of continuous self-development:

1. The increasing role of the knowledge worker.
2. The rapidity of technological change.
3. The growth of the systems concept.
4. The advances in knowledge which require a redefinition of managerial competence.

There are also these intrinsic reasons:

1. To be able to qualify for advancement in responsibility and organizational position.
2. To be able to identify new areas and ventures for corporate action.
3. To apply the latest concepts and acquired skills in approaching and solving problems.
4. To develop a sense of personal fruition that comes from deepening growth and progress.

Therefore, it is most important for the manager, early in his career, to recognize the need for continual development and to incorporate this concept as an integral element in his philosophy of life. Or as John Gardner puts it—and much more eloquently—"what we must reach for is a conception of perpetual self-discovery, perpetual reshaping to realize one's best self, to be the person one could be."[1]

A Test for Personal Growth

A test of a manager's acceptance of change is his willingness to adapt to changing times and conditions. Much change is evolutionary not revolutionary. The manager needs to view adoption of new technical approaches and reformed attitudes as a normal and regular activity of everyday management life.

On the other hand, and most important to remember, obsolescence can just as easily occur by default, by inaction, and failure to exercise certain "fundamentals" such as a lack of initiative or dedication of purpose. Personal obsolescence will come easily to a person who is satisfied with the status quo, who is comfortable with present techniques and methods, who hesitates to experiment,

---

[1] John W. Gardner, *Excellence* (New York: Harper & Row, Publishers, 1969), p. 162.

and who constantly avoids an introduction to the new and different.

The concerned manager can assess his present attitude of growth by honestly answering certain key questions that are definite barometers of progress.

1. Do I possess a sense of intellectual curiosity that compels me to find the answers to questions about myself, my profession, and my company?
2. Am I idealistic in wanting to improve the quality of the contributions and efforts of my subordinates?
3. Am I an achiever? Do I really enjoy making a contribution? Do I enjoy my work and its related activities?
4. Have I a keen awareness of my strengths and weaknesses? Do I maximize my strengths and make a serious effort to overcome weaknesses?
5. Do I discipline myself? Am I temperate? Do I have control over myself and my behavior? Can I manage my time, my emotions, and my personal inclinations toward food and drink?
6. Finally, do I have long-range as well as short-range goals? Do I know where I want to be 5 years, and 10 years, from now? Do I know and have ultimate, and yet realistic, objectives for myself?

In designing a program for growth, one that satisfies both personal and organizational needs, the executive should give real consideration to a model proposed here. Suggested is a dual track model, consisting of two distinct phases: a present phase and a future one.

1. *Present Phase.* In the process of developing a present phase program for continuous growth, the executive should consciously consider three essential sequences:

a) First of all, he needs a diagnosis of his present position in terms of its required knowledges, abilities, and skills. Some sources for this diagnosis are the job description itself, statements of objectives and performance standards for the position, along with the expressions and expectations indicated by his superior.

b) Secondly, there is an assessment by the manager himself as to the correlation between his actual performance and that required and desired of the position.

c) Finally, there is an agenda constructed for the satisfaction of those needs which represent the difference between the actual and desired levels as they evolve out of the manager's analysis.

2. Future Phase. The future phase of a recommended operational design for personal development consists of concurrent programming so as to avoid the threat of obsolescence. It consists of a deliberate attempt to forecast the future in terms of the knowledge and skills the executive should be concerned with. "What should be the present composition of such an agenda?" the student might inquire. Studies of developmental need areas seem to point out that there is a growing need to focus on the management sciences with their far-reaching extensions of knowledge. Increasingly, advanced techniques, both quantitative and qualitative, are being manifested in making decisions about production and production schedules, manpower planning, inventory control, financial and budgetary allocations, and marketing and distribution systems. More pronounced too, have been the manifold changes introduced by the computer in the handling of information and in facilitating planning and control and decision-making techniques. And, most importantly, there is a continuing need to study and apply the applications of the behavioral sciences as they relate to motivation, morale, and to individual and group behavior in the organization.

Simultaneously, during both the present and future phases of his functional model for development, the manager should consider an on-going development program in his own technical field in order to prevent knowledge erosion. To illustrate, it is estimated that the engineer of today without ongoing refreshment of his technical expertise will find himself obsolete in 10 years or less. This suggests, then, that the engineer must continue his technological education immediately after graduation from college.[2] Figure 25–1 represents a model of engineering obsolescence and its prevention over time through education. But it, the message, should be abundantly obvious, that it is certainly no less important, for any manager, irrespective of his field, to avoid dissipation of his acquired technical knowledge and to maintain currency with new knowledges and skills as they emerge and become evident. Throughout his career, the manager will have to engage in self-development activities including formal advanced study, membership in professional groups, seminars and conferences, selective reading programs, and so on. To the manager who does not keep pace, and to the manager who feels

---

[2] M. Scott Myers, *Every Employee a Manager* (New York: McGraw-Hill Book Co., 1970), p. 106.

FIGURE 25-1
Engineering Obsolescence Cantilever

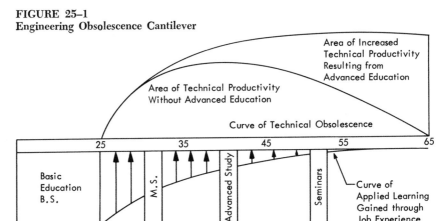

Source: Dean Alvah K. Borman, *Northeastern University Graduate Cooperative Programs in Engineering and Mathematics* (brochure), p. 3.

self-development is an interruption of his daily routine, there is the distinct threat of professional archaism, and with it the danger of premature extinction as a functioning and productive member of the organization.

Summarily then, this much should be apparent to the reader. Advancing accelerations of change in society, and more specifically, in the environment of the organization, will require a continuing and almost relentless adoption of new knowledges, attitudes, and skills. So much so that, perhaps, a new approach to the concept of learning and development is necessary. As one recent writer observed:

Given further acceleration, we can conclude that knowledge will grow increasingly perishable. Today's "fact" becomes tomorrow's "misinformation." This is no argument against learning facts or data—far from it. But a society in which the individual constantly changes his job, his place of residence, his social ties, and so forth, places an enormous premium on learning efficiency. Tomorrow's schools must, therefore, teach not merely data, but ways to manipulate it. Students must learn how to discard old ideas, how and when to replace them. They must in short, learn how to learn.[3]

The Manager and Change

1. *Some Basic Aspects of Change.* Within the past two decades more than at any other time in our economic history the executive

---

[3] Alvin Toffler, *Future Shock* (New York: Bantam Books, Inc., 1970), p. 414.

is confronted with wholesale change. The jarring significance of change is its resultant multidimensional impact on the organization, the groups it serves, and on the manager himself, in the exercise of his managerial responsibilities. Broadly speaking, and according to Webster, the verb *to change* means "to alter, by substituting something else for, or by giving up for something else; to put or take another or others in place of; or to make different; to convert." In an organizational context, change may further be defined as any modification or alteration purposefully induced by management in the work itself, work relationships, or work environment.

A wide range of forces or influences exert themselves upon the organization and require managerial decisions as to the need for innovation and change. These forces arise out of the economic, social, political, and technological climate of our times.

More specifically, those factors causing the need for managerial concern about change are:

a) Computer technology and its applications.
b) New management sciences and techniques.
c) Changes in manpower and its composition.
d) Technological innovation in products and services.
e) Competition, both domestic and international.
f) Trends toward the conglomerate corporation.
g) Social changes in society.
h) Changes in the political atmosphere.
i) Current economic climate.
j) Increasing government relations.

Varying in degrees of intensity, and occurring at different times, the influence of these factors is sometimes minimal and sometimes profound. But at all times, management must recognize and identify the specific causal force and its meaning to the industry, the firm, and to the manager himself. Specifically, and more pointedly, management must assess and evaluate the influence of change upon the objectives of the organization itself.

2. *Leadership, Objectives, and Change.* There appears to be a distinct linkage between change, leadership, and the objectives of the organization. In fact, there's a synergistic relationship among the three variables. A major corporate objective may be to improve product quality, design, or utility. This in itself may trigger a subsequent series of changes throughout the structure generally and in functions like research, engineering, and production specifically.

Also pressures for increasing sales volume and profits are important change-producing stimuli particularly on most marketing activities. Very significant, too, as an objective, is the constant need to improve the corporation's image with both the general and consuming public, and, not in the least, there is the eternal need to improve human relationships within one's own firm. All these are corporate targets regularly requiring changes in their definition by management and subsequent achievement—through delegation—by lower management and operating personnel.

Consequently, the processes of change are inextricably in lock-step with the objectives of the firm and with the leadership responsible for characterizing and accomplishing those objectives. Change, therefore, is expected of the firm's leadership by its many constituents, by society, government, labor, the consumer, and the employee himself. In this respect, the executive occupies a unique position when organization alterations, modifications, and adjustments are required since he performs a catalytic role in the firm's strategy for measured progress and growth through innovation. He must not only identify the need for change, function as an agent of change in creating and innovating change, but must also support it and encourage positive acceptance of it by his subordinates.

Change is an integral element in leadership and it can be either imitative or innovative. If the leader waits, follows, copies, and adopts the kinds of changes others have attempted, then it is imitative. Change has happened to him. But the true leader is a change agent who originates and changes things *before* anyone else. He *makes* change happen. Or as a president of a small liberal arts college recently and informally remarked, "What we need around here is more planned change and not changed plans."

3. Effects of Change. People, it seems, can be affected by change in various ways. The effects may be either technological, psychological, or sociological in character.

a) *Technological Effects.* By this is meant the effects of new technology, machinery and equipment, that cause change in the physical routines of people performing the work. For example, new production machinery may involve processes requiring changes in the sequencing of motor skills or the adoption of altogether new skills—or it may result in absolute displacement of some people.

b) *Psychological Effects.* The change may alter the persons attitudes and feelings about the work. Announced changes may generate questions, uncertainty, and doubt as to the personal impact of change. New techniques may be strange, threatening, and fraught with uncertainty. The person, for example, may question his ability to adjust to new machinery or to the new territory, in case of a required relocation.

c) *Sociological Effects.* Here the effects are adjustments that must transpire in the person's established patterns of interaction with his associates, with his immediate management, and with the organization as a whole. Organizational changes may require alterations in the informal relationships already established among those performing the work, their colleagues and supervisors. For example, a new supervisor may require a new pattern of relationships, including new communication networks, between the supervisor and his subordinates and even among the subordinates themselves.

4. Resistance to Change. While it is commonly generalized that "people resist change" it is more accurate to say that it is the *significance* of the negative aspects of change that engender resistance. Some changes are indeed welcomed. Salary increases, promotions, improvements in fringe benefits, ameliorated working conditions, reduced expenditures of physical energy—all are forms of change normally accepted by the average employee.

Important for consideration is that resistance to change is sometimes reflective of other and more basic problems in the organization. Firms with a history of good human relations and honest intentions, where management makes a real effort to develop understanding and rapport, find that people respond to change without serious incident. However, resistance to change seems more intense where there is distrust between management and its employee groups including labor.

An additional point to be remembered about resistance to change is the fact that the greater the change which is attempted, the greater will be the resistance encountered and the subsequent amount of time required to effect the change. Figure 25–2 projects graphically this concept of resistance and time span relationships.

Minimizing Resistance to Change

Since change in one form or another is inevitable for the organization, the question arises as to how the firm can reduce resistance

FIGURE 25–2
Levels of Resistance to Change

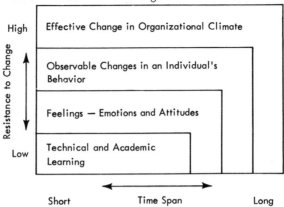

Source: *Modern Principles of Personnel Administration*, Middle East Industrial Relations Counselors, Inc. (Beirut, Lebanon: Heidelberg Press, 1970), p. 28. (Reprinted here with permission of Herbert C. Hayward, senior author.)

to its effects. What measures can be employed to assist the introduction and assimilation of change into the organizational systems without disruption or possible chaos. Obviously there is no panacea guaranteed to effect success, but there are indeed certain recommended actions for the executive's consideration. Among these are the following:

1. *Preparation for Change.* Whenever possible the organization should prepare for the forthcoming change. Its introduction or application for the most part should be announced *before* rather than *after* the occurrence.

2. *Communication of Change.* Again where possible, the rationale for organizational change should be communicated to all interested parties. Specific and honest reasons for necessary change should be given.

3. *Identification of the Specificity of Change.* It is important that management let its personnel know what exactly will be changed, *who* will be affected, and *when* the change is to take place. People will feel less threatened if their questions are answered before change takes place.

4. *Communication of Advantages.* The positive advantages of change should be made known to all those concerned. By the same token, any disadvantages accompanying change should be discussed openly within the firm.

5. *Allowance for Participation.* Oftentimes, it's efficacious to allow employees themselves to participate in discussions relating to change. There is real value in permitting employees to be voluntary partners in the implementations of change.

In the final analysis, there is no need for the effects of change to be shattering and disruptive within the firm. Change will be accepted and implemented by the people affected if they are aware of contemplated changes, their purpose and possible effects, and moreover if they are shown how they can satisfactorily accommodate to those changes.

QUESTIONS

1. Identify and discuss the different kinds of obsolescence that a manager may face.
2. Discuss the rationale for an ongoing program of self-development.
3. Describe what you believe to be the more important causes of change in the organization.
4. Of what influence is leader in adopting change?
5. Give illustrations as to how people may be affected by change—either technologically, psychologically, or sociologically.

CASE 25-1

"I would like my resignation to be effective two weeks from today," Arthur Wall said somewhat dejectedly. "I'll be taking a new job as a life insurance agent for the Puritan Life Company. It just isn't like it used to be around here."

A review of Art's personnel file would show that until now he was a regional sales manager for the New Era All Line Insurance Company. In his 49th year, of which 25 were spent with the firm, Art rose quickly during World War II, and immediately thereafter, from a life insurance agent to regional sales manager responsible for 7 district sales managers and some 70 agents in the New England area.

As RSM Art had no difficulty meeting his life insurance quotas, but he was generally average or below on his auto and health sales quotas. "These are accommodation lines," he used to say rather scornfully. Even though his territory covered a three-state area, Art steadfastly avoided air travel. "It doesn't give a person time enough to plan and think," was his regular excuse.

While Art attended the required company-sponsored, and usually marketing-oriented seminars, there is no record of his pursuing professional advancement activities. Furthermore, he rarely allocated budgetary funds for developmental activities for his district sales managers. "You learn how to manage by experience, not theory," he was heard to remark.

His sales region incidentally ranked among the highest in annual managerial turnover. When it was suggested by staff headquarters that he make better use of personnel testing services, he observed that "psychological testing is all gobbledegook. When the squares debug it, I'll try it."

The computer also seemed to incur Art's wrath. Once he sent a long letter to the vice president of marketing voicing his own misgivings about the myriad problems involved in converting his regional policyholder files to a computer-based system tied into the home office computer center. His was the last region to adopt its installation even though Art had assistance from the EDP people.

It is not known definitely when Art finalized his decision to leave the firm. However, his secretary noted that he seemed most distraught, the day before, upon receiving a memo from the vice president of personnel stressing the need for his voluntary compliance to Title VII of the Civil Rights Act of 1964.

1. What do you suppose were Art Wall's problems? Why did he resign?
2. What reasons would you advance for Art's resistant behavior to change?
3. Outline a program of development that would, for any manager in a similar situation, forestall personal obsolescence.

CASE 25-2

With expanding industrialization and increasing population, the Midwest Illuminating Company, an electric utility, found that demands for electric energy were overtaxing existing capacity and growing in such proportions that "a crisis of energy" was imminent unless immediate action was taken.

Consequently, the president authorized the purchase of 25 acres of land on a strip bordering one of the Great Lakes and he simultaneously approved a contract for the purchase of a nuclear power boiler to furnish the needed electricity. The board of directors applauded the president's decisions which would result in "satisfying electric energy needs for the next several generations."

The site of the proposed plant was considered ideal. It was proximate to the heavily industrialized, populated areas and yet far enough removed from any residential areas. It would furthermore generate substantial tax revenues in addition. to employment opportunities for the local population.

However, it seems that all is not going well with Midwest. The purchased area is near a lakeside resort community which voices objections to devaluation of property, ruination of recreational areas, an unsightly industrial plant, and most of all, the threat of radiation emanating from the nuclear core. The community is gathering signatures on a petition to halt the project.

1. What went wrong at Midwest? What actions should the president have taken to prevent community resistance to the plant?
2. What problems does Midwest now face which conceivably could create a barrier to the erection of the nuclear power plant?
3. Is the fundamental problem here simply resistance to change?

26

Trends in
Management

THE BUSINESS organization is a dynamic, changing entity operating in a complicated, changing environment. It simultaneously contributes to and receives from the societal environment within which it functions. It must seek, therefore, to adapt itself to ongoing changes, to support research for improved management techniques, and to incorporate new knowledges from other disciplines. The firm can neither stand still nor stand alone. It must be sensitive to the pervasive and compelling influences that emerge around it.

While it is difficult, to be sure, to predict the future, it is possible, though, to discern certain emerging trends or developments that will assume even larger significance for the firm and its management in the future. All this is to say that if there is one organizational requisite more germane than others, it is the need for creative innovation and adaption. This chapter will provide a brief summary of the more significant trends, and their implications, currently visible in management. The discussion will concern itself with:

1. The changing work force.
2. Computer technology and management science techniques.
3. Management of international operations.
4. Corporate social responsibility.

The Changing Work Force

An organization perpetuates itself by regularly drawing its leadership and productive human resources from the many groups it

476

serves. Through the 1970s distinctive differences will appear in the demographic makeup of our population. These differences will have profound implications for the business enterprise. First of all, in this decade, there will be an absolute decrease in males of the age group 35 to 44. This age group, the prime age group for management, technical, and professional positions, has been declining steadily. "In 1965, there were 10.4 million men; the projection is for 9.8 in 1970, in 1975, 9.6, and in 1980, 10.7 million."[1]

This, of course, is the age group from which management derives its experience and vitality. This is the age bracket of line officers and department and division heads. So unless there is more intensified and deliberate programming to develop more and younger managers (both men and women) a smaller number of managers will be forced to handle the many complex problems in the seventies and beyond.

The sex composition of the labor force has undergone pronounced changes. The force of womanhood will be more impressed upon the firm. Since 1920, there has been a marked increase in the numbers of adult women in the civilian work force. In April of 1960, female employment constituted 31.9 percent of a total employment of 66.1 million. In April of 1968, the percentage had risen to 37.4 percent of an employment total of 75.6 million.[2] The reasons for the growth of the female contingent of the labor force are a mixture of economic, sociological, psychological, and legislative influences. Women are entering the labor force with a higher degree of both education and emancipation. It appears, too, that business is recognizing both the challenge and necessity of recruiting increasing numbers of qualified women at the entry level of executive jobs. In more and more organizations women graduates are routinely getting business posts that were closed to their predecessors 10 years ago. Those with MBAs or advanced training in business often have their pick of well-paying, prestigious, first-rung jobs.[3] And this trend is certain to continue. Business will need to maximize the further contribution of women through providing increased developmental and promotional opportunities at all levels of the organization.

Another important demographic projection is this. In the age

[1] John T. Dunlop, "The Nations Manpower Arrangements," *The Conference Board Record*, Vol. 7, No. 3 (March, 1970), p. 27.

[2] Chester A. Morgan, *Labor Economics* (3d ed.: Austin, Texas: Business Publications, Inc., 1970), p. 24.

[3] "For Women, a Difficult Climb to the Top," *Business Week*, August 2, 1969, p. 42.

group 25 to 34 there will be a major expansion of men. "Starting at 9.5 million in 1965, it rises to 10.7 in 1970, 13.3 in 1975 and 15.5 in 1980."[4]

This age group of 25 to 34 will be made up of today's teen-agers and young adults whose behavior, at times, may seem questionable to senior management. Even so, management will have to adapt itself to the behavior and various life styles of this new generation. Tomorrow's young people will certainly no less question the values and constraints of society. Consequently, there will be a real challenge to management to provide opportunities and challenges which will interest these future managers if they are to contribute enthusiastically to the attainment of organizational objectives. Such considerations as job enlargement, broader job responsibilities, better utilization of talents, and increased business involvement in social problems will be necessary to attract young and capable people to industry from other alternatives now open to them.[5]

In summary, demographically we face the seventies in which there will be a significant growth of young men, more women in the labor force, and keen competition in bidding for men in the age group over 35 years of age. More than ever before, top management will be required to develop long-run strategies for manpower development.

Computer Technology and Management Science Techniques

The computer makes possible better management of the modern corporation and its social, economic, and managerial systems. It facilitates through the use of management science techniques the planning, measurement, and control of the organization's systems.

As early as 1958 forecasters spoke of the new technology called information technology:

It is composed of several related parts, one includes techniques for processing large amounts of information rapidly and it is epitomized by the high-speed computer. A second part centers around the application of statistical and mathematical methods to decision making problems; it is represented by techniques like mathematical programming and by methodologies like operations research. . . .[6]

---

[4] Dunlop, "The Nations Manpower Arrangements," p. 28.

[5] Charles A. Myers, "Management Decisions for the Next Decade," *Industrial Management Review*, Fall 1968, pp. 31–40.

[6] Harold J. Leavitt and Thomas L. Whisler, "Management in the 1980's," in Max D. Richards and William A. Nielander (eds.), *Readings in Management* (Cincinnati, Ohio: South-Western Publishing Co., 1963), p. 34.

At that time it was prognosticated that information technology would have its greatest effect upon middle and top management. It was predicted that the planning function would be taken from the middle manager and given to organizational specialists, "operations researchers," or "organizational analysts." Jobs at the middle management level would become highly structured with much more of the work being programmed and subject to firm operating rules governing the day-to-day decisions. It was also forecast that large organizations will recentralize with top management assuming an even larger share of the planning and innovative functions. Certain classes of middle managers would lose status by becoming routine technicians rather than thinkers (through loss of autonomy) and finally the line separating the top from the middle of the organization will be drawn more clearly and impenetrably than ever.[7] It is not yet in the 1980s, but such trends are already evident.

1. *Growth of Computerization in Business.* The computer has made the knowledge industry possible. In 1960 there were 4,500 computers in use; in 1970 there were 90,000; and by 1975, it's estimated there will be 160,000 in operation.[8] Also, a few years ago, investment in computers and related equipment as a percentage of new plant investment was very difficult to find on any curve. In 1965 the computer accounted for 8 percent of investment in new plants and equipment, and by the turn of the decade (1970), it will exceed 10 percent. The fact that the sheer hardware comes to 10 percent of our plant investment begins to make clear the fact that information technology as an industry has arrived, and its influence will be continuing.[9]

2. *Effects upon Different Management Levels.* The effect of the computer appears to vary with each level of management. The application of data processing has automated, for lower level management, normally decisions of a routine and menial nature. Furthermore, decisions on inventory control and manpower scheduling, formerly made by control supervisory staffs, are now being made by the computer. In turn, this is providing middle management with more accurate data for effectively evaluating the operating results of its supervision.

At the top management level, the computer is being utilized to

[7] Ibid., p. 35.

[8] John Diebold, "Diebold Research Program Report," *Administrative Management,* February, 1970, p. 58.

[9] John Diebold, "The Information Revolution," in Peter F. Drucker (ed.), *Preparing Tomorrow's Business Leaders Today* (Englewood Cliffs, N.J.: Prentice-Hall, Inc., 1969), p. 63.

better analyze data essential to a better understanding of the firm and relationships between it and its environment. It is being used in the ultimate to evaluate the effects of various corporate strategies over the long run. Furthermore, the computer is being enlisted to forecast, among other contingencies, the success potential of new products and services as well as the probable effectiveness of changes in sales, sales promotion, and distribution techniques.

3. *Effects upon the Manager.* In the previous chapter, obsolescence and its relationship to the manager was discussed. However, left unmentioned was the topic of managerial obsolescence generated by the computer itself. The computer is a dual-edged tool. Just as it will provide needed data for the manager of the future it will also hasten his obsolescence if he is not in tune with its expansive uses. If present and future managers want to maintain their productive vitality, they will certainly prepare for personal compatibility with computerized information systems. They will learn to adapt their operations to include the use of computer based skills and applications. The middle manager who incorporates and applies computer technology should not become extinct but will find increasing personal worth and satisfaction as he moves along in the responsibilities of management.

Management of International Operations

As successful organizations have grown in size, diversity, and geographical dispersion, they have tended to look to opportunities in other countries. However, unlike the trading companies of the 19th century, the multinational firm has moved the entire production system across the waters. Financial capital, technology, and management know-how have been exported to where markets and resources offer the largest payoff.

This trend, while not new, has burgeoned since World War II. Both the Bretton Woods agreements and the General Agreement on Tariffs and Trade (GATT) have established a favorable milieu for a new burst of trade and overseas investments. The forms of operations on an international footing are varied. Some are merely licensing arrangements whereby a foreign country is permitted to use the design and method owned by a domestic firm (or vice versa). In other cases, however, the firm may be domestically owned but managed by foreign nationals of the host company. In yet other instances the top management of the unit abroad may be Americans who are sent there to apply the management system of the parent company.

The movement toward international growth has generated several interesting developments for the parent firm. The first is the emergence of the corporate entity itself with its unique form and structure for doing business. Additionally, highly efficient transportation and communication networks have increased the capacity of the firm to plan, direct, and control far-flung operations. Finally, a major force and possibly the key to success is the capacity of the multinational firm to transfer technology across national boundaries and around the world. The transfer of technology not only permits the transplant of industrial skills and knowledge from the parent firm but also allows the host or foreign nation an opportunity to develop overnight, so to say, an industrial capability and economic thrust.

Today it is estimated that for approximately 80 of the top 200 U.S. corporations their foreign operations now account for at least one fourth of sales, earnings, assets, or employees. With the continuing growth of overseas markets more companies will join their ranks. As it now stands, U.S. multinationals produce an estimated $200 billion worth of goods and services annually overseas—which is just about equivalent to the gross national product of Japan.[10] In fact there is a new vocabulary of terms. There is a distinction made between international companies which are U.S. based and serve foreign markets and the multinational company which produces abroad. And a multinational company is considered "polycentric" if its foreign plants manufacture mostly for local markets and it's "geocentric" if both parent and subsidiary companies market worldwide. Also "transnational" companies—firms from two or more different countries—are emerging. Ultimately, "nonnational" firms incorporated under an international charter and transcending national boundaries with no distinction of personnel and devoid of national policy may yet appear.

Not surprising is the fact that some management problems result from multinational operations. In a number of cases, the parent company has superimposed its management system on the local organization, and this has sometimes produced obstacles and frictions which have not always been anticipated. Frequently the social environment has been one marked by different personal values and

---

[10] "A Rougher Road for Multinationals," *Business Week,* December 19, 1970, p. 57.

belief systems. Status and caste systems have not always permitted personnel selection and placement in the same way that these functions are exercised in this country. Attitudes toward work as a moral obligation may not be nearly so strong in certain cultures. Administration of disciplinary action may differ. Because of differing value systems, direction and motivation of personnel may have to be done on bases different from those which have proven successful in our own culture. The continued existence of marked status and educational lines between classes of people accounts in part for a continued authoritarianism in management in some countries.

The difficulties and challenges encountered in managing foreign operations have served to enlighten management on how to handle problems of operating in differing social, economic, and political environments. This analysis has helped American firms to plan more carefully their own programs for expansion in terms of local conditions. A division located in Western Europe will not be managed in the same way as one in the Middle East, for example. Parent companies have realized the need for modifications in their own policies and procedures. Personnel are selected with careful observance of their qualifications to work in the local environment.

In view of such varying managerial problems it is logical that management development programs have been initiated to better prepare both American personnel and foreign nationals for more effective administrative performance. Functional techniques, management philosophy, and human relations skills geared to the local culture are covered in educational programs for managers. If such efforts are even moderately successful, the developments in management of operations abroad will be among the more significant phenomena of the future.

Corporate Social Responsibility

Basic, and increasingly so, is the question of corporate social responsibility. It is discussed here in terms of, first, developing concepts; second, management and technology; and, third, management and human resources.

1. *Developing Concepts.* The question of whether or not business should exercise a sense of social responsibility is almost an academic one. This question is less and less debated, and presently the focus is on the *degree* of social involvement by business. By social responsibility is meant the obligation of the firm to consider

the impact of both its decisions and actions on the entire social system. Moreover, if the public interest is affected by management decisions and actions, then there is no question about the need to exercise social responsibility.

It is the position of the authors of this text that there is a decided interdependence, a distinct relationship between business and the social system within which it functions. Just as the business institution reflects the values and mores of a consuming society it also creates social values for that society. Why, the student may inquire, is there a growing concern about social responsibility? There appear to be several main reasons.

The first is that there is an increased sensitivity by business itself to its role and responsibility in the exercise of social consciousness. A progressive and professional management is aware more and more of the interdependencies of business and society. Business through the application of advancing technology is instrumental in causing social change and consequently feels increasingly responsible for ameliorating its effects upon society.

Second, there is pressure from society itself—composed of the many groups that business serves. More and more the parameters of corporate responsibility are felt to extend beyond the performance of economic functions alone. The social concerns—of unemployment, environmental pollution, resource conservation, and ecological stabilization—are felt to be considered along with the problems of market and profit performance. Since business possesses the resources and talent to assist in solving social problems the expectancy level of business behavior rises accordingly.

Finally, there is the recognition that the government will impose a model of required socially responsible behavior through controls and regulations as the need arises. Historically this has been the case. Obviously, preventative action by business would forestall increasing intervention by the public sector in defining business social responsibilities.

Spinning off from a discussion of social consciousness are two important problem derivatives. These are the impact and influence of technology upon the organization, and secondly, the responsibility of the firm in utilizing human resources.

2. Management and Technology. Our advanced civilization owes much of its economic progress to the innovation and application of technology. But a fundamental question is where will technological progress lead us? Will it be servant or master of management in its relationships to the concerns of society? In answer to these questions, management it appears will need to continually evaluate the applications of technology, for consumer benefits, in terms of the longer range benefits to mankind itself. Historically, in our affluent and consuming society, the overriding calculus of the enterprise has been the acceptable ratio of goods and services to factor inputs. However, with the newer wisdom—the quality of life—our economic operations will have to be conducted in the future, not only with an eye to the successive lessening of labor inputs relative to output but also, and increasingly, with a more deliberate approach to environmental and ecological concerns. Management will need to address itself to the use of technology for, among a growing list, the reduction of land, sea, and air pollution; the conservation of natural resources; and the renovation and redevelopment of our depressed urban and industrial areas.

3. *Management and Human Resources.* The firm of the future will assume even greater responsibility for the development of all its human resources. Its own survival is the primary objective of the organization. Markets, products, technology, and financial resources will no longer be the predominant assurances for economic and social achievement. The survival of the corporation in the future will depend increasingly on its capacity for adapting innovation. This will require well-educated and highly motivated people. Corporate survival, essentially then will derive from the quality of intellect and activation that its people possess.

As advancing technology accelerates the erosion of human physical skills, the organization will more concernedly plan for the development of its human assets through ongoing and continuing activities at all levels, and with all peoples, of the organization. The financial allocations for the development of human resources will not be considered optional allocations after all other monetary claims on the firm have been satisfied, but will be fixed charges or necessary costs incurred in the conduct of the corporation's social performance in conjunction with its profit performance.

QUESTIONS

1. Of what real significance to the organization is the changing composition of the work force?
2. Describe and discuss the impact of computerization upon the firm and upon management itself.

3. Will the experience of firms in international operations result in a change in basic management philosophy? Why or why not?

4. Explain the rationale for the social responsibility doctrine of the American enterprise. How does this doctrine differ from that exercised, say, about 100 years ago in the average firm?

5. What do you foresee in the way of future developments in the exercise of social responsibility by the business community?

6. Do you believe that management is now or will become a profession? What are your reasons for believing as you do?

7. Do you believe that concern with the social responsibility of management will change the basic nature of management, as some observers predict? Why or why not?

CASE 26–1

At a recent board meeting, a president of an automobile manufacturing firm remarked, "Our only responsibility is to our stockholders. It's our job to protect the investor's equity in our company and to appreciate that investment. In other words, our sole objective has got to be profits. If we cease in this, we're out of business. There are enough other groups in our pluralistic society who will satisfy the concern for social responsibility."

1. Do you agree or disagree with the president's remarks?

2. Develop a policy statement that in your opinion would satisfy the profit motive with a due respect for the exercise of social responsibility.

CASE 26–2

At a recent management seminar, three leading management experts were discussing "The Computer's Impact on the Centralization or Decentralization of Authority in the Organization."

The first speaker felt that the computer is essentially neutral with respect to the organization and that the firm can use the computer to move into whatever direction is necessary. The factors influencing direction include market changes, force of competition, and philosophy of the firm.

The second speaker argued that the future trend was toward decentralization of authority since managers are more likely to delegate decision-making powers to subordinates when they can be sure authority will be handled properly. The computer makes it possible to notify the delegating manager almost simultaneously of actual deviations from planned performance.

The concluding seminar speaker saw a recovery of previously delegated authority and it would now be recentralized at the top. New management reporting systems will permit top executives to make decisions formerly made by middle managers who will now be bypassed, and few managers, furthermore, will be needed.

1. Define the terms centralization and decentralization.
2. With what speaker do you most agree? Advance additional arguments to support your position.

Integrative Case

The Goodwill Steel Company

The Goodwill Steel Company had neither an employee evaluation program nor a formal salary administration program. The situation was unquestioned by the nonunion employees as they were satisfied to receive the same wage increases as were granted to the workers under the wage contract with the union. Although, the home office employees were not members of the bargaining unit, they were given the same benefits as member employees. Performance appraisal in the company was informally conducted by the immediate superior for supervisory employees, and increases accordingly were based on merit.

At the last contract settlement the wage demands of the union employees were settled without a strike. But this time the company decided in the case of nonunion employees to introduce a formal performance rating system in lieu of granting across-the-board salary increases, even though other member firms in the industry granted their nonunion employees the salary increases and changes in benefits. While the Goodwill officials procrastinated, the President of the United States announced the wage-increase freeze. The company immediately informed the employees they were unable to grant the increases as granted by other industry firms.

A credibility gap between management and employees suddenly became very apparent. Other local firms in the same industry it seemed were having no difficulty giving their employees the increases. Management, consequently, became aware of the hostility among their employees and the president of the company wrote to all employees informing them of his efforts to obtain permission from the government to grant the salary increases. The employees however were not convinced. Comments between individuals were within the following context:

—"The company owes this to us."
—"Other companies are giving their employees the increase why can't they?"
—"I don't believe a word they say."
—"The cost of living has gone up, college tuition is more, the price of a new dress is greater, and why should the employees in other companies who do the same kind of work we do receive the increase and we don't?"

Employees impatiently awaited the next word from top management. It was the topic of most conversations and discussions. Employees had been informed they would receive a letter from management confirming the information they had received as soon as it was available from Washington.

Meanwhile there was a proliferation of placating communications from top management that employees felt were a "mockery" of the letter employees were expected to receive. Soon, too, any communication from management was both ridiculed and disregarded by employees.

The next move made by management was to appoint a steering committee of carefully selected employees to meet with a member of top management to "improve the employee attitude by informing them about employee benefits they were entitled to as group employees," for example, discounts on purchases of certain items of merchandise, noon-recreation sports, movies in the auditorium, sports and travel clubs. There were a total of approximately 55 "fringe" items to be given to the employees, which included their participation in the implementation of the programs they desired. Many of the benefits the employees felt were unrealistic while others were needed improvements.

The reaction to the list of items was extremely negative. Comments from some of the employees were as follows:

—"We aren't supporting *ANY* of their 'crazy' programs until we receive our raise."
—"We don't want noon movies, or sports. We want what is due us."
—"Who are they trying to kid? This is the raise we should be having, and it's not fair."

—"We don't want any merit program. We can't trust our management to be fair about who will get a good rating. Only the boss's favorite people will get a good rating. We who are good workers but not favorites, we'll never get a raise."

—"The only fair way is to give everybody a raise just as the other companies have."

Management tried within their limited channels of communication and particularly through the members of the steering committee to convince employees that this recreation program was not intended in any way to be a substitution for the awaited permission to grant a wage increase. This too was greeted with disbelief.

Coincidentally, middle management itself had not been informed of the purpose of the steering committee, which was composed of nonmanagement personnel, and they resented being uninformed. Some of them, because of the lack of communication from top management, would not support the employee recreation program and began to resent their personnel being represented on the steering committee. This fact was made known to members of the committee. Employees on the committee suddenly found themselves in disfavor with their peers (for concurring with top management on the salary ruse), for being on the committee, and with their immediate superior for participating in it, even though meetings were held after office hours.

Finally the vice president of industrial relations, who had tried to develop the recreation program out of a genuine desire to benefit the employees, was made aware by confidants of the problem that had arisen. He took immediate steps to inform middle management, but it was too late, since by this time everyone was hostile to everyone else. For example, middle management was hostile to top management and to their own employees, top management was hostile to middle management for not supporting their new program, employees were hostile to each other for their individual ideas about the situation. Members of the steering committee were accused of being "members of an organization unit," and in turn were expressing to top management the problems they were encountering as a result of being on the committee.

However, and irrespective of all this controversy, the company continued to proceed with the new employee evaluation program by informing management of its role in evaluating their people. The program is of the forced choice type, and managers are required to distribute the rankings of their employees according to the classic "bell-shaped" curve. This was resented by some management personnel who did not want to judge their people in this manner.

Meanwhile, another letter was sent out by the president of the company which advised the employees that they were to receive the increase in salary comparable to that which had been received by other member firms in the steel industry. This communication appeared on the same day as the announcement of the new evaluation program. There was a mixed reaction from employees. Some were happy and pleased; others showed very little enthusiasm. Employees were confused about the real reason for the salary increase and viewed the entire action with trepidation. They were now asking each other the following questions:

—"Will they have another wave of dismissals, retirements, and layoffs?"

—"What will be expected of me now?"

—"How will my boss evaluate me and will I really be able to dispute his rating as they say I can . . . do I dare?"

—"Whose side is my manager on? My side or that of top management?"

—"Who do I believe now?"

Many employees who voiced strong objections and disbeliefs were now shamefacedly keeping quiet. Management personnel did not receive the salary increase; only nonmanagement clerical employees. Some members of management expressed resentment at this. "What will the president do next?" one middle manager asked.

QUESTIONS

1. Identify the basic problem(s) at the Goodwill Steel Company.
2. Develop what you feel would be a realistic communications program for Goodwill Steel.
3. Why do you feel the fringe benefits program was unacceptable to the employees?
4. Why did the company incur such resentment in their attempt to install the evaluation program?

Integrative Case

The Clarkson Hotel Company

The Clarkson Hotel Company is a solely owned, family operated chain consisting of five hotels in southern California. In 1958, Thomas Clarkson, president of Clarkson Hotels, left his position as eastern district manager of a large motel chain to establish his own hotel business. By 1961, through the pledging of personal securities and obtaining a long-term loan, Clarkson established two hotels. The Clarkson Hotels since have gained a fine reputation and subsequently have established a profit throughout the years.

However, the true efficiency of Clarkson's chain is somewhat questionable. Bob Reynolds, to whom Clarkson reported in the motel chain, states, "Maybe I should say first that Tom Clarkson is the type of guy who has to do everything himself. He is very efficient, and enjoys being in on everything that goes on, and feels that he would lose some power or prestige and wouldn't know what's going on if he turned over part of his job to a subordinate. When he left our organization, he unsuccessfully attempted to entice two of our local managers (Tom Jones and Bill Wilson) from their jobs by offering them more money to work for him. Tom Jones gave as his reason for refusing Clarkson's offer, "Tom is a good guy, but I need more freedom to exercise my effectiveness.' Bill Wilson replied, 'I could become stagnant within a year working for a president like that.'"

After the initial formation of Clarkson Hotels, Mr. Clarkson decided to bring some of his relatives into the organization and since has done very well running his one-man show. Harold Clarkson, Tom's brother and manager of one of the Clarkson Hotels, states,

"Tom has a firm hold on the inner workings of the organization, and he's the only man fully capable of making most of the decisions concerning us. However, while I often feel like tackling some of the problems that occur, I know that Tom's the only man who can effectively instigate any change to keep the entire system in balance."

By 1967 the Clarkson Hotel chain had expanded into five hotels in three other cities. Each hotel is managed as an independent unit by a relative of Clarkson. However, Mr. Clarkson continued to retain control over the five hotels, with the manager reporting solely to him. The company still operated under implied policies as Mr. Clarkson (1) defines a narrow scope of activity with the units; (2) specifies performance criteria for the hotels as to what standards, limits, policies, and procedures will be enforced within the hotels; (3) decides what performance will be rewarded or corrected and how; and (4) procures, conserves, and then deploys resources among competing demands from the hotels. Clarkson, however, remains in close personal contact with each of his managers receiving information and requests from each and instructing each of them individually.

In the past, the managers have often offered suggestions for improvements concerning their own hotels, but for the most part, the suggestions were never adopted. Ralph Evens, a recent graduate of New York University in Hotel School Studies, and one of the managers, states, "Tom believes that because of his former experience that he knows all there is about the hotel business and thinks he can carry the whole burden of our chain and make a profitable dollar." However, David Spencer, a close relative and manager, states, "I once had a serious problem concerning menus in my restaurant; Tom came to the rescue and solved my dilemma. I don't know what this chain would do without him!"

Invariably, when Clarkson instigated *any* change concerning his hotels, the effect was immediately felt throughout the channels and implemented with little or no disagreement. Some of the managers felt that the timing of certain changes was unpredictable and that many changes were not applicable to their own hotels. For example, hiring of employees was done solely by Clarkson when he considered the need pressing. Harold Clarkson said: "Once Tom sent me a new bartender when I already had two more than I needed. As it turned out, he did more barring than tending. I dismissed him, and that was the last I heard of it."

Also, Mr. Clarkson placed limits upon purchasing. It was implicit in the company that *any* order over $200 must be personally approved by Mr. Clarkson, himself.

Advertising was done solely by way of roadside billboards on the major highways. Marketing studies were not undertaken as Clarkson felt that they were too costly and not applicable to the urban hotel.

For the most part, record keeping was done by the individual units. Purchasing also was decentralized, with each unit preparing its own purchasing criteria, subject, of course, to Mr. Clarkson's approval. Jim Clarkson, a younger brother who had been the manager of one of the hotels for four years, was aggressive and intelligent. His past experience included systems work with an insurance company, three years with a CPA firm, and six years in the Air Force as a systems analyst. Jim felt that with each unit trying to handle its own records, there was much duplication and waste of time and materials; no standardized practices; and no uniform setup, proper coordination, or proper identification of the forms themselves. He saw this as an area for cutting cost. He also felt that under the present purchasing setup, the managers were so overloaded that they had a tendency not to treat this function as a primary one, and a neglect of it was proving costly, not only in actual dollars but also in errors of shipment, quantity, and control. In his judgment, these were areas that needed immediate attention if the Clarkson Hotels were to remain competitive.

There is no doubt that Mr. Clarkson is a hard-working executive. He is continually available to his managers. Also, he is very proud that his company has remained profitable under his supervision and close control. Periodically, Mr. Clarkson visits each of the five hotels to check on their current problems. During these visits he spends much time with the employees, "making them feel like they belong to Clarkson."

In 1968 the Clarkson Hotel company had an opportunity to expand the existing five-hotel chain. Mr. Clarkson purchased the right-of-way for constructing a chain of five additional motels along a newly completed stretch of interstate highway. By 1969 the five new motels were open and operating; however, with the expansion came no new organizational change. Mr. Clarkson remained as head of the one-man show. Subsequently, the chain immediately encountered new problems; the new managers who had been hired to run the new units were experiencing a very high turnover. A new manager usually lasted only a few months. Bob Graves, after recently leaving as manager of one of the new motels, stated: "Mr. Clarkson is an excellent man; however, the problems I encountered at my motel demanded his immediate attention. Furthermore, I had to have all my original purchases and hiring approved by him. It's a wonder my motel stayed in the black, since he just wasn't around when I needed him. I spent much time on the phone trying to contact him and when I finally did reach him, his schedule was too full to make a personal visit."

With the increased burden of the new motels plus keeping the existing hotels in effective operation, Clarkson suffered a heart attack in 1971. A few months after his illness, still convalescing, Mr. Clarkson was receiving reports that his entire chain was in complete chaos.

QUESTIONS

1. As the Clarkson Hotel chain grows, so will the scope of authority that Mr. Clarkson will have to exercise. Do you think that Mr. Clarkson should delegate a proportional amount of his authority to his subordinates? If so, why?

2. What underlying reasons could you cite as to why Mr. Clarkson has not delegated his authority in the past?

3. "If" Mr. Clarkson had tried to delegate some of his authority in the past, what assumptions could be made as to why his relatives did not attempt to use their increased lines of authority?

4. However, if Mr. Clarkson does delegate some additional authority to his relatives, and if they accept his authority, does this act alone mean that authority delegations will be effective? Explain.

5. In reference to Question No. 4, how specifically could an achievement-minded relative earn additional authority within the organization?

Integrative Case

Melbourne Appliances, Inc.

Melbourne Appliances, Inc., is a small, independently owned and operated retail appliance store located in the downtown section of a small southern town. Although the town is small in size with a population of only 30,000, it is highly industrialized with its two main industries employing over one half of the town's work force.

Melbourne is a widely known and respected name in the field of retailing within the town itself as well as the neighboring communities. Although in business under the name Melbourne Appliances for only seven years, its predecessor, a family-owned business, Frank Schmidt Electric, served the town for over 30 years in retail appliance sales. Upon Frank's death, Thomas Melbourne and Frank's youngest son Bill decided to carry on the family business. Since Tom was 20 years Bill's senior, the two agreed to organize under the name Melbourne Appliances. Upon the suggestion of a friend, the two decided to incorporate the business rather than organize as a partnership in order to take advantage of the tax savings. The stock of the corporation is owned entirely by Melbourne, his wife, and Bill Schmidt.

Ironically, the store was organized initially as a wholesale appliance outlet. Tom and Bill traveled throughout this and neighboring states wholesaling conventional washers in areas which did not have enough water pressure to utilize automatics. This became a profitable business for nearly eight years. But as modern technology advanced, the rural water conditions improved and the amount of water used by automatic washers decreased. Bill saw the "handwriting on the wall" and suggested now was the time to switch from wholesale to retail sales. Hence, the beginning of Melbourne Appliances, Inc. as it exists today.

Melbourne's emphasis from the beginning has been customer service. Frank Schmidt's reputation for fair and honest dealings and genuine interest in his customers' welfare was carried over into Melbourne Appliances' basic business philosophy. The cliche "almost a generation of family service to the community" characterized Melbourne's attitude toward the full-service approach to customer selling.

As an insight into the management of the business, it is well to briefly characterize Thomas Melbourne's and Bill Schmidt's ideas and attitudes concerning the business.

Thomas Melbourne is a dynamic personality; a tall, staunch, gray-haired man 62 years of age. "Good old Tom," as his friends affectionately refer to him, is a well-known and well-liked member of this small community. At one time a top-notch salesman, he is now at the point in his life where he is much more interested in having a good time than in how the business is operating. Ever since the store switched from wholesaling to retailing, Tom's interest in the business has gradually decreased. "I'm too old to learn about that new stuff we're selling. I've been in this business all my life and I don't want to work anymore; I just want to relax and enjoy myself. The switch from wholesaling to retailing wasn't my idea in the first place. Bill wanted to open the retail store and although I was quite content with leaving things as they were, I figured he was younger and still had quite a few years to work, so I agreed. As long as he keeps things running so that I still get my paycheck, everything is OK with me."

Although Tom's sales ability has decreased, he still attracts more business to the store than can be measured because of his warm, friendly personality—"you just can't help but like him." In fact, it is not uncommon for one of his old customers to call him on the phone and ask him to send out a refrigerator. For many a salesman, the temptation to send out the most expensive model or the model generating the biggest commission would be overpowering. But as one customer remarked, "I've known Tom all my life and I know he'll pick out the model that best suits my needs. He has never given me any reason to doubt his integrity throughout all my dealings with him."

Bill Schmidt, Tom's brother-in-law, is a short, stocky, dark-haired man in his middle 40s. Bill, the brains behind the operation, takes his job quite seriously, in fact too seriously at times. It is not uncommon to find his dark eyes squinting in a note of distress. Although Bill has only a high school education, his many years of experience working with his father and with Tom have been a valuable teacher. The store is literally his life, and he spends many hours of hard work for a paycheck which is hardly conducive to his effort. Since his father emphasized the customer-oriented business, Bill grew up with an understanding of the importance of personal selling. Through his own hard work, he became quite proficient in selling to the point of being offered lucrative selling jobs by various wholesalers, distributors, and competing retailers. But time and time again he would turn down sizable increases in pay to remain at the store. "I like being my own boss. I don't have to answer to anyone for my actions and I am able to see the outcome of my efforts not in personal gain but through the successful operation of the business. This is much more important to me than my weekly paycheck."

His total commitment to his work often presented problems in his relations with the store employees. It was difficult for him to conceive that for most of them, work was an eight-to-five job which paid an acceptable salary and nothing more. His attempts to motivate his employees by mere psychological stimulus, as you may imagine, failed more times than they succeeded. The sharp contrast between Bill's serious responsible nature and Tom's seeming indifference even resulted in periodic clashes between themselves. Bill was especially upset when the business was experiencing difficulties of some sort, but to try to consult with Tom on any matter of a serious nature was next to impossible. Tom could care less and he didn't care who knew it. Bill's German temper would flare, and an exchange of words could be heard by all.

Unfortunately, Bill's emphasis on total commitment has resulted in a lack of interest on the part of his sons in the business. Although his sons work part-time in the store while in school, it is evident to Bill that the boys have no interest in pursuing the business as a career in the family tradition. Thus, the reason for his emphasis on immediate short-range goals—goals whose fulfillment he will realize in his lifetime.

Melbourne Appliances emphasizes quality merchandise at competitive prices. Since the store is independently owned and operated, meeting competition—especially discount houses and chain stores on the basis of price alone—can at times be difficult. In order to augment pricing, the business in addition emphasizes a variety of customer services free of charge. As an example, the sale of a washer and dryer involves much more than its initial price. Melbourne's offers free delivery, free installation, including outside venting of the dryer, and provides free of charge the installation materials such as the electrical connection for the dryer and the vent kit. Melbourne's even offers the service of moving the old laundry equipment to another location if within a reasonable distance from the delivery area. The delivery men even fully explain and demonstrate the operation of the machine to the housewife. In contrast, a large competitive chain store provides none of these free of charge.

Melbourne's strongly supports the policy of handling only quality merchandise. Low-end budget lines are not even considered, irrespective of the low pricing and high profit the business could realize. By handling only high-grade merchandise, future service problems which in turn lead to customer ill-will are minimized. Melbourne's emphasizes not the initial sale but rather the future performance and service of the merchandise it sells. Keeping in line with this philosophy, Melbourne's merchandises only the highest quality national name-brand appliances.

Melbourne's considers its customers the lifeblood of its business and emphasizes the customer's interest above all else. Its total sales volume is comprised to a great extent of repeat business with past customers, many of whom have dealt with the family business from the time it was Frank Schmidt Electric.

Although repeat business is of major importance, it would not be valid to say that Melbourne's effort is directed only toward retaining the business of past customers. Melbourne's is always attempting to increase its appeal to potential customers who comprise that segment of the market which can be satisfied with Melbourne's offerings. Advertising plays somewhat of a minor role in the company's merchandising techniques, not by choice but by necessity. Bill Schmidt as manager of the store's operations has considered advertising funds a rather minimal appropriation. However, Bill was able to secure the necessary cooperative funds to daily fill a one minute spot prior to the noon news broadcast on a well-known and widely listened to radio station in the area. As a result of this type of advertising, Melbourne's is now reaching potential customers from a radius far exceeding its normal area of penetration.

The company's pricing policies, while seemingly too old-fashioned and traditional to some of its competitors, still appear to be satisfactory for the company. Melbourne's follows a one-price policy to all customers. This eliminates either discrimination or favoritism in customer contact and creates an atmosphere of equality of bargining power. Since Melbourne's offers no allowance for trading-in old merchandise, trade-ins in no way provide a hedge for the customer.

The sales staff therefore is the focal point of the organization. For the first five years of business, Tom and Bill handled the majority of the personal selling. But as the sales volume of the business gradually increased and the floor traffic along with it, it became necessary to consider hiring additional sales personnel. The administrative duties of the business increased in number, and the paper work became more voluminous. This work began to take up all of Bill's time and left little time for personal selling and customer contact. In addition, Tom's capabilities as a salesman had decreased along with his interest in the business, the natural result of which was an increasing number of lost sales. Melbourne's attempts in the past to hire qualified salespeople have been futile. The company could not afford to pay large salaries, so the only people it seemed to attract were those who were neither qualified nor interested in learning the business. Melbourne had hired one young man in his middle twenties about three years ago. Although he had no experience in selling, he was eager and quick to learn. After 10 months with the company, he was just becoming proficient enough to be a real asset to the firm when he quit his job to join a competitor who was willing and able to pay him a higher salary.

Melbourne's employee compensation plan has been based on a straight salary with no commission on sales. The company has always felt commissioned salesmen resulted in high-pressure selling—one of the main causes of customer alienation and ultimately lost sales. This policy had caused no problem in the past because the majority of the selling was handled by Tom and Bill.

Tom had a friend, Paul Haynes, a wholesale lumber salesman whose job involved quite a bit or travel. Since he is now in his early 60s, he wanted to find a job where he could stay closer to home. Tom suggested to Bill that Paul could possibly be the man they were looking for. Bill was impressed with Paul's neat appearance and pleasant manner and asked only whether he thought he could learn the appliance business. Paul expressed a willingness to try, and the conversation then turned to reminiscing of old times. They mutually agreed upon a salary figure. The firm was to provide hospitalization benefits, and salary raises would be based on performance.

Melbourne's had no formal training program, and Bill accumulated various manuals comprised of product information relating to the store's lines of merchandise. Bill told Paul that the distributors normally hold training seminars periodically and that he should plan to attend the next session. However, that was the last Paul ever heard about the training sessions. Gradually Paul acquired bits and pieces of information from the manuals and from observing Bill's selling techniques. He found it difficult if not impossible to become familiar with the features of every model of every product handled by Melbourne's. He continued reading and studying until he finally conceded, that at 60, he was no longer able to comprehend the volumes of information that were so dissimilar to his prior job. He became disillusioned and quit studying the materials altogether hoping that through repeated sales encounters he would gradually acquire a working knowledge of the appliances.

At this same time Bill was becoming ever more dissatisfied with Paul's progress. Paul's sales record was not at all what Bill expected of him. Bill was quick to criticize but slow to understand. He could not conceive of the problems that Paul was experiencing. Rather than discussing his dissatisfaction with Paul, Bill chose merely to ignore any performance on the part of Paul and considered any effort he made less than satisfactory. Since salary increases were based on performance, Paul received no increase in salary. At the same time Paul was growing increasingly dissatisfied. He remarked several times to the office girl, "Bill has never once complimented me on any sale I've made since I've been working here. I can't understand what he wants. I think I'm doing a darn good job but you would never know it from the pay I'm receiving." A stalemate resulted between Paul and Bill. Paul felt that nothing he did was or ever would be good enough for Bill. "Why should I do more? I'm never going to get anything better than I've got now. I'm too old to go looking for another job, so I'll just have to hang on until it's time to retire." Bill stubbornly refused to discover the source of the conflict between Paul and himself. "If it was up to me he would have been fired months ago. But he is Tom's friend and he doesn't want to do anything to hurt Paul's feelings. But if he thinks I'm going to give him a raise he's got another guess coming. Maybe if I wait long enough he'll get fed up and quit."

When Melbourne Appliances first started in the retail business, the delivery of merchandise was handled by an outside delivery service not affiliated with the store itself. Melbourne's felt it would be cheaper to pay the company a certain rate depending on the type and size of the appliance and the delivery distance rather than purchase a truck and hire and train men to do the delivering. The delivery company, in addition to delivering the merchandise, would install the appliance for the customer provided the installation was not too complicated. In order to determine how well this arrangement was working out, Bill composed a survey form to be completed by the customer and returned to the store after a delivery was made. In addition to questions concerning the installation and delivery of the appliances, the customer was questioned concerning the sales personnel and various operating policies of the company.

Bill would faithfully review each survey he received from the customer to determine what area of the company's operations needed improvement. He soon discovered that this type of delivery service was more of a detriment than a benefit to the company. Although he may have been saving money by operating in this fashion, the loss of customer goodwill more than offset this savings. It was discovered that the delivery company's only concern was getting in and out of the customer's home as quickly as possible. The men had very limited knowledge on the operation of the appliances, and even failed on various occasions to install the appliances properly. Based on the findings of the survey, Melbourne's decided to terminate the delivery service, purchase a truck, and hire its own personnel to do the delivery job. This system is currently in use by the company. The practice of sending the survey forms to the customers was terminated soon after the switch in the delivery system was made. When questioned as to why the survey was no longer in use, Bill replied, "We aren't getting any complaints on our delivery service since we've been doing it ourselves. If the customers weren't happy we would have heard about it. Let's leave well enough alone."

QUESTIONS

1. Discuss the relationship in this case between Bill Schmidt's own interests and personality with the objectives of the firm.
2. Evaluate Melbourne's compensation program. What is wrong with it and how does it affect the organization's objective of high quality service?

3. Is Melbourne too small an operation to develop a training program and a performance evaluation program for its employees? Devise what you feel would be adequate programs that would satisfy Melbourne's needs.

4. If you were Bill Schmidt would you have discarded the use of the consumer survey form? If not, why not? Of what use is the survey as a management tool?

Selected
Bibliography

1. The Field of Management

Athos, Anthony G., and Coffey, Robert E. *Behavior in Organizations*, pp. 1–34. Englewood Cliffs, N.J.: Prentice-Hall, Inc., 1968.

George, Claude S., Jr. *The History of Management Thought*, chaps. 10–12. 2d ed. Englewood Cliffs, N.J.: Prentice-Hall, Inc., 1968.

Koontz, Harold, and O'Donnell, Cyril. *Management: A Book of Readings*, pp. 3–52. New York: McGraw-Hill Book Co., 1972.

McFarland, Dalton E. (ed.). *Current Issues and Emerging Concepts in Management*, Vol. II, chaps. 2–4. Boston: Houghton Mifflin Co., 1966.

McGregor, Douglas. *The Professional Manager*, chap. 2. New York: McGraw-Hill Book Co., 1967.

2. Leadership

Davis, Ralph C. *The Fundamentals of Top Management*, chap. 3. New York: Harper & Bros., 1951.

Jones, Manley Howe. *Executive Decision Making*, chap. 7. Rev. ed. Homewood, Ill.: Richard D. Irwin, Inc., 1962.

Kelly, Joe. *Organizational Behaviour*, chap. 3. Homewood, Ill.: Richard D. Irwin, Inc., 1969.

Knowles, Henry P., and Saxberg, Borje O. *Personality and Leadership Behavior*, chaps. 7, 9, and 10. Reading, Mass.: Addison-Wesley Publishing Co., Inc., 1971.

Likert, Rensis. *The Human Organization*, chap. 3. New York: McGraw-Hill Book Co., 1967.

3. Philosophy of Management

Garrett, Thomas M. *Business Ethics,* chaps. 1 and 2. New York: Appleton-Century-Crofts, 1966.

Gellerman, Saul W. *The Management of Human Relations,* chap. 4. New York: Holt, Rinehart & Winston, Inc., 1966.

George, Claude S., Jr. *The History of Management Thought,* chaps. 6–9. Englewood Cliffs, N.J.: Prentice-Hall, Inc., 1968.

McGregor, Douglas. *The Professional Manager,* chaps. 1 and 5. New York: McGraw-Hill Book Co., 1967.

Newman, William H.; Summer, Charles E.; and Warren, E. Kirby. *The Process of Management,* chap. 1. Englewood Cliffs, N.J.: Prentice-Hall, Inc., 1972.

4. Decision Making

Deardon, John, and McFarlan, F. Warren. *Management Information Systems: Text and Cases,* chaps. 1–3. Homewood, Ill.: Richard D. Irwin, Inc., 1966.

Elliott, C. Orville, and Wasley, Robert S. *Business Information Processing Systems,* chap. 2. Homewood, Ill.: Richard D. Irwin, Inc., 1971.

Greenwood, William T. (ed.). *Decision Theory and Information Systems,* parts 1–4. Cincinnati: South-Western Publishing Co., 1969.

Koontz, Harold, and O'Donnell, Cyril. *Management: A Book of Readings,* pp. 164–207. New York: McGraw-Hill Book Co., 1972.

Miller, David W., and Starr, Martin K. *The Structure of Human Decisions,* chaps. 1–7. Englewood Cliffs, N.J.: Prentice-Hall, Inc., 1967.

Sanders, Donald H. *Computers and Management,* chaps. 2 and 8. New York: McGraw-Hill Book Co., 1970.

5. Planning

Elliott, C. Orville, and Wasley, Robert S. *Business Information Processing Systems,* chap. 3. Homewood, Ill.: Richard D. Irwin, Inc., 1971.

Hill, Walter A., and Egan, Douglas M. *Readings in Organization Theory,* chap. 3. Boston: Allyn & Bacon, Inc., 1966.

Koontz, Harold, and O'Donnell, Cyril. *Management: A Book of Readings,* pp. 99–116, 150–63. New York: McGraw-Hill Book Co., 1972.

McFarland, Dalton E. (ed.) *Current Issues and Emerging Concepts in Management,* Vol. II, chap. 24. Boston: Houghton Mifflin Co., 1968.

Newman, William H.; Summer, Charles E.; and Warren, E. Kirby. *The*

Process of Management, chaps. 16–19. Englewood Cliffs, N.J.: Prentice-Hall, Inc., 1972.

Starr, Martin K. *Management: A Modern Approach,* chaps. 8–10. New York: Harcourt, Brace, Jovanovich, 1971.

6. Organizing

Goliembiewski, Robert T. *Men, Management, and Morality,* chaps. 4–6. New York: McGraw-Hill Book Co., 1965.

Katz, Daniel, and Kahn, Robert L. *The Social Psychology of Organizations,* chap. 4. New York: John Wiley & Sons, Inc., 1966.

Koontz, Harold, and O'Donnell, Cyril. *Management: A Book of Readings,* pp. 262–303, 304–33, 393–415. New York: McGraw-Hill Book Co., 1972.

McFarland, Dalton E. (ed.). *Current Issues and Emerging Concepts in Management,* Vol. II, chaps. 11–12. Boston: Houghton Mifflin Co., 1968.

Newman, William H.; Summer, Charles E.; and Warren, E. Kirby. *The Process of Management,* chaps. 2–6. Englewood Cliffs, N.J.: Prentice-Hall, Inc., 1972.

Sexton, William P. (ed.). *Organization Theories,* chap. 3. Columbus, Ohio: Charles E. Merrill Publishing Co., 1970.

7. Directing

Gellerman, Saul W. *The Management of Human Relations,* chap. 3. New York: Holt, Rinehart & Winston, Inc., 1966.

Katz, Daniel, and Kahn, Robert L. *The Social Psychology of Organizations,* chap. 11. New York: John Wiley & Sons, Inc., 1966.

Koontz, Harold, and O'Donnell, Cyril. *Management: A Book of Readings,* pp. 517–49. New York: McGraw-Hill Book Co., 1972.

Leavitt, Harold, and Pondy, Louis R. (eds.). *Readings in Managerial Psychology,* chaps. 5 and 6. Chicago: The University of Chicago Press, 1964.

McGregor, Douglas. *The Professional Manager,* chaps. 3 and 4. New York: McGraw-Hill Book Co., 1967.

8. Controlling

Emery, James C. *Organization Planning and Control Systems,* chap. 5. Toronto, Canada: The Macmillan Co., 1969.

Hill, Walter A., and Egan, Douglas M. *Readings in Organization Theory,* pp. 521–54. Boston: Allyn & Bacon, Inc., 1966.

Koontz, Harold, and O'Donnell, Cyril. *Management: A Book of Readings*, pp. 652–63. New York: McGraw-Hill Book Co., 1972.

McGregor, Douglas. *The Professional Manager*, chaps. 8 and 9. New York: McGraw-Hill Book Co., 1967.

Newman, William H.; Summer, Charles E.; and Warren, E. Kirby. *The Process of Management*, chaps. 24–27. Englewood Cliffs, N.J.: Prentice-Hall, Inc., 1972.

Starr, Martin K. *Management: A Modern Approach*, chaps. 11–12. New York: Harcourt, Brace, Jovanovich, 1971.

9. Objectives

Ackoff, Russell L. *A Concept of Corporate Planning*, chap. 2. New York: Wiley-Interscience, Division of John Wiley & Sons, Inc., 1970.

Davis, Ralph C. *The Fundamentals of Top Management*, chap. 4. New York: Harper & Bros., 1951.

Koontz, Harold, and O'Donnell, Cyril. *Management: A Book of Readings*, pp. 117–49. New York: McGraw-Hill Book Co., 1972.

McFarland, Dalton E. *Management Principles and Practices*, chap. 7. New York: The Macmillan Co., 1970.

Miller, Ernest C. *Objectives and Standards: An Approach to Planning and Control.* AMA Research Study No. 74. New York: American Management Association, Inc., 1966.

10. Policies

Davis, Ralph C. *The Fundamentals of Top Management*, chap. 6. New York: Harper & Bros., 1951.

Gross, Alfred, and Gross, Walter. *Business Policy: Readings and Commentaries*, chaps. 3–4. New York: The Ronald Press Co., 1967.

McFarland, Dalton E. *Management: Principles and Practices*, chap. 9. New York: The Macmillan Co., 1970.

Newman, William H., and Logan, James P. *Strategy, Policy and Central Management*, part 2. Cincinnati: South-Western Publishing Co., 1971.

Petersen, Elmore, and Plowman, Grosvenor E. *Business Organization and Management*, chap. 11. Homewood, Ill.: Richard D. Irwin, Inc., 1962.

11. Functions and Procedures

Elliott, C. Orville, and Wasley, Robert S. *Business Information Processing Systems*, chaps. 5 and 14. Homewood, Ill.: Richard D. Irwin, Inc., 1971.

Hill, Walter A., and Egan, Douglas M. *Readings in Organization Theory,* pp. 364–73. Boston: Allyn & Bacon, Inc., 1966.

Katz, Daniel, and Kahn, Robert L. *The Social Psychology of Organizations,* chap. 2. New York: John Wiley & Sons, Inc., 1966.

McFarland, Dalton E. (ed.). *Current Issues and Emerging Concepts in Management,* Vol. II, chaps. 8 and 21. Boston: Houghton Mifflin Co., 1968.

McGregor, Douglas. *The Professional Manager,* chap. 6. New York: McGraw-Hill Book Co., 1967.

12. Organization Structure

Cleland, David I., and King, William R. *Systems Analysis and Project Management,* chap. 8. New York: McGraw-Hill Book Co., 1968.

Koontz, Harold, and O'Donnell, Cyril. *Principles of Management,* 5th ed., chaps. 12–15. New York: McGraw-Hill Book Co., 1972.

Litterer, Joseph A. *Organizations: Structure and Behavior,* Vol. I. New York: John Wiley & Sons, Inc., 1969.

Rice, George H., Jr., and Bishoprick, Dean W. *Conceptual Models of Organization,* chaps. 2 and 7. New York: Appleton-Century-Crofts, 1971.

Rubenstein, Albert H., and Haberstroh, Chadwick, J. *Some Theories of Organization,* chap. 2. Rev. ed. Homewood, Ill.: Richard D. Irwin, Inc., 1966.

13. Authority and Responsibility

Davis, Ralph C. *The Fundamentals of Top Management,* chap. 9. New York: Harper & Bros., 1951.

Jones, Manley H. *Executive Decision Making,* chap. 6. Homewood, Ill.: Richard D. Irwin, Inc., 1962.

Koontz, Harold, and O'Donnell, Cyril. *Principles of Management,* chap. 3. 5th ed. New York: McGraw-Hill Book Co., 1972.

Newman, William H.; Summer, Charles E.; and Warren, E. Kirby. *The Process of Management,* chap. 20. 3d ed. Englewood Cliffs, N.J.: Prentice-Hall, Inc., 1972.

14. Line and Staff Relationships

Albers, Henry H. *Principles of Organization and Management,* chap. 7. New York: John Wiley & Sons, Inc., 1965.

Davis, Keith. *Human Relations at Work: The Dynamics of Organizational Behavior,* chap. 10. New York: McGraw-Hill Book Co., 1967.

Koontz, Harold, and O'Donnell, Cyril. *Principles of Management,* chap. 16. 5th ed. New York: McGraw-Hill Book Co., 1972.

Newman, William H.; Summer, Charles E.; and Warren, E. Kirby. *The Process of Management,* chap. 4. 3d ed. Englewood Cliffs, N.J.: Prentice-Hall, Inc., 1972.

Richards, Max D., and Nielander, William A. (eds.). *Readings in Management,* pp. 718–50. Rev. ed. Cincinnati: South-Western Publishing Co., 1967.

15.   Informal Relationships

Davis, Keith. *Human Relations at Work,* chap. 13. New York: McGraw-Hill Book Co., 1967.

Gellerman, Saul W. *The Management of Human Relations,* chaps. 1–2. New York: Holt, Rinehart, & Winston, Inc., 1966.

Hill, Walter A., and Egan, Douglas M. *Readings in Organization Theory,* pp. 196–206. Boston: Allyn & Bacon, Inc., 1966.

Katz, Daniel, and Kahn, Robert L. *The Social Psychology of Organizations,* chap. 7. New York: John Wiley & Sons, Inc., 1966.

Leavitt, Harold, and Pondy, Louis R. (eds.). *Readings in Managerial Psychology,* chap. 8. Chicago: The University of Chicago Press, 1964.

16.   Human Relations

Athos, Anthony G., and Coffey, Robert E. *Behavior in Organizations,* pp. 82–133, 148–58, 266–74. Englewood Cliffs, N.J.: Prentice-Hall, Inc., 1968.

Hill, Walter A., and Egan, Douglas M. *Readings in Organization Theory,* pp. 374–402. Boston: Allyn & Bacon, Inc., 1966.

Koontz, Harold, and O'Donnell, Cyril. *Management: A Book of Readings,* pp. 517–49. New York: McGraw-Hill Book Co., 1972.

Leavitt, Harold, and Pondy, Louis. R. (eds.). *Readings in Managerial Psychology,* chap. 13. Chicago: The University of Chicago Press, 1964.

Wadia, Maneck. *The Nature and Scope of Management,* pp. 158–66, 229–37. Chicago: Scott, Foresman and Co., 1966.

17.   Morale

Chruden, Herbert J., and Sherman, Arthur W., Jr. *Personnel Management,* chap. 16, 3d ed. Cincinnati: South-Western Publishing Co., 1968.

Gellerman, Saul W. *The Management of Human Relations,* chap. 10. New York: Holt, Rinehart & Winston, Inc., 1966.

Hill, Walter A., and Egan, Douglas M. *Readings in Organization Theory*, pp. 207–27. Boston: Allyn & Bacon, Inc., 1966.

Koontz, Harold, and O'Donnell, Cyril. *Management: A Book of Readings*, pp. 577–87. New York: McGraw-Hill Book Co., 1972.

Wadia, Maneck. *The Nature and Scope of Management*, pp. 238–57. Chicago: Scott, Foresman and Co., 1966.

18. Motivation

Athos, Anthony G., and Coffey, Robert E. *Behavior in Organizations*, pp. 171–82. Englewood Cliffs, N.J.: Prentice-Hall, Inc., 1968.

Katz, Daniel, and Kahn, Robert L. *The Social Psychology of Organizations*, chap. 21. New York: John Wiley & Sons, Inc., 1966.

Koontz, Harold, and O'Donnell, Cyril. *Management: A Book of Readings*, pp. 550–76. New York: McGraw-Hill Book Co., 1972.

Leavitt, Harold, and Pondy, Louis R. (eds.). *Readings in Managerial Psychology*, chap. 1. Chicago: The University of Chicago Press, 1964.

Likert, Rensis. *The Human Organization*, chaps. 3–4. New York: McGraw-Hill Book Co., 1967.

19. The Executive and Ethics

Baumhart, Raymond. *Ethics in Business*, chaps. 2 and 3. New York: Holt, Rinehart & Winston, Inc., 1968.

Davis, Keith, and Blomstrom, Robert L. *Business Society and Environment*, chap. 9. New York: McGraw-Hill Book Co., 1971.

Garrett, Thomas M. *Business Ethics.*, pp. 133–59. New York: Appleton-Century-Crofts, 1966.

Towle, Joseph W. (ed.). *Ethics and the Standards in American Business*, pp. 41–77. Boston: Houghton-Mifflin Co., 1964.

Walton, Clarence C. *Ethos and the Executive*, chap 8. Englewood Cliffs, N.J.: Prentice-Hall, Inc., 1969.

20. Communications

Haney, William V. *Communication and Organizational Behavior: Text and Cases*, chaps. 3, 7 and 9. 3d. ed. Homewood, Ill.: Richard D. Irwin, Inc., 1973.

Kelly, Joe. *Organizational Behaviour*, chap. 11. Homewood, Ill.: Richard D. Irwin, Inc., 1969.

Leavitt, Harold J. *Managerial Psychology*, chaps. 11, 18, and 19. 3d ed. Chicago: The University of Chicago Press, 1972.

Sigband, Norman B. *Communication for Management,* chaps. 1–2. Glenview, Ill.: Scott, Foresman and Co., 1969.

Strauss, George, and Sayles, Leonard R. *Personnel: The Human Problems of Management,* chaps. 10–11. 3d ed. Englewood Cliffs, N.J.: Prentice-Hall, Inc., 1973.

21.   Managerial Manpower Procurement

Haimann, Theo., and Scott, William G. *Management in the Modern Organization,* chap. 20. Boston: Houghton Mifflin Co., 1970.

Jucius, Michael, J. *Personnel Management,* chaps. 6–8. 7th ed. Homewood, Ill.: Richard D. Irwin, Inc., 1971.

Newman, William H.; Summer, Charles E.; and Warren, E. Kirby. *The Process of Management,* chap. 10. 3d ed. Englewood Cliffs, N.J.: Prentice-Hall, Inc., 1972.

Patten, Thomas H., Jr. *Manpower Planning and the Development of Human Resources,* chap. 9. New York: Wiley-Interscience, Division of John Wiley & Sons, Inc., 1971.

Yoder, Dale. *Personnel Management and Industrial Relations,* chaps. 8–10. 6th ed. Englewood Cliffs, N.J.: Prentice-Hall, Inc., 1970.

22.   Developing the Managerial Team

Bellows, Roger; Gibson, Thomas Q.; and Odiorne, George S. *Executive Skills Their Dynamics and Development.* Englewood Cliffs, N.J.: Prentice-Hall, Inc., 1962.

Campbell, John P.; Dunnette, Marvin D.; Lawler, Edward E., III; and Weick, Karl E., Jr. *Managerial Behavior, Performance and Effectiveness,* chaps. 10–13. New York: McGraw-Hill Book Co., 1970.

Houston, George C. *Manager Development,* chaps. 9 and 10. Homewood, Ill.: Richard D. Irwin, Inc., 1961.

Lynton, Rolf P., and Pareek, Udai. *Training for Development.* Homewood, Ill.: Richard D. Irwin, Inc., 1967.

McLarney, William J., and Berliner, William M. *Management Training: Cases and Principles,* 5th ed. Homewood, Ill.: Richard D. Irwin, Inc., 1970.

23.   Appraisal of Manager Performance

Finkle, Robert B., and Jones, William S. *Assessing Corporate Talent,* New York: Wiley-Interscience, Division of John Wiley & Sons, Inc., 1970.

Humble, John W. (ed.). *Management by Objectives in Action.* London, England: McGraw-Hill Publishing Company Limited, 1970.

Kellogg, Marion. *What to Do about Performance Appraisal.* New York: American Management Association, 1965.

Miner, John B. *Personnel Psychology,* chap. 4. New York: The Macmillan Co., 1969.

Odiorne, George S. *Management by Objectives.* New York: Pitman Publishing Corp., 1965.

24. Compensation

Beach, Dale S. *Personnel: The Management of People at Work,* chap. 26. 2d ed. New York: The Macmillan Co., 1970.

Belcher, Daniel W. *Wage and Salary Administration,* chap. 19. 2d ed. Englewood Cliffs, N.J.: Prentice-Hall, Inc., 1962.

Burgess, Leonard R. *Wage and Salary Administration in a Dynamic Economy.* New York: Harcourt, Brace & World, Inc., 1968.

Moore, Franklin G. *Management Organization and Practice,* chap. 30. New York: Harper & Row, Publishers, 1964.

National Industrial Conference Board. *Top Executive Compensation.* Studies in Personnel Policy, No. 204. New York: National Industrial Conference Board, Inc., 1966.

25. Executive Behavior in a Changing Environment

Bennis, Warren G.; Benne, Kenneth D.; and Chin, Robert. *The Planning of Change,* chap. 9. 2d ed. New York: Holt, Rinehart & Winston, Inc., 1969.

Davis, Keith. *Human Relations at Work,* chap. 23. 3d ed. New York: McGraw-Hill Book Co., 1967.

Hodge, Billy J., and Johnson, Herbert J. *Management and Organizational Behavior,* chaps. 19–20. New York: John Wiley & Sons, Inc., 1970.

Judson, Arnold. *A Manager's Guide to Making Changes,* chaps. 1–2 and 6. New York: John Wiley & Sons, Inc., 1966.

Strauss, George, and Sayles, Leonard. *Personnel: The Human Problems of Management,* chap. 12. 3d ed. Englewood Cliffs, N.J.: Prentice-Hall, Inc., 1973.

26. Trends in Management

Blough, Roy. *International Business: Environment and Adaption,* chaps. 1–6. New York: McGraw-Hill Book Co., 1966.

The Conference Board. *Intercompany Transactions in the Multinational Firm: Managing International Business,* No. 6. New York: National Industrial Conference Board, Inc., 1970.

Davis, Keith, and Blomstrom, Robert L. *Business, Society, and Environment,* chaps. 6 and 21. New York: McGraw-Hill Book Co., 1971.

Davis, Stanley M. *Comparative Management: Organizational and Cultural Perspectives,* chap. 2. Englewood Cliffs, N.J.: Prentice-Hall, Inc., 1971.

Sanders, Donald H. *Computers and Management,* chap. 8. New York: McGraw-Hill Book Co., 1970.

Wren, Daniel A. *The Evolution of Management Thought,* chaps. 19 and 20. New York: The Ronald Press Co., 1972.

Index

513

This book has been set in 11 and 10 point Caledonia, leaded 2 points. Chapter numbers are 30 point Craw Modern; chapter titles are 18 point Craw Modern. The size of the type page is 27 by 46 picas.